Cold War Captives

The publisher gratefully acknowledges the generous support
of the Ahmanson Foundation Humanities Endowment Fund
of the University of California Press Foundation.

Cold War Captives

Imprisonment, Escape, and Brainwashing

Susan L. Carruthers

UNIVERSITY OF CALIFORNIA PRESS

Berkeley   Los Angeles   London

University of California Press, one of the most distinguished university presses in the United States, enriches lives around the world by advancing scholarship in the humanities, social sciences, and natural sciences. Its activities are supported by the UC Press Foundation and by philanthropic contributions from individuals and institutions. For more information, visit www.ucpress.edu.

University of California Press
Berkeley and Los Angeles, California

University of California Press, Ltd.
London, England

Library of Congress Cataloging-in-Publication Data

Carruthers, Susan L. (Susan Lisa).
    Cold War captives : imprisonment, escape, and brainwashing / Susan L. Carruthers.
        p.   cm.
    Includes bibliographical references and index.
    ISBN 978–0–520–25730–6 (cloth : alk. paper)
    ISBN 978–0–520–25731–3 (pbk. : alk. paper)
    1. Popular culture—United States—History—20th century.   2. Cold War—Social aspects—United States.   3. Captivity narratives.   4. Political prisoners—History—20th century.   5. Repatriation—History—20th century.   6. Defection—History—20th century.   7. Brainwashing—History—20th century.   8. Cold War in mass media.   9. Cold War in motion pictures.   10. Cold War in literature.   I. Title.

E169.12.C293   2009
909.82'5—dc22   2008047712

Manufactured in the United States of America

18   17   16   15   14   13   12   11   10   09
10   9   8   7   6   5   4   3   2   1

This book is printed on Cascades Enviro 100, a 100% post consumer waste, recycled, de-inked fiber. FSC recycled certified and processed chlorine free. It is acid free, Ecologo certified, and manufactured by BioGas energy.

For Patricia

CONTENTS

ILLUSTRATIONS

ACKNOWLEDGMENTS

Over the course of this book's extended gestation many debts have accumulated that I'm eager to acknowledge. Finally!

Research support was initially supplied by the College Research Fund of the University of Wales, Aberystwyth. Colleagues in "Interpol," particularly Tarak Barkawi, Jenny Edkins, Mike Foley, and Steve Hobden, were valued fellow travelers. The Arts and Humanities Research Board funded early archival forays in Washington, D.C., and in different ways Jim Deutsch, Kerric Harvey, Laureen Smith, and Wendy Wasserman eased my two sabbatical semesters there, making them memorably good times. Archivists at the Archives II facility in College Park, Maryland, and at the Library of Congress—especially Madeleine Matz of the Motion Picture Division—helped me unearth materials I would never otherwise have discovered. The Eisenhower World Affairs Forum provided funds for a visit to the Eisenhower Presidential Library. I gratefully acknowledge the assistance I received from staff there and from librarians and archivists at all the institutions where I've worked extensively: the Hugh Owen Library at the University of Wales, Aberystwyth; Yr Llyfrgell Genedlaethol Cymru; the Library of Congress; the New York Public Library, and the Dana Library at Rutgers University, Newark.

Since arriving at Rutgers in 2002, I have benefited from both the university's financial support and its generous leave policy. A fellowship during 2005–6 at the Rutgers Center for Historical Research in New Brunswick, headed by Michael Adas, gave me a productive opportunity to interact with an interdisciplinary circle of colleagues.

In Newark, I've found intellectual and social sustenance within and beyond the Rutgers/New Jersey Institute of Technology Federated History Department, and for this I'm especially grateful to Fran Bartkowski, Karen Caplan, Jon Cowans, Eva Giloi, Kent Harber, Gabriela Kütting, Jan Lewis, Neil Maher, Gary Roth, Beryl Satter, Mara Sidney, Doris Sher, and Rick Sher. David Hosford and Steven Diner deserve special thanks for hiring me in the first place. So too does Christina Strasburger for being the best administrator ever, a whiz with TIFFs, and wonderful in myriad ways. Prachi Deshpande and Miriam Petty are much missed former Conklin corridor-mates. Graduate students Neal Ziskind and Sarah Howard provided valuable research assistance, as did Andy Buchanan, who, together with Mary Nell Bockman, has been an unrivaled source of camaraderie, altitude, and Laphroaig for several years.

During the academic year 2006–7, I was particularly fortunate to receive a fellowship at the Charles Warren Center for Studies in American History at Harvard University, where Emerson Hall provided a stimulating setting in which to write much of this book. I'm grateful to Nancy Cott and Carol Oja for selecting me and for leading such a fine seminar; to fellow fellows, especially Beth Levy and Susan Zeiger, for lively engagement; and to Arthur Patton-Hock and Larissa Kennedy for administrative support. Off campus, Richard and Emmie Homonoff were the most delightful neighbors, friends, and landlords imaginable. Sara Fass, Carol Zall, Iain McCallum, and Sato also added to the enjoyment of this project's Fayerweather phase. Special thanks are also due to Matt Shurtleff for helping me find my feet in Cambridge and for providing green eggs and ham at a critical juncture.

Over the past decade, chunks of *Cold War Captives* and sundry offshoots have been presented at numerous conferences and seminars on both sides of the Atlantic. I'm grateful to all those who commented on or asked questions about this project while it matured. Two interlocutors deserve special thanks, however. Marilyn Young has been a tremendously supportive champion over several years. The seminar "The Cold War as Global Conflict," which she and Allen Hunter convened at New York University's International Center for Advanced Study, provided me a welcome Friday morning berth for two years when I had newly landed in New York. I'm further indebted to Marilyn for insightful comments on the manuscript—but, more than that, for her staunch friendship. Tom Doherty has also been a dogged supporter of this project and its author since its inception. For help with pictures, factoids, and subtitles, and for sustained encouragement, he has my sincere thanks.

At the University of California Press, Mary Francis and Niels Hooper gratifyingly showed much enthusiasm for the project. Thanks are also due to Nicholas Arrivo for issuing only the gentlest of reminders as deadlines loomed; to Elisabeth Magnus for eliminating the manuscript's many errant anglicisms; and to Marilyn Schwartz for shepherding the book through production.

Finally, and as ever, the last, best thanks go to my family in Galway: the Morrisons and the Carrutherses. For your patience when I've apparently been doing nothing but work, I thank you. I'm especially appreciative of my parents' consistent faith in me and what I do. This book is dedicated, with love and gratitude, to my mother—my first teacher and biggest fan.

Newark, NJ
July 25, 2008

Introduction

Between Camps

COLD WAR: SOMETHING PEOPLE CAN UNDERSTAND

When did the cold war begin? Was it in March 1946, when Winston Churchill asserted that an iron curtain had descended across Europe "from Stettin in the Baltic to Trieste in the Adriatic"? Or twelve months later, when President Truman committed the United States to the defense of "free peoples" wherever they were menaced by "armed minorities or outside pressures"? Alternatively, if the first volley was fired from the Soviet side, the triggerman may have been Andrei Zhdanov, the Politburo member who proclaimed in September 1947 that the world was divided between "democratic" and "imperialist" camps—the latter, led by Washington, bent on war. Or perhaps the United States and USSR had been waging a cold war ever since 1917, even if the phrase wasn't coined for another thirty years. Scholars have broached all these possibilities and numerous others.[1] But a voluminous literature crammed with opening salvoes, crisis points, and bellicose declarations yields no mention of August 12, 1948—the day when, in *Newsweek*'s estimation, the cold war became "Something People Can Understand."[2]

August 1948 was an especially eventful month in the cold war's infancy. In Berlin, American planes were engaged in a massive airlift to provision a city that the Soviets had attempted to blockade. In London, several athletes from eastern Europe announced their intention to defect after the first postwar Olympic games, protesting the lack of freedom in their newly Stalinized homelands. Washington, D.C., meanwhile, was reeling from testimony delivered by a disheveled *Time* magazine editor and repentant ex-communist named Whittaker Chambers. Appearing before the House Committee on Un-American Activities (HUAC), he claimed that

1

Alger Hiss, a former State Department official, had belonged to an underground party cell in the 1930s—proof positive, in some eyes at least, that the administration was riddled with Red subversives.[3] Yet it was neither the threat of war in Europe nor the specter of internal collapse that prompted *Newsweek* to announce that the cold war had, at last, become universally intelligible. Rather, the inspiration was a fifty-two-year-old chemistry teacher, Oksana Kasenkina, who on August 12, 1948, leapt from an upper story of the Soviet consulate in New York City.

Historians have failed to memorialize Kasenkina's role as a precipitant of the cold war, but for some weeks in 1948 the tale of a desperate Soviet schoolteacher who sought to avoid forcible repatriation to the USSR monopolized the headlines: "a melodrama more hair-raising than a Grade B-thriller." Full of baffling reversals, accusations, and counterclaims, the story reached its climax when Kasenkina plummeted from a third-floor window after five days' entrapment in the consulate. Captured by photographers, her fall was instantly dubbed a "Leap for Freedom"— a stirring example of the lengths to which a Soviet citizen would go to escape her state's tyrannous clutches. With her dramatic exit from the consulate, Kasenkina appeared to validate a fundamental truth about two antithetical ways of life. While the "workers' paradise" was a country one would court death to flee, the United States beckoned as an asylum for which one would risk life itself. "No casting director would ever have put Oksana Kasenkina in a dramatic role intended for an Ethel Barrymore or a Bette Davis," opined *Newsweek*. Nevertheless, this unlikely heroine had redeemed her unprepossessing appearance by providing the "Western democracies . . . their biggest break in the three year propaganda war" with Moscow.[4]

If these grandiloquent sentiments struck a eulogistic note, no obituary was required. Despite multiple fractures and contusions, Kasenkina lived, her fall broken by a tangle of telephone wires strung across the consulate's courtyard. Neither dead nor Red, she became a prominent icon of anticommunism, hastily leaping into the "high income bracket," thanks to the lucrative sale of her story to the Hearst press.[5] The schoolteacher's swift recovery and speedy reversal of fortune were not replicated at the level of intergovernmental relations, however. Kasenkina had triggered a "first-class diplomatic incident," with testy exchanges and consular expulsions marking a new nadir in U.S.-Soviet relations. In August 1948, the two countries' simmering dispute reached its "tensest point in recent years," announced the *Chicago Daily Tribune*—a judgment all the more remarkable given that columnists were simultaneously calculating odds on war breaking out in Berlin.[6] By the time the State Department declared the Kasenkina case shut in September, consular relations between the two states had been severed altogether. The rift would take sixteen years to close.

As 1948 drew to a conclusion, news reviews listed Kasenkina's fateful leap among the year's top ten stories, somewhere between the birth of Israel, the death of Babe

Ruth, and the assassination of Mahatma Gandhi.[7] But in the eyes of many columnists the biggest story wasn't a single event but a process of crystallization that rendered 1948 a "year of resolution." For *Time* magazine, it had been a "fighting year"—when Americans finally committed themselves to battle after "the last trace of doubt about the nature of the enemy" dissolved. "More than speeches, reports or eyewitness accounts of life under Communism," it was the action of a distressed schoolteacher that "nakedly revealed the bitter despair behind the glowing promises in Communism's workers' paradise."[8]

To disinter the long-buried story of Oksana Kasenkina (as chapter 1 does at greater length) is thus to propose a different kind of starting point for the cold war: the point at which that phenomenon became emotionally resonant for "ordinary Americans." By any other reckoning, confrontation between the two antagonistic blocs was well advanced by August 1948, as events in Europe attested. For months the White House had sought to rally support for an expanded U.S. role that would encompass not only assistance to embattled regimes in Greece and Turkey but defense of "free peoples" wherever they were imperiled by "terror and oppression." As every standard cold war history recounts, Truman heeded the advice of Republican Senator Arthur Vandenberg, who insisted that the only way to dispel Americans' innate isolationism and postwar lethargy was to "scare hell out of the country."[9] Announcing what would become known as the Truman Doctrine on March 12, 1947, the president did his best to electrify the nation. In a speech of some eighteen minutes' duration, the words *free* and *freedom* recurred no less than twenty-four times as Truman conjured a world riven between "alternative ways of life" in which freedom was everywhere imperiled.[10] It was "as cold a war speech against Russia as any President has ever made except on the occasion of going before Congress to ask for a declaration of war," editorialized the *Chicago Tribune,* though the Soviet Union was nowhere mentioned.[11]

Yet despite much press acclamation, Truman's exhortation apparently failed to fuel popular fervor for this all-out confrontation. To a war-weary population that had vigorously protested American troops' tardy demobilization in 1945, the notion of an embattled "free world" must have sounded as familiar as it was unwelcome. Elaborating national war aims, Franklin Delano Roosevelt and Vice President Wallace had repeatedly invoked a world "divided between human slavery and human freedom"—a motif that, in the opinion of intellectual historian Daniel Rodgers, "slipped unchanged into place as the controlling metaphor of the Cold War."[12] But "freedom" showed signs of battle fatigue after 1945, like many of those who had fought in its name. As a "fighting word" it required recuperation and reorientation for cold war service.[13]

It was for her role in resuscitating an exhausted abstraction that columnists and policy makers congratulated Oksana Kasenkina. "The incident on Sixty-first Street will strengthen popular resolve," the *New York Times* predicted, attributing the potency of *l'affaire Kasenkina* to its stirring properties and alarming proximity. That it *had* happened here demonstrated that the Red menace didn't simply lie beyond the Iron Curtain. It lurked in neighborhoods as exclusive as Manhattan's Upper East Side, where the Soviet consul had turned an elegant mansion into a miniature police state. This "house of fear" replicated the defining traits of the "slave world"—oppressive, confining, and impossible to leave except at mortal risk.[14] Rejecting slavery in favor of freedom, Kasenkina vividly illuminated the cold war's terms of engagement, providing a model for individuals and nations the world over.

To contemporary observers, the consular crisis of August 1948 provided a wake-up call to the high drama and moral imperatives of the age. "Life in these United States nowadays is not without some resemblance to life in wards seven and eight of the county insane asylum," noted a *Washington Post* editorial. "If you think you are about to perish of boredom, it is your own fault, because it shows that you haven't made use of the opportunities that await you on every side."[15] But if the saga of the Soviet schoolteacher seemed to brim with novelty, there was also something familiar about its plot. Kasenkina's was, at root, a *captivity* story. As such, it offered a cold war variation on a well-worn theme: the innocent captive beset by a savage captor.

From the colonial era onwards, captivity has occupied a privileged place in the American imaginary as a fixture of national speech, symbology, and statuary. Arriving in the New World, the Puritans understood their passage across the Atlantic as a recapitulation of the Israelites' flight over the Jordan.[16] As God's chosen people, they too were redeemed captives freed from bondage. Yet the North American wilderness appeared an insecure sanctuary to European settlers: the threat of death, dismemberment, or enslavement at the hands of marauding Indians seemed ever present. This national self-conception—a people under the perpetual shadow of a raised tomahawk—proved stubbornly persistent. For a century, Horatio Greenough's *The Rescue* stood at the east entrance to the U.S. Capitol Building: a massive tableau in which a classically attired, oversize European male rescues a huddling, partially disrobed woman and infant from a tomahawk-wielding, nearly nude Indian predator. Despite earlier protests that it represented an affront to Native Americans, the statue occupied this site until 1958, when the Capitol was remodeled.[17]

If captivity symbolically overshadowed the seat of U.S. government, it also provided a dominant motif in American storytelling, an enduring template for constructions of identity and difference. "Captivity narratives constitute the first coherent myth-literature developed in America for American audiences," proposes Richard Slotkin, "as if the only experience of intimacy with the Indians that New England readers would accept was the experience of the captive."[18] Similarly, the new republic's early encounters with Islam were filtered through the prism of captivity in accounts of American "enslavement" on the Barbary coast. Thereafter, parables of imperiled national virtue remained a staple of American literature, assuming increasingly secular and sentimental forms in the nineteenth century.[19]

Noting the genre's flexibility and longevity, literary scholars have identified captivity's tendency to resurface at times of insecurity, whether as an invitation to self-scrutiny or a prompt to patriotic outrage (if not both): an arc stretching from the kidnapping of Patty Hearst to the Iranian Embassy siege and the "rescue" of Jessica Lynch in Iraq.[20] Rarely, however, do cultural critics include the early cold war in this canon. Yet during the late 1940s and 1950s, captivity suffused American understandings of the eastern bloc and its inhabitants. Those "captive peoples" trapped behind the Iron Curtain were, as Dean Acheson put it, "prisoners of a tyranny" presided over by "prisoners of a dream of power and a doctrine of destiny."[21]

Enslavement was simultaneously corporeal, mental, and spiritual, a plight both figurative and literal. "The Russians do not grab merely real estate," Leland Stowe warned in *Reader's Digest* in 1952. "They also grab people. . . . No-one is too small or insignificant, too young or too old, to be shackled and regimented or pauperized and destroyed."[22] This threat to bodies, minds, and souls was not, however, confined to totalitarian states, nor was it exclusively a communist menace. In the 1950s, captivity served as a metaphor for a lengthening list of domestic social and psychological maladies, from the anomie of suburban housewives to the "slave world" of drug addiction, which, as the *Los Angeles Times* cautioned, trapped addicts in a "twilight world as vile and degrading and brutal as any slave camp behind the Iron Curtain."[23]

Like a fine mist, captivity saturated the language and thought of early cold war America, diffusing into the atmosphere without becoming an object of historical scrutiny. To many at the time, though, the prospect of "menticide"—the "rape of the mind," as the Columbia psychologist Joost Meerloo explained his coinage—appeared more terrifying than the threat of atomic annihilation. Even as Americans were learning to duck and cover in preparation for the looming nuclear apocalypse, leading figures warned (as John Foster Dulles did in his 1950 treatise *War or Peace*) that they should be as "concerned about the mass destruction of minds and spirits" as they were about weapons of mass destruction.[24]

Cold War Captives examines captivity as a dense matrix of ideas, images, and practices. It is, in part, a study of the storytelling that makes popular sense of geopolitics. Metaphors of enslavement played a crucial role in transforming the Soviet Union and China from courageous wartime allies into barbarous foes implacably opposed to the "free world." This cold war vision of a globe fractured between good and evil—half free, half slave—drew on a peculiarly American tradition of configuring any infringement of liberty as "slavery" and any such challenge as an existential threat to national survival that required total annihilation. In its denial of the antagonist's right to exist, the cold war was a U.S. ideology, the historian Anders Stephanson argues.[25] But the specter of enslavement that menaced postwar America was not simply a phantasm dredged from the deep reservoirs of collective memory. Captivity's ubiquity also reflected material circumstance in that millions of individuals experienced different forms of incarceration during and after the war. Confinement—of prisoners of war, forced laborers in the gulag, satellite populations, and isolated Americans behind the Iron Curtain—profoundly shaped both the early cold war's international politics and its imaginative practices.

THE INTERNATIONAL POLITICS OF IM/MOBILITY

Barely into middle age, the twentieth century had already attracted many sobriquets. For Henry Luce, writing in 1941, it was categorically the "American Century." One year later, Henry Wallace offered a more egalitarian alternative when he vowed that "the century which will come out of this war can and must be the century of the common man."[26] What soon emerged, however, was rather less elevating. With the war leaving millions of refugees in its wake, and postwar conflict uprooting approximately one thousand people a day, the twentieth century was better understood as the "century of the homeless man," proposed Dr. Elfan Rees (adviser on refugee affairs to the World Council of Churches) in 1952. The *New York Times* concurred, noting that "the displaced person is as much the symbol of this century as the broken atom."[27]

Twenty years later, the German author Heinrich Böll would offer a different summative verdict. "It may be that our century is the century of camps, of prisoners," he ventured in an essay on Alexander Solzhenitsyn, "and whoever has never been imprisoned, whether he boasts or is ashamed of his good or bad fortune—has been spared *the* experience of the century." If displacement and incarceration are conceived as opposite poles of an experiential spectrum, Böll's judgment might appear to contradict Rees's.[28] Yet mobility and immobilization were both prominent phenomena during a tumultuous century, and they were far from mutually exclusive. Millions of people were successively uprooted and confined, released and displaced, encamped then resettled—particularly in the decade that encompassed World War II and its chaotic aftermath. Camps were variously sites of shelter and places of perdition.

From a sixty-year remove, it is hard to comprehend how prevalent a plight captivity was at midcentury. Of ninety-six million men mobilized for war, more than one-third spent time as prisoners of war—an experience many did not survive. Soviet casualties, in this regard as in others, were staggeringly high. Approximately 3.3 million Red Army POWs perished in German camps, a death rate approaching 58 percent.[29] In all, some thirty-five million men were held as POWs during and after the war. This enormous figure includes neither the inmates of Nazi concentration and extermination camps nor the millions of forced laborers—men and women—conveyed from their homes and confined by the Third Reich, the USSR, and imperial Japan in various forms of war-related exploitation.[30]

U.S. servicemen experienced far lower rates of imprisonment than most other combatant forces, with fewer than 1 percent becoming POWs.[31] But wartime America was hardly a stranger to captivity. Nearly 120,000 Japanese Americans spent the war in internment camps, a sweeping move justified in the name of quarantining society against Japanese sabotage and "Americanizing" a population viewed as troublingly alien.[32] Since the first objective took precedence over the second, the encampments that housed these internees were purposely constructed in remote spots. Camps accommodating Italian and German POWs, by contrast, became a common enough sight across rural America during the latter stages of the war and for some time thereafter—from Michigan to Massachusetts, the Carolinas to California.

For millions of prisoners, the surrender of Germany and Japan did not bring a swift end to their confinement. From the defeated Axis powers, the Soviet government sought reparations in the form of human labor—an asset that could be stripped more readily than heavy industrial machinery, though that too was dismantled and carted off to aid the shattered motherland's reconstruction. Several thousand German and Japanese POWs would remain in the USSR until after Stalin's death in 1953. Meanwhile, many Red Army personnel newly released from German camps became the postwar captives of their own state. Reviled as traitors who had surrendered to (or even fought on behalf of) the enemy, and mistrusted on account of what they had observed of life beyond the USSR, many Soviet former POWs returned east to face imprisonment.[33]

Many others were incarcerated or impressed into forced labor for the first time in the wave of ethnic expulsions, population transfers, and refugee movements that followed the Third Reich's collapse. As the historian Tony Judt observes, "At the conclusion of the First World War it was borders that were invented and adjusted, while people were on the whole left in place. After 1945 what happened was rather the opposite: with one major exception boundaries stayed broadly intact and people were moved instead." During this violent convulsion some twelve to thirteen million Germans were "transferred" west from eastern Europe, while seven million refugees of other nationalities were forced from their homes in a frenzy of what would later be called "ethnic cleansing."[34] Across Europe, not just in the USSR, camps dotted the postwar landscape. No sooner had POW and concentration camps disgorged their inmates than new reception centers for displaced persons (DPs) sprang up. By late 1945, the United Nations Relief and Rehabilitation Administration (UNRRA) was operating 227 camps in Germany alone. In some cases, former Nazi concentration camps, like Dachau, abruptly changed function to become DP shelters. Within two years, UNRRA was running some 762 camps and relief centers in western Europe, and while these were ostensibly temporary places of accommodation, many refugees found themselves long-term residents of institutions that could feel decidedly punitive.[35]

As even this preliminary sketch indicates, the plight of POWs, camp survivors, forced laborers, and myriad others bombed out of their homes or too fearful to stay in them—an estimated thirty million people in Europe alone, with millions more refugees in Asia—constituted a humanitarian crisis of incomprehensible magnitude. Witnesses to this abjection struggled to convey the scale of human misery to distant Americans, who, by contrast, were "in the pleasant predicament of learning to live 50 percent better than they ever lived before."[36] Writing in the *New York Times* six weeks after V-E Day, Anne O'Hare McCormick chronicled a "story of retrogression that has no precedent since the collapse of the Roman Empire": "A considerable part of Europe is already living in this new cave age. . . . Millions of people are moving over the roads with all their possessions on their backs. Millions are moored where they are, with no means of getting anywhere else. Millions are living in all kinds of temporary shelters. When one sees people who once had homes, decent clothes, ambitions, human manners, grubbing in the fields like animals for roots to eat, one does not see revolutionary forces, or constructive forces, but only spent forces, the breakdown of a civilization."[37] In the judgment of Dean Acheson (then assistant secretary of state), the "whole world structure and order that we had inherited from the nineteenth century" lay in ruins.[38]

Within months, it became clear that Moscow and Washington favored incompatible designs for the postwar architecture that would arise from the rubble. Diplomatic historians commonly locate the sources of their estrangement in disputes over boundaries, successor regimes, and spheres of influence: realpolitik at its bluntest. Undoubtedly these questions preoccupied the fractious victors as they set about the daunting business of reconstruction. But Washington and Moscow weren't simply concerned with which parties would govern the reconstituted states of Europe and where these polities' boundaries would lie. They also disputed who, in effect, belonged to whom. The politics of mobile and immobilized humanity encompassed an array of interlocking issues: repatriation and reparations; the relocation of refugees; and the freedom with which people could (or could not) move across national borders. Since captive bodies represent a form of capital, and were explicitly regarded as such in 1945, these questions were no less the stuff of power politics than the boundary drawing, election rigging, and geopolitical jockeying more customarily considered under that rubric.

Yet since captive bodies are also considerably more than a source of symbolic lucre or disposable labor, their confinement stoked sentiment in ways that less corporeal issues often did not. Certainly, in the estimation of John Deane (commanding general of the U.S. military mission to the Red Army), the American people "had more sympathy" for their own POWs than for any other casualties of war.[39] While comparatively few U.S. servicemen were taken prisoner, their privations in cap-

tivity generated profound bitterness and a corresponding clamor for the early return of those who survived. But Soviet intransigence threatened to impede this goal.
In early 1945, American observers became concerned that the Soviets were failing
to expedite the return of U.S. personnel freed from German-run camps after their
liberation by Red Army troops. More alarming yet were the reports that Russian
soldiers were mistreating, starving, and stealing from American troops waiting to
be repatriated.

Anxiety over the welfare of these men was not restricted to civilians fretful over
the fate of loved ones in uniform. Statesmen also approached POW issues through
a haze of intense emotionality, taking umbrage at Moscow's reluctance to return
former prisoners of war and airmen downed in Poland. U.S. military and civilian
officials' reports bristled with incidences of "barbarism" perpetrated by the Red
Army against American soldiers. These estimations of Soviet mistreatment of
POWs may have been exaggerated. Nevertheless, a widespread perception prevailed
that Red Army troops handled Americans with callous disregard for their welfare
at best and calculated viciousness at worst. Moscow did little to alleviate American concerns, ignoring Washington's entreaties to respect reciprocal agreements
on repatriation. Over time, U.S. military personnel became increasingly uneasy
about maintaining their side of the bargain: namely, helping the Red Army repatriate some five million displaced Soviet citizens, thousands of whom had to be sent
back under duress.

Disputes over repatriation did not *cause* the cold war, as several scholars have
noted. Undoubtedly, though, they hastened the disintegration of the wartime alliance.[40] In 1949, cooperation over repatriation came to a halt after years of ever
more acrimonious dispute. By then U.S. personnel had helped dispatch approximately two million people to the USSR. All this is reasonably well known. Less fully
appreciated, however, is that Truman's administration didn't simply stop assisting Soviet repatriation efforts; it fashioned an elaborate agenda around a new declaratory "Fifth Freedom"—a development anticipated by *Life* in August 1948.
"When a frightened little Soviet schoolteacher, Mrs. Oksana Kasenkina, jumps from
the third-story window of the Russian consulate in New York to keep from being
sent back to the Russian Fatherland, the case for a Fifth Freedom—freedom of
movement—becomes incontrovertible," the magazine presciently editorialized.[41]

Over the course of the early cold war, the Truman and Eisenhower administrations in turn developed an array of unorthodox policies to promote defection,
assist (and variously exploit) eastern bloc escapees, embolden the "captive peoples,"
and champion POWs' right to *refuse* repatriation—a putative way to prevail in the
cold war by deterring the Kremlin from sending troops of unreliable loyalty into
the field. A radical departure from the Geneva Conventions, the principle of voluntary repatriation would bedevil the Korean War armistice talks. After all other
points of disagreement had been settled, hostilities continued for an additional fif-

teen months, with settlement frustrated by American insistence on "nonforcible repatriation." Intended to salvage a symbolic victory from military stalemate in the form of a mass refusal by North Korean and Chinese prisoners to return behind the "Bamboo Curtain," Washington's stance also prolonged the captivity of some four thousand American POWs. But as later chapters reveal, this was only one of many paradoxes inherent in a commitment to the "Fifth Freedom" that was tested and strained in numerous ways, not least by the decision of twenty-one American POWs to repudiate their country in favor of Mao's China—assuredly not a choice U.S. officials intended to promote.

THE CAMP AS MICROCOSM

Like all identities, America's self-conception as leader of the "free world" was relational, forged in opposition to an Other imagined as its absolute antithesis: the "slave world" of communism. As Moscow consolidated its grip over eastern Europe in the late 1940s and Mao triumphed over his nationalist adversaries in 1949, this area of darkness appeared to be expanding inexorably—"full of dead men's bones, and of all uncleanness," John Foster Dulles warned, quoting the Gospel of Matthew. In 1953, Dulles used his first televised appearance as secretary of state to map a zone of barbarism that extended from Berlin to Kamchatka, a short distance across the Bering Sea from Alaska. This vast landmass was home to some eight hundred million of America's "proclaimed enemies"—a proposition that would not necessarily have struck his audience as hyperbolic.[42] During the early cold war, Americans were constantly told that one-third of the world's population lived "in virtual bondage" and that communists—"Satan-inspired slave-men," in the phraseology of New York's Cardinal Spellman—languished in shackles at once mental and physical.[43]

The concept of totalitarianism did much to fix the "slave world" as a universe of irredeemable difference, hastily extinguishing more positive views of the USSR that had been common in the 1930s and more or less mandatory during the war years. This point bears stressing. Cold war constructions of the Soviet bloc were so uniform as to appear a transparent representation of life's uniformity behind the Iron Curtain. But we should not be misled by the tendency of dominant interpretive frames to erase their compositors' fingerprints. It required work to reimagine the Soviet bloc as the "slave world," not least because during the war Americans had been encouraged to conceive their Russian ally in entirely different terms. For four years, Washington's Office of War Information had worked hard to burnish the Soviets' image, with no little success. Moviegoers who watched wartime entertainments such as Samuel Goldwyn's *The North Star,* United Artists' *Three Russian Girls,* or MGM's *Song of Russia* (all released in 1943) would have found that ordinary Russians, while more prone to spontaneous singing and dancing than their

FIGURE 1. "Welcome to Moscow!" Jerry Costello's cartoon from the *Knickerbocker News,* June 10, 1952, imagines the "slave world" of communism as America's antithesis. Reproduced courtesy of the Library of Congress.

American counterparts, had very similar values and aspirations. Fighting to defend their motherland, they too nurtured hopes for a better, more peaceful and prosperous future for the "common man."[44]

This rosy image outlived the war, fortified by the Red Army's undeniable contribution to Germany's defeat and by the Soviets' unimaginable loss of some twenty-seven million lives. For several months after V-E Day, American correspondents continued to depict the Soviet Union as a rapidly modernizing society where optimism prevailed despite years of wartime privation and boundless suffering. Writing in July 1946, the *New York Times*'s Drew Middleton enthused over Moscow's "wide, magnificent streets," its "imposing shops whose full windows promise much," and the "physical strength and mental hope" of a citizenry dedicated to constructing a "richer future"; such was the "pro-Soviet euphoria of the period around the end of World War II" recalled by George Kennan in his memoirs.[45]

This enthusiasm did not survive the great postwar geopolitical reversal, however. By the late 1940s, the Soviet Union as a place of promise and plenty would be not only altogether absent from American popular commentary but regarded as an absurd inversion of what everyone knew to be true of the "slave world"—that it was a realm of deprivation and despair. With Middleton's soft-focus lens discarded, Soviet citizens were depicted shuffling through a drab landscape of identikit buildings, absorbing a sterile communist ideology that dulled resistance to the state that stunted their lives. No longer irrepressible workers, they appeared joyless automatons trapped in a giant prison or vast DP camp. "The saddest people on earth are those who are homeless at home, people forced to live under a system so alien to their own instincts and desires that their homelands are strange prisons," proposed Anne O'Hare McCormick in 1952, gesturing behind the Iron Curtain. "These are people who are displaced without moving; their spiritual exile is far worse than physical deportation."[46] Driven into inner emigration, Soviet citizens were simultaneously prisoners of their state and stateless refugees.

How did this discursive volte-face occur with such speed and totality? The answer owes much to the ascendancy of totalitarianism as the "great mobilizing and unifying concept of the Cold War." After hovering on the margins of political philosophy for two decades, this theory may not have been unique to postwar America, but it was uniquely serviceable.[47] Its central postulate was that regimes hitherto plotted as the outer extremes on a horizontal left-right axis in fact converged in circular fashion. Theorists of totalitarianism maintained that there was no fundamental difference between Nazi Germany and the Soviet Union: both were "total states" that shared the same annihilatory aspiration not only to regiment human behavior but to extinguish every last spark of inner vitality. Communism, J. Edgar Hoover asserted in 1947, was merely "red fascism."[48]

Since many distinctions had to be finessed in order to elide Nazism and Soviet communism, theorists of totalitarianism focused not on political ideology but metaphysical essence: on the will to absolute power that united Hitler and Stalin. Nowhere was this essence more palpable or more apparent as an emanation of absolute evil than in the concentration camp. As the total state's defining institution, the camp occupied center stage in theories of totalitarianism—the precise point where "obsolete political differentiations" between Nazi Germany and the Soviet Union collapsed and definitional hair-splitting became a moral obscenity. The camp, proposed Hannah Arendt in *The Origins of Totalitarianism* (1951), functioned as the "laboratory" in which totalitarians perfected the malign science of reducing humans to "mere bundles of reactions"—"ghastly marionettes with human faces, which all behave like the dog in Pavlov's experiments, which all react with perfect reliability even when going to their own death, and which do nothing but react."[49]

Americans knew well enough what these "laboratories" looked like. In the spring and summer of 1945 they had seen numerous still and moving images of Nazi concentration and extermination camps—shocking pictures of skeletal survivors and stacked corpses, of SS perpetrators and German bystanders.[50] Soviet camps, by contrast, remained invisible to western cameras, but they occupied an increasingly prominent place in postwar portrayals of the communist bloc. Containing millions of forced laborers, the vast network of camps scattered across the Soviet Union served to literalize the descriptor "slave world." Theorists of totalitarianism often made this point rather abstrusely; U.S. policy makers would popularize it in plain language, on the assumption that workers and peasants worldwide would reject communism once they became aware of its crimes.

As chapter 3 of *Cold War Captives* shows, Washington waged a concerted campaign to draw attention to the Soviet gulag during the late 1940s and early 1950s. However, the notion of the camp/prison as a microcosm of communist society was hardly unique to government publications. Literary representations of the "total state" also made confinement a central theme. Privileged fictions of the early cold war—Arthur Koestler's *Darkness at Noon* (1941) and George Orwell's *1984* (1949) in particular—rendered its quintessential milieu as a suffocating space with a door bolted shut and a grille through which the occupant could be observed but from which nothing could be glimpsed of the world beyond. The quintessence of totalitarianism, as these novels conceived it, lay in a dank prison cell or the dreaded Room 101.

Works of imagination seemingly shaped U.S. diplomats' perceptions and prescriptions just as much as intellectual theorizations of totalitarianism. George Kennan, who had served as a diplomat in both Nazi Germany and the USSR (before and after the war), insisted that fiction offered a *superior* way of apprehending "its power as a dream, or as a nightmare." It was the phantasmic dimension of the total state—a trick collectively played on and by captive minds—that Kennan regarded as its most singular, and ineffable, attribute. "When I try to picture totalitarianism to myself as a general phenomenon," he mused in 1953, "what comes into my mind most prominently is neither the Soviet picture nor the Nazi picture as I have known them in the flesh, but rather the fictional and symbolic images created by such people as Orwell or Kafka or Koestler or the early Soviet satirists."[51]

Whether derived from literature, political theory, or personal experience, carceral motifs loomed large in leading cold warriors' interpretations of Soviet behavior. Kennan's famous "Long Telegram" of February 22, 1946, portrayed the Soviet Union as a "dim half world" governed by "oriental" secretiveness—with rulers so fearful of "foreign penetration" that they kept their own citizens locked in and others shut out.[52] Sixteen months later, writing under the pseudonym "X" in *Foreign Affairs*, Kennan expanded his earlier depiction of mass immobilization to stress imprisonment at its most literal. Anticipating State Department initiatives to indict "slave labor," he noted that Soviet industrialization had "necessitated the use of forced labor on a scale unprecedented in modern times."[53]

The foundational document of cold war grand strategy, National Security Council Report 68 (NSC 68), fashioned its entire exegesis around the Soviet Union's enslaving tendencies, which threatened "the fulfillment or destruction not only of this Republic but of civilization itself." Imputing an eliminationist impulse to the "idea of slavery," Paul Nitze and his coauthors anticipated a war of extermination that brooked no possibility of coexistence or compromise. The "slave power" would not rest content until the "idea of freedom" had been annihilated, for the "implacable purpose of the slave state is to eliminate the challenge of freedom." The very existence of freedom—so irresistible in its allure—represented a mortal danger to the slave world. This "antipathy of slavery to freedom," NSC 68 proposed, explained "the iron curtain, the isolation, the autarchy of the society whose end is absolute power."[54]

In urging that the United States cultivate its inner vitality while applying pressure wherever the Soviet Union threatened to "penetrate" (or overwhelm) free institutions, NSC 68 sounded notes familiar from Kennan's earlier jeremiads. But its account of the sources of Soviet behavior exceeded the Long Telegram's elaboration of the compound of Russian "secretiveness," Marxist dogmatism, and postwar insecurity that impelled Stalin toward confrontation with the western powers. Minimizing the role of Marxist-Leninism in the Soviet worldview, NSC 68 advanced a psychosexual interpretation of the dynamics that shaped the "slave society." "Where the despot holds absolute power—the absolute power of the absolutely powerful will—all other wills must be subjugated in an act of willing submission, a degradation willed by the individual upon himself under the compulsion of a perverted faith." In the eyes of Nitze and his coauthors, the "slave state" not only sought but received its subjects' unconditional surrender to the pleasures of passivity and masochistic delights of "degradation."[55]

This remarkable account of the "perverted faith" that kept slaves in ecstatic thrall to their masters was not authored by students of Soviet politics, Russia specialists, or those who (at a later stage of the cold war) would become known as Kremlinologists. Elaborated over fifty dense pages, NSC 68's characterization of the "slave world"—swollen with metaphysical implications and sexual connotations—cited no concrete empirical evidence. Challenged later on its inflation of the total state's omnipotence, Nitze defensively cast his blueprint for containment as "very much a product of its times."[56] This it certainly was. NSC 68's vision of the slave power's sadistic desire for utter abnegation could have been lifted straight from *1984*, published the previous year. "Power is in inflicting pain and humiliation," the state interrogator O'Brien informs Winston Smith: "Power is in tearing human minds to pieces and putting them together again in new shapes of your own choosing." From these reassembled beings, Big Brother demands fervent assent, not mute acquiescence.[57]

What decisively marked NSC 68 as a product of its time was less its account of a leviathan's insatiable will to power—a recurrent figuration of political theory from Hobbes to Nietzsche—than its depiction of the "slavish" abandonment of those who gladly yielded to the "boot stamping on the human face." Here Nitze sounded a note that reverberated through the work of contemporaries in a range of fields: Erich Fromm on the "escape from freedom"; Bruno Bettelheim on the psychology of concentration camp inmates; and Stanley Elkins on the plantation mentality.[58] These authors' influential treatises all stressed the readiness with which individuals ceded their autonomy under "totalizing" circumstances that encouraged a relinquishment of the burdensome self. Fearful that there lurked (in Arthur Schlesinger's phrase) a "Stalin in every breast" surreptitiously whispering "Freedom is Slavery," American liberals conjured up the nightmarish prospect that not every subject might jealously guard and cherish his or her individual agency.[59] Modern selves seemed only too eager for submission. By the mid-1950s many critics had come to regard passivity as the greatest malaise to afflict postwar society. Plumped and coddled into complacency, Americans were turning into the affectless pod people of Don Siegel's *Invasion of the Body Snatchers* (1956). Abundance, wrote Schlesinger, "has burned up the mortgage, but at the same time sealed us in a subtler slavery."[60] For Betty Friedan, affluent suburbia was nothing but a "comfortable concentration camp."[61]

SENTIMENTAL ANTICOMMUNISM

Captivity occupied the commanding heights of the cold war's ideological economy in the United States. But as the fissile material of anticommunism, its effects proved more unpredictable than strategists like Kennan, Nitze, or Dulles may have anticipated or desired. This volatility of feeling was especially pronounced when Americans turned their attention from the eastern bloc's slave laborers and captive peoples to the plight of captured U.S. citizens. Before the Korean War delivered several thousand American soldiers and airmen into communist captivity in the winter of 1950–51, a handful of incarcerations in China and eastern Europe generated intensive publicity and equally intense emotion. Early cold war opinion formers ascribed revelatory power to these captivities, echoing Harriet Beecher Stowe's assertion that to "realize the miseries of captivity" it was necessary to turn from "the idea of hundreds of thousands languishing in dungeons" to "the picture of one poor, solitary captive pining in his cell."[62]

Over the course of two years, a series of cases claimed the headlines. In October 1948, Angus Ward, the flamboyant U.S. consul general in Mukden (the principal city in Manchuria), was placed under house arrest and held incommunicado for thirteen months by Chinese communist forces.[63] Several more Americans— as many as two hundred, *Life* speculated—met a similar fate.[64] In May 1950, Senator Joseph McCarthy took up the cause of Marine Sgt. Elmer Bender and Navy Chief Machinist's Mate William C. Smith, who had spent twenty months imprisoned in the People's Republic, and used their plight as a stick with which to beat the State Department for "losing" China and subsequently failing to retaliate against communist provocation with sufficient vigor.[65]

While thousands of American missionaries and businessmen joined the Nationalist scramble to flee the People's Republic, eastern Europe was also becoming a terra incognita for western travelers and traders. Several American businessmen were briefly imprisoned in Hungary in 1949 but released after confessing to sundry offenses and paying fines to Budapest's pro-Soviet government. This pattern of harassment assumed more alarming proportions in November 1949, when an IT&T executive, Robert A. Vogeler, was charged with leading a "pro-fascist" spy ring and sabotaging reconstruction efforts in the Hungarian people's democracy. In February 1950, Vogeler (the subject of chapter 4) became the first American to appear in what fellow citizens unhesitatingly called a "show trial," or, more provocatively, a "lynching under the cloak of law."[66] His imprisonment overlapped with a similar episode in neighboring Czechoslovakia, where William Oatis, the Associated Press bureau chief in Prague, was incarcerated on espionage charges in 1951. And while Americans continued to smart over this affront, four U.S. airmen, downed in Hungary in November 1951, were jailed and "ransomed" for $120,000 by Mátyas Rákosi's regime in a fresh manifestation of what reporters dubbed "communist gangsterism." "All that is lacking," proposed C. L. Sulzberger, the doyen of U.S. foreign correspondents, "is the traditional Albanian custom of sending together with the ransom note a small portion of the victim's body."[67]

Contemporary responses to these developments frequently invoked the horrible ordeal of earlier American captives, particularly those citizens of the fledgling republic "enslaved" by Barbary pirates a century and a half earlier. Communist blows to national honor aggravated old wounds, and vice versa. But at the same time history (to those minded to read it in a particular way) recommended proven responses to barbarism. Invariably, administration critics proposed tactics more bellicose than those favored by the State Department. The most pugnacious urged that communist ransom demands be parried with the defiant Jeffersonian riposte, "Not one cent for tribute!" Rather than succumb to blackmail, the United States should put its ballistic advantage to use, prompted Senator William Jenner (R-IN): "It is time to tell the government of Czechoslovakia to release Oatis or we will send an air missile to Prague and take him."[68] If freeing American captives meant war with the "communist world," then so be it.

By the time Jenner made his provocative recommendation, America *was* at war with the "communist world"—in Asia if not in Europe. Indeed, the imprisonment of some five thousand U.S. service personnel in camps along North Korea's Manchurian border stoked the rage with which many Americans responded to events behind the Iron Curtain. With the war in Korea at a military impasse, it was easy to interpret captivity as evidence of American powerlessness; frequent analogies with rape underscored the humiliatingly feminine character of this degradation. But in the eyes of many midcentury Americans, incarceration by communists was worse than a violation of bodily integrity or a deprivation of physical liberty, for the captive was also stripped of *mental* autonomy.

Such fears have a long history in North America. The captivity narratives of Puritan New England brimmed with anxiety that "unredeemed" captives would adopt Indian ways or (worse yet) lose their souls to papacy. Similarly, imprisonment on the Barbary coast raised the specter that beleaguered American sailors would "turn Turk," embracing their captors' Mohammedan religion. Yet while shadowed by the threat of transgression, most narratives affirmed the ultimate triumph of Christian faith and civilized ways over savagery. Early cold war stories, by contrast, reversed this pattern. Commonly, they were tales of American cowardice, confession, or even conversion in captivity that were all the more troubling for this antiheroic cast. What many Americans found most disturbing in the Vogeler story was that he had confessed to the "absurd" charges against him—as had Cardinal Mindszenty (prince-primate of the Hungarian Catholic Church) one year earlier.

At the time of Mindszenty's trial in February 1949, Americans lacked a term for the trancelike state in which the cardinal had delivered his mea culpa and the "diabolical" treatment that had rendered him so obedient—whether drugs, hypnosis, or torture had effected the transformation. Eighteen months later, they had a word for this perplexing process, *brainwashing,* now applied liberally to discussion of Vogeler's collapse and American POWs' collaboration with their captors. "Some people have asserted that there is no such thing as brain-washing, or individual psychological conquest," cautioned Gladwin Hill (the *New York Times* bureau chief in Los Angeles). "They can hardly have been aware of the Russian purge trials; evidently they did not read Arthur Koestler; or they did not believe the harrowing stories of Robert Vogeler and Williams Oatis, who came from behind the Iron Curtain." After brainwashing's "grisly success with civilians," it was only to be expected that "the Communists would try it out in the military field."[69]

No one knew, or could ever agree on, exactly *how* a brain was washed. There was similar disagreement over whether mental erasure could be reversed under benign influences or whether brainwashing was more akin to boiling a wool sweater: a process that left behind something forever shrunken and useless. Rather than limiting the term's utility, however, this mysterious vagueness made it all the more serviceable for an ever-expanding array of psychopathologies that purportedly rendered Americans suggestible, listless, and inclined to "give-up-itis."[70] Several of these conditions had nothing to do with communism and only an allusive connection to captivity, yet they all betokened a terrible corrosion of national character, or so numerous social critics insisted. As chapter 5 shows, by mid-decade many commentators had devoted far greater energy to probing the enfeebled American psyche—the *real* enemy within—than to exploring or excoriating the "communist threat" from without.

As in times past, captivity was generative of intense sentiment during the early cold war. Where tales of captivation in Puritan New England issued an invitation to Indian hating, their cold war counterparts rallied what we might call sentimental anticommunism, an unstable compound of empathy and fury. Understood as an affront to national pride, captivity stirred a retaliatory animus as sympathy for pitiable victims hardened into vengefulness, and vengeance in turn promised national "regeneration through violence."[71] Yet whatever violent impulses stories of victimization licensed, their real sting was often aimed less at the "captivating Other" than at the sinful self who had succumbed to captivity. Conceived as a test of individual and collective mettle, captivity, in early cold war America as on the colonial frontier, prompted ferocious self-criticism, replete with admonitions against the perils of sloth, greed, and heedlessness of the Almighty. When Kennan (writing as X) thanked Providence for providing the American people with an "implacable challenge" that stood to renew national cohesion and restore collective purpose, he struck a note redolent of Puritan sermons that had interpreted captivity as a divinely mandated ordeal, an opportunity for the elect to prove their worthiness and consecrate their covenant anew.[72]

At once thrilling and terrifying to contemplate, an appalling prospect and an appealing fantasy, captivity served as a stimulus to protest, prayer, and play in early cold war America. This double-edged character can be seen in an elaborately choreographed "Red take-over," staged in the small Wisconsin town of Mosinee on May Day, 1950. Aiming to heighten awareness of how grim daily life would be if communists took over and thereby to prove "how lucky we are to have a democracy," the American Legion hit on the idea of a municipal role-playing exercise with "smashing" pictorial possibilities.[73] With Joseph Zach Kornfeder and Ben Gitlow (two former Communist Party USA members who had become friendly witnesses

FIGURE 2. Playing at captivity. During a staged communist takeover at Mosinee, Wisconsin, on May Day, 1950, objectionable citizens are consigned by role-playing Red commissars to a makeshift "concentration camp." © The Associated Press.

for HUAC) on hand to ensure the verisimilitude of this performance, Mosinee's new rulers forced residents onto the streets to demonstrate fealty to the Red flag. Restaurants were compelled to serve a restricted menu of unedifying fare. And the movie theater was "nationalized," depriving townsfolk of the opportunity to watch *Guilty of Treason,* Felix Feist's dramatization of the Mindszenty story, which the "commissars" no doubt found especially objectionable.

The central artifact of Mosinee's takeover, however, was a "concentration camp" erected in the town's newly renamed Red Square, to which ideological reprobates were unceremoniously dispatched by what the *Washington Post* referred to as "red gorilla squads." A photograph carried in the *New York Times* showed three nuns behind the barbed wire: godless communism at its most sacrilegious. Meanwhile, the mayor's expulsion from his home, dressed only in polka-dot pajamas and robe, was a moment of such rich visual piquancy that it had to be rehearsed several times until photographers and cameramen were satisfied that they had captured its drama to best effect.[74] It was unfortunate, then, that within a week of the "communist coup" both Mayor Kronenwetter and a Mosinee clergyman, also consigned to the concentration camp, were dead—one the victim of an cerebral hemorrhage and the other of a heart attack. Two unscripted fatalities lent greater irrevocability to the simulation than the legionnaires doubtless intended, though neither these deaths nor any potentially discomforting wartime memories deterred the Legion from proposing at its annual convention (just two months later) that all "proven Communists" be interned in the interests of "national defense."[75]

A monstrous affront to individual dignity and civilized values when communists practiced it, confinement carried a different valence when Americans proposed it. Containment was, after all, the early cold war's grand strategic concept. Meanwhile, civil defense officials urged vigilant citizens to embrace another form of voluntary incarceration, conceiving the fallout shelter as a place of deliverance or even a subterranean site of erotic possibility—a point *Life* magazine elaborated by devoting an August 1959 photo story to one newlywed couple's "Sheltered Honeymoon."[76]

Truman's cold warriors invested "containment" with an array of positive connotations. More recently, though, cultural critics have recoded the term as shorthand for the scattershot smears and stigmatizing maneuvers that constrained speech, straitened subjectivity, and policed "deviance" in postwar America.[77] Not restricted to figurative closetings, "containment culture" also assumed more literal, and invasively punitive, forms. Several leftist intellectuals, artists, and activists who critiqued forms of "unfreedom" in America found themselves incarcerated and deported, like the Austrian-born communist leader Gerhart Eisler and Trinidadian Trotskyist C. L. R. James, or prohibited from traveling beyond U.S. borders, like Paul Robeson. At the Red Scare's zenith, the Truman and Eisenhower administrations proved as reluctant to let out "fellow-traveling" residents as to let in foreigners who had once been, or might remain, Communist Party members.

In assuming free world leadership, Washington wrestled with multiple inconsistencies—none sharper than the discrepancy between a declaratory language of freedom and the palpable legacies of slavery that continued to stratify black and white citizens along racialized lines. Such contradictions were, of course, grist to Moscow's mill. To State Department attacks on "slave labor," the Soviets replied by assailing the persistence of racial discrimination in the United States, the status of American women as "kitchen slaves," and, more broadly, the "wage slavery" of capitalism. To charges that Moscow had dropped an impenetrable iron curtain across Europe, Soviet commentators pointed to a color line every bit as rigid. U.S. cold warriors accordingly strove to recast, obfuscate, or disavow slavery's history in the "free world." When, for example, John Foster Dulles took an editorial pencil to a draft "Resolution on Enslavement of Peoples" in February 1953, he alighted on a sentence proclaiming that America would "never acquiesce" to the "enslavement of any people"—a declaration couched in the conditional future tense. This formulation evidently dissatisfied Dulles, who substituted a timeless historical assertion that "the people of the United States, in fidelity to their tradition and heritage of freedom, have never acquiesced in such enslavement of any people." At a stroke, he reconceived U.S. history as, in effect, always already abolitionist.[78]

This book explores captivity's contribution to the work of imagining the cold war as a contest between "slave world" and "free." Elements of this story have been told before. Other authors have anatomized cold war rhetoric, dissected the social construction of the "communist threat," analyzed the role of totalitarianism as a galvanizing concept, and pondered the origins of Americans' alarmist response to brainwashing. Over the past decade, the "cultural cold war" has received sustained scholarly attention, as have U.S. attempts to perforate the Iron Curtain and roll back communism by clandestine means. *Cold War Captives* pursues a different tack, however, showing how the rhetorical opposition between slavery and freedom took shape around concrete struggles over repatriation, defection, forced labor, incarceration, and mind control: issues that, to prominent opinion formers of the day, appeared just as consequential as the threat of atomic war.

America's cold war imaginary was, then, profoundly informed by the dichotomy between mobility and captivity. Yet standard diplomatic histories typically tell us little about how Washington's projections involving captives and escapees evolved, while most cultural critiques of the "cold war within" are similarly inattentive to captivity, whether as allegory or lived experience. To a striking degree, these two literatures have developed in near-isolation from one another. One of the larger objectives of this book is thus to transcend the schism between accounts of the cold war without and within. Even as scholars have deconstructed the categories "foreign" and "domestic," insisting on their mutually constitutive character, cold war history continues to be conceived in ways that implicitly reify the notion of a domestic "inside" distinct and separate from a foreign "outside."

Inwardly focused studies of the "age of McCarthy" often neglect the international context within which the man and his -ism flourished, treating the politics of the Red Scare and the blacklists as peculiarly introverted phenomena, the outgrowth of a long American tradition of witch-hunting and countersubversive demagoguery. On the other side of this historiographical iron curtain, we find analyses of a parallel cold war of arms races and missile gaps, puppet regimes and proxy wars, in which domestic opinion barely surfaces. Where "ordinary people" fleetingly appear in these externally oriented histories, it is generally with the assumption that their collective will was bludgeoned or duped into passive assent to the schemes of diplomats, premiers, and generals.

Placing captivity at the center of the early cold war's cultural and international politics offers a way to breach this conceptual boundary. Drawing on sources that range from declassified documents to glossy magazines and heavy-handed Hollywood B movies, *Cold War Captives* explores what it *meant* to Americans to be engaged in a cold war, asking why and how this peculiar conflict so often found expression in practices, images, and allegories of captivity—and to what effect. It seeks answers at the point where foreign and domestic intersect: where high politics coincides with popular culture and top-down pressure meets bottom-up agency.

Exploring the role of elite opinion formers in mobilizing support for a worldwide, open-ended struggle, this study is equally concerned with popular interpretations and appropriations of captivity, many of which surpassed officially mandated responses in their extravagant emotionalism. It was, after all, a curious thing to be mobilized for cold war, not least when America was simultaneously fighting—and failing to win (or perhaps even *refusing* to win)—a hot war in Korea. Captivity variously provided a reason to fight harder or to quit altogether. To some, it appeared a symptom of weakness that signaled the need to deploy superior strength; to others, it demonstrated the perils of overstretch and need for retrenchment. Infusing anticommunism with a volatile sentimentality, captivity animated displays of intolerance and venom toward enemies without and within. If there was indeed a "cold war consensus," it was neither mute nor passive, and certainly not lacking an adrenalin rush of anger.

Upper East Side Story

Repatriation, Romance, and Cold War Mobilization

THE HOUSE ON SIXTY-FIRST STREET

In August 1948 a ferocious heat wave claimed scores of lives and provoked a rash of unusual behavior across the United States. As a mass of tropical air drifted up the Mississippi Valley—"like a soldering iron being run slowly up a dowager's spine"—chickens dropped dead and asphalt sidewalks turned to molten taffy. Indianapolis experienced a "plague of Peeping Toms," while in Washington, D.C., Tom Collinses were the order of the day. Desperate to escape the heat, twenty thousand autoworkers in Detroit boycotted the assembly line, just as baseball fans nationwide stayed away from big league games. Louder, hotter, and more crowded than anywhere else, New York City formed the center of this maelstrom. As the New York Telephone Company answered 190,000 calls from individuals inquiring, "Hey, Mac—how hot?" the city's police were "driven wild by wrench-wielding gangs who turned on hundreds of hydrants," reported *Time*. Photographers, meanwhile, were driven wild by the city's fashion-conscious women, who were stripping down to nothing more than a sheet worn "toga-style" to have their hair set.[1] But none of this hot weather drama was more peculiar, or more compelling, than the events played out on August 12 at 7 East Sixty-first Street.

A sultry Thursday afternoon found numerous reporters and cameramen milling outside the ornate mansion that housed the Soviet consulate, smoking, chatting, or resting on car fenders. Their presence attracted a growing throng of curious loiterers. All were anxious for news of the woman being held captive inside, Oksana Kasenkina—a schoolteacher who had fled Manhattan some days earlier in a bid to avoid repatriation to the USSR by the diplomats whose children she had spent two years tutoring. Removed from her upstate sanctuary by the consul on August 7, Kasenkina had been confined in the consulate ever since. Her entrapment prompted the anticommunist organization Common Cause, Inc., to seek a habeas corpus writ that required Consul Lomakin to produce her in court on August 12. When Lomakin blithely ignored the summons he left the press braced for fresh developments in this baffling consular melodrama. A showdown seemed imminent. Yet its precise form surely caught even the most seasoned hacks off guard, for who could have anticipated that the suspense would be punctured not by further bluster from the consul but by the appearance of Kasenkina herself—plunging from a third-floor window?

This news broke at about 4:00 p.m., when a liveried employee of the private club next door to the consulate dashed out to alert the press pack to what he'd just seen. His cry—"Hey fellows! A woman just jumped out the back window!"—triggered a rush by reporters to clamber across the fence for a better view of the action in the adjacent courtyard.[2] Through the railings, they observed a woman on her back with telephone wires tangled around her legs, her body blocking a doorway from which Soviet staff members were trying to emerge. A skein of cables—ripped loose from the masonry by the impact of her descent—had broken the teacher's fall. "There was an instant of silence," related *Time*. "Then the whole neighborhood was in uproar."[3]

Police officers raced to reach the injured woman, while a trio of consular attachés struggled to push the door open from the inside. The latter succeeded after a couple of minutes, and as they started dragging Kasenkina across the threshold, she could be heard crying "*Ostavte, ostavte!*"—"Leave me alone, leave me alone." Meanwhile, a police officer managed to "hoist his 170 pounds over a 8 foot wall" with "the skill healthy young men have for such occasions." Shouldering his way into the consulate, he breached the "Red Iron Curtain," the *Chicago Daily Tribune* approvingly noted.[4] By the time an ambulance arrived at 4:35 p.m., a crowd of three hundred had amassed on the street outside. Within a few minutes, it had grown "considerably larger." Scuffles broke out between reporters and police patrolmen before an unconscious Kasenkina was stretchered out at 5:00 p.m. and whisked across town to the Roosevelt Hospital.[5] Thus the summer's most mysterious saga reached its cliff-hanging "Perils of Pauline" climax, as *Newsweek* put it, invoking the silent movie heroine who invariably managed to extricate herself from the jaws of disaster.[6]

A "first class diplomatic incident," the Kasenkina affair became an instant cause célèbre.[7] For several days, her vertiginous "leap for freedom" was indisputably *the* story, lavishly illustrated with photographic spreads and breathlessly narrated by the newsreels. Americans—seemingly unmoved by distant wrangling over Berlin and the creeping Stalinization of eastern Europe—thrilled to a drama that brought the opposition between two antithetical ways of life into sharp relief,

FIGURE 3. Kasenkina's "leap for freedom" captured the moment after she landed in the Soviet consulate's rear courtyard on August 12, 1948. © The Associated Press.

underscoring "the gulf between the philosophy of the ant heap and the philosophy of a free person in a free society."[8] But the story resonated far beyond U.S. borders. "The crash of her body on the pavement was heard around the world," one columnist remarked with little exaggeration. Voice of America broadcasters amplified the thud, boasting that they'd taken just forty-one minutes to beam news of Kasenkina's "leap for freedom" to audiences behind the Iron Curtain. "This is what we have been waiting for in our war of words," one official remarked. "This is something that can be easily understood by people all over the world."[9]

Many opinion formers were just as eager for the anti-Soviet ammunition that Kasenkina's story supplied, though it required some ingenuity to marshal meaning from events as hazy in circumstantial detail as they were rich in symbolic significance. Yet despite journalists' enthusiastic flame fanning, the actions of an obscure chemistry teacher *need* not have sparked a major international incident. Why, then, did Washington and Moscow choose to escalate what might otherwise have been an inconsequential episode? What was at stake in the fate of Oksana Kasenkina that so many parties rushed to wrangle over her?

Contemporary observers understood the larger significance of this episode in different ways. For some, most notably the influential columnists Joseph and Stewart Alsop, the tussle over Kasenkina was rooted in the conflicted postwar politics of repatriation. Viewed in this way, the chemistry teacher represented one among thousands of Soviet citizens who had resisted return to the USSR since 1945, her desperation mirroring the distress—or suicidal despair—of innumerable displaced persons (DPs). If the events on East Sixty-first Street shed oblique light on conditions in refugee camps across Europe, they also constituted an argument for a new U.S. policy to accommodate and employ this growing legion of "free world" recruits.[10]

Others interpreted the Kasenkina affair as a uniquely consular crisis, one that signaled the dangers of trying to conduct diplomacy as normal under increasingly abnormal conditions. Consul Lomakin's attempt to exercise "police power" over an exclusive portion of the Upper East Side called into question the desirability of permitting a Soviet presence on U.S. soil—or of sending American representatives to the USSR only to be harassed and surveilled.[11] With the two states curtailing movement and association within and between their territories, U.S. diplomats in Moscow soon concluded that they too had become cold war captives.

If the "case of the defenestrated schoolteacher," as the Alsops called it, lowered the temperature of U.S.-Soviet relations by several degrees, it also quickened the pulse of domestic anticommunism, pumping oxygen through the capillaries that connect high politics and popular culture.[12] A diplomatic crisis, the incident on Sixty-first Street was in rapid succession a media event and a cultural phenomenon. Soon after her fateful leap, Kasenkina announced that she had been emboldened by a biopic on the Soviet defector Igor Gouzenko, William Wellman's *The Iron Curtain*. Roused to action by Hollywood's fictional version of a real-life defection, she in turn inspired both cultural producers and consumers. While she may have been no Ethel Barrymore or Bette Davis, the "little Russian schoolteacher" agitated popular feeling in unexpected ways, catalyzing a string of copycat escapes and kindling a variety of rescue fantasies that were charged with both ideological and emotional significance.

THE MYSTERY OF THE KIDNAPPED RUSSIAN

For a clarifying moment, the Kasenkina story was remarkably muddled. Even columnists who hailed its capacity to crystallize the cold war's terms of engagement acknowledged that readers had to negotiate no less than three competing versions of the schoolteacher's "three-story jump"—a conservative estimate, given the sizable array of parties vying to stamp their authority over a convoluted sequence of events and the woman at its center.[13] "At first," wrote *Life* magazine, "only one fact was clear. When the Russian steamship *Pobeda* sailed from New York harbor on July 31 . . . Mrs. Kosenkina, a 52-year old woman who dressed carelessly but liked to use large amounts of US cosmetics, was not on board."[14]

American newspaper readers received their first introduction to this ungainly character on August 8, 1948. Under front-page headlines, reporters recounted a "bizarre tug-of-war between White and Red Russians."[15] At a press conference convened in the Soviet consulate on August 7, Jakov Lomakin, the Soviet consul general, related a gripping cloak-and-dagger tale that cast the FBI and "white Russian bandits" as malign conspirators in an abduction plot. His story went as follows. On July 31, three teachers, colleagues at the school for Soviet diplomats' children in Manhattan, vanished shortly before they were due to board a ship bound for home. Two members of this trio, Mikhail and Klavdia Samarin, remained at large, spirited away by the FBI. The third, Oksana Kasenkina, had fallen foul of the machinations of anticommunist émigrés—"white Russian bandits" in Lomakin's terminology—determined to prevent her return to the USSR. Intent on spreading vicious calumnies about the Soviet Union to disoriented Russians in America, Kasenkina's shadowy pursuers had latched onto the impassive woman who now sat before the press corps. Dressed in a black skirt, white blouse, turquoise-colored bobby socks, and red moccasins, with eyes lowered and legs demurely crossed at the ankle, Kasenkina did indeed appear adrift between generations and cultures—a fifty-two-year-old widow approximating the attire of an American adolescent.[16]

White Russian gangsters had thrown this helpless woman into turmoil, Lomakin announced. They had bamboozled her with repeated assertions that she would be sent to Siberia on return to the USSR; that her soldier son was dead; that her husband, missing since 1937, had been "liquidated." Not content with poisoning her mind, one of these "bandits" had lured the teacher to a shady spot on Riverside Drive, where he had plunged a hypodermic needle into her arm. (Kasenkina, almost mute throughout, obligingly rolled up her sleeve to reveal a blotchy rash.) Whatever mind-altering substance the syringe contained had left the poor creature quite devoid of will. "Everything went black," Lomakin theatrically intoned. Insensible, Kasenkina had permitted her abductors to drive her some thirty miles north of New York City to Reed Farm, a hostel for "reactionaries" run by Alexandra Tolstoy, the author's youngest daughter.

When Kasenkina had regained her senses, Lomakin continued, she had immediately written him—a letter smuggled out of the White Russian vipers' nest by a passing stranger with a vegetable cart. She had implored the consul to fetch her at once, terrified lest her captors prevent her return to the beloved Soviet homeland. At his point, Lomakin brandished a two-page letter and read a couple of impassioned sentences: "Once more I beg you not to let me perish here. . . . I have been deprived of my freedom."[17] He and his staff had duly responded to her cry for help, arriving at Reed Farm to find the poor woman at the kitchen sink, subjected to "slave labor." Despite the best efforts of Tolstoy's reactionaries to prevent their departure, the consular motorcade had managed to get away under a hail of sticks and stones.

Not surprisingly, reporters greeted this "lurid" tale with much skepticism. Dismissing Lomakin's story as a "lot of baloney," Alexandra Tolstoy offered an alternative version that reversed the identities of rescuer and kidnapper, assigning the

FIGURE 4. Meet the Press. Soviet consul Jakov Lomakin introduces Oksana Kasenkina to American reporters on August 7, 1948, displaying the letter in which she asked to be rescued from Reed Farm. © The Associated Press.

virtuous role to Russian émigrés and attributing an abduction (or something akin to it) to the consul and his staff. In Tolstoy's telling, Kasenkina had come to Reed Farm willingly, after making contact with various anti-Soviet Russians in Manhattan. Tolstoy confessed initial doubt as to whether Kasenkina was a plant who was posing as a defector to glean intelligence for the Soviets on the "underground railway" for fugitive Russians that she helped operate.[18] But Tolstoy's suspicions had been allayed by the teacher's agitated demeanor: the woman had been so fearful for her life that she refused to sleep in a room alone at night. Had she wished to leave, she could have done so at any time. Reed Farm, its proprietor pointedly remarked, was not a prison camp. Since no one policed its perimeter, Kasenkina had only to summon a taxi or walk to a bus stop if she wished to leave. She did not, and when consular staff suddenly appeared six days later, the hysterical teacher accompanied them in a state of suicidal resignation, having abandoned herself to the prospect of imminent liquidation. Kasenkina's parting words—"If they shoot me maybe it's the best way out"—did not suggest tremendous eagerness for return either to the consulate or to the Soviet Union.[19]

Clearly, these two accounts were incompatible, yet neither one added up to a coherent whole. In Lomakin's narrative, the influence of mind-altering drugs was required to explain the oddity of Kasenkina placing herself in the hands of her alleged abductors. As Tolstoy recounted events, it was unclear why the schoolteacher—if she were eager to evade return to the USSR—would write a letter alerting the consul to her whereabouts, possibly even inviting him to come and fetch her from a place of sanctuary. (Or had she, perhaps, written no such letter at all?) In both stories, Kasenkina appeared perplexingly acquiescent to her own captivity, whether at the hands of White Russians or Soviet officials.

Something curious was going on. However, the predicament of a discombobulated Soviet schoolteacher—once again in the custody of her consulate—was not necessarily dry tinder for a major diplomatic conflagration. Conceivably, the affair might have ended after this initial flurry of accusations had various protagonists not wished to bring matters to a head by enlisting the law to substantiate their version of events. The Soviets attempted to initiate a criminal investigation into Kasenkina's "kidnapping," the illicit activities of White Russian "gangster" organizations, and the FBI's role in the disappearance of three teachers.[20] From Foreign Minister Molotov downwards, Soviet officials furiously repudiated the State Department's claim that Lomakin had imprisoned Kasenkina against her will in the consulate. The very suggestion that he had detained "a citizeness" was "incompatible with the dignity of a Soviet Consul."[21] Tolstoy, meanwhile, filed a report with the New York State Police regarding the seizure of Kasenkina from Reed Farm by consular personnel.

Into this melee stepped Representative Karl Mundt, acting chair of the House Committee on Un-American Activities (HUAC), determined to bring the runaway teachers into the committee's ambit—and sensing, no doubt, an opportunity to attract further media attention to its activities.[22] Not that publicity was lacking. In August 1948, HUAC was very visibly investigating allegations of a communist espionage ring within the U.S. government in hearings that introduced audiences to Elizabeth Bentley, the so-called red spy queen, and produced the first airing of Whittaker Chambers's explosive claims regarding the subversive activities of Alger Hiss.[23] With their inside knowledge of the consulate, the Samarins and Kasenkina might be able to shed further light on Soviet spying operations, Mundt asserted.

Claiming to know that Kasenkina wished to make herself a "stateless person" and eager to appraise HUAC of "the whole Soviet system of world controls," Mundt planned to subpoena her: an unorthodox means of extending U.S. state protection over a woman he cast as the consulate's unwilling captive. "To have what amounts to a branch of the NKVD [Narodnyi Komissariat Vnutrennikh Del (People's Commissariat of Internal Affairs), the Russian secret police] pick up a person in a private American home and put them in virtual seclusion—in what amounts to house arrest—seems to us unprecedented," he announced. His point was clear, if not eloquently expressed: "We feel that that kind of goings-on cannot be tolerated." But rescuing Kasenkina required adjudication of the extraterritoriality of consular property, which in Mundt's words occupied a "twilight zone"—claiming the same immunities as embassies, though possibly without equivalent entitlement.[24]

Was the Soviets' elegant Upper East Side mansion beyond the reach of U.S. police officers as they investigated competing criminal allegations made about Kasenkina's removal to and then from Reed Farm? Could HUAC subpoena a woman now apparently immured within the consulate if she wasn't allowed out and they weren't allowed in?[25] By this stage, the initially tight-lipped State Department was also embroiled in the affair. Consul Lomakin and Ambassador Panyushkin had leveled serious allegations of criminal malfeasance against U.S. state agencies, taking their lead from the Soviet foreign minister, who delivered a "vigorously worded protest" to U.S. ambassador Walter Bedell Smith in Moscow. Summoning the American at midnight, the "usually coldly self-possessed" Molotov appeared incoherent with rage—the only time Smith ever saw him "really flustered," stuttering over a messily drafted protest note, his entire office in disarray.[26] Meanwhile in New York, a Supreme Court judge approved a habeas corpus writ sought by Common Cause, Inc., requiring Lomakin to produce Kasenkina in court.[27] The teacher would then have "the chance to be free if she really wants to be," explained Christopher Emmet, its chairman.[28]

Thus was the scene set for the climactic events of August 12 that left Kasenkina suffering fractures to her femur, patella, and lumbar vertebrae, a broken pelvis, multiple contusions, and traumatic shock.[29] While she recovered in hospital—every fluctuation of her temperature, blood transfusions, and surgical procedures attentively monitored by the press—U.S. and Soviet officials waged war over her future, simultaneously disputing the motives behind, and meaning of, her leap.

Had Kasenkina leapt rather than tumbled? Did her action represent a bid for freedom or for death? Having gained entry to the consulate, New York police officers searched for "a suicide note or any other evidence that she had intended to destroy herself."[30] Or had she, perhaps, been pushed? Six months earlier, the ousted Czech foreign minister Jan Masaryk had fallen to his death from an open window in Prague. U.S. news media reported his death "in mysterious circumstances" as a wake-up call to Americans who still harbored fraternal sentiments toward "Uncle Joe." Whether Czech (or Soviet) communists had actually delivered the coup de grâce or whether their coup d'état had simply extinguished Masaryk's will to live, his fatal fall struck many observers as the result of Soviet propulsion. "It was the communists who killed him," the popular travel writer John Gunther pronounced, "for his death was murder—even if a suicide."[31] In Kasenkina's case, while foul play could not be ruled out, it seemed unlikely that consular staff would

choose such an unreliable method of ridding themselves of so very public a problem as the errant schoolteacher.

Over the next few days, Soviet sources produced several explanations for the
teacher's misadventure. According to *Pravda*, Kasenkina had fallen by accident
through an open window, disoriented by her traumatic weeklong abduction at Reed
Farm.[32] Lomakin's version, however, held that she had jumped in suicidal despair—
terrified of the gathering crowd outside the consulate, whom she took to be a mob
of White Russians. ("It looks as if they are coming to get me," Kasenkina cried before "losing control of herself," Vice-Consul Chepurnykh related.) In a precarious
emotional state, she had heard a radio broadcast announce HUAC's intention to
serve her a subpoena and had assumed her enemies were now determined to brand
her a spy. No wonder the poor woman decided to put an end to her miseries rather
than face framed-up charges.[33]

These explanations—unintentional accident, intended suicide, or bungled assassination—found little favor among American commentators, especially since
Kasenkina herself was quickly reported as confirming that her aim had been to escape Soviet control. A few hours after her leap, when consular personnel demanded
access to her hospital bedside, the patient emphatically protested. She would see
no one from the consulate. Accepting only anticommunist visitors, Kasenkina apparently told one such confidante, Vladimir Zenzinov: "I was like a bird in a cage.
I had to get out."[34] A gift for less inventive cartoonists, this cliché seemed to clinch
the matter. "As soon as she was able to talk, Oksana Kasenkina knocked all the Soviet protests into a cocked hat," declared *Time* magazine.[35] "Even in the most fanciful tales of crime and adventure there is no example of a person jumping out of
a window and breaking his bones in order to get free from his rescuers," a sardonic
columnist noted in the liberal Catholic weekly *Commonweal*. Whatever confusion
surrounded Kasenkina's abortive flight to Reed Farm, "no sane person could believe" the Russian version any longer.[36]

Only the Soviets refused to accept Kasenkina's word as final. How could anyone determine the true sentiments of a critically injured woman, still barely conscious and in great pain, with White Russians and Russian-speaking police officers
serving round-the-clock duty as the invalid's mouthpiece, minder, and puppet master? consular officials inquired. They emphatically denied press reports that Kasenkina had dispatched Vice-Consul Chepurnykh from her hospital bed with the
decisive rejoinder, "You kept me a prisoner. You would not let me go."[37] On this
occasion, as on others, her Russian had been maliciously mistranslated into English by Detective William Dyczko, whose deceptions formed part of a larger plot
to deny Soviet consular personnel their right to extend protection over a fellow citizen. With a full-fledged intergovernmental crisis now well advanced, Soviet
protests proliferated: against FBI connivance in criminal acts; police violations of
consular extraterritoriality; and obstruction of consular access to a "citizeness" who,

they insisted, enjoyed no right to repudiate her state's "protection." In short order, Kasenkina must be returned to Soviet custody, along with the Samarins.[38]

In response, the State Department let it be known that the New York Police Department was investigating criminal charges against consular personnel for detaining Kasenkina. No charges were in fact pressed, but Washington's response to Soviet protests was categorical. President Truman himself intimated that Kasenkina would be granted asylum.[39] A decisive rebuke to the Soviets, this announcement did not, however, bring the saga to an end. With all the righteous indignation of the unjustly accused, the State Department lambasted Lomakin for having "deliberately designed to mislead the American public in regard to a serious charge involving the United States Government," namely, the preposterous accusation of FBI participation in Kasenkina's "kidnapping." On August 19, Undersecretary of State Lovett requested that Truman revoke the exequatur issued to Lomakin. The consul general would be obliged to leave the United States "within a reasonable time."[40]

This step caused quite a stir. "More extraordinary than the brusqueness of the note's language was its request—tantamount to an expulsion order—that Lomakin be recalled by his government," editorialized *Newsweek*.[41] Since recognizing the USSR in 1933, Washington had never expelled a Soviet representative. Moscow responded by upping the ante, announcing the imminent closure of its two consulates in New York and San Francisco because "circumstances in the United States [did] not permit proper carrying out of consular functions." Diplomatic convention dictated that American representatives in turn quit the U.S. consulate in Vladivostok, while negotiations over a proposed second facility at Leningrad came to an abrupt halt.[42] By the time State Department officials declared the case shut on September 19, consular relations between the two states had been completely severed—a development that press commentators greeted with enthusiasm if not outright exultation. Kasenkina would stay, and Lomakin had to go. "Good Reddance," crowed Jack Tarver in the *Atlanta Constitution*. Alone the *New Republic* rued the "enormous harm to Soviet-American relations" wrought by *l'affaire Kasenkina*.[43]

UNHAPPY RETURNS: THE POLITICS
OF FORCED REPATRIATION

The Kasenkina episode gave every appearance of uniqueness, with a plot "so lurid that a good professional cloak and dagger writer would be obliged to tone it down to make it even faintly credible." Yet as several contemporaries pointed out, this drama was less novel than its idiosyncratic elements implied. Although the schoolteacher drew Americans' attention to communist "captive taking"—their furious reluctance to let even a single subject go—she was scarcely the first Soviet citizen to balk at the prospect of returning home. Viewed from a wider angle, Kasenkina was one among thousands of *nyevozvrashchentzi* (nonreturners). According to the influential columnists Joseph and Stewart Alsop, *the* story in August 1948 was Soviet citizens' wholesale rejection of their state, not Kasenkina's singular exit strategy. That there existed "in the western zones of Germany and Austria alone, some hundreds of thousands of Soviet citizens who have obeyed precisely the same impulse as moved Mme. Kosenkina to her desperate expedient" formed the consular melodrama's "real meaning." Choosing the "half-life of fugitives or displaced persons," these individuals were united by "one desire—to stay out of the Soviet Union." Their desperation and their number suggested something far more significant about the "deep inner weakness of the Soviet state"—exposed by this mass exodus as a "ghastly and tragic failure"—than one cause célèbre possibly could.[44]

Of these nonreturners, the majority were Soviet citizens displaced during the war, or nationals of the Baltic states—invaded by the Red Army in 1939—over whom Moscow contentiously claimed sovereignty.[45] Some *nyevozvrashchentzi* had been shunted west during the war as forced labor for Germany and its new eastern empire. (By January 1945, the Third Reich alone contained an estimated 2.75 million involuntary *Ostarbeiter*.)[46] Others had been German prisoners of war, Red Army personnel reluctant to return home following Hitler's collapse.[47] A third sizable group comprised soldiers captured in German uniforms by British and U.S. forces but subsequently revealed as Soviet citizens—whether willing volunteers for the "Russian Liberation Army" loosely grouped around General Andrei Vlasov or coerced conscripts for the Wehrmacht, prepared to take up arms on their captors' behalf rather than enter German POW camps from which a high proportion never returned.[48] Then there were those who had fled west as German troops retreated from Soviet soil, fearing punishment for collaboration or simply seizing an opportunity to escape. Altogether, displaced Soviet citizens in mid-1945 numbered approximately five and a half million, of whom between two hundred thousand and one million resisted repatriation.[49]

This mass of Soviet DPs had been supplemented by a smaller, but nevertheless sizable, number of *post*war refugees. Primarily these comprised Soviet military and civilian personnel stationed in the occupation zones of Germany and Austria—dispatched west to oversee the "Sovietization" of east/central Europe. How many had managed to escape wasn't easy to tally, given the covert circumstances under which such individuals fled and then struggled to reinvent their identities, but the Alsops estimated the total somewhere between five thousand and twenty thousand.

By 1948, displacement, repatriation, and defection had become thoroughly vexed issues in the relationship between Washington and Moscow—both a symptom and a source of the wartime alliance's disintegration. That the politics of mobility would come to be so divisive was not obvious during the war itself. Anticipating a massive postwar refugee problem, the Allies agreed to deal with it by the simplest expedient possible: returning the displaced home. The western allies' concurrence on

FIGURE 5. "The Homing Instinct of Russian Pigeons." "Ding" Darling illustrates the larger meaning of Kasenkina's resistance to repatriation in a cartoon that appeared the day after her leap, August 13, 1948. Reproduced courtesy of the "Ding" Darling Wildlife

this principle was to be expected. Ever since an international refugee regime emerged in the wake of World War I, the principle of repatriation has underpinned the operations of international relief organizations—a reflection of states' tendency to regard population in proprietary terms.[50] When the Allies established the United Nations Relief and Rehabilitation Administration (UNRRA) in 1943, repatriation duly formed its core responsibility. Similarly, wartime discussions between Washington, London, and Moscow over future arrangements for POWs released from German captivity, while fraught with evasions, rested on an understanding that all parties would expedite the return of one another's prisoners and refugees.

These ad hoc agreements took more solid shape at the Yalta conference of February 1945, where U.S. and Soviet military representatives signed a bilateral agreement on the reciprocal repatriation of personnel. Throughout the cold war, detractors of FDR and Truman strove to make "Yalta" a dirty word akin to "Munich"—shorthand for appeasement, if not a synonym for treason.[51] But however repugnant these critics found the forced return of reluctant Soviet citizens, the "pawns of Yalta" in Mark Elliott's phrase, the principle of involuntary repatriation did not represent a departure from precedent. The Geneva Conventions of 1929 contained no provision for former prisoners of war to *choose* their postwar destinations or to repudiate their citizenship while encamped. When hostilities ceased, prisoners were to be exchanged—returned, as it were, to sender.[52]

What looked straightforward on paper proved extremely difficult to effect in practice. Not only was the sheer scale of displacement overwhelming, but the meaning and location of "home" had become moot for hundreds of thousands of mobile individuals as borders shifted, regimes were reconstituted, and people moved and resettled in unprecedented numbers. Under these conditions, the idea of returning home carried a hollow ring of irony. For many, the slim possibility of finding a house still standing, property intact, a familiar community, and a welcoming state was outweighed by the probability of discovering everything destroyed, looted, or appropriated, an alien set of neighbors, and scant chance of redress from an unsympathetic regime. No wonder, then, that many DPs preferred the "half-life" of refugees, irrespective of dismal camp conditions and dim prospects for resettlement.[53] For Soviet troops who had fallen into German hands repatriation assumed an even bleaker aspect, since the Stalinist state treated prisoners of war as traitors—the fact of capture proving a soldier's insufficient dedication to the motherland. Decree Number 270 of 1942 declared "a prisoner captured alive by the enemy *ipso facto* a traitor." "Liberation" from captivity was likely to mean the rapid exchange of one camp regime for another, with most Red Army returnees "now either dead or in the slave camps in Central Asia or Siberia or . . . the dread Kolyma gold mines," as the Alsops noted in 1948. Vividly aware of these lethal possibilities, former prisoners were among the most obdurate nonreturners.[54]

Why hundreds of thousands of Soviet citizens would resist repatriation is readily understood; and resist they strenuously did. In September 1945, Robert Murphy (U.S. political advisor for Germany) cabled Secretary of State Byrnes to alert him to what respecting the Yalta agreement entailed in practice: "In applying the policy of forcible repatriation there has been a number of unpleasant incidents involving violence such as the forcible seizure by our troops of 100 Russians at a church service resulting in serious injuries on both sides. A considerable number of suicides by Russians . . . apparently are also taking place."[55] In view of cold war Washington's subsequent encouragement of flight from the eastern bloc, what is puzzling is the degree and duration of U.S. cooperation with Soviet authorities in facilitating the return of its fugitive population—at gunpoint if necessary.

During the Kasenkina episode, Washington's role in repatriating reluctant Soviet citizens was rarely mentioned, and certainly not by government officials.[56] In August 1948 the president represented the right of asylum as a fixed point in U.S. policy. Asked if "the same right of asylum in the United States, promised to the teachers, would apply to other Soviet citizens in similar circumstances," Truman replied that "this right has always applied in such cases."[57] His assertion was disingenuous. Asylum—a right of states to adjudicate, not an automatic entitlement of stateless refugees—had figured nowhere in wartime intergovernmental agreements on repatriation. Indeed, the State Department treated with considerable wariness individuals such as Victor Kravchenko, a member of the Soviet Purchasing Commission in Washington, D.C., who defected in 1944. Some U.S. officials even urged that he be returned to Moscow to face court-martial as a deserter.[58] While a powerful set of allies lobbied hard on Kravchenko's behalf to ensure that he was granted leave to remain, other disaffected Soviet citizens were less fortunate.

"Unpleasant incidents" pitting suicidal Soviets against American enforcers were not confined to Europe. One such episode occurred at Fort Dix, New Jersey, where a group of Soviet prisoners—men captured in German uniform—had been temporarily housed. In June 1945, they were scheduled to set sail from New York City, bound for the Soviet Union. But they had no intention of following their repatriation orders; on the eve of embarkation, the group of 154 men staged an insurrection in their barracks with the aim of provoking their guards to retaliate with lethal force. The plan failed. Three men hanged themselves from barracks' rafters during the disturbance. Seven others sustained gunshot wounds from the American enlisted men under attack, who responded in the anticipated fashion with tear gas and bullets but not on the scale that an assisted mass suicide bid required.[59] Two days later, the prisoners' embarkation—presided over by two hundred armed soldiers and eighty military police with submachine guns—was abruptly halted at Pier 51 in lower Manhattan, while a crowd of three hundred looked on.[60] But this dockside volte-face proved only a temporary suspension, not a reprieve. On August 9, Secretary of State Byrnes confirmed that "under commitments made at the Crimea Conference [Yalta], the United States Government undertakes to return to the Soviet Union all Soviet citizens."[61] On August 31, the group was again marched on board—or, if some reports are to be believed, herded aboard under heavy sedation.

This episode failed to attract more than glancing press attention. Perhaps empathy for these reluctant repatriates required more effort than most newspaper editors wished to make or believed their readers willing to expend. The men had, after all, been captured in German uniforms. Was Washington beholden to dispatch them to the Soviet Union, honoring Moscow's right to punish its own war criminals and collaborators? Needless to say, this represented the Kremlin's position. International prisoner-of-war conventions pointed in a different direction, however. Since the Geneva Convention of 1929 takes citizenship to correspond with the uniform worn at the moment of capture, the Fort Dix prisoners argued that Washington was obliged to treat the men as German POWs.[62] Critics of U.S. repatriation policy argued that Truman's administration should have respected the 1929 convention. But in mid-1945, although the Fort Dix case divided opinion in Washington, the dilemmas were resolved in favor of conciliating the Soviets.[63]

As the discrepancy between the events of June 1945 and August 1948 makes clear, Washington's position on matters of repatriation shifted considerably over the course of three years. No one moment marks a decisive reversal. Nor, as chapter 2 details, did the extension of asylum to Kasenkina and the Samarins herald a new era in which *all* Soviet nonreturners, defectors, and DPs were warmly embraced by the United States. Even as Truman made this announcement, Congress rejected a Displaced Persons Act that would have admitted more eastern bloc refugees into the United States.[64]

If Washington's reorientation was fitful, repatriation nevertheless played a significant role in souring relations between Moscow and Washington after the initial incentive for cooperation dissolved. In 1945, U.S. authorities wanted to expedite the return of perhaps as many as twenty-eight thousand American POWs from areas under Red Army control, fearing that the Soviets would use these men as bargaining chips if Washington challenged Moscow's dilatory pace and prevarications with any vigor or if U.S. officials reneged on their own commitment to reciprocity undertaken at Yalta.[65] To prolong the ordeal of U.S. former prisoners—under conditions believed to be barbaric—was not something the administration could countenance lightly. "The Soviet attitude toward liberated American prisoners is the same as the Soviet attitude toward the countries they have liberated," noted an aide to General John R. Deane (the Pentagon's liaison to the Red Army). "Prisoners are spoils of war won by Soviet arms. They may be robbed, starved, and abused—and no one has the right to question such treatment."[66]

Once the majority of U.S. prisoners had come home, however, Washington showed less inclination to let Soviet behavior go unchallenged. By late 1945 it was evident that Moscow had no intention of relinquishing thousands of Axis POWs in the near future—or perhaps at all—though it continued to press for the immediate repatriation of Soviet citizens from western occupation zones. In addition, the USSR was replenishing this reservoir of expendable labor by forced population movements from various areas of eastern/central Europe and the Baltic states.[67] U.S.-Soviet differences received an acrimonious airing at the foreign ministers' conference of February 1947, where Generals Mark Clark and Fedov Gusev vehemently disagreed over the "disposal" of four hundred thousand DPs and former POWs in Europe who continued to resist repatriation. Clark made public the U.S. military's opposition to involuntary repatriation, claiming that force had never been mandated at Yalta.[68] For their part, Soviet officials insisted that western Europe's DP camps had become, with U.S. connivance, sites of anticommunist coercion. In squalid and disorienting conditions, "quislings and war criminals" psychologically browbeat camp inmates into resisting repatriaticn, spreading vicious lies about the treatment that would await them on return home and resorting to physical force when less crude forms of persuasion failed—charges that anticipate those made by Lomakin about the "White Russians'" abuse of Kasenkina.

For Moscow, the mass resistance of citizens to repatriation after the war, coupled with the attempt of thousands more to flee west after 1945, constituted a stain that no amount of patriotic propaganda could bleach. In the Alsops' heightened language, "Defection is the most unthinkable of all the crimes that their slave-peoples can commit."[69] For Washington, opposition to forced repatriation became (however belatedly) an emblem of the free world's commitment to individual rights—a position staked definitively by Truman during the Korean War armistice talks. But to burnish America's image as a place of asylum required the effacement of its history of collaboration with Red Army repatriation teams. "If the American people and their representatives were agents of the Kremlin, they could scarcely have done more to deliver those refugees to the assassin and the slave master," chided *Life,* noting that "quite a few went back tied up in ropes, delivered like African slaves in the blackbirding days."[70] If many Americans remained oblivious to their state's role in pursuing fugitive Soviets, U.S. participation in forced repatriation was painfully apparent to discontented residents of Soviet-dominated Europe and the USSR. Granting asylum to Kasenkina offered an opportunity to make public, if very partial, amends: a signal that Washington now wished to encourage and reward defection.

DIPLOMATIC IMMUNITY
AND COMMUNIST CONTAGION

For opinion formers like the Alsops and the *Time/Life* group, the Kasenkina affair underscored the need for a more generous attitude toward the thousands of refugees in Europe who had escaped Soviet control and continued to risk death in order to flee west. Others extracted a quite different lesson, however, focusing not on what the schoolteacher represented but on what the presence of the Soviet consulate on East Sixty-first Street meant for U.S. security. Their response to this consular crisis draws attention to the constriction of diplomatic channels that occurred during the late 1940s: a strangulation symptomatic of the condition of persistent estrangement dubbed "cold war."

As Anders Stephanson has noted, while use of that term became ubiquitous soon after Walter Lippmann popularized it in 1947, few paused—either then or later—to elucidate what constitutes a cold war. Were one to codify a definition, the cessation of "diplomatic dialogue, normal relations, probing negotiation, and resolution of issues of mutual interest" would loom large. "This is what made the cold war a cold *war*," Stephanson asserts.[71] But since a cold war was also, by definition, *not* a war proper, diplomatic relations between the antagonists were formally maintained. Even during the most fractious phases of this protracted confrontation, Washington continued to dispatch diplomats to Moscow and to receive the Soviet Union's representatives. Embassies remained open, if not exactly for business as normal. As "contact zones" in and around which Soviets and Americans encountered one another more or less directly, embassies and consulates formed the staging ground for intimate and invasive cold war maneuvers. Diplomats—surveilled, restricted, and vilified by hostile host states and populations—also came to regard themselves as cold war captives, and the Kasenkina episode played an instrumental role in sharpening such perceptions.

Diplomacy doesn't often excite high feeling. So long as relations remain cordial, the implications of assigning small portions of "national space" to foreign powers generally pass unremarked. But during the early cold war long-standing conventions governing diplomatic exchange suddenly appeared as unnatural as they were unwelcome to many Americans, with the Kasenkina affair focusing attention on processes—and persons—usually invisible to popular scrutiny. In particular, the imbroglio on East Sixty-first Street prompted a heated debate over the principle of extraterritoriality.

To many U.S. press commentators it now seemed remarkable, unconscionable even, that Washington would willingly surrender territory to Soviet control during what increasingly resembled a time of war. The "basic issue" under dispute in the Kasenkina case, editorialized the *Washington Post,* was "American sovereignty in America itself."[72] Soviet diplomats had abused extraterritoriality to transform small pockets of America into miniature police states (though the opulence of consular life in a thirty-three-room mansion rented from a niece of John D. Rockefeller did not pass unnoted either).[73] From these impregnable centers, Moscow spun its web of espionage and subversion, infiltrating even the most sensitive inner sanctums of American government.

Conjuring Soviet subversion in unmistakably sexualized terms, conservative columnists played on fears of violation and contamination. To them it was all of a piece that Lomakin and his aides would imprison a helpless woman in the consulate while spies who masqueraded as diplomats surreptitiously penetrated American institutions. Both activities hinted at rape, a common metaphor for Soviet expansionism made literal by the Red Army's marauding rampage across Europe. Kennan's Long Telegram famously depicted the Kremlin exerting "insistent, unceasing pressure for penetration" of foreign countries, while also "ravishing its own supine population."[74] And what the Soviets did to their own citizens they certainly wouldn't hesitate to do to Americans. Soviet agents were thus understood as exploiting the convention of diplomatic immunity to spread the "contagion" of communism—a venereal condition whose unobserved symptoms threatened to ravage the American body politic. Yet far from engaging in precautionary prophylaxis, the U.S. government sanctioned an obvious deficiency in its quarantine arrangements, permitting the Soviet consulate to remain terra incognita. Such recklessness left America's vital organs exposed. To these anticommunist opinion formers, the niceties of diplomatic reciprocity belonged to a vanished era of gentlemanly statecraft. From the Kasenkina episode they derived confirmation that accommodating Soviet diplomats was not just naive but dangerous—suicidal, even.

Press commentary on Lomakin reflected this hardening attitude. A trim, forty-four-year-old father of two with a playfully bantering manner, Lomakin appeared to defy the familiar Soviet stereotype—an oversized, vodka-soused buffoon of the kind invariably personified by Oscar Homolka on screen.[75] But in assailing the "bandit-like morals of the American intelligence service," he had overplayed his hand and "made an ass of himself." In the characterization of the New York Daily Mirror, Lomakin was a "rough-and-tumble skullbuster" who should be sent packing. "If the State Department had any courage, it would have ruled promptly and emphatically that America will NOT countenance any cossack goon squads," the Mirror editorialized. When Secretary of State Marshall moved to expel Lomakin, many columnists envisaged the bleak future that awaited a returning Soviet representative careless enough to have "misplaced" no less than three citizens in the United States. Few sympathized with the consul's predicament, however. "If Comrade Lomakin should leap from a window I would not be greatly surprised," observed Ralph McGill dryly in the Atlanta Constitution.[76]

That the Kremlin had badly bungled the case of the errant schoolteachers and would suffer the boomerang effects of this misjudgment was a theme repeated in press evaluations of the consular shutdowns. Since diplomatic representation functioned as cover for Soviet espionage activities, Moscow's peevish announcement that it would not simply recall Lomakin but vacate its consular facilities in New York City and San Francisco amounted to a self-denying ordinance. In shutting these "two excellent listening posts," the Soviets were curtailing their opportunities for spying, while the U.S. lost nothing but "an isolated consular outpost in Vladivostock."[77] Conservative columnists cheered the Soviets' departure but pressed for more stringent quarantine measures. Approximately two thousand citizens of the USSR remained in America as holders of diplomatic passports. The United Nations' location in Manhattan—a source of deep chagrin to many—furnished Moscow a permanent reason to maintain a large staff there, irrespective of the consular expulsions. For the Chicago Daily Tribune, the Kasenkina debacle demonstrated the "utter folly of allowing the United Nations to set up its head-quarters in the largest city and principal port of the United States:"

> It would be bad enough if UN headquarters were in the Nevada desert, where it would be relatively difficult for a foreign power to set up an effective spy headquarters. UN is in New York City, where people can come and go relatively unnoticed.
>
> It isn't pleasant to think of what a well organized spy service might do to poison the New York City water supply, damage the docks, or wreck the bridges and tunnels, but those are dangers which were invited when UN was invited to set up house-keeping on Manhattan Island.[78]

Diplomat, spy, and "terrorist," the Soviet official appeared insidiously protean. Yet to emphasize the danger posed to Americans by Soviet representatives was to minimize the vulnerability of diplomats—whether Soviets in the United States or Americans in the USSR—to spontaneous and orchestrated forms of retaliation. As relations between Washington and Moscow soured and human traffic between East and West stalled, diplomats on both sides were left increasingly exposed to reprisal. Visible symbols of a suspect alien presence, subject to malign construction as enemy spies, they acted as magnets for popular protest. After June 1946, the New York Police Department stepped up its watch over the Soviet consulate in Manhattan—not because of the possible harm consular officials might do to unsuspecting New Yorkers but because an unknown American had marched into the lobby and assaulted the receptionist on duty. In the wake of the Kasenkina episode, a more vocal but less violent protester—a "full-blooded Sioux Indian and a war veteran living in Ridgewood, Queens"—appeared outside the consulate with a placard "informing Mr Lomakin that he would not be missed if he left the country," as the *New York Times* euphemistically paraphrased the message.[79]

Bearing the brunt of popular frustrations and animosities, foreign representatives presented an easy target for official retaliatory moves. Insulted, ostracized, curbed, and harassed, diplomats found conditions more and more onerous during the early cold war. In Moscow, U.S. diplomats were certain that their premises were bugged and that local ancillary staff supplied further details that audio surveillance failed to pick up.[80] Under these impossible conditions, diplomats took to conducting more sensitive conversations outdoors, though never without the shadowy accompaniment of Soviet minders. Between 1945 and Stalin's death in 1953, "daily life in the embassy proceeded in an atmosphere of sullen isolation," notes the historian David Mayers.[81]

It wasn't ever thus, however. For a brief honeymoon period after the embassy opened in 1933, American diplomats were neither isolated nor sullen. The men who worked under Ambassador Bullitt, including Chip Bohlen, Charles Thayer, and George Kennan, relished their pioneering role on the eastern front of foreign affairs, embraced by surprisingly effusive Soviet hosts. "These Russians—they know how to treat one like royalty even if they once forgot how to treat royalty itself," quipped Thayer in a letter to his mother, "Muzzy."[82] During these halcyon days, champagne and vodka flowed freely, street urchins hailed "Comrade Bullitt" as he sped through Moscow's streets, and Stalin had been known to kiss the new ambassador "full on the mouth." A ballerina, "by far the greatest advertisement for Communism we have seen," was locked in an embassy closet—with Bullitt, Bohlen, and Thayer fighting over the key.[83] The diplomatic corps recognized that their pas de deux (or trois) with the corps de ballet provided the NKVD with an opportunity to practice undercover surveillance at its most literal. But since this form of espionage was so pleasurable, the intentions behind it so transparent, American diplomats continued to tangle with these lithe Mata Haris. When everyone tacitly acknowledged the terms of engagement, being spied on merely imparted an additional frisson to the fun and games. "What an Embassy!" Thayer exclaimed—with good reason.[84]

Such exuberant high jinks could not, and did not, persist. After Sergei Kirov's murder in December 1934, Stalin's purges claimed several former embassy guests such as Nikolai Bukharin and Karl Radek. U.S. representatives confronted heavy-handed surveillance, coupled with tight limitations on their travel around and beyond Moscow—the radius narrowing still further in the immediate aftermath of the Kasenkina affair.[85] Worse yet, the Kremlin drastically curtailed Americans' interaction with Soviet citizens. According to Kennan, vestigial contact was relegated to a "furtive no man's land of personal relations between the Soviet world and ours"—a formulation that implied closeted couplings of a very particular type.[86] Men who had delighted in holding ballerinas hostage now conceived of themselves as prisoners of the Kremlin. It was a crushing reversal, starkly contrasting with the heady days of 1933–34 that Kennan recollected as the "highpoint of life . . . in comradeship, in gaiety, in intensity of experience."[87] Asked in September 1952 how he found life in Moscow, Kennan (then ambassador to the USSR) replied that it closely approximated his incarceration by the Nazis following Hitler's declaration of war against the United States. "Had the Nazis permitted us to walk the streets without having the right to talk to any Germans," Kennan informed the Berlin-based journalist, "that would be exactly how we have to live in Moscow today."[88]

ENTANGLING ALLIANCES: AFFAIRS
OF STATE AND AFFAIRS OF THE HEART

Kennan's impolitic outburst gave voice to mounting frustration over restrictions aimed at Americans in the Soviet Union, diplomats and "civilians" alike. The State Secrets Act of 1947 limited "even the possibility of spoken or written communications between Soviet citizens and foreign diplomats." Social contact having been criminalized, U.S. diplomats' circle shrank to approximately four hundred non-communist foreigners also resident in the USSR—and if social mingling was radically circumscribed, marriage became utterly taboo.[89] On February 15, 1947, Moscow outlawed unions between foreigners and Soviet citizens. Preexisting marriages could scarcely be rescinded by an act of state, but the Soviet government did what it could to disrupt them, especially when couples attempted to depart the USSR. Exit visas became almost impossible to obtain. Although foreigners were generally permitted to leave, their Soviet spouses were often forced to remain behind.

During the late 1940s and 1950s, hundreds of husbands, wives, and children were separated in this way.[90] One American journalist explained this "grotesque attempt to legislate affairs of the heart" as a move to "liquidate" actually existing marriages by "forcing husband and wife to live in different parts of the world," between which movement was near impossible. Having sundered couples geographically, Soviet officials then sought to engineer their emotional estrangement. Separated spouses, waiting for endlessly deferred visas, were encouraged to reconsider the wisdom of their life choices: Did Soviet women *really* expect to find connubial bliss under capitalist conditions? Was it worth squandering prime years—and other matrimonial opportunities—in pursuit of a foreign husband who would surely prove himself unworthy before all the bureaucratic hurdles had been traversed?[91]

In the West, the plight of these "Russian brides" animated much outrage, taking most pointed expression in April 1949 when Chile brought the Soviets' "feudal conception of sovereignty" before the United Nations.[92] By a margin of 39 to 6, the General Assembly deemed that the USSR had violated both the UN Charter and the recently proclaimed Universal Declaration of Human Rights, Article II of which stated that "everyone has the right to leave any country, including his own, and to return to that country."[93] But despite this condemnatory resolution, Eleanor Roosevelt cautioned against premature optimism on behalf of the 65 Russian husbands and 350 wives of U.S. citizens trapped behind the Iron Curtain. Her pessimism proved warranted. Moscow deflected UN criticism—the charge that it was, in effect, keeping its citizens captive—with counteraccusations of slavery. The Soviet representative Alexei Pavlov claimed that his state sought only to protect Russian women who had recklessly married foreigners from reduction to "slave status," the condition of many Soviet wives with "dishpan hands" in Britain, France, and the United States.[94] Inverting Washington's cold war idiom, Moscow sought to expose the "free world," the United States in particular, as the past and present locus of slavery—a rhetorical strategy that it deployed repeatedly, on this issue and others.

It seems unlikely that Moscow's "kitchen slaves" theme resonated widely in the United States. The late 1940s may have seen a concerted redomestication of American women after the wartime expansion of opportunities, but no matter how constrained postwar housewives felt, nothing in popular representations of the USSR presented Soviet women's lot as more enviable than the stultification of suburbia.

Typically, American media portrayed women in the USSR as groaning under a double burden of manual labor and housework: hence Eleanor Roosevelt's caustic riposte to Soviet invocations of female slavery in the United States: "We might ask, by the way, who does the housework in the Soviet Union—the men?"[95] Stripped of femininity by their conscription into the industrial economy yet scarcely emancipated from domestic drudgery, they craved—like Ernst Lubitsch's celebrated creation, Ninotchka—cosmetics, glamorous gowns, high heels, silk stockings. Oksana Kasenkina herself confirmed this picture of deprivation. During her first public appearance in March 1949 she told journalists that while career girls were "generally single" with "mannish haircuts," clothing, and mannerisms, Russian women compelled to work as "blacksmiths, miners, stevedores, lumberjacks and railroad track tenders" typically "aged fast and died prematurely."[96]

Far from instigating a reappraisal of gender roles, Soviet intransigence over the "plight of the stranded wives" provided another rallying point for sentimental anticommunism.[97] After President Truman decried Moscow's stance again in August 1951, Charles Bohlen (Kennan's successor as U.S. ambassador) pressed the issue more forcefully with Foreign Minister Molotov in May 1953 to achieve the first significant breakthrough: a clutch of exit visas.[98] With American press correspondents in Moscow among those personally affected by the Soviet Union's "inflexible rigidity," the question received steady media attention, bolstering representations of Soviet communism as both godless and heartless.[99] That Stalin, of all men, presumed to set asunder unions that God had joined together was a particularly galling affront to Christian America.

Popular cultural treatments of this vexed issue did not scruple to attribute the Kremlin's jealous possessiveness over its female citizens to the sexual rapacity of Stalin himself—nowhere more explicitly than in *Never Let Me Go,* an MGM romance starring Clark Gable as an American newspaperman in Moscow and Gene Tierney as Marya Lamarkina, the Russian ballerina bride he is forced to leave behind. Released in June 1953, just days after Bohlen had secured visas on behalf of the wives of four British and American press representatives in Moscow, *Never Let Me Go* boasted what *Variety* called a "topical provocative theme."[100]

Early scenes find the ever-ebullient Gable optimistic that a visa will prove forthcoming for the young bride he has just married in the U.S. Embassy under Abraham Lincoln's benignly approving gaze. "You know how it is with red tape," he reassures Marya, "and naturally the Reds have more and redder tape." But it soon becomes clear that the Kremlin's intransigence owes less to bureaucratic bungling than to concupiscent calculation. The Russians may be inscrutable—"put two and two together, make nine, add seven, divide by four and give up," Gable's character quips—but Moscow's motives in blocking the exit of his adoring wife are thoroughly transparent. "The Russian bear is the only creature that can eat his honey and have it," a savvy colleague warns the American. And so it would seem—for the Kremlin's grizzliest bear clearly wants *Gable's* honey.

The troublesome reporter is duly ejected from the country, leaving Marya to the predatory designs of the Kremlin. At Stalin's behest, a special command performance of *Swan Lake* is arranged in Tallin. But the Baltic resort, susceptible to an American amphibious assault, proves a careless choice of locale in which to exercise droit de seigneur over the corps de ballet. After sailing a small dinghy through the English Channel into the North Sea and across the Baltic, outdrinking a bunch of Russian sailors en route, and stealing the uniform of a Red Army medical corps colonel in order to sneak into Tallin's closely guarded theater (where, incidentally, the imposter must administer emergency medical assistance to an ailing Soviet officer along the way), Gable forestalls whatever private performance Stalin planned to command from the lead swan. Needless to say, he pulls all this off "with the coolness of a big boy taking candy away from kids"—or honey from a grizzly.[101]

Reprising the plot of King Vidor's 1940 comedy *Comrade X* (in which Gable smuggles Hedy Lamarr out of Russia), *Never Let Me Go* reworked familiar elements of the captivity genre: imperiled womanhood rescued by Euro-American ingenuity and derring-do from sexual degradation at the mauling hands of barbarians. Despite its strong whiff of implausibility, the movie earned plaudits from contemporary critics. "It is cheering to have the reassurance that Clark Gable is one fellow, at least, who can still make the Soviet Union tough guys look like absolute monkeys—and does," nodded Bosley Crowther in the *New York Times*. Silliness aside, *Never Let Me Go* delivered a gratifying romantic payoff. Gable "winds up caressing Miss Tierney in the dinghy while the seas moan, which is exactly as it should be," noted the *New Yorker*. More than that, the movie afforded the satisfaction of seeing a lone American "rip through the Iron Curtain with all the breeziness of a demonstrator showing off the very latest can opener in Gimbel's basement"—all the more welcome given the movie's appearance at a fragile moment in negotiations over the release of POWs in Korea, two months before the final armistice was signed.[102]

Hollywood was not alone in recognizing the potential of captivity as a rich seam to be mined. So did American diplomats, while growing ever more frustrated by their inability to protect the rights of U.S. citizens in the Soviet Union, including their right to depart. "With the exception of the period preceding the War of 1812, perhaps never have so many American citizens been subjected to comparable discriminations, threats, police interrogations, and administrative punishments," complained one official to his State Department superiors. "Never, unfortunately, has a United States Embassy been quite so powerless to protect American citizens."[103] But impotence could be turned to advantage. What clearer or more universally affecting demonstration of Soviet monstrosity than the Kremlin's calculated efforts to part husbands from wives and sever children from parents? By never letting go, Moscow had snarled itself into a bind from which there could be no disentanglement without further injury. Whether it let dissatisfied residents out or continued to detain them, the Politburo could only damage the facade it had assiduously erected of a society so perfect that no one would wish to leave. American diplomats appraised their antagonists' predicament with some satisfaction: "Either they must present the West with further propaganda opportunities of the nature created by the wives question or they must accept the consequences of discharging a flood of new Kravchenkos and Kasenkinas upon the free world."[104]

But for all the dynamite that entrapped wives and escaped schoolteachers provided Washington in detonating the Soviet "big lie," Moscow mustered a forceful retaliatory strike. In fact, the Kremlin already possessed a Kasenkina figure of its own: thirty-three-year-old Annabelle Bucar, a former U.S. Embassy employee. In February 1948, she had resigned her post as an information officer with the U.S. Information Service, informing Ambassador Bedell Smith that she had no truck with America's virulent anti-Sovietism, preferring to live among the Russian people, for whom she had developed a warm admiration. Naturally, the Soviet state was happy to assist in this aspiration; a defector from the U.S. Embassy represented a premium asset. Moreover, this particular turncoat was (in the estimation of her own scorned ambassador) "rather attractive." With luminous eyes and blonde hair plaited around her crown, Bucar made an appealing advertisement for anti-Americanism.[105] Soon she was reported to be lecturing Soviet factory workers on the superior conditions they enjoyed over their American counterparts. These public performances were supplemented by a series of "true confessions" in *Pravda,* followed in February 1949 by an incendiary volume entitled *The Truth about American Diplomats,* a slim tract bristling with large claims about the "anti-Soviet clique" in control of the U.S. Embassy—a gang of rapacious racketeers and warmongers.[106]

In the United States, this defection received only glancing attention as a cautionary tale of romantic misadventure abroad. Bucar, it seemed, hadn't just developed a comradely regard for the Soviet Union's "fine people who are doing [their] utmost toward making the world a better place to live in." She had surreptitiously married a Russian and given birth to his child.[107] According to Ambassador Smith, popular, pretty Annabelle had fallen for the well-rehearsed charms of one Constantin Lapschin, "an operetta singer whom we knew best for his reputation as having courted, at one time or another, almost every unattached young foreign woman in Moscow."[108] Besotted, she had repudiated her citizenship and embassy connection as the sole way to persuade the unfeeling Soviet authorities to relax their prohibition against foreign marriages. If only America could have "exchanged" Miss Bucar for "one of the Russian wives of United States soldiers who wanted to come to the United States to join their husbands," Smith joked with U.S. reporters.[109]

Echoing the ambassador, Joseph B. Phillips in *Newsweek* wrote knowingly that

"Lapshin had been frequenting [sic] Americans in Moscow long before Miss Bucar came there." In other words, Soviet intelligence had set a honey trap into which
smitten Annabelle tumbled headlong. As for *The Truth about American Diplomats,*
in Phillips's judgment, "Part of the book came from Miss Bucar and most of it from
File Cabinet 'A'—'American, Anti—' in the propaganda office."[110] Couched in this
way, the sting of defection subsided, with further balm supplied by Bucar's father,
a fifty-one-year-old immigrant from Yugoslavia, who disowned his daughter just
as decisively as she had rejected the family's adoptive homeland. "I won't let her
come home," he huffed, ignoring the single most important point in this drama—
his daughter's emphatic desire *not* to return. "I will not recognize her. I do not approve of her becoming a Russian and I do not approve of Russia." At a loss to explain her "leaving the best country in the world to go to a country that isn't good,"
he speculated that "too much education" had inclined Annabelle to "high people
and high society" when she "didn't have the money for either."[111] What had the
University of Pittsburgh done?

American readers thus encountered Bucar's defection (if they scanned the small
print at all) as a sorry saga of entrapment: a woman in love, cornered into re-
nouncing her citizenship by Soviet machinations of the most emotionally manip-
ulative sort. Her misfortune merited a brief entry in the expanding encyclopedia
of Moscow's misdeeds, alongside the tale of a young army cryptographer working
in the U.S. Embassy, James McMillin. "As a protest against the anti-Soviet policies
of the capitalists who presently rule America, I refuse to go back to America and
am remaining in the Soviet Union," McMillin wrote his father (a U.S. Army colonel)
on May 15, 1948—the day his two-year tour of duty in Moscow was due to end.
Behind this bold assertion, however, embassy officials suspected another defection
by seduction. McMillin was known to have been consorting with the estranged wife
of a U.S. sergeant, Mrs. Galina Dunaeva Biconish. Like Lapshin, she appeared sus-
piciously eager to fraternize with Americans at a time when such liaisons had been
criminalized. "A most naïve, unskilled socially and in fact timid young man," James
had been "captivated by a more mature woman"; he was "an easy prey for a romantic attachment with no knowledge of the world to aid in his decision as to
whether the girl might or might not be good or bad," his aunt ventured in a long
explanatory epistle to the State Department.[112]

Neither defection received much attention in the domestic press. American officials successfully presented the stories of Bucar and McMillin in terms of Washington's willingness to let citizens make individual choices about where and how
they lived, however ill-considered. McMillin's "desertion" was pitched to reporters
as a "result not of any political ideas but of youthful, inexperienced infatuation and
attachment to [a] Soviet married woman with whom he has secretly carried on relations for some time despite repeated warnings and specific instructions from his
superiors."[113] With their criticisms of U.S. policy dismissed as mere ventriloquism,

McMillin and Bucar were, at most, objects of passing pity: victims of Soviet "seduction and exploitation." It remained an article of faith that no one crossed the Iron Curtain from west to east unless ensnared. As a *New York Times* editorial noted during the Kasenkina episode, "The only exodus to the East, barring the cases of two American Embassy employes [sic] in Moscow trapped by amorous ties, is that of slave laborers deported from their home lands and sent to a slow death in the Siberian mines. If any proof were needed as to the rival merits of the Western way of life and the Communist 'paradise,' that contrast alone provides it."[114]

In the USSR, however, American diplomats could hardly deny Bucar's impact, even as they distanced the woman from the scurrilous pronouncements issued in her name. "The book is obvious Soviet propaganda," noted a ruffled embassy employee of *The Truth about American Diplomats*. "It is quite clear that the main sections were written or at least the content provided by someone other than Miss Bucar, since she was never in a position in the Embassy to know either the personalities or the general policy matters so freely discussed," implying both that the claims were not all unfounded and that the embassy must have been "penetrated" at a high level.[115] Whoever had written the book also knew how to command an audience. A first print run of ten thousand copies sold out so quickly that embassy employees—hardly well placed to elbow to the front of the line—failed to secure a copy. A second batch of one hundred thousand copies did not "appreciably relieve the situation." "It was obvious that the average Soviet citizen, so starved for color and spice in his drab daily life, was finding *The Truth about American Diplomats* of exceptional interest," one U.S. diplomat remarked. Having found a winning formula, the Soviets hastily repackaged Bucar's "truths" as a stage play, announcing plans for a feature film, *Goodbye America,* in December 1950.[116] Before long, the same spicy fare was warmed over in translation—with Hungarian-, English-, and Indian-language editions catering to anti-American appetites worldwide.[117]

None of this augured well for America's global reputation, nor did it make local conditions in the embassy any easier. On the contrary, the rising tide of popular anti-Americanism evident among Muscovites made the already parlous position of the embassy's few remaining Russian staff well nigh untenable. Deprived of local translators, secretaries, caterers, and housekeepers, American officials contemplated a bleak existence under conditions akin to house arrest. Bohlen's enraptured exclamation "What an Embassy!" now carried quite a different charge.

COLD WAR PROJECTIONS

While Annabelle Bucar achieved celebrity in the Soviet Union as an anti-American emissary, Oksana Kasenkina found herself transformed overnight into an anticommunist icon in the United States. After her valorous leap from the consulate she ceased to be the frowzy and befuddled schoolteacher of early press reports: a

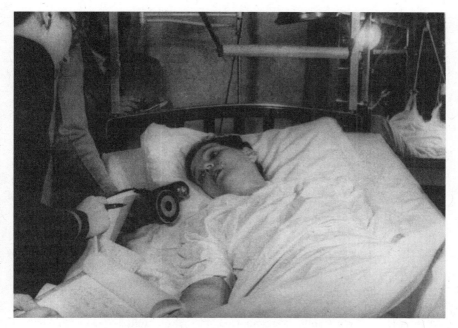

FIGURE 6. "Previous pictures did not do her justice." Kasenkina receives an admiring, if insistent, press corps at her Roosevelt Hospital bedside on August 24, 1948, two weeks after plunging from the Soviet consulate. © The Associated Press.

"stubby little woman," according to the *Washington Post*. Hitherto "dumpy," "plump" and "matronly"—or "middly, brunette, stoute" (as described by Consul Lomakin)—she was now alluringly "diminutive."[118] When she received the press in the hospital on August 24, an interview that "brought about one of the greatest outpourings of newspapermen in recent years," many remarked that she looked "much younger than her reported age of 52 years." "Previous pictures did not do her justice," gushed one photographer.[119] Reporters who made the pilgrimage to her bedside found the schoolteacher not only beautified but beatified: "The sun shone through one of two windows upon the room's white walls. A lithographed card, with a picture of Madonna and child, was propped upon a bureau, alongside the nail-polish bottle."[120] This air of sanctity was combined with something pleasingly familiar in her appearance. "If you saw her on a train and did not know that she is a Russian who can hardly speak English, you would say: 'There goes my high school teacher from Lincoln, Neb., or Atlanta, Ga., or Burlington, Vt.'"[121] The Soviet schoolteacher whose story was that "of all the women in the Soviet Union" could also pass as an American everywoman.[122]

Any lingering doubt as to her motives—whether she intended to commit suicide or seek sanctuary in America—evaporated as columnists endowed the episode with a range of affirmative meanings. For some, Kasenkina stood as a universal emblem of humanity's unquenchable desire for freedom, proof that "man" was not, after all, "a sorry sort of animal." Imbuing her leap with redemptive power, several commentators cast her story as a Christian allegory. She had offered to die "that freedom might live," rhapsodized Fulton Oursler in *Reader's Digest*. Like Christ, Kasenkina was a resurrected martyr, even if it did take the injured schoolteacher three months to rise again.[123]

For those of a more secular bent, the courageous chemistry teacher provided heartening evidence that *Homo sovieticus* retained an appetite for liberty despite three decades of communist tyranny. According to Victor Kravchenko, whose defection memoir *I Chose Freedom* enjoyed pride of place in the early cold war canon, Kasenkina's "great political significance" lay in her demonstration "that ordinary people are now beginning to break with the Soviet regime."[124] This too was the lesson extracted by Isaac Don Levine, the founder of *Plain Talk,* who was hired to "edit" a twenty-eight-part serialization of Kasenkina's story run by the *New York Journal-American* between September 26 and October 23, 1948. "To come to know Oksana Kasenkina," he advised readers, "is to renew one's love for the gifted Russian people and one's faith in their ability to regain freedom." She supplied a reminder that "the warm people made familiar to the Western world by Tolstoy, Tchaikowsky and Chekhov, are still alive in Russia"—quite a different breed "from that of the Molotovs and Gromykos and Lomakins, the taskmasters of her people."[125]

If Kasenkina humanized "the Russians," she also heightened animosity against "the Soviets." In the opinion of many columnists, the consul's refusal to let her go made tangible for U.S. audiences a political system as alien ideologically as it was distant geographically. "The enormity of the Russian tyranny over the human spirit is indeed difficult for free Americans to realize," opined Kathryn Stone, prescribing Kasenkina's memoir as an antidote to incomprehension.[126] That the Soviets had dared treat America like a "semi colonial" state in eastern Europe—and Americans like credulous dupes who would fall for preposterous tall tales—added insult to injury. "Mr. Lomakin appears to have wandered into the supreme folly of assuming that a great American city was as helpless against Soviet lies and Soviet coercions as some little capital of a pseudo-independent Communist nation east of the Iron Curtain," carped an editorial in the *New York Times,* adopting an aggrieved tone not restricted to elite press commentary. Letters and telegrams addressed to President Truman on the Kasenkina issue pressed the White House to challenge and punish the Soviets more forcefully.[127]

In the State Department's estimation, no other issue had "so dramatically raised before the world the conflict between a way of life based on personal freedom and a political ideology based on State domination of individual rights." U.S. news media understood the salience of Kasenkina's action in similar terms. "Personalized in the decision of one human being" were "the great issues in the struggle between East and West": a cold war parable tingling with life-or-death drama.[128] Confronted with a decision between "slavery" and "freedom," the schoolteacher had elected the latter, but hers was no abstract adjudication of the relative merits of rival political systems. Ultimately, Kasenkina's choice represented less a "leap from Marxism"— as *Newsweek* captioned its photo-story of the events of August 12—than a choice *for America*.

At a time of intense effort to burnish U.S. credentials as leader of the "free world," opinion formers eagerly appropriated Kasenkina's leap. When, for example, Republican presidential candidate and New York governor Thomas E. Dewey proclaimed that "we are the last, best hope of earth. Neither barbed wire nor bayonet have been able to suppress the will of men and women to cross from tyranny to freedom," he rhetorically summoned Kasenkina to bear witness. She "could not even understand the language of our country, but in her heart she came to understand America," Dewey told a campaign rally in Des Moines in September 1948.[129] Admiration for the United States, in other words, had galvanized her leap as much as revulsion against the Soviet Union. In the same vein, a *Chicago Daily Tribune* editorial informed readers that "the freedom she saw about her in America crystallized Mrs. Kasenkina's dissatisfaction with her status as the helot of a slave state."[130]

Orotund diction aside, such assertions are striking for the assurance with which they characterized Kasenkina's motives and aspirations. Depicting her leap as a move magnetized by "freedom"—in its uniquely American incarnation—these commentators stamped the "mystery of the kidnapped schoolteacher" as an uncomplicated allegory of slavery and redemption: a tale as old as Exodus, as American as the *Mayflower*. In cold war storytelling of this kind, the episode's most puzzling aspects were resolved: Kasenkina had been "abducted" and incarcerated by Soviet consular staff, from whom she had escaped through the only route available—an open window—because she had been inspired by "the freedom she saw about her." This was a gratifying notion, but it rested less on privileged insight into Kasenkina's consciousness than on a determination to make muddled actions enunciate a clear and congenial message.

Deciphering how Kasenkina herself made sense of the events of August 1948 is no easy task. Repeatedly spoken for, she rarely made public statements without others' mediation. Her "own story" as related first by the *New York Journal-American* and then a memoir, *Leap to Freedom* (1949), was ghosted by Isaac Don Levine, although his name appeared nowhere in a memoir that claimed to be set "down from the heart": "For if the leap is meaningful, only the life behind it makes it so."[131] For the Hearst press, this massive front-page serialization afforded an opportunity to familiarize readers with a sweeping survey of the Soviet Union, from the Bolshevik revolution to the horrors of collectivization and the purges. With a husband lost to the gulag, a daughter claimed by famine, and a son surrendered to the great patriotic war, Kasenkina's family saga encompassed Soviet history's grimmest chapters.

Narrated in the lunging style of sentimental anticommunism, *Leap to Freedom* offers an unreliable guide to its purported author's state of mind in August 1948. Surely the "plucky woman who planned for years to gain the shelter of democracy" was considerably more complex than the one-dimensional heroine of anti-Soviet hagiography?[132] An alternative, albeit inconclusive, interpretation arises from the one extant document seemingly written by Kasenkina herself: the letter she dispatched from Reed Farm to the Soviet consulate. This was the impassioned missive from which Lomakin read aloud at his August 7 press conference—a document later requested by the State Department to assist the criminal inquiry into Kasenkina's alleged abduction and detention in the consulate.

Senior State Department personnel assumed that this letter had been either fabricated in its entirety or amended to support the Soviet version of events—suspicions bolstered by the willingness with which Lomakin handed over the document. Scenting imminent victory in this tug-of-war, Ernest Gross (the State Department's legal adviser) and Chip Bohlen playfully envisioned Ambassador Panyushkin sitting up late into the night, feverishly practicing Kasenkina's handwriting—a ruse that FBI handwriting specialists would soon rumble, they imagined. Exposed as fraudulent, the letter would affirm Soviet mendacity by demolishing Lomakin's claim that the schoolteacher had *asked* to be retrieved from Reed Farm.[133]

Contrary to State Department expectations, however, graphologists found no discrepancies in the handwriting of various samples available to them. Kasenkina, it seemed, was the letter's sole author.[134] She insisted otherwise, yet when interviewed by detectives (on at least two different occasions soon after her leap) she proved reluctant or unable to establish where material had been inserted into her original text. Perhaps she had penned it in a state of such confusion that she retained no subsequent recollection of composing it. Or perhaps, still in shock when questioned, she was incapable of bringing that moment back into focus. Conceivably, though, Kasenkina may have wished to distance herself from a document that did less to clarify her intentions than to call her lucidity into question, casting doubt over constructions of her leap as a move "magnetized by freedom." The letter certainly imparted no suggestion that its author was driven by an overwhelming desire to begin life over in the United States, borne aloft by her ardor for freedom and hatred of Soviet tyranny.[135]

Other than disparaging the "capitalistic system," the author says nothing of America. Nor does she directly express an intention to defect. Formulaic expressions of love for "the fatherland" and hatred of "traitors" aside—"never in my life shall I go against the dictatorship of the working class"—the document is overwhelmingly personal and confessional in tone, intimate and imploring. The writer presents herself as a soul in torment: a mother distraught by the unconfirmed supposition that her soldier son has perished; a devoted teacher "persecuted" by her colleagues, tormented by pupils taught to revile her. ("They threw nails, books, screwdrivers and penholders, and all kinds of objects at me. The thing that was dearest to me, the thing I lived by, was killed.") For reasons unclear, she has been vilified as a thief. Her mind is in turmoil: "I was in despair, ready to commit suicide.... I was alone, in the silence of the grave." Nothing is mentioned of a refusal to return to the Soviet Union. Her plea is for a sympathetic ear, a word of understanding from the consul general, who (she says) pushed her away: "I admire you infinitely as a person who is worthy of our fatherland. And I should have told you everything, but you would not receive me. I was crushed. You should have drawn closer to me and understood my state of mind." The tone is that of a rejected lover, begging for reconsideration.

This anguished cri de coeur concludes with an entreaty that the consul fetch her from Reed Farm: "I implore you, I implore you once more, don't let me perish here. I am without will-power."[136] Lomakin had not, then, misrepresented the overall sense of the letter when he read from it on August 7, though it contained no reference to her kidnapping by "white Russian bandits" as Soviet protest notes later alleged.[137] Had Kasenkina's dispatch been forged or strategically doctored, one would expect it to corroborate her abduction by reactionaries and FBI gangsters, while expressing a fervent desire to return to the USSR. Yet the letter contains no such material, and its tremulous register—suggestive of a woman perilously close to breakdown rather than a resolute patriot—would seem a curious choice for any Soviet forger. Given the peculiar tone and content, it appears more likely that Lomakin handed over a letter written by Kasenkina herself, convinced that it would resolve in his favor a central issue in the dispute. After all, the letter's most unambiguous statement is its concluding plea that the consul retrieve its author from Reed Farm.

Much discussed while it remained in Soviet hands as the key to a mystifying affair, this document was never publicized once delivered into State Department keeping. Unsurprisingly, U.S. officials exhibited scant enthusiasm for making its contents known, despite legal advice that sanctioned its publication. What good would be served by releasing this opaque document to the press? Ideological investors in Kasenkina's "daring spirit" had little use for inner conflict or messily human irresolution. Suggesting a woman in extremis, the letter disrupted a core element of the dominant narrative: the schoolteacher's kidnapping by Lomakin.[138] While it remained unclear why Kasenkina, having sought assistance in escaping Reed Farm, would then leap from the consulate window on August 12, the letter hinted at a suicidal state of mind. Asked by a police detective why she had jumped, some six hours after the event, Kasenkina's reply indicated a stronger desire for deliverance than for asylum: "I was considering my position and what would happen if I returned to the Soviet Union and I came to the conclusion that I would only have a bad life there and have a very bad situation and there was nothing else for me to do."[139]

Naturally, Kasenkina's memoir presented her as a heroic freedom seeker, though it could hardly avoid some explanation of her faltering resolve. In *Leap for Freedom* the author confesses a desire to have the consul understand her break with "the soviet," attributing the compulsion that led her to write a "silly and hysterical" letter from Reed Farm to the thrall still exercised over her by a Svengali-like Lomakin. But the memoir hinges less on August 12 as the moment of decision than an earlier epiphany that inspired the schoolteacher to plot her escape—a chain of events set in motion with a brisk injunction, "To the Roxy!"[140]

IRON CURTAIN, SILVER SCREEN

Attentive readers of Kasenkina's memoir would immediately have appreciated the significance of this destination—for Manhattan's Roxy Theater had also made headline news in 1948. On the night of May 11 it had been the scene of a violent clash between two thousand demonstrators and counterpicketers over the movie set to enjoy its theatrical premiere inside.[141] Pro-Soviet demonstrators against a feature they billed as "Propaganda for World War III" jammed Seventh Avenue, while fifteen thousand bystanders crowded the sidewalks all the way to Times Square, many spilling across town as a Henry Wallace campaign rally in Madison Square Garden concluded. Police officers "swinging two-foot-long nightsticks like polo mallets" struggled to separate the placard-wielding "red hot crusaders"— "Wallaceites, Communists, fellow travelers and troubled innocents," in *Time*'s partisan characterization—from their opposite numbers: members of the Catholic War Veterans, the American Legion, and Veterans of Foreign Wars who had been drinking in nearby taverns. Scuffles, punches, and a handful of arrests ensued as "picket signs were splintered, leaflets shredded, clothing ripped."[142]

The attraction that caused this "randan at the Roxy" was Twentieth-Century-Fox's *The Iron Curtain*. Hollywood's "first shot in the 'cold war,'" Darryl F. Zanuck's ballyhooed pet project dramatized the high-profile defection of Igor Gouzenko in September 1945.[143] A disillusioned twenty-six-year-old cipher clerk, "Eager Igor" had deserted his post at the Soviet Embassy in Ottawa, brandishing evidence of a transatlantic atomic spy ring. Filmed on location in Canada, *The Iron Curtain* depicted Gouzenko's growing repugnance for his Soviet masters' atomic acquisitiveness—"delight[ed] every time somebody slips them the dope that there's such a thing as uranium," noted the *New Yorker*'s skeptical critic.[144] Impressed by North Americans' hospitality, affluence, and godliness, Gouzenko (Dana Andrews) makes elaborate plans to defect with his pregnant wife (Gene Tierney). After initial skepticism from the Canadian officials, whom he approaches with evidence daringly smuggled from embassy vaults, Gouzenko's claims are finally taken seriously—just before the net of Soviet counterintelligence closes in.

Faulting this production for its paranoid outlook and exaggeratedly villainous Soviets, liberal critics castigated Zanuck for his attribution of malign intentions to the Kremlin, a contemporary intervention that could only aggravate East-West tensions. "I am old-fashioned enough to want my wars declared for me by the President, and not by a motion-picture company," announced Robert Hatch in the *New Republic*.[145] Naturally, though, the heroine of *Leap to Freedom* didn't see it that way, enraptured by the heady sensation of watching her own fate foretold on the big screen:

> For although I understood little of the dialogue I knew it was my story that was being told. Igor Gouzenko and I were one growing up in Russia; learning to fear the Soviets, to whom life meant nothing; getting to detest their lives, hypocrisy and lust for power; becoming oppressed in body and spirit; coming to the New World and passionately craving freedom—and daring to escape. Again I caught my breath as we were about to fail. Again I wept from anger and helplessness when the Canadian authorities, one after another, displayed an incredible indifference and lack of understanding. Then dawning comprehension; quick, desperate last-minute moves; and finally, wonderful, ecstatic freedom![146]

Kasenkina's story and Gouzenko's did indeed have common elements. Having monopolized the headlines with their defections, both enjoyed considerable celebrity thereafter. Gouzenko, living under protection in Canada, garnered an impressive sum for the sale of his story to *Cosmopolitan* magazine and Twentieth Century-Fox. His memoir appeared in May 1948, opportunistically timed to coincide with release of *The Iron Curtain*. (If Kasenkina's autobiography sounded remarkably similar, that perhaps owed something to their shared ghostwriter.) Five years later, Gouzenko followed it with a best-selling novel, *Fall of a Titan*, the screen rights to which he sold for $100,000.[147] In similar fashion, Kasenkina's "leap for freedom" was quickly bankrolled into a leap into the "high income bracket." While still in the hospital, she hired an attorney to negotiate the sale of her story and earned $45,000 from its serialization—a sum that far outstripped the spontaneous public donations to a fund for her assistance. With her royalty check, Kasenkina settled her medical bills, buying a four-room apartment in Queens and spending $2,050 on a new Buick sedan. Soon her attorney playfully reported that his client was "such a good American that she got arrested for speeding the other day."[148] Financially secure, she had no use for any of the offers of accommodation that admirers around the country extended while she recuperated, including "marriage proposals from far and wide." One horse breeder from Michigan even enclosed pictures of his horses as well as a likeness of himself—to no avail. Kasenkina declared herself "too old to marry again."[149]

The consulate's celebrated escapee clearly aroused sentimental anticommunism at its most amorous, continuing to receive between forty and fifty congratulatory letters a week months after August 1948.[150] But she didn't inspire only romantic projections. Quickly, she joined a growing number of witnesses—exiles from either the USSR or the party (if not both)—whose testimony on communism derived heightened credence from its claim to firsthand authority. In the inverted epistemology of the early cold war, to see was to *disbelieve*, a formula attested by a steady stream of memoirs written by those who having "kissed communism now, under the imprint of good old-fashioned capitalist publishers, wish to tell."[151] Of these, Whittaker Chambers's blockbuster *Witness* (1952) cornered the most lucrative market, even if the author's "descent into the inferno of totalitarianism" was made "tourist class," without his ever venturing east of the Elbe.[152] Chambers's spiritual odyssey was by no means the sole exemplar of this genre, however. The memoirs of both Kravchenko and Gouzenko had earlier lingered on best-seller lists. And if the canonical apostates were predominantly male—Arthur Koestler, André Malraux, Ignacio Silone, Richard Wright—their company was expanded by former agents such as Elizabeth Bentley and Angela Calomiris. Both produced accounts of their underground lives that promised as much kissing as telling, accentuating thralldom to the party as "an intellectual and moral slavery that was far worse than any prison."[153]

Many of these "ex-communist anticommunists" made careers not only from their literary endeavors but by serving as expert witnesses before congressional committees. Not so Kasenkina. She did, however, perform a similar—if somewhat more ornamental—function for various anticommunist groups and gatherings that sought to derive luster from her celebrated leap. In March 1949, for example, Kasenkina appeared alongside Sidney Hook, Alexander Kerensky, Max Eastman, and others at the inaugural meeting of Americans for Intellectual Freedom, a gathering convened to counter the "Communist-controlled" Cultural and Scientific Conference for World Peace concurrently assembled at New York's Waldorf-Astoria Hotel. Eighteen months later, she spoke at a rally in Manhattan to observe "Freedom Sunday"—an event that formed part of a larger "Crusade for Freedom" aimed at mobilizing "the forces of truth to pierce the Iron Curtain and defeat the 'Big Lie' of Communism." Still intermittently in the spotlight in 1951, Kasenkina (whose conversion to Catholicism had been widely reported) contributed an essay entitled "We Worship GOD Again" to an audacious issue of *Collier's* that anticipated Russia's "defeat and occupation, 1952–60" after a nuclear war won by the United States.[154]

Hollywood also took notice of this unlikely celebrity whose melodramatic story was invariably narrated in cinematic terms. The studios may not have snapped up *Leap to Freedom* as they had Gouzenko's *The Iron Curtain,* but in different ways Kasenkina made her mark, on screen and off.[155] The "escapee"—a prototype she

FIGURE 7. Janet Leigh, playing a Russian ballerina in occupied Austria, recoils from the approach of Red Army colonel Piniev (Louis Calhern), while Angela Lansbury watches frostily in MGM's *Red Danube* (1949). Courtesy of Photofest.

did much to inaugurate—made a starring appearance in several Hollywood productions, often transmuted from widowed schoolteacher into willowy ballerina. MGM's *The Red Danube* (1949) typified this genre. An overwrought treatment of forcible repatriation from the western zones of occupied Austria, it starred Janet Leigh as a displaced Russian ballerina relentlessly pursued by the Red Army. In no danger of being described as dumpy, poorly dressed, or excessively made up, the twenty-two-year-old Leigh appeared "disarmingly pathetic as the tormented ballerina," the *New York Times*'s critic noted.[156] But if *The Red Danube* improved on Kasenkina in the tragic character of Maria Bühlen, it also made a striking amendment to the novel on which its screenplay was based. In Bruce Marshall's *Vespers in Vienna,* the dancer "shoots herself in the breast" as the Red Army closes in. In MGM's movie, however, Maria regards "the freedom of an open window as preferable to a resumption of her dancing career under Russian sponsorship"—with fatal consequences.[157]

Whether or not this plot change intentionally gestured toward Kasenkina, contemporary critics certainly noted the fluidity with which "actual events" inspired cinematic scenarios and vice versa. Claiming inspiration from Hollywood's dramatization of a true story, the Soviet schoolteacher had upped the ante for cultural producers. "What's the use of paying 50 cents to see dull unimaginative movies or paying 25 cents to the lending library for silly stupid detective yarns in a country where you can have adventures like Mme. Kosenkina's for nothing?" inquired a *Washington Post* editorial in August 1948.[158]

Hollywood was not to be outdone, however. Anticommunist thrillers like *Sofia,* a B-movie yarn of American agents venturing behind the curtain to kidnap a team of Russian atomic scientists, rose to the challenge. Patently ludicrous, its plot was retrieved from outright disbelief by the improbable melodrama of its real-world referents. "With Soviet captives hopping out of consulate windows and testimony of derring-do unfolding in Washington as the current headliners, *Sofia* is promoted from the implausible to a strictly exploitable film, synchronized to the news of the day," *Variety* observed.[159] At least one director attributed to Kasenkina a more personal epiphany. Edward Dmytryk, imprisoned for some months as one of the recalcitrant Hollywood Ten, told a *Saturday Evening Post* reporter that the schoolteacher's leap had sparked a stirring of conscience that heralded the onset of his political maturity.[160]

Everyone, it seemed, wanted to congratulate, copy, or court Kasenkina— eastern bloc dissidents, New York intellectuals, Michigan horse breeders, and Hollywood directors alike. In tumbling from the consulate, she became a beacon for others to follow, boldly advertising the attractions of life in the United States while tearing a "sudden rent in the Iron Curtain." *Time* attributed the anti-Soviet consensus that coalesced in 1948 largely to Kasenkina's bold act, which hastened the "slow swelling of resolve in many hearts"—"at the corner store and the village market, at the tea table and the union meeting." Yet the woman who turned 1948 into a "year of resolution" appeared prone to crippling, and ultimately unfathomable, indecision.[161] She may have made the cold war "Something That People Can Understand," but what propelled her through the third floor window of East Sixty-first Street remains as mysterious now as it was on August 12, 1948.

2

Bloc-Busters

The Politics and Pageantry of Escape from the East

RUSSIAN FLIERS "TAKE" VIRGINIA

"I is Russian pilot!" With this idiosyncratic salutation, Piotr Pirogov greeted U.S. authorities at Camp McCauley airstrip in October 1948, initiating an East-West encounter that captivated U.S. reporters. According to *Newsweek*, the disaffected twenty-eight-year-old lieutenant had "taken French leave of the Soviet air force." With Captain Anatoly Barsov, he had borrowed a bomber and flown from Lwow to the most westerly point marked on their truncated map of Europe. Their objective? To reach Linz, in the U.S. zone of occupied Austria. Crash-landing somewhat short of the runway, the unannounced duo nevertheless met a genial reception, reporters claimed—even if the pair did find American habits thoroughly baffling. Never having encountered a modern bathtub before, Pirogov and Barsov apparently tried to climb in with their shorts on, mistaking the tub for a "small swimming pool." A child on roller skates caused the pair almost as much bemusement. But the Russian airmen seemed more than happy to substitute gin, the U.S. Air Force tipple of choice, for deicing fluid, the Soviets' supposed intoxicant of necessity. So began the Americanization of Anatoly and Piotr—as recorded by a U.S. press at once adulatory and arch.[1]

To all outward appearances, the two pilots perfectly embodied a new cold war type: the eastern bloc "escapee." Fresh faced and of seemingly impeccable ideological pedigree, Pirogov and Barsov lost no time in denouncing the evils of Soviet communism—a system loathed by 70 percent of all Russians, they insisted. With table-thumping emphasis, they protested the lack of free elections and the reviled system of collectivization that made life a misery for rural Russians.[2] At the same time, they radiated zeal for the free world. As *Life* pointed out, they'd been "listening to the Voice of America when they should have been reading *Pravda*."[3] From its broadcasts, the two fliers had learned not only of life in the United States but of Kasenkina's "leap for freedom." These reports, Pirogov claimed, had played a crucial role in stiffening their resolve to initiate an escape plan that had been gestating for a year. If a mere woman could do it, so could they! Washington's refusal to hand the schoolteacher back had given the airmen confidence that they too would be safe as soon as they reached U.S.-controlled territory.[4]

In February 1949 the pair arrived in the United States. Although journalists related that this was to be a two-month stay, after which Pirogov and Barsov would return to Germany, the Russian airmen entertained different ideas. No sooner had they disembarked than they announced a desire to make America their home. To stress the point, the fliers expressed willingness to do *anything* Washington might ask of them, including military service, so long as their new masters did "not use force."[5] But first they had to see the sights. Virginia topped the list—a state they'd formed a particular yen to see, thanks to Voice of America. "Maybe beat biscuits were mentioned, maybe ham, maybe scenery, maybe climate, maybe George Washington and Robert E. Lee, and maybe not," mused an editorial in the *New York Times*. "Anyhow, they just had to see it." Obligingly, the state chamber of commerce offered the pair a weeklong tour. "It is to be hoped they will like Virginia," the *Times* continued. "Many people do. The Chamber of Commerce will doubtless supplement the information already furnished by the Voice of America. It will do its level best to keep them from drifting off to other states, such as Florida and California. But it won't shoot them if they do."[6]

The visit attracted nationwide coverage. Coinciding with the trial of Cardinal Mindszenty in Hungary, it came at a time when popular anticommunism had reached a new pitch of emotional intensity. Barsov and Pirogov commanded "more attention than Gargantua and his mate," *Time* quipped, referencing "the mightiest, most frightful beast ever shown to the public"—Barnum and Bailey's star attraction, a scowling 550-pound ape.[7] Where the gorilla had drawn capacity crowds at Madison Square Garden the previous April, the Russian fliers' much-publicized tour allowed Americans to appraise an equally fascinating species, the "new Soviet man," "structurally so different from Western man in personality, morality and behavior that he is an object of profound curiosity to us." Born shortly after the Bolshevik revolution, the two airmen belonged to the first generation to have grown up under communism. Their road show gave Americans a rare chance to marvel over Soviet man's peculiar psychology and stunted range of experience as the pair embarked on an adventure "comparable with that of Columbus when he set out on an unknown ocean on the way to an unsuspected continent."[8] As such, this reverse encounter of savagery with civilization afforded an opportunity for self-admiration. To witness the Russians' astonishment was to see America flatteringly mirrored through the eyes of fugitives from the "slave world." Their every reaction, "popeyed with amazement," accentuated the allure of "capitalistic delights" over the wretched conditions they'd fled, abandoning wives and a child in the process.[9]

Virginia's compensations were many, however. With Monticello and Robert E. Lee's statue out of the way, the two guests were introduced to the *real* business of America, while their responses were closely monitored by a crowd of reporters and throngs of Virginians drawn to the spectacle. "Few things are more likely to make the US citizen walk a mile with a smile," *Time* proposed, "than a chance to get a look at a real, live Russian: he gawks at them with the same delighted curiosity that his grandfather turned on for Barnum and Bailey's wild man from Borneo."[10] As marquee attractions, Barsov and Pirogov did not disappoint. Dazzled by a lavishly stocked department store in Richmond, the thirty-two-year-old Barsov demanded to know whether this was "unquestionably a people's store." Models, just like movie stars, paraded in a selection of evening gowns, cocktail dresses, and beach "playsuits" for the fliers' delectation. Their satisfied response, "using the international eyebrow code," needed no translation.[11] And everywhere new sensations: their first encounter with ice cream cones and Coca-Cola, with "Negro" shoeshine boys and "jive" musicians—to say nothing of Sweet Briar's ingenuous coeds, whose polite inquiries as to whether the airmen would be returning to Russia caused some alarm as to the soundness of their "mental processes."[12]

Barsov, having nearly been run over twice in Richmond, announced himself particularly fascinated by American automobiles. His enthusiasm soon generated an invitation to visit the Ford plant at Edgewater, New Jersey, where the pair gasped not only at the assembly line's productivity but at the flabbergasting fact that factory workers themselves owned cars and earned as much as $100 a week. Requested to identify the single "most impressive" thing he'd seen, Pirogov demurred: "It is the abundance, the absolute abundance of everything, that amazes—the traffic, the lights at night, the women's shoes in the department store, the lightheartedness." Asked by the Ford manager whether they'd head back east, the two airmen responded in unison with an impassioned "*Nyet!*"[13]

But by the end of the tour cracks in this smooth reflective surface had already appeared. Not all Americans were equally entranced with their Soviet visitors, it seemed. The Staunton-Augusta Chamber of Commerce withdrew its lunch invitation to the fliers after protests from the local AmVets chapter, which regarded the Russians as "deserters and unauthorized aliens"—undeserving recipients, in other words, of Virginia taxpayers' largesse. Tensions abated when the national organization stepped in to announce that the fliers were "political refugees, not deserters," and should be embraced as such.[14] But Pirogov and Barsov themselves appeared less than gracious guests on occasion. Their inspection of Virginia concluded with a testy press conference at which Pirogov complained that the press corps and the air force major who had served as the pair's interpreter had caused offense with

FIGURES 8 and 9. "Russian Fliers Take Virginia." Anatoly Barsov (left) and Piotr Pirogov (right) are introduced to American freedom—Southern style—during their February 1949 tour. As reporters interpreted the Russians' reactions, they were "bemused" by these Richmond street performers, enjoyed their first ice cream cones, and "admired" the grapefruit. Top, photo by Thomas D. McAvoy/Time Life Pictures/Getty Images; bottom, © The Associated Press.

ceaseless requests to divulge military intelligence about Soviet capacities and to "paint a black picture about everything in Russia."[15]

As journalists rendered this fractious incident, the real source of Pirogov's dissatisfaction wasn't that he'd been made to "feel more like a criminal than a guest" or that everything in the USSR was "not black" (though he did make both these points). Rather, he resented reporters' erosion of his prime asset. Keen to protect the capital vested in his dramatic tale, the savvy lieutenant feared that constant cross-questioning by reporters would depreciate its market value. Perhaps having heard of Kasenkina's leap into the top income bracket, Pirogov imagined that his story's sale would raise "a million dollars." Such acquisitiveness could have been read as a welcome sign that entrepreneurialism had claimed another convert, but several columnists instead castigated the ingrate for having overstepped the mark. Pirogov's uppity behavior exposed the dangers of lionizing Soviet "apostates." An editorial in the *Washington Post,* though recommending that "refugees from totalitarianism be afforded asylum," cautioned that "the Russian visitors are flying too high. They ought to be disabused of their Hollywood notions of America before they are displayed like a sideshow."[16]

These words proved prophetic. The perils of feting Soviet defectors became all too apparent just seven months later. In September 1949, Barsov suddenly reappeared in the headlines—back in the USSR. Quite how this "flight from freedom" had come about drew much speculation.[17] More sympathetic commentators imagined that he had succumbed to ferocious pangs of homesickness, missing the wife and son he'd abandoned a year earlier. It couldn't have been easy, some conceded, to adjust to the unglamorous life of the newly arrived, non-English-speaking immigrant. With $100 apiece from Voice of America, the pair had been "turned loose in the land of opportunity and all but forgotten." While Barsov's better-looking and better-adjusted comrade set to work on his memoir—"no less terrifying than Dante's description of the inferno," a critic later effused—the former captain found himself pressing women's pants in a Brooklyn factory, then digging ditches as a day laborer in Stratford, Connecticut, a "bitter comedown for an officer."[18] It was also widely reported that Soviet personnel had made a concerted effort to engineer Barsov's "redefection." Preying on his insecurities, Soviet agents had reportedly encouraged the prodigal flier to believe that if he could also secure Pirogov's return neither would face punishment. Press stories related a meeting between the two men in a Washington restaurant, an encounter that ended with FBI agents (tipped off by Pirogov) seizing Barsov and deporting him to Austria, where he was hand-delivered to Soviet authorities.[19]

Few columnists queried the ethical or legal probity of a "preemptive" deportation designed, U.S. officials announced, to facilitate the unhappy man's freedom of choice. Overwhelmingly, American opinion formers construed the perversity of Barsov's decision in terms as racially stigmatizing as they were ideologically laden:

a "tortured Slavic mind" incapable of adjusting to the demands of freedom. Initially described as more jovial than his younger companion, Barsov's inferior character now appeared somatically inscribed in his "thick-knuckled peasant hands," "short, husky" frame, and face "pitted by small pox."[20] Where Kasenkina had been beautified by her leap for freedom, Barsov's reverse defection disfigured him.

Life carried extensive extracts from a journal and notebook left in the shabby hotel where Barsov had spent his final days in America. This "gloomy diary of a Russian deserter" represented the work of an "extremely confused and pathetic man," a jealous, neurotic, emotionally incontinent drunk. Moreover, the notebook's author appeared to be in tormented thrall to communism, whether animated by vestigial allegiance to the Soviet state or attempting to impress its agents with an exaggerated display of penitence. Contemptuous of American consumerism's hollow pretensions—"What mud there is here. . . . What a craving to make money!"— Barsov's journal anticipated his own thoroughly deserved punishment by the state he'd betrayed. "Now I have to be destroyed if I shall not be corrected by the labor camps," he wrote in a final entry on February 27.[21] Yet despite anticipating the worst, he felt moved (or forced?) to return.

Exemplifying the tenor of much editorial comment, the *New York Times* anchored its analysis of Barsov in Orwell's *1984*, published that June:

> Barsov was clearly a man whose mind was enslaved, even when his body was free. One cannot help thinking of the terrifying picture that the English author, George Orwell, has written for us in his novel *1984*. Barsov was born in 1920, which is to say that until his escape last October he never knew or thought or felt anything that was outside the closed, totalitarian orbit of the Soviet State machine.
>
> Out here in the free air of democracy he must have felt like an animal born in captivity who was suddenly set loose to roam the forests and open fields. He could not have been a very intelligent man. . . . At any rate, he did not have the resources within himself to make a life in a new world, a world so different that he might just as well have been translated to Mars. . . .
>
> The accounts say that he took "a book of Russian poetry and a Russian poem" with him when he crossed the line into the Soviet Zone of Austria. There was the Dostoievsky touch, the brooding Russian mind, which is so tragic and sometimes so pathetic.

The *Times* concluded by encouraging Americans to extend sympathy to this wretched specimen of Soviet manhood. His days were numbered, but he had "harmed only himself." Pirogov likewise predicted that within six months Barsov would "die like a dog."[22]

From triumphant reception to ignominious exit, Barsov's story hinted at the difficulties that would beset subsequent schemes to encourage and exploit defection from the eastern bloc. On paper, it all seemed straightforward. What better way of underscoring the superior allure of the free world or of undermining the "slave world" than by encouraging captive peoples, who couldn't cast a vote of no confidence in communism at the ballot box, to do so with their feet? Yet as the pilots' tour intimated, Soviet escapees could behave unpredictably, and the same was true of domestic opinion. Citizens and their elected representatives remained torn "between their sense of hospitality and their sense of suspicion," like the residents of Virginia in February 1949.[23] With Moscow taking vigilant steps to ensure that fewer residents departed—and that more, like Barsov, subsequently came back— defection would prove a volatile phenomenon for Washington to manage.

INSPIRING DEFECTION

States do not typically urge foreign citizens to flee their own countries. Yet in the late 1940s, U.S. policy makers decided to do just that, eyeing high-profile defectors from the Soviet bloc as prized assets who could help win the cold war in numerous ways. As early as February 1948, George Kennan's Policy Planning Staff (PPS) advised that defection should be not merely welcomed but positively promoted. Departures from the "slave world" would humiliate and demoralize a Kremlin already rattled by the scale of wartime defection from Red Army ranks and by the obdurate resistance of its errant citizens to going back. At the same time, defectors would supplement the stock of intelligence, expertise, and creativity at the West's disposal. As the eastern bloc became a terra incognita, shrinking the "area of American knowledge," refugees promised to illuminate conditions behind the Iron Curtain. Their revelations about the "true nature of the Soviet world" would, Kennan believed, render hitherto uninformed Americans less vulnerable to "Fifth Column operations." Broadcast back behind the Iron Curtain, news of successful escapes would also fortify the resolve of others minded to undertake the perilous journey west, assuring them that the free world was a safe haven they too might reach. In short, defection was a zero-sum game in which Moscow's infuriating losses would directly profit Washington.[24]

Oksana Kasenkina's fabled "leap for freedom" boosted this appreciation of what defectors could do for cold war America. Three days after her dramatic exit from the Soviet consulate, newspapers reported that "athletes of Red Nations" were "seeking escape" in London, where the Olympic games had just concluded. "Finding the atmosphere of political freedom to their liking," three Hungarians and two Czechs had secured leave to remain, while several Yugoslavs and Poles hoped either to stay in Britain or to strike out for North America.[25] The *Los Angeles Times* hastily followed with the case of a nineteen-year-old pianist "prodigy," Lydia Makarova— "Sweden's 'Kosenkina'"—who had fled Leningrad in 1944 and was now scorning the insistent demands of the Soviet Embassy in Stockholm that she return. Later that year, Pirogov and Barsov acknowledged their own debt to the schoolteacher, thereby attesting the potency of U.S. radio broadcasts. Then in May 1949 the *Wash-*

ington Post reported a Turkish version of "the Kasenkina kidnap case," with Soviet officials chasing after the errant wife of a former embassy employee, recalled after a copy of Victor Kravchenko's *I Chose Freedom* was found in the couple's home.[26]

All this was grist to Kennan's mill. "Kravchenko's book, Gouzenko's testimony in Canada and the defection of Mrs. Kasenkina in New York probably did more to arouse the Western world to the realities of the nature of communist tyranny than anything else since the end of the war," a PPS report concluded in June 1949.[27] Agents of enlightenment in the West, escapees also blazed a trail for others in the East to follow, as the Kasenkina copycats seemed to attest. In theory, these effects were easy to orchestrate. Washington had apparently located a superweapon that Moscow couldn't possibly hope to replicate. While thousands of Soviet bloc citizens had headed west since the war, very few Americans—a handful of gullible dupes and lovesick naïfs aside—had rejected the free world in favor of communism. This imbalance told its own story, one that merited loud amplification.

PPS personnel valued Soviet-orbit defectors primarily for their potential contribution to the "psychological" dimensions of cold war. However, the repertoire of possible roles quickly expanded, as did expectations about the scale of exodus that Washington might hope to inspire. In April 1951, the National Security Council endorsed "unlimited and indiscriminate encouragement of defection" from the USSR as a secret objective of U.S. strategy.[28] Those eager to "roll back" the postwar expansion of Soviet power regarded eastern bloc refugees as a valuable reservoir of military manpower, a source that the Nazis had failed to exploit because they had been too wedded to their view of Slavs as *untermenschen* to trust General Vlasov with the command of thousands of Red Army defectors. Washington should learn from this error. Trained as guerrillas, saboteurs, and espionage agents, anticommunist "fighters for freedom" could be dispatched back east, taking the war against communism behind the Iron Curtain. As far as some hawkish lawmakers and columnists were concerned, nothing less than the outcome of World War III depended on America's successful deployment of eastern bloc escapees.[29]

But if the rewards of encouraging defection seemed limitless, this unorthodox practice also generated considerable conflict and irresolution. One early episode helps explain why. Six days after Kasenkina made her leap, Chip Bohlen received word from a contact at the *New York Post* that the Soviet vice-consul, Zot Chepurnykh, had confidentially informed her that he "did not wish to return to the Soviet Union and would not do so if there was any opportunity of staying in the United States." In response, Bohlen told the reporter that "this Government was not in the business of attempting to seduce Soviet officials" and that he didn't know "whether there was anything we could do in the matter."[30] At one level, such nonchalance is mystifying. Wouldn't a Soviet diplomat represent a yet more stunning coup for Washington than an unknown chemistry teacher? Surely Chepurnykh was exactly the kind of "outstanding personality" that Kennan hoped to woo. Why, then, did

Bohlen resist consummating this arrangement with a Soviet official who seemed more than eager to elope?

State Department correspondence supplies several reasons for Bohlen's reticence, all indicative of larger tensions that surrounded defection. Perhaps most fundamentally, U.S. strategists hesitated over how far to go in needling and harassing the Kremlin. Whereas some ardent cold warriors strove to push confrontation to the brink of war or beyond, others advocated less nakedly provocative tactics. Active enticement of defectors by Washington represented a frontal challenge to norms of sovereign statehood—a direct affront to Moscow. Even those who championed unorthodox means of waging cold war recognized that some discretion was required. Subversive tactics required an element of "plausible deniability." It was one thing for the Voice of America to broadcast stories of successful escapes back behind the Iron Curtain, with their implicit message that others should follow suit. But for the State Department to be seen "seducing" a vice-consul, especially one so recently embroiled in a major diplomatic incident, was a more delicate proposition.

Such scruples clearly colored Bohlen's reaction to Chepurnykh's overture. So too did suspicion of the man's motives. Filling J. Edgar Hoover in on the case, one State Department official raised the concern that the vice-consul might be "playing the role of an agent provocateur," seeking to entrap U.S. personnel into extending asylum, only then to expose their "seduction" efforts.[31] This anxiety reflected a persistent fear that individuals who purported to be victims of communist oppression might actually be Soviet espionage agents—spies or sleepers sent west to subvert the free world.

Mistrust didn't stop there. In the State Department's idealized view, defectors were (or ought to be) driven by purely ideological motives: nothing less elevated or more complex than a hatred of communism and desire for freedom. By the lights of the PPS's complex definitional taxonomy, a defector was "a person who places himself at the disposition of US authorities and seeks sanctuary because he has become convinced the Stalinist system is evil and he therefore desires to escape its power." Yet as policy makers privately acknowledged, the reasons for flight varied greatly. In contrast to the pristine defector, the "refugee" was someone who departed "Soviet controlled-territory for primarily economic, personal or other reasons not essentially of a political nature." Then there were "ordinary military deserters or other persons escaping from Soviet or satellite jurisdiction to escape the consequence of a crime or misconduct not of a political nature." As these value-laden categorizations suggest, while every defection represented a net gain for the free world, some defectors were more equal than others.[32]

As for Chepurnykh, State Department officials speculated that even if his eagerness to evade the USSR were genuine, he was surely driven more by an instinct for self-preservation than by a conviction that "the Stalinist system is evil." It took no imagination to see why a man in his position would "wish not to return to the Soviet Union." There would be "no maidens flinging roses in his path," Ralph McGill tartly observed in the *Atlanta Constitution*. Other columnists were yet more blunt in anticipating that it would be "next stop Siberia" for Lomakin and Chepurnykh—intimations of doom later confirmed by a *New York Times* report that the vice-consul had received a fifteen-year prison sentence on return to the USSR, that his wife had been exiled to Vorkuta in Siberia, and that his two U.S.-born daughters had been sent to a "re-education institution."[33] That Bohlen and colleagues preferred to let Chepurnykh face this fate than facilitate his defection suggests an underlying disjuncture in attitudes toward defection and defectors. Steeped in symbolic and strategic potential, the phenomenon of defection found favor. But individual defectors did not.

Suspicion assumed many forms. With a domestic housing shortage causing social distress, and price increases frustrating expectations of prosperity, assistance to displaced persons (DPs) was not a popular postwar cause. Truman struggled (and failed) to gain congressional approval for a Displaced Persons Act in 1948 that would have brought four hundred thousand refugees to the United States, packaging it as a security measure to stabilize fragile European states and as an opportunity to redress shortfalls in America's own agricultural labor market.[34] But if refugee assistance in general met deep resistance, émigrés from the eastern bloc engendered more specific antagonism.

Who were these voluntarily stateless people, critics of immigration liberalization asked? Analyzing the desertion of a substantial number of Soviet military personnel from their postings in eastern Europe in 1948, *Newsweek* attributed this exodus to "the almost glandular Russian instinct for adventure and romance." But the magazine simultaneously noted, as did the State Department, that anticommunist impulses "were mixed with the insignificant and the grotesque": "Some Russian soldiers were lured into deserting by their German girlfriends. Others feared disciplinary action or sought to escape from the increasingly tighter discipline practiced by the Soviet Army. One former collective farmer frankly admitted that he had enjoyed the war, when he murdered Jews and raped German women. Peacetime discipline had made him desert."[35] Such individuals hardly seemed deserving recipients of American largesse, let alone desirable new residents.

Distinguishing the worthy from the unscrupulous was not easy. Eastern bloc escapees were suspect not only because their motives could never be satisfactorily established but also because they were *Russians*—or members of other ethnic groups subject to malign construction at a time when the admission of "undesirables" was both stringently controlled and under intense legislative scrutiny. Worse yet, they came from *communist* states. To those who regarded Marxist-Leninism as a dangerous pathology, these refugees were thus putative bearers of contagion.

With anticommunism and nativist chauvinism finding common cause, there was scant enthusiasm for admitting Soviet bloc refugees en masse into early cold war America—a point often misunderstood. Many commentators have assumed that escapees were ushered straight in because "the West scored ideological points by welcoming refugees from the East."[36] In reality, anticommunism did not automatically open doors for escapees. If anything, fears of Red subversion, aligned with skepticism over the caliber of Slavs' "whiteness," worked to push the door shut and keep it bolted. Many of the most bellicose cold warriors—ardent champions of the captive peoples' liberation—were equally staunch opponents of refugee admission. Tellingly, when the PPS originally recommended that premium-grade defectors be recruited for active service, it proposed admission of only 150 specialized recruits whose expertise would directly benefit U.S. psychological warfare programs, a suggestion enacted in the 1950 Central Intelligence Act. Kennan and his staff had no intention of offering carte blanche to escapees in general. They didn't even debate such an unpalatable move. A shared assumption that "no significant proportion" of escapees could "be brought to the US" structured all high-level policy deliberations, barely requiring articulation.[37]

In 1950, prospects for eastern European refugees' admission received a further setback with passage of the Internal Security (McCarran) Act, which denied entry to anyone who either was or had been a Communist Party member. Since many of those fleeing the Soviet bloc had been compelled to join the party or were under suspicion of having done so, the McCarran Act made it extremely difficult for many eastern European and former Soviet citizens to enter the United States.[38] Its stipulation that former party members must spend a decade "in the clear" before they could be considered for naturalization ensured that when Piotr (now Peter) Pirogov applied for citizenship in 1955 his request would be turned down. As a boy, he had been required to join the Komsomol youth movement.[39]

Early cold war schemes to manipulate defection would struggle to resolve these many tensions: between a mass exodus and targeted "poachings," between extravagant promises and parsimonious practice, and between past assistance to Soviet repatriation efforts and present aspirations to encourage citizens' flight from the countries of the eastern bloc. Above all, though, such projects had to reckon with Americans' stubborn reluctance to accommodate a rhetorically valorized character often vilified in person: the eastern bloc escapee.

YOUNG, SINGLE, AND STATELESS: THE REFUGEE MOBILIZED

Whether or not Washington took active steps to encourage defection, U.S. policy makers in the late 1940s couldn't ignore the fact that hundreds of thousands of Soviet and eastern European refugees were already *in* western Europe, as the Alsops had pointed out at the time of Kasenkina's leap. PPS reports estimated the total at seven hundred thousand in February 1948.[40] Of these, some had been in the West since the war, evading Soviet and United Nations Relief and Rehabilitation Administration (UNRRA) repatriation efforts. Others arrived later as the Stalinist grip over eastern/central Europe tightened, squeezing through borders guarded with increasing zeal, or (if they lived in Berlin) simply crossing the street from the Soviet zone to the western sectors. Before the erection of the wall in 1961 brought *Republikflucht* to a near halt, thousands left East Berlin every month, including a significant number of Soviet military personnel who abandoned their postings in the satellite states.[41] In October 1948, the month of Pirogov and Barsov's flight, *Newsweek* estimated the number of deserters from the Red Army at between thirty thousand and one hundred thousand—"the greatest body of expatriates since the French Revolution."[42]

To enthusiasts of schemes to "roll back" Soviet power, these disaffected soldiers were ripe for recruitment, either by direct enlistment into the U.S. military or through the formation of a new Volunteer Freedom Corps (VFC).[43] With 1.4 million young American men drafted, nearly five hundred thousand at war in Korea, and American occupation forces still heavily deployed in Europe and Asia, military manpower was stretched thin. Mobilization of eastern bloc "volunteers" would help alleviate this burden. Republican Congressman Charles J. Kersten, together with Senators Alexander Wiley and Henry Cabot Lodge, led the way, lauding escapees as potentially "the biggest, single, constructive, creative element" in U.S. foreign policy.[44] "Stateless, single, anti-Communist young men" cried out for an organization to harness their energies, Eisenhower announced.[45] In Lodge's pet project for the VFC, U.S. officers would command units of defectors organized along national lines. When general war broke out again in Europe—sooner rather than later, many anticipated (or even hoped)—these troops would form the vanguard, leading the charge to liberate their respective "captive nations."

Machinations of this kind resulted in various legislative moves, both before and after Eisenhower took office in 1953. The Lodge Bill of 1950 authorized the U.S. Army to enlist 12,500 "unmarried aliens." Processing proved so cumbersome, however, that none were enlisted in 1950 and only 113 in 1951.[46] This dilatory pace made another plan seem more compelling: to bring bands of eastern bloc recruits under NATO command. In October 1951, during congressional deliberations over the Mutual Security Act, Kersten proposed an amendment that would make available $100 million "for any selected persons who are *residing in or escapees from* the Soviet Union, Poland, Czechoslovakia, Hungary, Rumania, Bulgaria, Albania, Lithuania, Latvia, and Estonia, or the Communist dominated or Communist occupied areas of Germany and Austria, and any other countries absorbed by the Soviet Union either to form such persons into elements of the military forces supporting the North Atlantic Treaty Organization or for other purposes" (emphasis added).[47] The Kersten Amendment thus marked the congressional debut of persons specifically identified as "escapees."

FIGURE 10. "He's gone A.W.O.L. with over 100,000 others." A maudlin Stalin sobs over his errant citizens in "Ding" Darling's cartoon, dated August 27, 1948. Reproduced courtesy of the "Ding" Darling Wildlife Society.

Eisenhower enthusiastically endorsed the VFC plan, adopted as NSC 154 in 1953. Yet despite presidential backing, obstacles to mobilization proved insuperable. Champions of rollback envisioned escapees as "patriots with a burning desire to bring freedom back to their own nation."[48] However, many who left the satellite states neither wished to go back nor regarded their departure as merely temporary. Every new arrival from the East faced intensive interrogation by a battery of military and civilian intelligence agencies. These debriefings revealed a considerable discrepancy between the ideal-typical "freedom volunteer" and the majority of Red Army deserters—many of whom had fled for (or from) women, to evade military discipline, or simply because the opportunity had presented itself. Asked in March 1953 whether potential recruits left their countries "to get out of them or in the hope of going back to liberate them," CIA director Allen Dulles equivocally ventured, "A little of both."[49] Many were neither fervent anticommunists nor ardent nationalists, and a substantial number aspired to leave Europe altogether. The United States was a favored destination. Australia trailed in second place, while Latin America, another common resettlement destination for DPs, was viewed with such disfavor that many new arrivals announced that they would sooner stay encamped in Europe than head south.[50]

In imagining the "freedom volunteer" as an idealist whose "lust for adventure" was matched by courage in evading communist border controls, these cold warriors invariably gendered the escapee as male. But Europe's refugee camps contained many women and a significant population of both sexes who were either too old, too young, or too infirm for strenuous labor of any sort, let alone guerrilla warfare.[51] As plans to devise what was infelicitously referred to as a "final solution" for DPs made clear, the sick, frail, and elderly represented the intractable "hard core" for resettlement agencies. What to do with the least wanted among the unwanted? Plans for a VFC made no provision for the myriad refugees from the East who could not be inducted into such a force.

Leaving aside the corps' incompleteness as a "solution" to flight from the Soviet bloc, military projections of this kind were snarled with logistical knots and anomalies. If the corps' structure were nationally based, how many "captive nations" would receive their own unit? Would *all* the nationalities subsumed by the USSR be separately represented? If so, how would U.S. authorities arbitrate competing claims to sovereign status? The State Department cautioned strongly against enumerating the precise number of "captive nations," fearing that Washington would confront demands for separate battalions "for Slovaks (as distinct from Czechs), Ukrainians, Byelorussians, Georgians, and possibly even for North Caucassians, Armenians, Turkelis, etc." Any departure from the current policy of "non-predetermination of national separatist questions" risked submerging the administration in the shifting currents of émigré politics.[52]

Another set of difficulties emerged when some planners recommended inclusion of former North Korean and Chinese POWs in the VFC. Expansion of the corps's field of operations offered a potential means to employ thousands of prisoners who refused repatriation after the Korean War (a phenomenon discussed in chapter 5). But anti-Asian discrimination in both the services and the United States complicated this prospect. Over time, planners had to acknowledge that their pre-

ferred scenario—in which escapee units would liberate their homelands from communism and then stay put—might not come to pass, at least not anytime soon. As
the 1950s wore on, it seemed increasingly probable that eastern Europe and China
would remain under communist rule indefinitely. What, then, would become of
demobilized freedom volunteers once their military service ended? Some, including Eisenhower, favored conferral of U.S. citizenship as the reward for loyalty.
Others fretted that such an incentive contradicted the liberationist ethos of the
corps, threatening to attract more mercenary-minded recruits who would see enlistment as an easy route to U.S. citizenship. Moreover, none of the VFC's most ardent advocates supported the idea of offering citizenship to Korean and Chinese
volunteers at a time when prohibitions against Asian immigration into America
had barely been lifted.[53]

The trick, Lodge proposed, was to "give as little as you can and still get your
man"—applying midcentury premarital mores to martial recruitment. Yet in practice he and others envisaged offering freedom volunteers little more than an opportunity to fight America's wars for less than half the pay of regular U.S. forces.[54]
Buckling under the weight of these contradictions, combative escapee plans were
ultimately undone in the mid-1950s by their own pugnacity. Proponents of rollback often made little attempt to mask their enthusiasm for pushing confrontation
with Moscow to the point of implosion, believing that another general war offered
the best, or only, chance of liberation for the "captive peoples." Such apocalyptic
visions doubtless appealed to a particular strain of U.S. opinion—the same segment
that, during the long military stalemate in Korea, exhibited mounting impatience
to drop atomic bombs on China. But others blanched.

Washington's sponsorship of subversion behind the Iron Curtain had already
generated one major international showdown. In authorizing funds not only for
"escapees from" but also those *"residing in"* the satellite states—for recruitment by
the U.S. military or NATO or "for *other purposes"*—the Kersten Amendment appeared to license plots to sabotage eastern bloc regimes from within. When the Soviets protested the illegitimacy of this move at the UN in December 1951, American delegates vociferously rebutted the charge. "We Americans—immigrants and
descendants of immigrants from every corner of the world—have no aggressive
ambitions. Everything we do we discuss in the open for all the world to hear,"
protested Senator Michael Mansfield, depicting America's melting pot as "the greatest goldfish bowl in the world."[55] This rebuttal was thoroughly tendentious. Kersten himself boasted, none too quietly, that his amendment paved the way to "make
some trouble for Joe Stalin in his own back yard."[56] Covertly, the CIA had already
launched clandestine schemes to "detach" Soviet satellites using guerrilla units mustered from escapees. In one official's opinion such forces were a "closer approximation to the absolute weapon than the atomic bomb," though attempts to deto-
nate this weapon backfired disastrously.[57]

After Mansfield's unconvincing performance at the UN, State Department officials lamented the "beating" Washington had taken over a hand recklessly overplayed. Over successive months, several western European governments also expressed determined opposition to militarized escapee recruitment schemes. For those on the eastern bloc's perimeter, the prospect of housing units of recruits itching for World War III was more alarming than reassuring. A pointed challenge to the Soviets, the VFC's deployment in western Europe threatened to destabilize the continent's precarious status quo. Altering that balance in the free world's favor was, after all, the VFC's raison d'être. Yet without the support of those states in which its units would be based, nothing of this sort could be done. And in the end, after many years of inconclusive planning, nothing was.[58]

CONJURING THE ESCAPEE

Plans for a VFC held a particular appeal for lawmakers drawn both to its liberationist potential and to the continental remove at which the corps promised to keep eastern bloc refugees.[59] Occupying a privileged place in national security deliberations, military schemes represented only one way in which policy makers hoped to profit from defection. While plans for recruitment stumbled from one obstacle to the next, other avenues were simultaneously explored for stimulating further departures and for accommodating refugees and defectors already in western Europe.

By the early 1950s, U.S. strategists could no longer insulate their projections for winning the covert cold war from the day-to-day misery of life in Europe's DP camps. Thousands of refugees, homeless since the war, were joined by a dwindling number of new arrivals who had been led by U.S. radio broadcasts to believe that their bold choice for freedom would be rewarded in the West. Often the reality fell considerably short of expectations. With prominent journalists drawing attention to this discrepancy, policy makers came to appreciate that unless they did more to assist refugees—including those of little "practical" value to Washington— grandiose schemes to win the cold war with escapees' assistance were liable to founder amid a welter of bitter recriminations. One question required particularly urgent attention. Refugees who had managed to evade their own states' vigilant border guards were frequently turned back at the perimeter of the "free world" by *western* authorities—sometimes by American soldiers. Michael Hoffmann of the *New York Times* reported in September 1951 that a putative escapee stood a "better than two-to-one chance of being jailed promptly like a common criminal" on arrival in the western zones of Austria and Germany. To its chagrin, the State Department corroborated Hoffman's findings: "Because every person who crosses the frontier of the West clandestinely is a lawbreaker, all who escape get treatment more consistent with the presumption that they are criminals than with the presumption that they are political refugees."[60]

Worse yet, this dispiriting news came four months after the U.S. commissioner for Germany, John McCloy, had explicitly assured asylum seekers that American personnel would *not* deliver them back into communist custody: an announcement intended to draw a firm line under Washington's past assistance to Soviet repatriation efforts.[61] Pirogov and Barsov had been fortunate, in this sense at least. When their plane bumped down near Linz in 1948 it was by no means a foregone conclusion that they would be allowed to remain in Austria. Only after lengthy deliberations did U.S. officials decide not to hand them over to Red Army officers. Many others—not having arrived in so dramatic a fashion—met a much frostier response.[62]

For the lucky ones allowed in, confinement in a "virtual concentration camp" followed. "Incarcerated under needlessly unpleasant conditions for long periods," refugees were subjected to intensive screening interviews as numerous agencies looked to extract every ounce of serviceable intelligence from individuals regarded as rapidly wasting assets. Refugees who weren't simply sent back were then turned "loose to shift for themselves," having been "squeezed dry of information." These bitter characterizations appeared in a secret government report. Yet American authorities were slow to streamline a screening process that they themselves had determined was as inefficient as it was inhumane.[63]

Not surprisingly, some new arrivals succumbed to "Barsovism." According to Pirogov's translator, this morbid condition quickly set in when "the new Bolshevik man, suddenly turned rebel," came to regard himself as "rudderless, useless and abandoned."[64] In growing numbers, sufferers were drearily retracing their steps and heading back east. Press columnists drew attention to this shameful indictment of Washington's inconsistency, noting (among other episodes) that some two thousand refugees had returned to Russia in 1951, disillusioned with their new careers as coal miners in Belgium. "All had come hoping for much from the free world. All had got nothing, except to be utterly cut off from the world they knew," Joseph Alsop protested.[65] The situation in West Germany was particularly dismal as the new Federal Republic struggled to absorb not only eight million *Volksdeutsche* expellees from the East but "a constant trickle of escapees from Soviet-occupied countries." According to Anne O'Hare McCormick, many of these fugitives were individuals otherwise destined for the Soviet gulag: "But the cruel quirk in the situation is that conditions on the other side of the line are so hopeless that 500 are now returning out of the 1000 who escape daily. There is no place for them in Germany.... Nothing reveals the present state of affairs more clearly than the fact that people who risk their lives to get out of Soviet territory take the greater risk of going back when they see what awaits them outside."[66]

McCormick joined the Alsop brothers, Drew Pearson, and various prominent

Russian émigré opinion formers, including Eugene Lyons, David Dallin, and Isaac Don Levine, to entreat Washington to improve its treatment of escapees—or, if it intended to do nothing, to promise less. Harry Rosenfield, the U.S. displaced persons commissioner, pointedly announced at a Vienna press conference in December 1951 that the United States "should either look after the escapees or tell them to stay at home."[67] A secret government-sponsored study of means by which the Iron Curtain could be "perforated," code-named Project TROY, made the point yet more starkly: "We have failed to supply physical protection and opportunities for decent livelihoods to defectors, even those who have defected at our direct instigation. Our covert agents have made promises, sometimes extravagant promises, which have not been kept. Our treatment has had the effect of saying 'We know perfectly well that you are traitors and undesirable citizens. We shan't trust you to the slightest degree either.'"[68]

After such an inauspicious beginning, Washington clearly had much to remedy, and 1951 proved a decisive year both for U.S. escapee plans and international refugee politics. The final year of the International Refugee Organization's activities, it also witnessed the promulgation of the Geneva Convention Relating to the Status of Refugees. This new statute defined the refugee as one whose "well-founded fear of being persecuted for reasons of race, religion, nationality, membership of a particular social group or political opinion" led to "his [being] outside the country of his nationality" and unable to return.[69] Privileging persecution as the precipitant of statelessness, the Geneva Convention has often been interpreted as a cold war implement designed to favor fugitives from communism over other refugees whose reasons for flight were less ideologically serviceable to the West and whose darker skin made them less palatable as prospective entrants.[70] But the politics surrounding the 1951 Convention were more complicated than this schematic interpretation implies. If it is no surprise that Moscow was not among the signatories, it requires more explanation as to why Washington did not subscribe either: why, precisely as the refugee category assumed sharper definition, U.S. policy makers chose instead to fashion the *escapee* as America's preeminent object of concern.

This idiosyncratic approach derived, in part, from increasing frustration with UN relief agencies, which fell under suspicion of undue neutrality toward the Soviet bloc. As tension with Moscow over issues of defection and repatriation mounted, U.S. policy makers exhibited growing reluctance to cooperate with international organizations not under exclusive American control. This unilateral turn was evident in Washington's response to the 1951 Convention. Rather than work with the UN High Commission for Refugees and endorse the open-ended commitment to stateless victims of persecution implicit in the convention, Truman's administration established parallel intergovernmental agencies to assist selective beneficiaries of American largesse.[71]

Washington's calculated investment in flight from the eastern bloc assumed its most concrete expression in March 1952, when Truman launched the United States Escapee Program (USEP). Unveiled with much fanfare, this welfare and resettlement assistance scheme aspired to reverse and redeem the administration's earlier missteps, notably Washington's postwar assistance of Red Army repatriation efforts and more recent failure to bring practical policy into alignment with rhetorical promises. Locating the Escapee Program within "long-established humanitarian traditions," Truman strove to bolster America's credentials as a champion of human rights, while reassuring dissatisfied residents of the Soviet orbit that the West was "a desirable place to which to flee, or with which to cooperate."[72] With Truman simultaneously assuring thousands of North Korean and Chinese POWs that they would not be sent back behind the "Bamboo Curtain" against their will, the moment for mass defection had seemingly come.

Packaged as a charitable venture, the Escapee Program shared the same cold war–winning objectives vested in more combative plans to deploy refugees as spies, saboteurs, and "psywarriors" in clandestine or open combat with the Soviet bloc. Behind the scenes, State and Defense Department officials reassured "rollback" Republicans that the Escapee Program wasn't an exercise in wishy-washy do-gooding. Kersten was duly reassured that "the primary purpose of escapee provision as a whole [was] to contribute directly toward the military strength of free Europe rather than to provide for the care of refugees in general." But Psychological Strategy Board personnel also cautioned that without being seen to do more for eastern bloc refugees as a whole, Washington would fail to recruit "enough able-bodied, male escapees to create meaningful military units."[73]

Meanwhile, Americans had to be sold on the unpopular idea of reassigning $4.3 million from the Mutual Security Act for relief and resettlement assistance—an initiative that required eastern bloc refugees' exemption from the stigma that surrounded DPs more broadly. Launching the Escapee Program, Truman self-consciously extolled "fugitives from Soviet terror" as "friends of freedom" and "courageous fighters against communism."[74] In so doing, he was acting on the express recommendation of the Psychological Strategy Board that "some definitive language should be used for escapees as persons who have actually escaped from the Iron Curtain to differentiate [them] from people who are otherwise called refugees."[75] Peculiarly calculated for effect, escapee status sought to transform mistrusted refugees into more deserving recipients of U.S. assistance.

Applauded as "courageous fighters against communism," migrants from the eastern bloc were assigned a clear moral identity, free from the taint of economic opportunism. Unlike refugees from noncommunist states, those fleeing the Soviet orbit did not have to prove that they were victims of *direct* political persecution. Oppression was, after all, taken to be a fixed point in the experience of all who languished under the "dark curtain of tyranny." Every resident of the eastern bloc thus appeared to be an escapee-in-waiting—if only they could get through the Iron Curtain.

FROM IRON CURTAIN TO "PAPER WALL"

In practice, it was no more self-evident who qualified as an escapee than what the entitlements of this status were. For different reasons Germans, Yugoslavs, and Chinese—the three largest groups of anticommunist refugees—were *denied* USEP assistance: East Germans because they enjoyed West German citizenship; Yugoslavs because the State Department didn't want a "major fuss with Tito," whose dissidence it was keen to encourage; and Nationalist Chinese because they were so numerous as to represent an expense Washington wasn't prepared to underwrite. Delimited by fiscal, ideological, and racialized concerns, escapees were duly defined as "persons from the territory or control of the USSR, the Baltic States, Poland, Czechoslovakia, Hungary, Bulgaria, Rumania, and Albania, who escape into Western Europe, ranging from Turkey to Sweden."[76]

To flee a communist state was thus not automatically to find oneself hailed in the West as an "escapee." Furthermore, the privileges of escapee status were often less impressive than the term's valorizing connotations implied. As a priority, the Foreign Operations Administration (which administered the Escapee Program in Europe with an American staff of forty-five) hoped to improve the dismal camp conditions that led a significant number of escapees to retreat back east. Initially, the State Department pushed West German authorities to house escapees in separate facilities. Since one clandestine objective of the Escapee Program was the extraction of superior intelligence, everything about segregated camps could be designed to facilitate the "psychological impression" made on new arrivals, thereby softening them up for subsequent interrogation.[77]

The scale of Germany's refugee crisis made it impossible to institute separate camps for escapees, however. This left the Foreign Operations Administration with a different predicament: How to improve the lot of only some encamped residents? A system of discriminatory humanitarianism—inscribed in the Escapee Program's anomalous terms—threatened to stoke bitter resentment among refugees who were unlikely to appreciate the logic or fairness of its remit. With residents subject to coercion from both anticommunist activists and Soviet agents, DP centers were already volatile environments. Overt favoritism by U.S. welfare agencies risked aggravating the tensions of camp life, while irking European governments and international relief agencies troubled by Washington's self-serving "investment in humanity." Partiality was also operationally unworkable. Since disease showed no respect for classificatory hierarchy, it was impossible to "partly decontaminate" a camp for the exclusive benefit of escapees, as one U.S. official ruefully observed. Sanitation was improved either for all or for none.[78]

For some escapees, their special status delivered little more than a care package containing a toothbrush, razor, and soap—"A Gift from the People of the United States." Better food, secondhand clothing, and footwear were also sometimes forthcoming. Few, though, received what many wanted most of all: speedy resettlement, preferably in the United States. Initiating the Escapee Program, Truman urged Congress to liberalize immigration restrictions, linking these "unfortunate victims of oppression" with Europe's "surplus population" in that both groups required homes elsewhere if fragile western and southern European states weren't to become dangerously overstretched. Truman thus appealed to Congress to authorize a Special Migration Assistance Act, granting visas for some three hundred thousand new entrants and earmarking seven thousand of these (issued over the next three years) for "religious and political refugees from communism in eastern Europe." Congress remained unmoved. Or rather, lawmakers were *more* moved by arguments that shaped the Immigration and Nationalities Act, passed on June 21, 1952, over the president's express veto.[79]

This landmark piece of immigration legislation, better known as the McCarran-Walter Act, largely reaffirmed the discriminatory biases of the national-origins quota system in place since the 1920s. Congressman Walter announced himself "particularly bothered" by Truman's proposal to bring "more Italian Catholics into the United States." But if this prospect caused alarm, how much more troubling was the specter of thousands of eastern Europeans and Slavs from communist states, tainted both by ethnicity and by proximity to a noxious ideology? Migrants from the eastern bloc were not "the kind of people our ancestors were," Walter insisted.[80]

As accounts of Barsov's reverse defection made clear, during the early cold war Slavs were often constructed as indelibly Other, more Asiatic than Caucasian in prevalent racial typologies. James Burnham's assertion in *The Struggle for the World* (1947) that Russia was not "part of Western civilization" encapsulated this mid-century common sense. Many commentators similarly stressed communism's "oriental" propensities toward barbarism, despotism, and cruelty.[81] When Walter Bedell Smith (former U.S. ambassador to Moscow, then director of the CIA) introduced a 1953 edition of the Marquis de Custine's *Journey for Our Time,* he commended the durability of an aperçu penned in the 1840s: "I do not blame the Russians for being what they are. I blame them for pretending to be what we are." Like Custine, Smith believed that a "Chinese wall"—the "Slavonic language and character"—separated Russians from the West as effectively as the Iron Curtain.[82] No matter how hard Slavs tried to "pass," they, like others "untutored in the habits of liberty," were deemed incapable of assimilation. Embellishing the point, Kennan expressed alarm at Soviet refugees' views of democracy, which he regarded as "primitive and curious in the extreme": the refugees, he observed, itched to line their adversaries up against a wall "with a ruthlessness no smaller than that to which they professed to be reacting."[83]

Before the McCarran-Walter Act was passed in 1952, two attempts had been made to deny visas to *all* citizens of the USSR and its satellites.[84] The failure of these legislative moves did not nullify perceptions of eastern bloc refugees as cunning tricksters trying to pass themselves off as what they were not—and never could be. In early cold war debates over immigration, some opponents of liberalization drew attention to a different dimension of Slavic slipperiness when they noted the large number of Russians and Ukrainians who had populated Europe's camps since 1945. Many of these men had been so eager to resist return that they fraudulently assumed new nationalities, hoping to dupe Red Army repatriation officers into believing that they weren't in fact Soviet citizens. Such mendacity—over something as intrinsic to personhood as national identity—suggested that they wouldn't hesitate to lie about past criminal or political convictions in order to gain entry to the United States. And without official documentation (which many escapees lacked) how could U.S. authorities really be sure of such individuals' bona fides? Eastern bloc émigrés existed in an alarming epistemological vacuum. Not just stateless, they were also nameless, paperless, and unknowable.[85]

Fears over imposture and "phoniness"—pervasive fifties preoccupations—also stoked suspicion that the Soviets might exploit the Escapee Program as a Trojan horse with which to smuggle communist agents "posing as DPs" into America. Others wondered whether the Kremlin hadn't, or wouldn't, purposely dispatch "unreliable and feeble" elements west, an accusation later made of Fidel Castro with regard to the *Mariel* exodus in 1980.[86]

Conceived at a moment of acute national anxiety during which many of the Capitol's most ardent anticommunists preferred to deploy escapees overseas than admit them into America, the McCarran-Walter Act did its best simply to sidestep the question of refugee resettlement. While it provided for temporary admission of aliens at the discretion of the attorney general ("for reasons deemed strictly in the public interest"), it mortgaged these entrances against national quotas. New legislation modified the 1950 Internal Security Act to allow the admittance of select former Communist Party members who could prove, under stringent screening, that they had joined under duress or as a minor, but it made no provision for a more sweeping relaxation of existing prohibitions.[87] Rejecting Truman's recommendation that a right of asylum be enshrined in U.S. immigration law, McCarran-Walter extended sanctuary only "to the disenchanted diplomat who chose to stay in the country," one caustic critic remarked.[88]

Despite Truman's failure to ease admission for DPs and escapees, arguments playing on "enlightened self-interest" gathered steam: Washington must "keep the doors to freedom open for those who dare to escape from the lands behind the dark curtain of tyranny" or tarnish its reputation. Truman's Commission on Immigration and Naturalization condemned the McCarran-Walter Act's parsimony in a report, *Whom We Shall Welcome,* published in January 1953. With a new president in the White House, and a secretary of state who styled himself an ardent champion of the "captive peoples," a Refugee Relief Act that passed in 1953 promised 120,000 special nonquota visas for each of the two following years. Yet as liberal critics pointed out, this new act not only left McCarran-Walter's racially discriminatory clauses firmly in place but contained "new ones, so drastic in scope as to destroy the hopes of many who have been dreaming of a safe haven in the United States." In its amended final version, it allowed for fifty-eight thousand refugee admissions. In practice, though, the total was much lower, since the conditions of issuance were willfully prohibitive.[89]

Many eligible petitioners spent years in limbo, for the Refugee Relief Act stipulated that admission required a *documented* two-year history, corroborating "character, reputation, mental and physical health, history and eligibility."[90] Because most refugees had no other way to prove their ideological, moral, and physical health, they had to remain encamped while evidence slowly amassed, "wait[ing] out their two years' probation in a state of such exemplary grace as to prove to the most skeptical that they just *couldn't* be Communists." Western Europe's camps thus gained more long-term inmates while the rate of admissions into the United States slowed down yet further.[91] From June to December 1954, the United States admitted only fifty escapees. Two years after the act's passage, the former solicitor general doubted whether as many as a thousand "actual escapees, expellees and refugees not eligible under any other category" had entered the United States. A *Harper's* feature, lambasting the "national disgrace" of this "compassion by slide rule," put the total (in April 1955) at only 563 visas for refugees and escapees. As for those who did squeeze in, they remained susceptible to hostile construction as "a Communist, a chiseler, and a competitor for some American boy's job."[92]

FLIGHTS OF FANCY: THE ESCAPEE
IN COLD WAR CULTURE AND PAGEANTRY

Escapee projects weren't only exercises in instrumental humanitarianism or covert warfare against the Soviet bloc; they also played a crucial role in cold war identity construction and domestic mobilization. When the Psychological Strategy Board urged policy makers in December 1951 to "exploit all aspects of the psychological value inherent in escape from Soviet tyranny," a key objective was to consolidate popular conceptions of the eastern bloc as the "slave world" while affirming America as "a free community with basic concern for the dignity and worth of the individual."[93] By rejecting slavery in favor of freedom, the escapee threw the antithetical character of these two worlds into sharp relief. But if this fearless voyager made palpable the schism between East and West, his mobility also gestured optimistically toward a moment when, under U.S. guidance, the world would be reconstituted as a single free space across which goods, ideas, and people could move without restriction.

A Gallup poll conducted in November 1951 found that 65 percent of respondents had a correct or "probably correct" understanding of the term *Iron Curtain* and that only 6 percent thought it was a "Russian underground organization" or shorthand for the Soviet attitude toward capitalism ("pull curtain and have nothing to do with").[94] Over the next few years, opinion formers strove to eradicate such misconceptions. Tales of escapees' heroism in evading guards ordered to shoot on sight solidified the Iron Curtain as a harsh concrete reality, not a figurative conceit. "Merely as a physical barrier it is formidable," a *New York Times* reporter observed in August 1953, describing the "deadly line" that stretched along the Hungarian frontier into Czechoslovakia. "What is visible are two rows of barbed wire with a strip of ground behind that is plowed up and sown with mines. Low wooden watchtowers, about five hundred yards apart, are fitted with powerful searchlights and manned day and night by Russian soldiers." Since many guards were "graduates of the concentration camps or of the tough postwar underworld school which rates none too highly the value of human life," crossing this frontier was, as the *Saturday Evening Post* put it, "no game for sissies."[95] That thousands risked their lives in the attempt not only stressed the Soviet bloc's carceral character but affirmed the free world as a pacific and prosperous place where universal aspirations for a dignified life unhampered by state interference could be comfortably realized.

Who formed the audience for these constructions? Washington's psychological strategists clearly hoped to reassure the "captive peoples" that they had not been forgotten, that their fate was not irreversible, and that they would find a warm welcome on the "sunny side of the iron curtain." Rather less explicitly, however, these psywarriors also included the American public in their calculations. Despite legal prohibitions against government agencies' propagandizing U.S. citizens, the Psychological Strategy Board actively sought the assistance of "men of the press and radio" in building support for cold war objectives in general and escapee projects in particular.

Throughout the 1950s, policy makers fretted that Americans lacked the kind of "emotional support" for U.S. foreign policy goals that would sustain a "larger degree of mobilization for a long time."[96] Citizens were "restless to take a personal part in the East-West struggle," officials believed. But they lacked direction, leaving the United States lagging dangerously behind a competitor believed to excel at channeling the human desire to belong.[97] Verdicts like that of the English military historian J. F. C. Fuller, who characterized the cold war as a contest of "the Soviet idea vs. the American dollar," cut deep.[98] Why, U.S. officials wondered, wasn't America better at waging a war of ideas both at home and overseas? This question preoccupied the Truman and Eisenhower administrations as they strove not only to kindle popular enthusiasm for an epochal struggle but to provide an energized citizenry with avenues for activity. Properly manipulated, escapee endeavors could impart the "sense of meaning and purpose in life that comes from being a participator"—something believed sorely lacking in atomized postwar America.[99]

The White House found many willing aides in this enterprise, including the Ford Foundation and the International Rescue Committee. The centerpiece, however, was an ostensibly private initiative, the National Committee for a Free Europe (NCFE), which set out to awaken popular outrage over the captive nations' plight. At the same time, a Crusade for Freedom would raise money for a new broadcasting station, Radio Free Europe, which could adopt a more strident anticommunism in its broadcasts behind the Iron Curtain than the state-supported Voice of America.[100] No one would be permitted to contribute more than $1 to the crusade's campaign kitty. That way, "*Pravda* cannot truthfully charge that any 'big interests' are behind the scheme," the *Los Angeles Times* explained on its launch in August 1950—ignorant, like almost everyone else until the 1970s, that Radio Free Europe was financed far more extensively by the CIA than by individual Americans' "truth dollars."[101]

Leadership of this national campaign indicates the extensive overlap between the policy and intelligence community and the realms of publishing, broadcasting, and philanthropy. C. D. Jackson, chair of the NCFE, was a former editor of *Fortune* who (as Eisenhower's PR impresario) became the VFC's most ardent champion. Henry Luce and DeWitt Wallace, who served on the board, were, respectively, the publishers of *Time/Life* and *Reader's Digest,* while David Sarnoff, head of the Crusade for Freedom, was president of RCA. Luce was also active on the International Rescue Committee, which had launched its own one-million-dollar fundraising drive in 1949, aided by General William Donovan (former head of the wartime Office of Strategic Services, the CIA's forerunner) and Lucius Clay (military governor of West Germany). No wonder, then, that the national press proved "exceptionally sympathetic to anti-Communist escapees—and to the foreign policy objectives their migration would promote."[102]

Americans who read newspapers and magazines, went to the movies, listened to the radio, or watched television—nearly everyone in other words—could hardly avoid exposure to escapee exploits in the early 1950s. The NCFE even arranged speaker tours so that business leaders and workers could quiz those with intimate knowledge of conditions behind the Iron Curtain. Having "taken" Virginia in 1949, Peter Pirogov appeared regularly on television, on the radio, and at fund-raising events on behalf of the "captive peoples."[103]

Hollywood contributed to the stock of escapee representations with movies like Ralph Thomas's *The Iron Petticoat* (1956) and Howard Hughes's *Jet Pilot* (1957), which, respectively, starred Katharine Hepburn as a Soviet pilot lured west by Bob Hope's comic charms and Janet Leigh as a MiG pilot seduced into defecting by John

Wayne. In a more high-minded vein, Elia Kazan's 1953 feature, *Man on a Tightrope*, focused on a Czech circus troupe that is constantly harassed by communist authorities who insist that the clown act dramatize the oppression of an "American Negro worker" by a "Wall Street capitalist." Finding life ever less bearable, the circus owner finally stages a carnivalesque rupture of the Iron Curtain involving lions, fire-eaters, strongmen, and all.[104]

Kazan's story line was little more far-fetched than reports regularly surfacing in the press.[105] "Escape plots thrilling enough for a movie scenario have been skillfully carried out by everyday laborers, clerks and housewives who were determined to escape Communist domination," enthused Eleanor Harris in a long feature for the *Los Angeles Times*, entitled "Too Smart for the Reds." Surveying various schemes devised by "average people, turned suddenly into bold adventurers," Harris noted a common characteristic of successful breakouts: "They were odd." Often they combined ingenuity with intoxication. Harris noted one story, akin to *Man on a Tightrope*, in which a band of "gypsy entertainers" in Hungary danced across the border, mixing "gaiety with shrewd psychology": "Singing loudly, they approached the guards at the border. Here they paused to dance, laugh, flirt and serve befuddling drinks. Then, still dancing and singing, they disappeared across the border right in front of the drunken guards!" Other feats of escapology displayed a Houdini touch. A Hungarian couple concealed themselves in wine barrels destined for export to Austria, while a railroad worker smuggled himself out of Czechoslovakia in an iron box inserted into a freight car full of coal.[106]

Many escape stories hinged on hijacking trains, planes, trucks, or tanks or, in the grand tradition of POW movies, tunneling to freedom. In the early 1950s, readers of popular magazines met the Ollarek family from Czechoslovakia, who had fled in a "freedom duck"—an amphibious jeep stolen and steered across the Morava River into Austria after a communist functionary had been distracted "with alcohol and some rabbits." They also encountered Ivan Pluhar, a Czech who had tunneled out of a prison camp near uranium mines where he had been sentenced for anticommunist activity, and who later gained admission to Yale Law School.[107] Some, like Hana Pavlickova and Jaroslav Konvalinka, escaped in airplanes; others, such as nine crew members from the tanker *Tuapse*, were rescued from Soviet ships. A handful defected from diplomatic missions, while many more deserted their army postings.[108]

Whereas refugees are often insistently spoken for—"speechless emissaries," in Liisa Malkki's phrase—escapees themselves were generally granted at least one line in the drama of curtain crossing. Almost all such tales ended with a euphoric endorsement of the "free world" that explicated the larger significance of escape. Having lost a leg when a land mine exploded, impeding (but not preventing) her escape, Mrs. Kapus apparently told her American rescuers: "I shall be happier with one leg in America than I would have been with two legs in Communist

Hungary." *Life* reported that a Polish pilot who had flown his MiG to Denmark jubilantly announced, "Kommunizm Kaput!" Likewise, when a Czech "freedom train" crashed into West Germany in September 1951, carrying an engineer and thirty-two asylum-seeking passengers, the engineer told reporters, "We are all here in the West—and the climate is wonderful!"[109]

Such stories, gathered by the U.S. Information Agency and fed to organizations such as the NCFE, provided rich material for cold war pageantry.[110] While the State Department billed the Escapee Program as an "investment in humanity," enterprises such as the Crusade for Freedom presented citizens with the chance to make their own personal contribution to fund-raising drives and to participate in the symbolic restaging of escapee drama. During the early 1950s, a cavalcade of vehicles toured America, capitalizing on the success in 1947 of the "Freedom Train," which had shunted key constitutional documents around the country in an effort to vivify civic commitment to democracy. In 1950 the Crusade for Freedom attempted to replicate this venture with an inaugural campaign that centered on a "Freedom Bell" to be erected in Berlin. As the bell visited various American cities, the NCFE staged ceremonies to collect ten million signatures for scrolls to be placed at its base. Signatories affirmed that "all men derive the right to freedom equally from God" and pledged to "resist aggression and tyranny wherever they appear on earth."[111] Stunts of this kind would be repeated many times over. In 1954, a "Freedom Tank"—already the subject of newsreel stories and a proposed Hollywood movie—also toured the country. Onlookers were entreated to place donations to support broadcasting behind the Iron Curtain in this "piggy bank for freedom," a "homemade" armored car in which eight "plucky Czechs" had steered through the Iron Curtain.[112]

Contemporary commentators attributed Americans' appetite for Iron Curtain escapology in part to its adventure-story dimension: the dread of imagining oneself captive offset by the exhilaration of "outwitting the Reds." While 4,400 American GIs remained in North Korean and Chinese POW camps (until release in the summer and fall of 1953), escape narratives perhaps served a particularly reassuring function—not least because very few U.S. prisoners successfully managed to evade their communist captors in the inhospitable terrain of North Korea.[113]

Action-adventure was not the sole mode of emplotment, however. In a more sentimental register, cold war storytelling reprised themes from the Indian captivity narratives of colonial New England, offering tableaux of loving homes cruelly sundered. These tales of entrapment and redemption were quintessentially family stories. At their happiest, they ended in reunion—often engineered by American intervention or influence. According to the *New York Times,* one Harvard-educated German citizen prised his daughters from the clutches of their communist East German grandfather in March 1954 with "promises to take them to a Gregory Peck movie."[114] With its testament to the magnetism of American cinema, this

FIGURE 11. The escapee life cycle. An illustration from a 1955 U.S. government brochure, *Escape to Freedom*, reassures Americans that only deserving escapees—here a nuclear family—receive assistance from the United States Escapee Program in resettling "abroad."

vignette replicated the central premise of Hollywood's own defection dramas: the irresistible allure of a culture of glamor, sophistication, and consumption. For nowhere was "the absolute abundance of everything"—the heady "lightheartedness" that elated Pirogov on arrival in America—more evident than on the silver screen, as Barsov soon discovered.

Such affirmative family sagas not only reinforced the superior desirability of life in the free world but also bolstered the escapee's positive image. Strikingly, publicity for the Escapee Program didn't depict single, stateless young men—putative "freedom volunteers"—as the model escapees. Government-issued brochures preferred to show whole families collectively undertaking the "perilous contest between life and death." Illustrated with affecting pictures of child refugees, these pamphlets reassured American readers of escapees' wholesome, unthreatening character and of their own generosity in supporting a program that built playgrounds and nurseries, provided pediatric health care, and offered these valiant pioneers an opportunity to "enrich the fabric of democracy" in the free world.[115]

FREEDOM TO LEAVE?

"The fact that the US was founded by escapees from oppression is precedence for US solicitude for escapees behind the Iron Curtain," announced Henry Cabot Lodge (U.S. ambassador to the UN) in March 1953, insisting that "the thing that bothers the Russians most is our escapee program."[116] This congratulatory self-understanding of America as the "asylum of all asylums" drew on an extended tradition of national self-fashioning that obscured the fact that this "nation of escapees" had also been built on Africans' enslavement. But for all the familiarity of Lodge's formula, America's ideological investment in escape—in captive peoples' right to flight—also belonged to a distinct historical moment.

In the wake of World War II, Washington placed itself in the vanguard of a global movement to codify human rights. Freedom of movement bulked large on this agenda. The right to "leave any country" (including an individual's place of citizenship) and to return to it was enshrined in the 1948 Universal Declaration of Human Rights. For some American opinion formers, this fundamental entitlement merited adoption alongside freedom of expression and worship, and security from want and fear, as a "Fifth Freedom." In such commentary, the schism between the "free world" and the "slave world" found expression in the polarity of their attitudes toward population movement. On one side of the Iron Curtain was a society that welcomed immigrants, associated mobility with betterment, and allowed its citizens to go wherever they pleased; on the other, a state that hermetically sealed its perimeter, issued internal passports to keep citizens rooted to designated places, and refused to let anyone out.

Cold war internationalists championed freedom of movement as a right at once universal and absolute. Anyone ought to be able to travel anywhere at any time—to leave and return as they wished. State-imposed fetters to motion not only left the globe fractured but carried dire implications for confined populations and humanity as a whole. "A world without easy cross-border movements is a world of concentration camps, forced labor, and cold war," opined *Life* magazine in August 1948, congratulating the White House on granting Kasenkina asylum. In stark contrast to the Soviet Union, the United States was conceived as a state that freely granted the right of entry to foreigners and exit to its own citizens. "A nation which honors the Pilgrim Fathers can see how the right to life and the right to move are inextricably linked," *Life* remarked.[117] Similarly, a *New York Times* editorial on the defection (in March 1950) of a Czech figure-skating champion in London inquired: "Can anyone imagine an American government withholding a passport for fear that an American traveller once out of its jurisdiction would refuse to come home?"[118]

Much discrepant evidence had to be overlooked, however, to sustain the belief that America unwaveringly championed a vital new "Fifth Freedom." Time and again in the late 1940s and early 1950s, Congress refused to make room for significant numbers of DPs, escapees, and sundry other refugees in the "asylum of all asylums." On the contrary, as one acerbic critic of the McCarran-Walter Act pointed out, "Those who became enmeshed in the dragnet of 'undesirable' categories were excluded irrespective of their status as political refugees in dire need of sanctuary."[119] Such discrimination struck some as a self-destructive anachronism—"fantastic," in the opinion of Harry Truman, who expressed disbelief that Americans were sandbagging themselves "against being flooded by immigrants from Eastern Europe" as in 1924.[120] But that was precisely the impulse at work.

In practice, then, the United States was less welcoming to mobile humanity than advocates of the Fifth Freedom implied. Zealously guarding its borders, Washington also proved unwilling during the early cold war to let some citizens *out*. This reluctance stemmed, not from a fear that they, like the Czech athletes in London, would never return, but from concern over what these fellow travelers would say about home while abroad. Several prominent African American Marxists who criticized U.S. policy, including Paul Robeson and W. E. B DuBois, found themselves immobilized in the United States, their freedom of movement severely curtailed or suspended altogether for years.

In August 1950, the State Department revoked Robeson's passport, asserting discretionary power to prevent this "political meddler" from using his worldwide celebrity to promote "the independence of the colonial peoples of Africa." Under the department's instruction, U.S. immigration officials even prevented Robeson from traveling to Canada, a border crossing that required no passport. Supporters protested his "virtual imprisonment in the United States," launching legal suits in defense of his constitutional right to travel and earn a living unimpeded by a government that did not find his politics "pleasant."[121] But the State Department continued to subject him to a form of national house arrest until 1958. Freedom of exit, it seemed, was not an absolute right. Rather, it was the privilege of those who (in Washington's eyes) would not abuse foreign travel as an opportunity for "diplomatically embarrassing" activism overseas.

Neither Robeson nor DuBois sought to settle abroad permanently. What they asserted was the right to circulate freely: to leave the United States and return, irrespective of the views they might express while overseas—rights enshrined in the 1948 Declaration. During the early cold war some citizens *did* seek to travel east without a return ticket, though. Where emigration to the USSR affected American-born children, the American state's declaratory commitment to freedom of exit was strained beyond endurance, as was its adherence to another principle incorporated in the 1948 Declaration: that "the family is the natural and fundamental group unit of society and is entitled to protection by society and the state."

Did naturalized citizens have the right to emigrate to the USSR with their American-born children? This issue was tested in a 1947 legal battle (reopened in 1950) concerning the custody of three Armenian American children—a protracted case that pitted the state's assertion of protective power over minors against the right of parents to retrieve children from care and remove them from the United States. Press interest in this case was inversely proportional to the gravity of what lay under arbitration. As the *Christian Century* pointed out, such fundamental constitutional rights were at stake that journalists' inattention was baffling—or would have been had the petitioner sought to reclaim and raise his children anywhere other than the USSR. An editorial in March 1950 sardonically noted: "The Federal Supreme Court has refused to review the Choolokian case. Does that sound very important? The name is only that of an Armenian shoemaker. Well, Dred Scott was only the name of a Negro slave."[122]

The *Dred Scott* verdict turned on the question of whether slaves and former slaves could legally be considered U.S. citizens, with Chief Justice Roger B. Taney insisting they could not. Choolokian's case, by contrast, hinged on the court's determination to *uphold* the citizenship of children whose departure from the United States threatened to alienate their entitlement to it—even if that meant refusing parents custody of their offspring, denying those children the right to leave the country, and splitting a family between the cold war's two worlds.

At the center of this struggle was Hamportzoon Choolokian, a forty-eight-year-old naturalized U.S. citizen who had fled his native Armenia in 1913. Thirty-three years later he decided to leave the United States for his home country, now absorbed into the Soviet Union. But first he sought legal assistance in securing custody of his three youngest children, two boys and a girl, aged twelve, eleven, and six at the time of the initial hearing in December 1947. These infants had been taken into the care of two Catholic welfare institutions in 1942 when their mother suffered a mental breakdown and was committed to an asylum by the Albany Department of Mental Hygiene—a misfortune that left Hamportzoon to raise six young children singlehandedly. This soon proved impossible. Two sons were subsequently given up to the Mission of the Immaculate Virgin in Staten Island, while a newborn daughter was taken in by the New York Foundling Hospital.

With his wife and children institutionalized in three different locations, and no imminent prospect of family reunion, Choolokian decided to accept an offer extended by the Soviet government to members of the scattered Armenian diaspora in 1946: to return home, passage paid. The State Department consented to this arrangement with respect to 160 Armenian Americans, seizing the moment to press Moscow for a reciprocal easing of its exit controls—especially with regard to Soviet wives of U.S. citizens trapped in the USSR.[123]

In October 1947, the Choolokian family received confirmation that its passage had been booked on a ship due to sail in late December. Albany's mental hygienicists consented (after five years) to discharge Mrs. Choolokian, but the two Catholic organizations entrusted with the couple's three youngest children proved less willing to relinquish their charges. The Welfare Department prevaricated. "Do you know what he wants to *do* to those children?" officials presiding over the case enquired of Choolokian's attorney, Samuel Blinken. "He wants to take them to *Russia!*"[124]

However emotionally rousing this horrified exclamation may have been in December 1947, it constituted flimsy legal grounds on which to deny a father access to his children. Under pressure from Blinken, the Welfare Department reviewed the case and reversed its initially obstructive position. Now pronouncing Choolokian a fit parent who had contributed to his children's upkeep and maintained an "immaculately clean" apartment, the department agreed that the Mission of the Immaculate Virgin must release the two boys from its care. At the eleventh hour the mission again refused, leaving Choolokian to file a habeas corpus writ just two hours before his ship was due to sail. As the court tarried, he was compelled to embark without his three children—assured by U.S. authorities that departure would not prejudice his chances of regaining them.

As the case played out, parents' natural rights counted for little. The crux of the issue for both Justice Lumbard and Monsignor John Corrigan (head of the Mission of the Immaculate Virgin) was that Choolokian wanted to transplant his children to *Soviet* soil. "We consider the children American boys adapted to American ways of living," Corrigan announced, "and we consider it unfair to subject them to foreign influences contrary to our ideals and to our American way of life." Asked by Blinken whether he would be as intransigent if Franco's Spain were the destination in question, Monsignor Corrigan demurred.[125]

Lumbard denied Choolokian custody of his children on two grounds: his alleged unfitness as a parent and the state's duty to protect children's citizenship rights. On the first count, despite the Welfare Department's recent commendation of Choolokian, Lumbard expressed concern that the petitioner spoke only "pigeon English."[126] His second contention was more substantive. Under U.S. law, American-born children who leave the country during their infancy enjoy a right to reassert their citizenship on reaching adulthood. However, this entitlement—conferred at birth—becomes void if unclaimed between the ages of twenty-one and twenty-three. In denying Choolokian the right to remove his children from the United States, Justice Lumbard turned to *Soviet* exit controls for his crowning argument: "Probably at no time in our history as a nation have we been confronted with a situation where our citizens have been treated virtually as prisoners by a foreign power with whom we are at peace."[127] Years hence, he projected, Soviet authorities would block American-born emigrants' departure from Soviet Armenia, thus dispossessing the now-adult Choolokians of their U.S. citizenship.

In other words, Choolokian could not be permitted to remove his children from America in 1947 because, in the future, they would not be permitted to leave the USSR. To allow the whole family to emigrate risked placing the infants in the "irretrievable position" of being unable to assert their claim to U.S. citizenship. A father could not be allowed to "dissipate beyond redemption these priceless rights of the children," Lumbard ruled.[128]

The state's obligation to preserve the "precious and transcendent" gift of citizenship thus trumped parents' rights, the State Department's formal consent to the Armenian repatriation arrangement, and (though this featured nowhere in the verdict) the three children's own preference as documented by the Welfare Department: to sail with their siblings and parents to Armenia.[129] In an ironic twist, a subsequent appeal ruling stipulated that only Choolokian's personal appearance in a U.S. court—to reestablish his fitness as a parent—would satisfy judicial scrupulosity.[130] Yet the initial ruling had been predicated precisely on the *impossibility* of passage back from the prison world of Soviet communism.[131]

Subsequent appeals all failed. In 1950 the U.S. Supreme Court refused to hear the case, despite prompting from the American Civil Liberties Union and various Protestant organizations that had championed the cause of the Armenian shoemaker since 1947.[132] Hamportzoon Choolokian never did become a Dred Scott. His case barely even made the news—other than a half-dozen modest columns tucked deep inside the *New York Times*. As the *Christian Century* caustically observed:

> The aggravating factor in the whole affair is probably the fact that Mr. Choolokian has gone to a communist state and now wants to have his children come to him there. It is perhaps not surprising that the sisters of the Mission of the Immaculate Virgin should view with horror the sending of their lambs into what must seem to them to be a den of atheistic wolves. The Armenians are, in general, Christians in their own way, but a Soviet Armenia *must* be a sinkhole of godlessness. Certainly there are many, besides Roman Catholics, who are of the same opinion.[133]

FIGURE 12. Apprehended by a London bobby, Alexis Chwastow is interrupted en route to the USSR in October 1956 and compelled to surrender his daughter, Tatiana (age two), for return to the United States. © The Associated Press.

In 1955, Moscow initiated a further fruitless bid to secure passage to Soviet Armenia for the three youngest Choolokians, the eldest of whom was now a corporal in the Marine Corps.[134] Again the case went almost unreported. Few Americans leapt to defend a parent's right to remove an American-born child to the USSR, having for years received strong prompts from the judicial system that "communists" had no business to be rearing children, let alone removing them from the United States. This position was made clear in August 1948, when a divorced father petitioned the New York Supreme Court to have his two-year-old daughter removed from the custody of his ex-wife because she was a "Communist sympathizer"—a charge she hotly denied, maintaining that she intended to raise her daughter to be "a fine American citizen, happy, contented, normal." Ruling on the case, Justice Bertram Newman announced that if the charge of "Communist influence" were established (which it had not been to his satisfaction), he would "not hesitate to change custody." "This child is entitled to be reared as an American under American influences," he proclaimed. Asked whether he would take a child from Wallace-supporting parents, he stated: "I believe I would."[135]

The absence of sympathy for parents who wished to raise their children under alternative "influences" was further demonstrated by the case of Alexis Chwastow and his two-year-old daughter, Tatiana—a cause célèbre that generated abundant copy and a photospread in *Life* in the fall of 1956. Unlike Choolokian, Chwastow (a fifty-eight-year-old Soviet escapee resident in the United States since 1951) initially succeeded in setting sail for Russia with his toddler in tow. According to his estranged twenty-four-year-old partner (a naturalized citizen who had entered the United States as a Czech DP), Chwastow had been pressured by Soviet agents to return east. Despite her protests, he had insisted on taking their daughter.[136] Responding to the mother's pleas, the U.S. Immigration and Naturalization Service stepped in. Commissioner Joseph Swing instructed his officers to prevent Tatiana's departure "at any cost."[137] But a search of the *Queen Mary* left them empty-handed. Soviet agents had concealed the infant so effectively that the search team found "only luggage and bottles of baby formula" in the Chwastows' cabin.[138] This failure sounded a dolorous note of national shame for the "first time in our history that the US Government has permitted an American citizen to be kidnapped from this country by a foreign Government," in the words of Senator Herbert Lehman.[139]

British immigration authorities and courts subsequently succeeded where their U.S. counterparts had failed. At the urging of the Church World Service of New York, the London High Court declared Tatiana its ward before she and her father could sail from Southampton to Russia.[140] Soon the toddler was heading back to Detroit with her mother, while the Soviet diplomat accused of plotting her kidnapping was sent packing on the recommendation of the Senate Internal Security Subcommittee. To the delight of press reporters, longshoremen on the Hudson River refused to handle the departing diplomat's luggage. While Konstantin Ekimov grappled with

his excess baggage, the longshoremen offered some well-chosen "unkind words"—
a moment that recapitulated the departure of Consul Lomakin to cheers and jeers
eight years earlier.[141]

THE TOURISTS OF TOMORROW

When Senator Mansfield rebutted Soviet charges at the UN that Washington was
planning to recruit and arm refugees as anticommunist guerrillas, he urged the
Kremlin to adopt America's attitude toward mobility: "The interests of the Soviet
Union and the peoples of Eastern Europe will best be served if the Iron Curtain
refugees of today can become the tourists of tomorrow."[142] His plea anticipated a
time when those daring souls who escaped from behind the Iron Curtain would
be able to travel abroad freely—just like the millions of Americans who annually
vacationed overseas. But Mansfield's characterization of Iron Curtain refugees as
putative tourists also unintentionally signaled the ambivalent reception these foreign travelers received in the West. Often escapees found themselves in limbo:
stalled between two worlds, encamped between hostile blocs, poised between past
and present.

Many U.S. policy makers and opinion formers, ascribing an indelibly nationalist subjectivity to eastern bloc escapees, persisted in viewing them as temporary so-
journers in the West, guardians of the national flame during an exile that would
end with the collapse of Soviet communism.[143] But even those who anticipated this
cataclysm within the foreseeable future still had to identify an interim destination
for eastern bloc refugees. As ever more states sealed their borders against immigrants, U.S. planners' visions became increasingly fanciful. Project TROY urged
"boldness and imagination" in this domain. Its authors broached "the possibility
of establishing a center on one of the Virgin Islands, from which all other inhabitants were evacuated, or on some other insular possession," qualifying this idea with
an afterthought that "Nova Scotia would be more suitable for climatic reasons and
because of the absence of a 'racial' problem if arrangements could be made with
the Canadian government."[144] "Men without a country," as eastern bloc escapees
were often construed, should be found a country without men.

Isaac Don Levine, writing in *Life* in March 1953, further elaborated the case for
a self-governing Russian republic in exile as the antidote to a policy of neglect:

> We could transform unused areas all over the world into places where communities
> can grow, and where millions of refugees, former Soviet occupation troops included,
> can find their freedom and their security, too. Thus could old-fashioned home-
> steading, on a gigantic, modern, worldwide scale, become the hope of the disillusioned
> Russian soldier who now thinks he has no choice but to continue his servitude under
> his Soviet masters.

And a further inducement could be offered to offset the very real love Russians have for their own society, customs and culture. Certain of these areas could be set aside exclusively for Russian refugees. Here they would find their own kind, speaking their own language, following their own traditions, but enjoying the freedom they can no longer find in their homeland. . . . We must offer the escapee the promise of private property and the satisfaction of ownership.[145]

However far-fetched, imperialist visions of this kind were neither passing pipe dreams nor confined to the hallucinatory realm of cold war psychological strategy in which no proposal was too outré for consideration. As late as December 1955, the U.S. government continued to express interest in "land settlement projects in Latin America."[146]

In a rather literal fashion, these fantasies cast eastern bloc refugees as latter-day Pilgrim Fathers, reenacting America's founding myth. Fleeing tyranny in Europe, these "redeemed captives" would claim underpopulated, unproductive land in the New World. Preserving their cultural heritage in splendid isolation, they would nurture a new political tradition: in place of serfdom, private property; in place of tyranny, the yeoman farmer's republican virtues. Viewed from another angle, however, such visions more closely approximate schemes for freed slaves' emigration from the United States. Just as some opponents of immigration reform in 1952 insisted that eastern bloc refugees possessed neither the desire nor the capacity to assimilate, so nineteenth-century emigrationists asserted that former slaves, untutored in self-rule, would be more content establishing new communities far from the sorrowful site of their former bondage.[147] Since neither emancipated slaves nor escapee Slavs properly belonged in a nation fearful of "blotting and mixing," the trick was to locate an alternative homeland; Nova Scotia figured in schemes for both.

However we interpret these projections, they further underscore escapees' undesirability as putative citizens in early cold war America. Indeed, during the first eighteen months of the Escapee Program, only 1,952 escapees were resettled in the United States. Four years after its inauguration, 250,000 refugees eligible for assistance were "still languishing" in West German and Austrian camps.[148] Rarely, then, was the escapee enthusiastically embraced except during choreographed stunts such as the two pilots' tour in February 1949 or the civic pageantry concocted around the Crusade for Freedom. As a USEP progress report acknowledged in 1954: "The hard fact of the matter is that most escapees find it necessary to remain in reception centers for some time before the process of arranging acceptable resettlement is completed." Cautioning against "overselling" the program, the author also noted that many experienced "major difficulty in adjusting to and fitting themselves constructively into the life of resettlement" once a destination had been found.[149]

The bleak conditions and frustrating immobilization endured by many refugees gave Moscow an opportunity to encourage the disillusioned to reconsider, as had Anatoly Barsov and Alexis Chwastow. One year after Stalin's death, during an ostensible thaw in the cold war, U.S. officials noted with alarm in 1954 that the Soviets had launched a systematic "Come Home" campaign. Eager to stimulate "re-defection," as U.S. officials termed this phenomenon, Moscow had announced an amnesty for those in exile, requesting assistance from the UN High Commission for Refugees in distributing repatriation literature in western European camps.[150] Soon eastern bloc refugees as far afield as North and South America began to receive letters that stressed the ease with which they could return and the warm reception that awaited. That Soviet intelligence possessed "uncannily accurate" mailing lists for individuals who had often lived for years under assumed names heightened the powerful impression made by this material. So too did the inclusion of handwritten notes and recent photographs from family members urging loved ones to come home.[151]

In *Newsweek*'s opinion, the Soviets' were spinning a "red web of return" to discourage further flight, thereby "destroy[ing] the effectiveness of the West's best propaganda weapon in the cold war: the living testimony of those who have renounced Communism for freedom."[152] Others stressed the positive uses to which returnees would be put, plugging intelligence gaps and ventriloquizing familiar messages about the unemployment, degradation, and racialized inequities of life under capitalism, before their unceremonious dispatch to labor camps. According to an article in the *Los Angeles Times*, the Soviets divulged their true intentions in code-naming the redefection drive "Operation Snow": "This designation suggests that the Reds have borrowed an idea from American slang and mean to take their victims for a sleigh ride. A long one."[153]

The *L.A. Times* was not alone in suggesting that most "redefectors" would end up in the gulag, a proposition that the Soviet state was keen to disprove. Exhibit A in this endeavor was none other than Anatoly Barsov, the prodigal flier whose execution on return to the USSR had been widely rumored in 1949. Appearing somewhat shakily at a Moscow press conference in May 1957, Barsov announced that he had been treated with greater lenience than his American tormentors had led him to expect. After five years of "corrective labor," he was now a free man.[154]

In September 1956, USEP reports tallied 5,579 redefections. Of these, 3,407 were from South America, but the North was by no means immune from this phenomenon. Eighty-six escapees had left new homes in Canada and the United States to head back east.[155] Some cases received prominent press coverage—most notably five Soviet sailors who, with some fanfare, had been retrieved from their grounded tanker in Taiwan and brought to the United States in October 1955, only to redefect six months later. Reporters generally ascribed these disturbing departures to communist coercion and skill in manipulating human weakness.[156] Nevertheless, "redefection" threatened to direct unwelcome attention to the grim conditions that confronted newly arrived escapees. As one anonymous U.S. official remarked to the reporter Harrison E. Salisbury, "The wonder isn't that a few of them go back.

The wonder is that more of them don't go."[157] At least in the short term, these "tourists of tomorrow" often found themselves third-class citizens in the first world.

If State Department personnel derived modest gratification from the fact that most refugees did *not* head back east, they also noted that a dwindling number were traveling west in the first place. Although Charles Kersten had hailed congressional assistance to escapees as a "bright beacon to induce large scale defections from satellite Europe," departures from the eastern bloc declined sharply during the early and mid-1950s.[158] The louder Washington called for defection from the Soviet orbit, the less success its efforts apparently met in generating escapees.[159] Where cold war strategists set out with the assumption that defection inspired defection, their schemes arguably made flight much harder as eastern bloc regimes intensified their border controls. As the Iron Curtain solidified in westerners' imaginations through daring acts of escape, it also became ever less penetrable for those attempting to slip under or around it.

3

Stalin's Slaves

The Rise of Gulag Consciousness

MAPPING THE GULAG

Six years after V-J Day, Dean Acheson and John Foster Dulles brokered a belated peace treaty with Japan in September 1951. When the signatories—watched by some forty million American television viewers—met in San Francisco's Opera House to inscribe a "bulky parchment," the event was hailed as a triumph of U.S. statesmanship. "Like no other diplomatic event since World War II, the signing exhibited the impressive unity of the anti-Communist world," trumpeted *Life* magazine.[1] That the Soviets had agreed to attend caused some surprise.[2] At the UN, walkouts, vetoes, intemperate invective, and fist pounding had become staples of international diplomacy—or markers of its abandonment. But far from reviving camaraderie between Washington and Moscow, the San Francisco conference emphasized the complete reversal of wartime patterns of enmity and amity. Having "embraced defeat," Japan was now thoroughly enmeshed in the U.S. alliance system. Hostility between the Soviet Union and United States, by contrast, appeared irremediable.[3]

This antagonism assumed various forms during the conference. The chief Soviet delegate, Deputy Foreign Minister Andrei Gromyko, survived a mysterious road accident (rumored to be an assassination attempt) only to face a more bruising—and more extensively reported—encounter the following day.[4] During a lull in the formal talks on September 6, Missouri congressman O. K. Armstrong approached Gromyko, ostensibly on a goodwill mission. Asking whether the latter would care to inspect a map of the Soviet Union, Armstrong revealed his true intent as he unfolded the document. "It happens to contain an accurate portrayal of every slave labor camp in the Soviet Union," Armstrong explained. According to press reports, Gromyko "blinked at the map, mumbled 'No comment,' and handed it to an aide who tossed

FIGURE 13. "Anti-Red Housewives" in a New York protest, in September 1951, against Gromyko. "The foxiest, two-faced diplomat just arrived" to attend the San Francisco Peace Treaty Conference, his passage paid by the wages of slave labor. Photo by Keystone/Getty Images.

it into the aisle." While some newspapers ran a photograph of this testy exchange, *Time* devoted two complete pages to a color reproduction of the map itself.[5]

Captioned "GULAG—Slavery, Inc.," the map indicated labor camps by red dots and shaded areas. Hammer-and-sickle motifs denoted smaller camps. Five hundred and thirty-two blots of red on a black-and-white topographical background created a strong visual impression, highlighting not only distant exile settlements in Siberia and the Central Asian republics but the heavy concentration of camps on Russia's *western* periphery. Lest the gulag's extent and extremity weren't clear from this cartographic representation alone, further visual and textual material around the edges amplified the point. A collage of photostatic copies of GULAG (Glavnoye Upravlenye Lagerei, Department of Penal Labor Camps) "passports" framed the map's borders. Underneath, photographs of emaciated children with protruding ribs and shaven heads (one conspicuously adorned by a crucifix) appeared in a red semicircle with the caption "victims of the GULAG system." These images could hardly fail to evoke the pictures of skeletal Nazi concentration camp survivors familiar from extensive photojournalism and newsreel coverage devoted to the camps' liberation in 1945.

Visually, the map signaled the equivalence of Nazi and Soviet camps. Textually, it detailed specific features of the system administered by GULAG:

> There are over 14,000,000 forced laborers in GULAG, scattered through scores of penal colonies, each a Devil's Island at its worst. This state monopoly in expendable human flesh is a chief source of revenue for the Soviet regime. Incontrovertible proof of the existence of GULAG and its vast ramifications is presented here. Nearly 14,000 affidavits, assembled by the High Command of the Polish Army during the last war, served as the basis of this map. . . .
>
> It has been established that the average mortality rate in GULAG exceeds 12% a year, i.e., every eight years its total population perishes and is constantly replenished with prison manpower. All the territory controlled by GULAG, if consolidated, would make a submerged empire the size of Western Europe.

A $1,000 reward was offered to anyone with "evidence disproving the authenticity of Soviet documents here."

Gromyko reportedly parried Armstrong's gesture by inquiring which "capitalist slave" was responsible for the map. Had he scanned the small print, he would have seen that it appeared under the aegis of the Free Trade Union Committee of the American Federation of Labor (AFL), though *Time* assured readers that the "map's accuracy is vouched for by high US Government agencies."[6] In fact, the U.S. government had done rather more than corroborate its veracity. During the late 1940s and 1950s, the State Department devoted considerable energy to charting the gulag—elucidating its contours and working to etch them on the map of domestic and international consciousness.[7] What appeared to be an independent AFL venture thus received considerable state support. Voice of America broadcasts, targeting Latin America in particular, worked to generate a receptive audience for the map's distribution.[8] Meanwhile, in occupied Vienna, a U.S. government–funded newspaper, *Wiener Kurier,* planned to distribute half a million free copies—only to find that the printer assigned this job, along with the bulk order of maps, had been seized by Soviet authorities a month after Gromyko rejected Armstrong's offering. "To the free world this frantic activity, by its very contrast with the previous silence, will seem the most eloquent proof that the map was irrefutable with logic or with facts," editorialized the *New York Times.* "It had to be answered, as it has been in Vienna, by the brute force of police."[9]

Of the Truman administration's multiple initiatives to discredit Soviet communism, exposure of the gulag occupied the commanding heights. Dramatic ruptures of the Iron Curtain underscored the repressive character of Stalinist states that effectively incarcerated their citizens. But cold war opinion formers were adamant that the inculcation of anticommunist sentiment required more than a *figurative* appreciation of the eastern bloc as one vast prison. People had to understand that the "Soviet monolith" was "held together by the iron curtain around it and the iron bars within it," as NSC 68 put it, with thousands of camps containing millions of forced laborers. By demonstrating that the phrase *slave world* wasn't "mere abuse, but a precisely accurate term," U.S. officials aspired to demolish communism's emancipatory pretensions, thereby shattering the appeal of Marxist-Leninism to oppressed peoples worldwide.[10]

Bertram Wolfe, a prominent Sovietologist who played a key role in this enterprise, made the case explicitly: "Forced labor is the Achilles' Heel of the Soviet system. The entire propaganda appeal of Soviet Communism vanishes if we can show that 'The Worker's Paradise' is really a vast forced labor camp and that the major achievement of the Russian Revolution has been to re-introduce mass slavery into the modern world as an instrument of Government and as an essential part of 'Socialist' state economy. If this can be proved with human, graphic and statistical evidence—and it can—then the hypocrisy of all the claims and propaganda campaigns of the Kremlin become self-evident."[11] With its emotive symbolism, didactic mode of address, emphasis on hard-and-fast evidence, and direct challenge to acquisitive disbelievers, "GULAG—Slavery, Inc." condensed many key features of a concerted campaign to uncover and indict the Soviets' empire of enslavement. In the estimation of the *Chicago Daily Tribune,* the map clarified "more perfectly than a million words could do the essential character of the rulers of Russia and the creed they espouse."[12]

The gulag's exposure forms a compelling case study in the transnational politics of knowledge. To historicize the emergence of "camp consciousness" is to appreciate how thoroughly an expanded awareness of the Soviet gulag was born of a distinct geopolitical moment and a determined effort to make known what had hitherto been only dimly, partially, or selectively understood. Most commentators tie westerners' first stirrings of awareness to the onset of détente, crediting Alexander Solzhenitsyn with transforming an administrative acronym into an emblem of moral outrage.[13] Yet while Solzhenitsyn illuminated the Soviet camps for a fresh generation, they had not hitherto passed entirely unnoticed. Indeed, when the feted dissident visited Washington, D.C., in 1975 he explicitly congratulated the AFL and Isaac Don Levine for their work in mapping the gulag.[14]

During the early cold war, numerous individuals and organizations strove to make Stalin's camps as widely known and thoroughly condemned as Hitler's: scholarly Sovietologists, Menshevik émigrés, ex-communist anticommunists, survivors of Nazi and Soviet camps, and trade unionists on both sides of the Atlantic. Their efforts resulted in a flood of camp survivors' memoirs, press exposés, court cases, international investigations, condemnatory resolutions, and bans on Soviet products. U.S. policy makers were quick to perceive the strategic utility of channeling these endeavors. In conjunction with Clement Attlee's Labour government, the State Department forged a transatlantic coalition to crusade against the resurgence of "slavery" on an epic scale.[15]

Adherents of disparate political traditions, the gulag's many publicists had divergent stakes in making visible what Moscow attempted to shield from view. But they shared a conviction that the Kremlin was uniquely vulnerable on this score: that there was no more "surefire device for tweaking the Russian bear's tail" than forced labor.[16] A small item from *Newsweek* in May 1951—ringing with the apocryphal—conveys the potency ascribed to such revelations:

> The East Berlin Communists thought they had a smart idea for a publicity stunt. One of their brighter members would enter a West Berlin radio quiz that paid cash prizes and then publicly hand over the winnings to the party.
>
> But, as the Voice of America told the story last week, the station director learned what was up. The Red was allowed to win until he came to the final, $98 question: "How many slave laborers are there in the Soviet Union—4,000,000, 6,000,000 or 8,000,000?" The Communist burst into a cold sweat and fainted.[17]

In fact, very few contemporary estimates of the gulag's population pitched the figure as low as eight million, let alone four. By scouring the letters column of leftist publications like the *New Statesman,* one might find the number tallied at just two million. But many estimates were significantly higher. The era's single most widely read book on the USSR, Victor Kravchenko's *I Chose Freedom* (1946), calculated the total at twenty million, or 10 percent of the entire Soviet population.[18] When an early version of the GULAG map appeared in 1947, the *Chicago Daily Tribune* proposed that the camps contained "as many as 14 million slaves, and surely not less than 8 million." The higher figure was endorsed by David Dallin and Boris Nicolaevsky in their influential *Forced Labor in Russia* (1947).[19] Three years later, at a dinner welcoming UN delegates to New York, Governor Thomas E. Dewey (R-NY) lambasted the Soviets for incarcerating ten to fifteen million slave laborers. Although press editors lamented his breach of etiquette—"the first time that a Soviet walkout was justified"—they didn't quibble with Dewey's figures.[20]

The numbers, in other words, reflected the statistician's particular stake in revealing, or minimizing, the extent of the gulag. As the historian Catherine Merridale points out, opponents of the Soviet system often "exaggerated the crimes of the totalitarian state (as if they needed such exaggeration to be real)," while its defenders found ways to ignore, deny, or rationalize the camps. "Blinkered by the universal lack of reliable evidence," estimations of the USSR's prison population remained inextricably tangled in the warp and weft of ideological struggle.[21] In this sense, camp inmates were not only "Stalin's slaves" but also cold war captives.

KNOWLEDGE OF THE GULAG BEFORE THE COLD WAR

Dissenting from the great gush of acclaim that greeted *One Day in the Life of Ivan Denisovich* on its American publication in 1963, one reviewer candidly pointed out that Solzhenitsyn's novella contained little revelatory material. More remarkable was the fact that this story was "being told by a Soviet writer for Soviet readers." Its appearance in the USSR represented an unexpected gesture of *glasnost* (openness) on Khrushchev's part. But the details of camp life Solzhenitsyn conveyed were hardly fresh to American readers—or not, at any rate, to those who'd been paying attention.[22] In the United States, camp consciousness depended less on Moscow's willingness to acknowledge the gulag's existence than Americans' own fluctuating receptivity to reports that had begun to filter from the Soviet Union as early as the 1920s.

Long before the Bolshevik revolution, western representations of Russia had accentuated enslavement and incarceration as pillars of the czarist state, with peasants trapped in serfdom and political opponents expelled to the empire's inhospitable periphery. Nineteenth-century works such as Fyodor Dostoyevsky's *Notes from the House of the Dead* and Anton Chekhov's *A Journey to Sakhalin* fixed Siberia's reputation as a destination of dread: a site of exile and exertion from which return was at best uncertain. Descriptions of this bleak physical and psychological landscape weren't restricted to a literary elite. *Century Magazine,* for example, published a lengthy series of articles in 1888 and 1889 by George Kennan (granduncle of the eminent diplomat) detailing "Siberia and the Exile System."[23] Early cold war excavations of the gulag often invoked this czarist history. If totalitarianism was by definition tyrannical and the concentration camp was its prototypical institution, the Bolshevik state's punitive excess was also ascribed to an engrained Russian propensity toward despotism, secrecy, and paranoia. As alumni of the czarist exile system, the Bolshevik leaders had subsequently "improved" it, uncoupling punishment from crime by sweeping suspect classes and national groups into the camps en masse.

Postwar accounts of the Soviet camps also drew on pioneering studies published in the interwar period, many written from firsthand experience and a position on the anti-Stalinist left. Boris Souvarine (a former leading member of the French Communist Party) and Victor Serge both discussed the camps in works published in the 1930s. In *Russia Twenty Years After,* the Belgian-born anarchist Serge vividly rendered the Soviet Union's "filthy corners from which there is rarely a return," using the term *concentration camps* before it had found a place in *Webster's Dictionary:*

> The routine in these penitentiaries has infinite variations. Its gradations run from the model establishment and semi-freedom to the most miserable conditions, to physical decay, to terror, to sadistically inflicted torture. It is no secret to anybody that a certain number of camp chiefs are shot every year for having conducted themselves criminally towards the interned. What cannot happen in a detachment of condemned men lost in the Siberian brush, including bandits, desperate or exasperated peasants, stool pigeons ready for anything, intellectuals and technicians, harshly treated politicals, all of them bound to a hard task, badly fed, and submitted to the absolute power of a policeman who is himself a condemned man![24]

A few did return, however, and to survivors fell the task of documenting how there was, in fact, nothing that "could not happen" in the Soviet camps. Anyone familiar with either Vladimir Tchernavin's *I Speak for the Silent* or George Kitchin's *Prisoner of the OGPU* (both published in 1935) would have found few unfamiliar revelations in gulag testimony from the 1940s and 1950s.[25]

These autobiographical testimonies bore witness to the gulag's massive expansion in the 1930s. As collectivization uprooted millions of kulaks and as schemes for breakneck industrialization sought to transform mineral-rich, population-poor regions above the Arctic Circle and in Central Asia, prisoners were "*literally* sold to regional administrations."[26] The gulag became the state's chief employment bureau. In settings where accumulation was at its most primitive, prisoners compensated for the undercapitalization of Soviet industry and agriculture. As Tchernavin explained, the camp population

> is actually the invested capital of the GPU enterprises; it takes the place of expensive equipment and machinery. Machines require buildings, care, and fuel of a certain quality and in fixed quantity. Not so with these prisoner-slaves. They need no care, they can exist in unheated barracks which they build themselves. Their fuel ration—food—can be regulated according to circumstances: one kilogram of bread can be reduced to 400 grams, sugar can be omitted entirely; they work equally well on rotten salted horse or camel meat. Finally, the slave is a universal machine; today he digs a canal, tomorrow he fells trees, and the next day he catches fish. The only requisite is an efficient organization for compelling him to work—that is the "speciality" of the GPU.[27]

Such trenchant descriptions of the exhaustion of human life on a mass scale obscured nothing of the scale or function of the gulag. They did not typify writings from or about the USSR during the halcyon years of the Popular Front, however. As André Gide pointed out in *Retour de l'URSS*—a tortured reappraisal of his "admiration" and "love" for the USSR that appeared in English in 1937—those who discerned in the Soviet state an "impetus capable of carrying forward in its stride the whole human race" hesitated to find fault. As depression gripped the capitalist world, many liberals and socialists regarded the Soviet Union as a model for what state planning allied to progressive social policy could accomplish. Rather than confront the USSR's metastasizing camps, they turned a blind eye.[28]

Soviet authorities encouraged foreign visitors to do so by mystifying the character of their penal institutions. Much was made of the great strides taken by state penologists in pioneering modern and humane correctional institutions—manufactories of the "new Soviet man," redeemed through ideological instruction and the purgative power of constructive work. Louis Fischer, who later repudiated his progressive past, devoted a laudatory chapter of his *Soviet Journey* (1935) to the topic of "health through labor." A year later Sidney and Beatrice Webb proposed in their two-volume opus *Soviet Communism: A New Civilization?* that Bolshevik reformatories were "as free from physical cruelty as any prisons in any country are ever likely to be."[29]

Many enthusiastic political travelogues of the 1930s offered descriptions of Bolshevo, an establishment on the outskirts of Moscow dedicated to the reclamation of young male delinquents. A steady stream of foreign luminaries passed through the doors of what served, in effect, as a Potemkin reformatory: a facade carefully erected to impress onlookers, complete with lecture halls, a library, laboratories, a gymnasium, a bathhouse, a cinema, a theater, and a "very good restaurant." George Bernard Shaw and Lady Astor visited, playing football with the inmates. Fischer made glowing reference to this remarkable example of enlightened social policy, while Jerzy Gliksman described how during his visit to Bolshevo in 1935 "an elderly English lady" wept "tears of appreciation and joy" at the Soviets' parturition of "new, re-born beings."[30]

Few western visitors saw beyond, or through, what they were intended to see. Where outside observers gained access to less exemplary sites, the "politicals" (especially those fluent in foreign languages) were kept in isolation, while criminal prisoners—who invariably received superior treatment and surplus calories—gave the appearance of well-fed satisfaction.[31] Before foreign inspectors visited, camp commanders were instructed to evacuate their premises, "efface all external marks of the penal camps, such as barbed-wire enclosures, watch-turrets and signboards," and costume guards in civilian clothes.[32] One gulag memoirist recounted the prelude to such an inspection as a violent frenzy of vodka-driven activity. Scores of prisoners were casually sacrificed to subzero conditions to satisfy foreign journalists that all reports of forced labor in the USSR—briefly a topic of international concern in 1930—were false.[33] Prominent Soviet authors lent their imprimatur to this message. Most famously, Gorky lauded the redemptive properties of hard work in an inspirational account of how thousands of workers had been "salvaged" by their contribution to constructing the Baltic–White Sea canal.[34]

If myopia characterized the most prominent interwar accounts, what were the preconditions of the gulag's later emergence as an object of knowledge? Clearly, America's wartime alliance with Stalin militated against heightened attention to the camps so long as the Soviet Union remained a vital partner in combating the Wehrmacht. The Office of War Information entreated cultural producers to provide sympathetic depictions of the USSR—"Yes, we Americans reject communism. But we do not reject our Russian ally!"—just as it urged Hollywood to stifle criticism of British imperialism and abandon demeaning representations of the Chinese as a "little people who run laundries."[35] Many publishers, writers, and filmmakers duly stressed the fundamental similarity between Russians and Americans, united by shared aspirations for postwar peace and prosperity.[36] But while flattering portraits of the USSR proliferated in wartime America, the gulag itself expanded exponentially during the war. As rations shrank and work quotas rose, rates of camp mortality reached their highest recorded levels: a death toll estimated at over two million.[37] The high-water mark of Soviet-American amity thus coincided with the gulag's zenith.

While Moscow conscripted some camp inmates into the Red Army, it also shunted millions of fresh replacements into compulsory labor in the struggle to expand and sustain an overstretched war economy. When Soviet troops advanced west in 1939, approximately one million men and women from eastern Poland, the Baltic countries, and Bessarabia were herded in the opposite direction, approximately a quarter of them consigned to the gulag.[38] Meanwhile, Soviet civilians deemed guilty of absenteeism and idleness found themselves subject to draconian punishments, including *katorga*: lifelong exile and servitude. Whole categories of "suspect" nationalities accused of collaboration with the Germans—Volga Germans, Chechens, Ingush, Crimean Tartars—were deported to the camps. And when the tide of battle shifted in the Red Army's favor, vast numbers of German soldiers were prodded into makeshift POW compounds, if they weren't simply shot or left to die of exposure first. Although Moscow never divulged statistics detailing German prisoners in its custody, historians estimate the total at three to four million, together with a smaller number of Finns, Hungarians, Italians, and Romanians.[39] In August 1945, the final push into Manchuria delivered approximately half a million Japanese prisoners into captivity.[40] For all these men, forced labor formed a fixed point of camp life.

When the war ended, Moscow sought to retain this workforce for as long as possible. With much of eastern/central Europe under Red Army occupation, the Soviets also began forcibly relocating thousands of able-bodied civilians to the USSR. From eastern Germany, Soviet occupation authorities prioritized the removal of skilled laborers, technicians, and scientists as well as those branded as political "undesirables." At the same time, the NKVD (Narodnyi Komissariat Vnutrennikh Del, People's Commissariat of Internal Affairs) presided over group deportations of ethnic Germans *(Volksdeutsche)* from eastern and southeastern Europe, systematically issuing notice to men and women, as young as sixteen, to pack appropriate clothing and a fifteen-day supply of food.[41]

None of this caused a great outcry in 1945, however. On the contrary, the victors shared a desire to extract whatever recompense they could from the defeated aggressors. "Elementary justice naturally demands that those guilty of the war and destruction be forced to repair the damage they have wrought," announced the *New Republic* in May 1945, giving voice to a widely held sentiment.[42] Having agreed at Yalta that Germany would offer reparations in labor, since other forms of capital would undoubtedly be in such short supply, the Allied powers collectively set their POWs to work. The British and French governments clung tenaciously to this cheap labor force. Not all U.S. employers were keen to relinquish their POW workforce either. In 1946 several cotton farmers and pulpwood producers petitioned the Truman administration for permission to keep their POWs at least until the end of the season. Some, in due course, would fill the gap left by the Germans' return home with displaced persons (DPs) recruited from Europe's refugee camps.[43]

The sheer scale of devastation suffered by the USSR, coupled with the fact that Germany had deported more than three million Soviet citizens as forced laborers during the war, fostered sympathy for Moscow's demand for reparations in human form.[44] Soviet estimates that thirty-five to forty billion dollars could be collected from the expropriation of five million Germans' labor over a decade may have occasioned some skepticism, but few quibbled with the underlying principle.[45] In May 1945, the *New Republic* went so far as to anticipate—on the basis of the "entire character of the Soviet social order" and the "attitude of the Soviet population toward labor and skill"—that German workers "rendering labor duty as part of Germany's reparations [would] receive the same wages, housing accommodations and food as Soviet citizens."[46]

Sustained criticism of Soviet "forced labor" became pronounced only when the great powers' wartime coalition splintered. Gulag consciousness in the West, in other words, was neither an outgrowth of détente nor a function of de-Stalinization but a correlate of cold war tension. By 1946, negative representations of the USSR had begun to displace the rosier wartime depictions, with critics of Soviet totalitarianism returning to themes never entirely dormant. As the descriptor *slave world* shifted from Germany to the Soviet Union, Moscow's reliance on "forced labor" became a dominant motif. In February 1946, Congresswoman Clare Boothe Luce condemned the Soviet system as one "which keeps eighteen million people out of 180 million in concentration and forced labor camps."[47] Similarly unflinching attacks appeared in diverse outlets, from political weeklies like the Menshevik-dominated *New Leader* to popular works of reportage that soon multiplied as Moscow-based correspondents returned home after the war.[48] Typically these travelogue-cum-memoirs contained passing reference to the gulag if they didn't offer more sustained treatment. William van Narvig's *East of the Iron Curtain,* to take but one example, contained a chapter jarringly entitled, "What Ho! Concentration Camps?"—a dig angled at fellow travelers who had rhapsodized over Bolshevo, or perhaps more pointedly at Henry Wallace. Visiting Magadan in 1946, Truman's secretary of commerce had saluted the "big, husky young men" who worked its mines, likening their rugged spirit to the pioneers of the American West. "Men born in wide free spaces will not brook injustice and tyranny," he proclaimed. "They will not live even temporarily in slavery."[49]

Drawing on a substantial body of witness testimony, cold war opinion formers strove to show that slavery was precisely the condition endured by these men and millions more. While the epic mobilizations, incarcerations, and displacements of wartime resulted in millions of fatalities, they also left myriad survivors with evidence to offer. Although Moscow did not surrender its last Axis POWs until the mid-1950s, certain groups of inmates were released considerably earlier. In 1939, under the terms of the Ribbentrop-Molotov agreement, the NKVD delivered prisoners of German nationality (mostly Trotskyists summoned to the USSR after 1933) to the Third Reich in exchange for Soviet citizens in German custody: a pact that, for its victims, meant the substitution of one camp regimen for another. Remarkably, some survived both. Two years later, in July 1941, the Soviets freed hundreds of thousands of Poles under the terms of an amnesty signed with the Polish government in exile of General Sikorski, many subsequently joining an army of "free Poles" under the leadership of General Anders. These men formed the earliest group from whom systematic evidence was gathered on conditions in Soviet camps. Housed at the Hoover Institution at Stanford University, this archive formed an important evidentiary cache for U.S. government initiatives and postwar publications on the gulag, such as *The Dark Side of the Moon* (a collection of autobiographical writings published in 1947 with a preface by T. S. Eliot).[50]

Within months of the war's end, then, the preconditions of expanded "gulag consciousness" were all in place: a group of energetic activists dedicated to raising awareness; a body of witnesses with compelling testimony to offer; and an audience in the United States and western Europe receptive to negative reports about the USSR at a time of rising animosity and mistrust.

THE GULAG IN THE DOCK: *L'AFFAIRE KRAVCHENKO*

In the postwar reorientation—or reconsolidation—of opinion toward Soviet communism, no single volume left a deeper imprint than Victor Kravchenko's *I Chose Freedom,* "one of the most important books of our time," in the estimation of the *New York Times.*[51] After abridged serialization in the Hearst press and condensation in *Reader's Digest,* this sweeping five-hundred-page memoir reached American bookstores in April 1946. It would subsequently sell five million copies in twenty-two languages, its foreign translation and distribution subsidized by British and U.S. intelligence agencies.[52] Beyond these phenomenal sales, the book also sparked what contemporary commentators described as a "major East-West propaganda duel" that is still recalled as "one of the great cold war 'affairs.'"[53]

According to historian Martin Malia, *I Chose Freedom* was the first volume to offer "hard evidence" about the "central postwar issue," the "question of terror and concentration camps."[54] This was far from true. Earlier authors including Anton Ciliga, Alexandre Barmine, and Walter Krivitsky had already published damning accounts of life in the USSR, and, as we've seen, they and others had specifically attended to questions of terror and the camps.[55] Even the most favorable reviewers of Kravchenko's book admitted that it contained "little that is essentially new," including the author's "horrified discovery of the character and extent of the slave labor system."[56] But the privileged position Malia accords Kravchenko underscores his function as an early cold war bellwether, a role solidified not only by the book's prodigious popularity but by the controversy that accompanied it. Having been acclaimed and attacked with equal vehemence, Kravchenko launched a libel suit against the communist literary weekly *Les Lettres Françaises* in January 1949. What followed was a three-month-long piece of political theater that confirmed the gulag's new centrality to reckonings with Soviet communism. As the titles of two French volumes published shortly after the Paris trial—*Kravchenko contre Moscou* and *Le goulag en correctionnelle*—made clear, the defendant in this "anticommunist publicity extravaganza" was less *Les Letters Françaises* than Moscow itself. Ultimately, the gulag was in the dock.[57]

With embarrassing prematurity, Victor Kravchenko had abandoned his post as an officer with the Soviet Purchasing Commission in Washington, D.C., in April 1944. While State Department officials pondered their Soviet ally's demand for the return of this "traitor," the defector drew support from a group of Menshevik émigrés who embraced him as a kindred spirit. Far from suspecting his motives or ruing his timing, this circle regarded Kravchenko as a natural democrat who had "instinctively come to speak Menshevik prose," in the opinion of Raphael Abrahamovitch.[58] To cultivate this voice, David Dallin put Kravchenko in touch with the *New York Times* labor correspondent Joseph Shaplen.[59] Dallin also worked to furnish a ghostwriter for the memoir that invariably followed a high-profile defection.[60] Initially, this role fell to another Russian émigré, the prolific editor of *Plain Talk,* Isaac Don Levine. (A specialist in such work, he had polished Krivitsky's *In Stalin's Secret Service* and would later write the twenty-eight-part serialization of Oksana Kasenkina's life story.) The resultant articles on Kravchenko's defection, "I Broke with Stalin's Russia," ran in *Cosmopolitan* magazine between June and September 1944, with Levine's contribution prominently acknowledged.[61]

The authorial hand behind *I Chose Freedom* was hidden, however. Only later was Kravchenko's ghost disclosed as Eugene Lyons, ex-communist editor of the *American Mercury* and author of numerous anti-Soviet volumes.[62] Working from an "unreadable" Russian typescript of 1,500 pages, Lyons produced a volume that was as much an epic narrative of Soviet history—dwelling heavily on the horrors of collectivization, mass famine, the purges, and incarceration—as an individual life story. Rendered in the tremulous vibrato of popular anticommunist prose, it read, as some reviewers pointed out, like fiction—"and Russian fiction at that."[63]

Publication of *I Chose Freedom* in April 1946 cleaved opinion along partisan lines. Critics of the USSR swooned over what Dorothy Thompson called a "throbbing book." "Dynamite under illusions," *I Chose Freedom* represented "the most remarkable and most revelatory report to have come out of the Soviet Union from any source whatsoever." Others joined the chorus, entreating "Americans—particularly Americans of good will—to absorb and understand" what Kravchenko had to tell them. While Ed Sullivan chivvied "local commies" to "learn about the bees and the flowers of Soviet gestation—and then decide that the United States is a pretty fine place in which to live!" advocates of ongoing cooperation with Moscow were repulsed.[64] The *New Republic* found the "latest spicy dish from the Red-baiters' kitchen" thoroughly unsavory: "Take one Soviet renegade. Mix with several professional Russophobes. Stir well so that ingredients are no longer lumpy. Flavor with sex and a dash of Chekhov or Dostoevesky. Boil with concentrated extract of Boris Karloff and Bela Lugosi. Cover thickly with Liberty sauce. Serve piping hot. List on menu as 'The Real Truth: Honest to God.' Will sell like hot cakes."[65] And so it did.

Yet even admirers certain that Kravchenko's damning portrait of the USSR was essentially accurate regretted that *I Chose Freedom* struck some false notes. "The suspicion that attends apostasy dies hard," noted Homer Metz in the *Christian Science Monitor*.[66] In a postscript, Kravchenko acknowledged that he had written the book in his native tongue. The translated English text had accordingly been "edited from an American vantage point"—albeit "under the stipulation that all facts, incidents, personal experiences, political events, pictures and individual characteristics, down to the minutest detail, follow faithfully [the] Russian manuscript." Who had performed these tasks neither author nor publisher would reveal.[67]

Kravchenko's slipperiness, the secrecy cloaking his ghost's identity, and the phalanx of Mensheviks that surrounded him all provided ample ammunition for detractors in the United States and beyond. In France, *J'ai choisi la liberté* (which sold almost half a million copies) intervened in an already heated debate on the left that had seen Albert Camus break with Jean-Paul Sartre over the function and character of Stalin's camps. With Sartre maintaining that condemnation of the gulag was simply anticommunist cant, the two authors' acrimonious falling-out emblematized a larger national schism between socialists and Stalinists.[68] In this volatile climate, it is hardly surprising that the *Les Lettres Françaises*—a publication "fully and enthusiastically in the Communist camp"—should have savaged a book that threatened to galvanize further defections from the ranks of the French Communist Party.[69] *J'ai choisi la liberté* was denounced as a work of CIA (or even Nazi) agents to which Kravchenko's name had been appended. The man himself was "morally insane," "so illiterate as to be incapable of writing a book."[70] A drunkard and a thief who had defected because he feared exposure for embezzlement, Kravchenko was a "puppet whose clumsy strings are 'made in the USA.'"[71]

These slurs provoked Kravchenko's one-million-franc ($3,150) libel suit, though they were not significantly more slanderous than insults published elsewhere. However, as the plaintiff let slip during one of the trial's many impassioned moments, his motives in taking legal action against *Les Lettres Françaises,* its editor, André Wurmser, and its director, Claude Morgan, were governed not by the magnitude of their libel but by the maximum impact a court case in France would generate. "I didn't sue the United States Communists because they aren't worth it," Kravchenko declared in an unguarded outburst, "but the French Communists should be unmasked for the good of the whole world."[72]

With remarks like this, Kravchenko strengthened communist charges that he was not his own man and that this politically motivated suit had been launched at Washington's behest. "Of course it was not Kravchenko, but his masters, who chose the place of the trial and decided at what time it would be most advantageous," proclaimed a strident article in *Pravda*.[73] It seems more probable, though, that Kravchenko's Menshevik circle urged him to pursue legal action, eager to find a new arena in which to air the case against Soviet totalitarianism. In 1947, Dallin and Nicolaevsky had threatened a one-million-dollar suit against the Soviet representative to the UN, Andrei Vyshinsky, for slanderous remarks made about *Forced Labor in Soviet Russia*, only to find him protected by diplomatic immunity.[74]

The CIA may neither have fabricated the defector's memoir nor prompted him to sue *Les Lettres*, but Washington certainly took an active interest in the case. Kravchenko's view of France as a vital staging ground of the cold war replicated the State Department's own estimation of a country still insecurely tethered to the Atlantic alliance, in which the PCF bulked alarmingly large. Through open channels carved by the provision of Marshall aid and covert initiatives to undermine the communist left, U.S. government agencies actively sought to propel French political culture in a centrist direction. Subsidized distribution of books like *I Chose Freedom* constituted one tactic in an extensive ideological war of maneuver against "intellectual defeatism."

Clandestine U.S. involvement with Kravchenko did not end there. As the trial approached in January 1949, the American Embassy in Paris helped him secure a visa, advising that he travel under an assumed name—another intervention that lent credence to communist charges that the defector was an American stooge who lacked a stable or autonomous identity.[75]

If Washington had a significant stake in Kravchenko's case against *Les Lettres Françaises*, so did Paris and Moscow. The latter helped furnish the defense with witnesses, while the former—partisan on the side of the plaintiff—opened the Palais de Justice to hundreds of observers and journalists. This unprecedented departure from standard judicial procedure was further accentuated by the fact that, as one American reporter wryly observed, "Justice has gone so far as to install a special telephone service at the door of the courtroom, from which the official information agency of the government, *France Presse*, every quarter hour sends around the world an analytical description of everything that takes place in the room." This voracious publicity machine was kept steadily fueled by the "vaudeville-like" antics of defendants and plaintiff.[76]

Proceedings opened in January 1949 "in a blaze of publicity unequalled since Marshal Henri-Philippe Petain was tried for high treason in 1945," noted the *New York Times*.[77] Several hundred observers thronged a courtroom thick with anticipation for a "wild session marked by bitter statements of political opinion by all sides and the presentation of numerous witnesses."[78] Kravchenko cut a flamboyant figure with his "marcelled hair and well manicured fingers," sporting a "mysterious black eye" whose provenance he refused to divulge.[79] For the defense, Maîtres Nordmann and Blumel had been sharpening their tongues if not buffing their nails, stopping at nothing to impugn Kravchenko's credibility. They even produced an embittered ex-wife "in a billowing New Look dress under a drab Old Look coat," who asserted that her former spouse ("an ignorant Don Juan") had forced her to abort a pregnancy.[80] But while such incidents heightened the Punch and Judy character of the proceedings, the substance of Les Lettres' libelous accusation— that Kravchenko had not written I Chose Freedom—soon shrank to subsidiary importance, an "evident pretext."[81] The central question under adjudication was not the book's authorship but the validity of its depiction of Soviet communism.

The defense called on the atomic physicist Frederic Joliot-Curie, the Reverend Hewlett Johnson (known as the "Red Dean" of Canterbury), and the Labour MP for East London, Konni Zilliacus, to testify (in the sardonic language of the New York Times) that "the Soviet Union was a very pleasant place indeed and bore no resemblance to the terror-stricken nation that Mr. Kravchenko had described."[82] Edward Dmytryk, a repentant member of the Hollywood Ten, claimed that "the commie paper" had also tried to procure him as a witness to "prove that Russia was right in contrast to America"—an assignment that he "turned down cold," and then decried as evidence of communists' utter disregard for national loyalty.[83] For his part, the plaintiff introduced thirty witnesses to corroborate his characterization of a "barbaric regime."[84] In the main, they were Soviet refugees brought to Paris from DP camps in West Germany—ordinary people (or "mad fanatics, murderers and moral degenerates" according to Pravda) with extraordinary stories to tell.[85] Olga Marchenko, "a sturdy Ukrainian in her fifties and a complete picture of the Russian peasant," tearfully told of being evicted from her home in the 1930s during "dekulakization" and giving birth to a stillborn child "thrown out in the snow" by callous Red officials. Another woman, who had lived in Russia for forty-five years, insisted that Kravchenko's book didn't "go far enough in telling about 'the terrible regime' in the Soviet Union."[86]

To some observers, the extremity of these witnesses' autobiographical sketches rendered them suspect—caricatures modeled on Kravchenko's crude original. But amid the raucous outbursts, flailing fists, and ripe invective that typified these sessions, one witness reduced the unruly courtroom to chastened silence. Expecting to be greeted with jeers of "sales Boches," Margarete Buber-Neumann instead met hushed respect as she took the witness stand on the fourteenth day of proceedings, at the start of the trial's fifth week.[87] The forty-eight-year-old Buber-Neumann bore an impressive pedigree: former daughter-in-law of the renowned German philosopher Martin Buber and latterly the partner of Heinz Neumann, onetime German

FIGURE 14. *J'accuse!* Victor Kravchenko takes umbrage at his ex-wife's assertion that he is an "ignorant Don Juan"—too stupid to have written *I Chose Freedom*—during his libel suit against *Les Lettres Françaises,* Paris, February 1949. © The Associated Press.

communist leader. Herself a member of the Communist Youth from 1921 to 1926 and of the KPD (Communist Party of Germany) until 1937, Buber-Neumann couldn't be dismissed (as some of Kravchenko's witnesses were) as a rancorous class enemy or fascist collaborator. She had been a convinced and active party member for years, an opponent of Nazism summoned to the USSR by the Comintern only to find herself dispatched to the gulag as a "socially undesirable element."

That her political sympathies had rested with the Comintern for so long made her subsequent treatment by Moscow all the more astonishing, for Buber-Neumann was one of those German prisoners handed over to the Nazis under the terms of the Molotov-Ribbentrop pact in 1940. Her two years in the gulag were thus followed by five more at Ravensbrück. At a time when comparisons between Nazi and Soviet camps were increasingly commonplace, Buber-Neumann was one of only a handful of survivors whose evaluative judgments derived from firsthand experience of life "under two dictators." Her personal history constituted its own unique indictment of totalitarianism.[88]

In court, much of Buber-Neumann's testimony was devoted to her experience at Karaganda—a vast encampment in Kazakhstan to which she had been summarily dispatched in 1938. For two years she performed heavy agricultural labor on a diet that barely sustained subsistence. Like other postwar witnesses to the gulag, she stressed starvation as an instrument of coercion. Prisoners who met punitive work quotas were "rewarded" with barely adequate rations, while those who either could not or would not work received such scant sustenance that their choice lay between slow starvation or compliance with the work regimen. For the infirm, all that awaited was a long descent through infirmity and incapacitation to death.

As this grim picture began to emerge, the defendants' counsel began a series of interruptions aiming to prove that Karaganda was not *really* a camp as the French would understand that term. "*Ce n'est pas en francais 'un camp,' c'est une zone,*" insisted Maître Blumel, trying to moderate perceptions of what Buber-Neumann described by finding some less damaging comparison than the most obvious point of reference: a Nazi concentration camp. The defense team plied Buber-Neumann with further questions—whether this "zone" was enclosed by a wall; whether she could walk freely around its extensive interior; whether her work was paid—in the hopes that Karaganda might appear more like an internment camp, or even (in the presiding judge's term) a hotel. Under provocation, Buber-Neumann's answers remained calm and succinct. Yes, one could walk unguarded along a road of some two kilometers (within a camp that extended for some fifty or sixty), but the camp was surrounded by barbed wire and guarded by armed soldiers with dogs. Accommodation was a clay hut infested by millions of fleas and lice—hardly a "hotel."

These points clarified, Buber-Neumann continued her testimony uninterrupted to the point of her handover by the NKVD to the SS at Brest-Litovsk, along with several Germans and Austrians, one Hungarian Jew, and an elderly professor— the only member of the group of thirty who had never belonged to the Communist Party. Recounting that, after interrogation by the Gestapo, she had spent five years in Ravensbrück concentration camp, Buber-Neumann faced no questions about conditions there. Not keen to pursue a comparison between Nazi and Soviet camps, Blumel returned to his line that Karaganda was more akin to the internment camps established by Daladier's government in 1939. Warming to his theme, he proposed that a degree of freedom *(une certaine liberté)* prevailed at Karaganda. Were there not shops and houses in this zone? Weren't married couples permitted to cohabit? What Buber-Neumann bluntly outlined in response was an altogether different sexual economy. Formally outlawed by the camp authorities (who not only separated married couples but did their best to prohibit any friendship between male and female prisoners), sex became the currency of survival for female prisoners forced to trade their bodies for food from better-fed male inmates and guards. To redress the dietary deficit, tipping the balance of probabilities from starvation to subsistence, most women needed to find not just one male provider but two or three.

Evidence of this sort abruptly dispelled the burlesque atmosphere that had prevailed hitherto in the courtroom. Observers unanimously recognized Buber-Neumann's testimony as the most damning indictment of the Soviet Union presented during the trial. A British Embassy official, unimpressed by the "dreary procession of displaced persons, who testified to the sternness which accompanied the extermination of the Kulaks in the Ukraine and the horrors suffered by recalcitrants at the hands of the secret police," reported that Buber-Neumann had provided the "most eloquent testimony against the Soviet way of life." After the preceding cacophony of profanities, this dignified witness recounted her "barbarous treatment . . . with obvious sincerity and emotion."[89]

More tellingly, Buber-Neumann's account of Karaganda also produced a chastening effect on observers reluctant to indict Soviet communism. Simone de Beauvoir, having attended one of the hearings with Sartre, expressed deep distaste for Kravchenko's "lies" and "venality." Buber-Neumann's testimony, by contrast, was chillingly credible: logical, unembellished, irrefutable. For all its histrionics, the trial had placed the Soviet camps' existence beyond dispute, de Beauvoir later wrote in *La force des choses*. Stalinists now had to ask whether the USSR and its satellites deserved to be called "socialist."[90]

Where Buber-Neumann lent gravitas to *l'affaire Kravchenko*, the judicial verdict exposed the flimsy character of the trial as a libel case. On April 4, Judge Henri Durkheim ruled in Kravchenko's favor, but his sympathies were clearly divided. Although he deemed the plaintiff a "cultured man" fully capable of having written the book, he ruled that *I Chose Freedom* had been "subject to some editing and possibly some 'romancing.'" He awarded Kravchenko $500 in damages, a sum reduced on subsequent appeal by *Les Lettres* to a token $1. At the same time, Judge Durkheim fined the journal $314 for its libelous statements—a relatively modest sum since the defendants' records proved them to be "patriots."[91] These mixed signals allowed both sides to claim a moral victory.[92] But if Kravchenko's reputation did not emerge unblemished and his triumph was partial, he was still hailed by admirers as a conquering hero tinged with the luminous aura of a matinee idol. As the verdict was announced, a mob of "frenzied women" overwhelmed one hundred police officers who had been detailed to protect the courtroom from communist protesters. Instead, the gendarmes found themselves "helpless" against a crowd of women, biting and clawing "to approach Kravchenko and kiss his hands or cheeks."[93]

While Kravchenko emerged daubed in lipstick, the Kremlin was covered in ignominy—at least as American commentators tallied the outcome of this strenuous slugging match. In an editorial entitled "The Big Red Team Loses a Road Game," the *Chicago Daily Tribune* contrasted the Kravchenko case with a series of recent show trials in eastern Europe, most notably that of Cardinal Mindszenty, which had concluded on February 8 with his conviction on charges of espionage, conspiracy, and treason. To the appalled consternation of western observers, the cardinal himself confessed to these charges, leading many to conclude that he had been tortured, drugged, or hypnotized into mouthing his own guilt. In the *Daily Tribune*'s opinion, these parallel courtroom dramas proved that only by rigging the outcome in the most pernicious way could communists hope to prevail: "The Stalinists prefer to try their legal showpieces in more sympathetic surroundings, where the shirt to fit the culprit can be starched and ironed in advance and the collar button never rolls out of the interlocutor's hands and disappears under the dresser."[94] Where they couldn't "soften up" witnesses in advance and coerce them into making false confessions, the Reds would fall flat, their crimes exposed and arraigned.

After the popular outcry occasioned in America by the cardinal's conviction, this was encouraging news. Kravchenko, it seemed, had performed a far greater service for the "free world" than merely securing token damages from a French literary magazine.

"A HORRIBLE CHORUS OF ACCUSATION": FORCED LABOR INDICTED

U.S. policy makers reached much the same conclusion. One American diplomat cabled home from Paris that as a propaganda victory Kravchenko's ranked "second in importance only to the signing of the Atlantic Pact": two momentous events that occurred on the same day.[95] State Department officials took due note of the trial's gladiatorial aspect. As the plaintiff sparred with the defendants and lawyers locked horns with witnesses, spectators appeared transfixed by the spectacle of hand-to-hand ideological combat. Kravchenko became a household name in France; the competing claims of East and West received a memorable airing, and the camps were established as fact—even by those loath to concede the point.

Impressed by the performative dimensions of judicial procedure, U.S. officials espoused the tribunal as an ideal mechanism through which to indict Soviet slave labor. Since Moscow claimed to possess the key to proletarian emancipation, a core objective of Washington's global campaign for allegiance was exposure of the "workers' paradise" as a hellish landscape dotted with forced labor camps. "Instead of nothing to lose but their chains, as the original communist theory predicted, the people have acquired chains that are better forged than ever," wrote *New York Times* Moscow correspondent Brooks Atkinson, a verdict with which the State Department was in perfect accord.[96] To this end, it aimed to do "everything possible to show those who at this time may be flirting with totalitarian disaster the ugly realities of Fascist or Communist rule—and there are few realities as ugly as the concentration camps which are the tools both of Fascist and Communist dictatorship."[97] Recognizing that there would be a limited audience for statistic-laden reports and dry factual pamphlets on Soviet "slave labor," U.S. government officials attempted to replicate the effect of the Kravchenko libel case in the international arena. What the Palais de Justice had been for Kravchenko, the UN—and its third committee, the Economic and Social Council (ECOSOC), in particular—could become for Washington, or so U.S. policy makers hoped.

The campaign against slave labor began in 1948, the year in which London and Paris reluctantly agreed to surrender their remaining Axis POWs.[98] Waged with some intensity for five years, this initiative coincided with (and contributed to) the UN's growing polarization. On both sides, protagonists struggled to monopolize the language of human rights, manipulating the symbolic spillover of the Nuremberg trials, at which "forced labor" had formed a key charge against the arraigned Nazi leadership. At the UN and its associated agencies, claims and counterclaims were now couched in terms of universal rights, "crimes against humanity," and "genocide." While Moscow loudly decried discriminatory practices in the United States and the Civil Rights Congress leveled its own indictment of U.S. racism, *We Charge Genocide,* Truman countered by casting Soviet forced labor as "the most extreme violation of human rights on the face of the earth today."[99]

Washington found many willing partners in this condemnatory enterprise. Indeed, the administration was not always in the vanguard of a movement pioneered by trade unionists on both sides of the Atlantic, a proactive Labour government in Westminster, and the ceaseless efforts of Dallin and Nicolaevsky. Their *Forced Labor in Soviet Russia* had sparked a fiery exchange at the UN in 1947. Provoked by the South African delegate's quotation from a volume that argued the gulag's centrality to the Soviet economy, Andrei Vyshinsky denounced it as the work of "gangsters" and "idiots," based on "information from Hitlerite agents."[100] This fractious episode confounded Orville Prescott's prediction in the *New York Times* that *Forced Labor in Soviet Russia* was destined "not to be widely read" since a postwar audience jaded by Nazi atrocities would "shrink from contact with further horrors."[101] Instead, the book became a touchstone of the international campaign against Soviet "slave labor," its authors liaising closely with the AFL to place forced labor on the agenda of ECOSOC in 1948.[102]

This initiative failed. It did serve, however, to inaugurate years of close cooperation between the U.S. government and ostensibly private actors and organizations, cementing the role of organized labor as a key cold war protagonist. Dallin, with others from the *New Leader* circle and representatives of the AFL and the International Confederation of Free Trade Unions, regularly attended meetings of the State Department's planning committee on forced labor.[103] Embroiled in its own two-front war against communists in the British Labour movement and overseas, Attlee's government formed another key player in this transatlantic network, sharing the State Department's view that slave labor represented their trump card in "political warfare" against the USSR. As such, it was a "leading theme" for the Foreign Office's dedicated anticommunist propaganda unit, the Information Research Department.[104]

FIGURE 15. "See, he's *free!*" The Congress of Industrial Organizations joins the chorus of indictments of Soviet "slave labor" with this cartoon from the *CIO News,* August 22, 1949. Reproduced by permission of the George Meany Memorial Archives.

In 1948, the British delegate Sir Christopher Mayhew took up the AFL's case to have forced labor discussed at ECOSOC. This move was "part of a new technique adapted by the United States and the Western European powers in meeting the Soviet accusations of exploitation of colonial peoples and of 'lynch law' in the Southern United States," explained the *New York Times.*[105] Undeterred when the motion was again voted down, British and American delegates returned to the fray in 1949, supported by the AFL's submission of a sixty-page document containing stories "grimly reminiscent of the Nazi concentration camp atrocities."[106] That February, with the Kravchenko trial at its height, British and U.S. representatives jointly pressed for an "impartial investigation into forced labor." This time, ECOSOC agreed to approach all member governments to ascertain their willingness to cooperate.[107]

U.S. and British officials invested considerable ideological capital in this campaign, a bold initiative that Mayhew believed would reanimate the spirit of nineteenth-century abolitionism, mobilizing worldwide moral outrage against the Soviets' reintroduction of slavery after its ostensible demise some eighty years earlier.[108] Yet these grandiose ambitions were never entirely realized. Fissures in the transatlantic alliance soon developed, triggered by Washington's unilateral insistence on a commission of inquiry with extensive powers of on-site investigation. In August 1949, Willard Thorp, the assistant secretary of state, called for the establishment of an eleven-person UN commission of experts, "empowered to visit any member country of the world organization and to hold hearings concerning forced labor practices anywhere in the world." This move, wrote Michael Hoffman in the *New York Times,* stressed not only the high moral seriousness with which the U.S. government regarded forced labor but also its commitment to the commission as an investigatory model:

> The United States is convinced that millions of persons, who still believe that the Soviet Union is a progressive country, with a government for, if not by or of, workers, would be convinced effectively of such a procedure more than by any number of United Nations reports or resolutions. A vast amount of material already exists concerning individual experiences in Soviet camps, but as the recent Victor Kravchenko libel trial in Paris proved, the European masses will read avidly stories about what somebody said under the dramatic circumstances of court hearings while ignoring completely what governments say on the subject because they feel that it is simply "propaganda."[109]

If the appeal of a procedure that involved public hearings, inspection visits, and harrowing eyewitness testimony was obvious, so too were its pitfalls. In the matter of labor practices, no state boasted a clean slate. Few governments wanted to see an independent commission investigate the more egregious forms of exploitation that occurred under their own jurisdiction. Fearful that indefensible practices in their colonies would be exposed, Washington's closest allies pushed for an investigation trained exclusively on the Soviet Union and its satellites. Clearly, though, such undisguised partisanship would never secure a consensus at ECOSOC. With some hesitancy Washington duly accepted that willingness to face domestic scrutiny was the price to be paid for rallying international opinion against Soviet forced labor.[110]

This strategy paid off, and in March 1951 a three-person ad hoc committee of inquiry was appointed under the aegis of the International Labour Organization and the UN, chaired by the eminent Indian statesman Sir Ramaswami Mudaliar.[111]

Slowly, his team set about the Herculean task of investigating what it parsed as two distinct aspects of the issue: "corrective" labor as a punishment for dissident political convictions, and forced labor that contributed significantly to a state's economy.

Predictably, Moscow refused to cooperate with the investigation, though it no longer absolutely denied the existence of the camps, as it had at the height of the Stalinist terror. A caustic editorial in the *Washington Post* noted that the "latest fashion is rather to describe them as places which combine all the best features of American country clubs, Viennese amusement parks, English country houses and Swiss sanatoria."[112] In the main, however, the Soviets devoted less energy to self-defense than to an offensive that aimed to redefine the terms of engagement, turning the language of slavery back on its capitalist proponents. Moscow thus countercharged that the United States "wished to raise a hue and cry on that particular subject in order to divert the attention of the working masses in capitalist countries from their own status, which was no better than that of wage slaves."[113] Under capitalism all labor was unfree, but some workers remained strikingly less free than others.

Moscow's litany of corroborative examples was compendious. In the United States alone, the Soviets pointed to the predicament of "fourteen million negroes . . . virtually deprived of the opportunity to engage in any but the most menial labour"; extensive use of convict labor; and widespread peonage in the South and Southwest, to say nothing of the unemployed millions whose plight was a structural feature of capitalism. The misery of these oppressed groups—African Americans in particular—already figured prominently in Soviet propaganda, but Washington's proactive stance on forced labor redoubled the vigor with which Moscow lambasted the wretched conditions that persisted wherever "the means of production were in the hands of private enterprise." Varieties of peonage, indenture, and corvée in Europe's colonies formed another substantial target of Soviet attack.[114] In June 1952, Moscow's delegate to ECOSOC also made much of a *Daily Worker* story that the U.S. government was constructing concentration camps in the southwestern states "to accommodate 'progressive' elements in a crisis."[115]

State Department officials scoffed at the "blind dogma that workers employed by capitalist employers are exploited." Yet however specious they found this contention, they could hardly debar Mudaliar's committee from probing America's alleged labor abuses, having pressed for open inspections.[116] To their chagrin, U.S. policy makers acknowledged that some Soviet claims were not without foundation. In Japan, where State Department personnel recognized that America's own wartime record of mistreatment regarding Japanese prisoners would not "very well bear the light of investigation," and where postwar occupation authorities had taken rigorous measures to outlaw communist-dominated labor unions, MacArthur bridled against accommodating the investigators, doing so only when Washington insisted that obstruction would afford the Soviets a cheap propaganda victory.[117]

Confronted with these challenges, U.S. officials swamped Mudaliar with as much detailed evidence on the Soviet camps as they could muster, delivering forty-four pounds of documents to the ad hoc committee in June 1952.[118] In pursuit of this material, researchers combed through sixty thousand pages of the Hoover Library's collection of fifteen thousand depositions given by the Polish prisoners released from the gulag in 1940. They also sought more recent interview testimony from hundreds of refugees who had fled the Soviet Union after the war (names supplied by Dallin) and from Japanese and Korean former inmates of the Far Eastern camps whose POW experiences remained "altogether unknown." The aim was to offer a picture as "complete and rich" as possible of the entire network of Soviet camps.[119]

To the State Department's disappointment, Mudaliar's committee attached greater weight to legal documents and printed evidence than to witness testimony. This wasn't what U.S. officials had anticipated when, with the Kravchenko trial fresh in mind, they conjured images of gulag survivors lending their voices to a "horrible chorus of accusation" that would reverberate worldwide. Nevertheless, the protracted inquiry allowed State Department officials to keep forced labor recurrently in the public eye, and they considered their publication *Forced Labor in the Soviet Union* (issued in September 1952) "undoubtedly the best propaganda pamphlet our Government ever got out." Truman personally commended it to the press corps with the backhanded compliment that it didn't contain "too many State Department words."[120]

Proud of their own efforts, U.S. officials evinced considerably less satisfaction with Mudaliar's committee. Its report—"huge and horrifying," in *Life* magazine's judgment—finally appeared in May 1953.[121] But from the State Department's perspective, this 619-page volume didn't horrify for quite the right reasons. With no little irritation, they found that it condemned "forced labor in South Africa almost as thoroughly as that in the Soviet Union." The report's ecumenical approach left the U.S. government embarrassingly exposed, as Pretoria was considered a necessary—if troublesome—cold war ally. Yet a refusal on Washington's part to condemn apartheid labor practices that turned southern Africa's indigenous population into a vast reservoir of highly exploited migrant labor would antagonize "colored" opinion throughout the world, exposing America's investment in forced labor for exactly what it was: a sharpened blade angled specifically toward the USSR. As Henry Cabot Lodge (U.S. ambassador to the UN) flatly concluded, "We will not get the Asian-African votes if we defend only the persecuted white people."[122]

As for allegations against the United States, the report was less damning than it might have been. A series of front-page articles run by the *New York Times* in 1951 had likened the plight of Mexican migrant workers to "the days of slavery, when the systematic exploitation of an underprivileged class of humanity as cheap labor was an accepted part of the American social and economic order."[123] Investigating these and similar charges, the committee adopted a lenient approach. Since peonage was outlawed in the United States and the committee had uncovered no direct evidence that the federal government failed to enforce the law when offenses were brought to light, the report concluded that "these practices [did] not constitute forced labor."[124]

Washington meanwhile deployed its standard response to accusations of discrimination. Concurring that America's copybook was blotted (albeit not hideously disfigured in the way Moscow alleged), U.S. representatives stressed that these minor imperfections were being rectified as democracy marched ever onwards toward full racial equality. Many journalists were happy to contribute to this work of rebuttal, concurring that comparison between Soviet "slavery" and the unenviable— but *self-assigned*—lot of migrant workers was invidious. *Time* typified this vein: "The Mexican wetbacks entered the United States illegally to work on farms and orchards. They swam the Rio Grande seeking this 'slavery.' But there is no record of anyone crossing any body of water to reach a Russian concentration camp. To pretend that the two evils are at all comparable is to perpetrate an enormous and dangerous falsehood."[125]

Publicly applauding Mudaliar's report, Lodge privately chalked up forced labor among his defeats at the United Nations in 1953.[126] Since Washington's interest in human rights abuses bore such a markedly strategic character, timeliness was of the essence. American policy makers anticipated in 1952 that "the whole issue" of forced labor "might be dead as a door nail" by 1954, the earliest date at which the General Assembly was likely to consider the ad hoc committee's final report.[127] And so it proved.

By the time of publication, Stalin had been dead for two months, and his successors were busily (if temporarily) dismantling aspects of his legacy. At the very moment that Moscow stood accused of employing forced labor on a gigantic scale, the Soviet government had "lost its appetite for forced labour camps," closing many of them over the course of the 1950s.[128] With Georgy Malenkov installed in the Kremlin, the Korean War finally over, and prisoners heading home, cold war animosities had started to abate—albeit fitfully, as the GDR's harsh repression of a workers' uprising in June 1953 attested. Although Eisenhower's administration remained mistrustful of Moscow's vaunted peace initiatives, other NATO members found them more persuasive, leading U.S. diplomats to surmise that Europeans hesitated to push the forced labor issue for fear of offending Moscow at this delicate moment.[129] A scathing editorial in *Life* reached the same conclusion, noting that European delegates had voted to *remove* forced labor from ECOSOC's fall agenda: "The excuse of ECOSOC's European delegates for hastily sweeping forced labor under the carpet was that they hadn't had time to read the report; moreover, this session's agenda was already hopelessly overcrowded. Translated from delegatese into plain English, this means, 'Oh dear, do we have to vex the Russians now? The mere mention of forced labor always throws them into a rage and, with the way things have been going in Russia lately, they'll be just too awful if we bring it up.' So ECOSOC will avoid Russia-vexing until its next session."[130]

After much lobbying, the U.S. delegation successfully championed a resolution condemning forced labor at the General Assembly. But the administration's attitude toward this issue, and the UN more broadly, was in transition. Under pressure from the isolationist right—in the shape of the looming Bricker Amendment—to distance itself from international agencies and treaties, Eisenhower repudiated the UN Covenant on Human Rights.[131] The forced labor question remained on the agenda of the International Labour Office throughout the 1950s. Now, though, the roles were reversed: Washington dragged its feet while Moscow took the lead in pressing for a new convention. Where U.S. representatives had hitherto argued that human rights questions were by definition matters for international adjudication, by the mid-1950s Washington had retreated behind the protective shield of sovereignty, refusing to subscribe to any new statute on forced labor on the grounds that it would infringe U.S. federal authority.[132]

TWO CAMPS COMPARED:
NAZI GERMANY AND THE SOVIET GULAG

As a device with which to pillory the Soviets, "slave labor" had a limited life span. In 1956, Washington didn't even deign to respond to an International Labour Organization questionnaire on the subject. But by then, and not merely as a result of governmental prompting, the camps had come to occupy a prominent position in American commentary on and consciousness of Soviet communism.

Historical comparisons proliferated. Constant substitution of the term *slavery* for *forced labor* accentuated parallels with both the empires of antiquity and chattel slavery in the Americas. Many commentators stressed, though, that neither precedent offered an adequate analogue. Nothing in the past foreshadowed the peculiar malignance of a system that was designed not only to extract labor from an expendable underclass but to keep an entire population in a condition of terror, mute in the face of state tyranny. Unlike the slavery of yesteryear, the Soviet gulag fused economic and political functions. When America's delegate to ECOSOC, Dr. Kotschnig, decried the shocking "return in the twentieth century to practices of ancient slavery," he added that Soviet forced labor was "worse than the slavery of the past because it is being used to suppress any dissident political thought."[133]

Those who imagined the Soviet camps as vaguely akin to the plantations of antebellum America (if colder) were chided with a reminder that southern slaveholders had treated their property much better than the Soviet state treated its helots. "One need only read *Uncle Tom's Cabin* and one of the Soviet slave books together to see that conventional chattel slavery was a mild and benevolent thing compared with what has evolved in the 'homeland of socialism,'" opined Eugene Lyons.[134] Chattel slavery, however "shameful and abhorrent," was a "capital investment: the slave owner fed, clothed and cared for his slaves; it was against his economic interests to work them to death," *Life* similarly informed its readers. In communist countries, by contrast, "the state owns the slaves and doesn't mind working them to death in the least. In fact, to destroy individuals and classes which it considers dangerous, it works them to death deliberately, for the death of such slaves is considered no loss. Virtually the only capital outlay required is the cost of seizing the slaves, transporting them to the slave pens and prodding them on with loaded guns until they drop dead."[135] Appraised in this way, the gulag not only attested the monstrosity of Stalin's regime but confirmed the meliorative character of capitalism.

If no historical analogy sufficed to capture the gulag's grim reality, the recent past offered a closer approximation. Indeed, the Soviet camps were rarely discussed without an invocation of their German counterpart. In complex and underappreciated ways, the Soviet and Nazi camps came to define and also distort one another during the early cold war. To a significant degree, American awareness of the gulag was contingent on shifting attitudes toward Germany set in motion by the former enemy's rapid rehabilitation as a cold war partner.

That the Soviet camps should have been twinned with Nazi atrocities in postwar U.S. discourse is hardly surprising. In the spring of 1945, any American who had opened a newspaper or gone to the movies would have seen images shot by Soviet, British, and American photographers as Allied forces liberated the concentration and extermination camps that the Nazis had erected across eastern and central Europe. All five U.S. newsreel companies carried extensive footage from the camps in special issues that jettisoned censorship conventions to offer an unexpurgated depiction of human suffering more explicit than anything American cinemagoers had ever confronted. No one who had seen the naked and the dead ("stacked like cordwood"), the corpses bulldozed into pits, the crematoria, and the showers—the abhorrent architecture and aftermath of genocide—was likely to have forgotten these images. The newsreels themselves expressly confronted cinemagoers with a moral obligation to view. "Don't turn away. Look!" Universal's commentator commanded viewers who might be tempted to avert their gaze.[136] Nor was this imagery confined to newsreels. An exhibit of photographs taken at several Nazi camps, depicting the victims, perpetrators, and German civilian bystanders who had been forced to inspect the "death mills" by American GIs, toured cities across the country in 1945.[137]

Discussion of the Soviet camps in the late 1940s self-consciously evoked some of the most repugnant features of the Third Reich. Sometimes latent, the comparison was frequently more calculated. Since it was the Nazi camps that had finally "roused the conscience of the world" by appealing to "the personal, human angle," exposure of the gulag could be expected to have the same effect, wrote Ralph Murray, the British Foreign Office executive responsible for anticommunist propaganda policy. The Soviet "concentration camps" were "far the most damaging aspect of the communist regime as seen through western eyes."[138]

A moral yardstick for the evaluation of evil, the Nazi camps also supplied a visual register for the "concentrationary universe" that the gulag otherwise lacked. Even as written reports and oral testimony from the Soviet camps amassed in the 1940s and 1950s, what these hidden sites of abjection looked like was largely confined to a few charcoal and pencil impressions smuggled out by survivors or drawn later from memory. In September 1948, *Life* printed a series of sketches by Vladimir Kowanko, a Pole imprisoned in the gulag from 1939 to 1941, who had surreptitiously produced scenes of camp life on cigarette papers. His drawings depicted the guards' calculated brutality; prisoners' backbreaking work in freezing conditions; their crude accommodation in wooden huts; and the degradation of female inmates who had "lost all sense of shame and dignity" (one vignette depicted a bare-breasted woman who had "traded her blouse for bread").[139]

These stark images were a rarity, however. For obvious reasons, no photographs or footage of the gulag circulated during the early cold war. Beyond the reach of cameras, the camps also defied the cinematic imagination. Hollywood's contribution to anticommunism did not extend to a Siberian excursion, even though during a speculative boom in 1948, inspired by the House Committee on Un-American Activities, titles such as *Shanghaied to Siberia* had been optioned.[140] This blank screen left the Nazi concentration camps to provide a projective stand-in, however inadequate the likeness.

The imaginative substitution of German camps for their Soviet counterparts functioned, at one level, through implied association. But parties to the cold war dispute over forced labor often invoked Nazism more directly. When British, U.S., and AFL delegates to ECOSOC likened forced labor in the USSR to that practiced by the Third Reich, Soviet delegates retaliated by pointing out that Josef Goebbels had been the first to level tendentious charges of "slave labor" at the USSR, in an article published in 1936. Turning the Soviet camps into the central plank of their anticommunist campaign, the capitalist/imperialist powers were simply replicating a fascist tactic, drawing on testimony derived from collaborators who had defected from the Red Army's ranks to serve the German war effort. Kravchenko was similarly slurred as a Nazi agent, the author of a vicious anti-Soviet tract published in France during the war. Embroidering the same motif, Moscow couched its refusal to grant access to international investigators as opposition to the violation of Soviet sovereignty by "American *gauleiters*."[141]

Meanwhile, U.S. newspapers reported that Soviet officials in occupied Germany had put vacated Nazi camps back into use, turning Sachsenhausen, outside Berlin, into a depot from which to dispatch German civilians as "slave laborers" to the

USSR.[142] That Stalin had seamlessly picked up where Hitler left off made literal a contention more abstrusely posited in theories of totalitarianism: that the concentration camp represented "the most consequential institution of totalitarian rule"—a crucial marker of the identical ambitions of Nazi Germany and Soviet Russia. In the judgment of Hannah Arendt, totalitarianism's most consequential theorist, the camps' purpose was far more radical in its annihilatory intent than the economic functionalism ascribed to the gulag by analysts like David Dallin. For Arendt, the camps' vital service to the total state lay not in extraction of surplus labor but in reduction of human life to nullity. The camps functioned as "laboratories in which the fundamental belief of totalitarianism that everything is possible is being verified"; their goal was to reduce human beings to mere "bundles of reactions" that could be "exchanged at random for any other." The camps thus represented the terminus of a will to absolute power.[143]

Arendt's metaphysical conception of "radical evil," expounded over five hundred dense pages in *The Origins of Totalitarianism,* was not intended for mass readership. But in less sophisticated form, the notion that Nazi Germany and Soviet Russia bore an essential kinship enjoyed wide circulation and was a mainstay of U.S. cold war ideology.[144] The camps were often invoked as article A in this elision. As intrinsic to the totalitarian state as the hump to the camel (in Dallin's analogy), the camps offered incontrovertible proof of the dictatorships' convergence and as such were often considered in conjunction.[145] Indeed, in 1950 an organization of Nazi camp survivors, led by the French Trotskyist David Rousset, proposed that *only* those who had themselves inhabited *l'univers concentrationnaire* could properly pass judgment on other camp systems that continued to scar the postwar world.[146]

In May 1951, six black-robed men and one woman—drawn from the ranks of the one-hundred-thousand-member International Commission against Concentration Camps—gathered at Brussels' Egmont Palace. "For the first time, the men who lived at Auschwitz and Buchenwald are going to hear men who lived through Kolyma and Magadan," announced Rousset, the proceedings' self-appointed "public prosecutor." After sifting through "mountains of documents" and three hundred written depositions, the jury heard the testimony of twenty-five witnesses, including Margarete Buber-Neumann, Elinor Lipper, another German communist victim of the gulag, and the Spanish Republican commander General Valentin Gonzalez (El Campesino), who had served as a fictional model for Hemingway in *For Whom the Bell Tolls.* After four days of hearings, the tribunal concluded that concentration camps undoubtedly existed in the Soviet Union, though they differed in significant respects from those established by the Nazis. The Soviets did not perform scientific experiments on their inmates, nor did they practice "racial extermination," and since the gulag was not designed to advance a premeditated program of genocide, some inmates obtained release.[147]

These differentiations offered a salutary corrective to the notion that the Soviet and Nazi regimes were exact replicas of one another, stamped from the same mold. The conceit of totalitarianism encouraged this belief, but perceptions of "Red Fascism"'s undifferentiated sameness quickly gave way to a conviction that the Soviet Union was not, in fact, identical to the Third Reich. It was worse. When observers held Stalin up to Hitler's mirror, they didn't invariably see the features blur into the same indistinguishable face of Big Brother; some observed the greater monstrosity of Joseph Vissarionovich. In the estimation of historian Peter Novick, not only did cold war imperatives make "invocation of the Holocaust the 'wrong atrocity' for purposes of mobilizing the new consciousness," but theories of totalitarianism served to marginalize the Holocaust: "Anticipating what some time later became a common theme, *Time* magazine, within a month of the liberation of the concentration camps, was warning against viewing their horrors as a German crime. Rather, they were the product of totalitarianism, and its victims' deaths would be meaningful only if we drew the appropriate anti-Soviet moral."[148]

In making (or insinuating) this case, critics of Soviet communism did not confront an impossible challenge. By the end of the twentieth century, the Holocaust had come to serve as its defining atrocity. Today, Belsen, Auschwitz, Treblinka, and Dachau register in collective memory in a way that Kolyma, Magadan, and Vorkuta do not. But if Nazism has come to epitomize evil, to earlier generations things looked rather different—so different that from 1937 to 1939, confronted with a hypothetical choice between communism or fascism, a majority of Americans expressed greater enthusiasm for fascism. This attitude shifted somewhat after Germany invaded the USSR, though in the fall of 1941 roughly a third of Americans still considered the two governments "equally bad." Only in 1942, with the Soviet Union besieged, did the number of those who said they couldn't decide between two such noxious alternatives fall below 50 percent. At this point, a majority favored communism over fascism, but this grudging preference did not erase a profound mistrust of the Soviet Union among those who had never rallied behind the popular front.[149] Cold war opinion formers didn't have to dig very far to tap this bedrock of latent anti-Soviet sentiment.

While Hitler's atrocities provided an initial benchmark to gauge and envisage the gulag's depravity, as anti-Soviet sentiment surged it became common for American commentators to insist that the Nazi camps were a pale imitation of those across the Elbe. Thus, for example, a journalistic account of the USSR entitled *East of the Iron Curtain*, published in 1946, strove to correct what its author viewed as an egregious misperception: "There is a general belief in this country that Hitler was the originator of the concentration camp system for the muzzling of political opponents. This is a completely erroneous belief. Hitler was not a producer of anything new but a mere copyist of things existing long before him. He copied his concentration camps from the Russians in much the same way he modeled his Gestapo after the Russian Secret Police."[150]

To relativize Nazi atrocities did not require an insistence that "the Russians" *invented* the concentration camp. This line of inquiry risked running into an awkward historical roadblock, after all, since both British and U.S. authorities had established concentration camps in turn-of-the-century imperial wars in South Africa and the Philippines, respectively. More common was the assertion that if Soviet and Nazi crimes were weighed in the same moral balance, the scales would tip against the former. "People who have survived both the Soviet and Nazi concentration camps . . . reluctantly admit that the Soviet brand is more horrible," opined Eugene Lyons. "At their worst, the Brown-Red choice is between a quick death in a gas chamber and a protracted death by overwork, undernourishment and filthy living conditions."[151] Margarete Buber-Neumann, as one such survivor, provided valuable ammunition to those eager to press this point on "all the fellow travelers, the Stalinoids, the double-standard 'liberals' and the phony 'progressives' who have acted as Stalin's stooges."[152] Several American commentators seized on her twin descriptions of Karaganda and Ravensbrück to claim that "Karaganda was worse"—though she herself reminded readers of *Under Two Dictators* that if Karaganda appeared bleaker in certain respects, her experiences of Ravensbrück were hardly typical. There was a salient reason why she survived while many around her, including her dear friend Milena Jesenka, were murdered. Buber-Neumann was not Jewish.[153]

SLAVES TOO LONG: EDITH SAMPSON
AND GERMAN POWS IN THE GULAG

The subordination of Nazi atrocities to an anti-Soviet program points to the role that West Germany's rehabilitation played in shaping "gulag consciousness." Eager to resuscitate a former enemy as a bulwark against Stalin, Washington quickly abandoned its initial insistence on Germans' "collective guilt," jettisoning ambitious plans to de-Nazify the country root and branch. One measure of this rapid normalization of relations lay in shifting U.S. attitudes toward the Third Reich's soldiers. In 1945, General Eisenhower insisted that the Wehrmacht "had been identical with Hitler and his exponents of the rule of force." By 1951 his tune had altered beyond recognition. With Washington maneuvering the new Federal Republic into NATO and the Korean War having paved the way for remilitarization, Eisenhower remarked "a real difference between the German soldier and officer and Hitler and his criminal group."[154]

With this volte-face came an American commitment to press Moscow for the release of German POWs still in its custody years after the war's conclusion. Precisely how many Axis prisoners remained in Soviet camps was hard to determine. Moscow had never issued figures, and in 1949 its news agency TASS claimed that the USSR had released all POWs except for the war criminals, whom it was under no obligation to relinquish. German estimates, by contrast, tended to include every soldier lost on the eastern front, though many had undoubtedly died in combat or perished as a result of maltreatment in (or before reaching) Soviet camps. Unsurprisingly, the disappearance of innumerable German men into the void of Soviet captivity was a galvanic issue in the fledgling Federal Republic—Chancellor Konrad Adenauer asserting before the new parliament that 1.5 to 2 million German prisoners of war remained unaccounted for in September 1949.[155] Of that total, some sixty thousand to one hundred thousand were still being held in the USSR, he maintained. That the misfortune of these Wehrmacht POWs also became an American cause célèbre indicates how far geopolitical priorities had shifted since the collapse of the Third Reich.

In 1950, U.S. delegates to the UN embraced the Axis prisoners' cause, with the twin aims of placating Washington's new German and Japanese allies and supplementing the roster of human rights abuses laid at Moscow's door.[156] The POWs' prolonged incarceration provided another opportunity to focus attention on the Soviet camps. And while the State Department nurtured no expectation that the prisoners would duly be released, they appreciated the "nuisance value" of scratching at this sore spot.[157] As one might expect, U.S. representations offered no indication that these inmates of the gulag—whose illicit imprisonment was likened to the plight of postwar refugees and victims of genocide—were the same Wehrmacht soldiers who, five years earlier, Eisenhower had insisted were indivisible from Hitler. More striking was the fact that the U.S. delegate tasked with pressing the Axis prisoners' case was an African American woman.

In August 1950, Truman had appointed Edith Sampson, a well-connected attorney from Chicago's South Side, as an alternate delegate to the UN in a blaze of publicity that clumsily underlined the strategic calculation behind the decision. Sampson's award of this prominent diplomatic position, announced the *Chicago Daily News,* served as a "dramatic backfire to Russian use of the color issue to set the nations of Asia against this country."[158] What better rejoinder to Soviet slurs that America's "fifteen million American Negroes lived behind barbed wire"—like so many concentration camp inmates—than this accomplished attorney, the first African American to receive a law degree from Loyola University? Blessed with a "hearty manner," an infectious smile, and a throaty contralto "like Tallulah Bankhead's," there was "nothing downtrodden about Edith Sampson," the *Des Moines Tribune* approvingly remarked.[159]

Sampson seemed more than happy to embrace both the official remit and an unofficial role flagged just as prominently. The POW issue provided an ideal platform from which to dismiss Moscow's repeated assertions that oppression inclined African Americans favorably toward communism. "Any white man who's a communist is a fool," Sampson announced briskly. "Any Negro who is a communist is a damned fool." Having yet to overcome the "slave mentality," these pathetic char-

FIGURE 16. Edith Sampson inquires of children at the Wegscheid displaced persons camp in West Germany, "Who wants to emigrate to the U.S.?" United States Information Bureau, May 21, 1951, reproduced by permission of The Schlesinger Library, Radcliffe Institute, Harvard University.

acters hankered for submission to Moscow in place of Massa—a barb "Miss Edith" fired specifically at Paul Robeson.[160] "Anyone who makes a compact with the devil to gain their immediate aspirations will not only fail to win those ends but will share the fate of all others in the hell to which their short-sightedness delivered them," she warned ominously.[161]

Communists, Sampson insisted, were "pushing their own people back into slavery."[162] That the Soviets continued to hold *other* people in slavery merely added grist to her mill. She thus stressed that her ancestry as a descendant of slaves made her not a paradoxical recipient of the POW assignment—a demeaned "subhuman" urging the release of Hitler's foot soldiers—but the natural choice: "We Negroes know something about the slave system. We know that it delivers a kind of security. We know that slaves never have to worry about unemployment, for example. The masters—and many of them were benevolent—look after the essentials of food, clothing, and shelter. And we also know the cruel marks of dictatorship, suppression, and the whip. We know what it is like to be forced to say that a lie is the truth. We know how it feels to be helpless in the face of arbitrary authority. It is a part of our folklore."[163] Sampson's presentations at the UN and her statements to the press constantly emphasized the fittingness of her appointment. Release of these pitiable "captives of war," as she termed them, wasn't an issue of power politics. It was a "human problem" that touched the hearts of people around the world who empathized with the anguish of families aching for their loved ones' return. An unconscionable deprivation of liberty, Axis prisoners' incarceration spoke to African Americans with particular clarity. "Those who themselves have suffered and struggled hardest for their human rights will feel this situation most acutely," Sampson asserted. "They know that the rights of men are involved in the struggle for the rights of any group of men."[164]

In Sampson, then, the State Department had found a woman of color whose condemnation of the "slave world" reverberated with peculiar effect. In Sampson's hands the elision of chattel slavery and communist enslavement was a weapon applied bluntly to both the USSR and that inconsequential minority of African Americans foolish enough to be duped by communist doublespeak. "We Negroes aren't interested in Communism," she was frequently quoted as saying. "We were slaves too long for that."[165]

Despite Sampson's forceful interventions at the UN General Assembly, the Axis POWs were not immediately released in 1950—just as State Department personnel anticipated. Before many more months had elapsed, though, families in Germany and Hungary began receiving mail from imprisoned relatives who had sent no word in years. Then, without advance notice, some men long absent suddenly arrived home. This unobtrusive about-turn was later formalized. Soon after Stalin's death, the Soviets had released twelve thousand POWs, and, with a visit to Moscow in 1955, Adenauer secured the return of ten thousand remaining Germans in captivity. Their homecomings received considerable attention from U.S. news media. Newsreels and illustrated magazines carried numerous stories devoted to this drama: embraces between gaunt, vacant-eyed sons and mothers whose faces bore witness to years of suddenly dissolved grief. Aspiring to the status of universal truth—the fraught rapture of reunion with profoundly altered loved ones—these poignant photographs surely struck a responsive chord with Americans in 1953, a year that saw the mass return not only of German prisoners from the USSR but of Americans from Korea.[166]

Both groups returned with captivity narratives to deliver. Redeemed by their suffering in the Soviet Union, the former Wehrmacht soldiers were valorized in the Federal Republic as sacrificial victims who had performed penance on behalf of all Germans.[167] In the United States, successive waves of prisoner releases provided opinion formers with fresh opportunities to deepen their readers' acquaintance with the Soviet camps—"the Russia only a few know"—based on "50,000 man-years behind the iron curtain":

Without a fork, without a knife,
The shirt reaching only the navel.
Mornings no water, evening no light,
This is the way of Soviet life.

Thus ran a "doleful" verse printed in *Life* in November 1953. The accompanying essay ended with what was related as an "old North German saying," "Better death than slavery." A reformulation of the more familiar North American saying "Better dead than red," this Prussian proverb reaffirmed a message endlessly reiterated in stories from the USSR: that there was no place like home and no place closer to hell than the Soviet Union.[168]

SERIAL REDISCOVERY

In the West the gulag has been uncovered, reburied, and disinterred several times over. The writings of Victor Serge, Boris Souvarine, and Vladimir Tchernavin were easily (and extensively) overlooked at the height of popular enthusiasm for the great utopian experiment that many took the USSR to represent in the 1930s. When the Soviet camps were rediscovered during the early cold war, these pioneering accounts found a fresh audience alongside an expanding collection of scholarly studies and firsthand testaments. Memoirs such as Buber-Neumann's *Under Two Dictators,* Elinor Lipper's *Eleven Years in Soviet Prison Camps,* Vladimir Petrov's *Soviet Gold,* and Gustaw Herling's *A World Apart* graphically charted their authors' progress through the Soviet carceral system. Arrest in the middle of the night was followed by confinement in a dank prison cell; charges of sabotage, wrecking, and "social undesirability" preceded a sentence fixed in advance of the perfunctory trial. Then came a journey by fetid boxcar to a featureless destination in the taiga, where life consisted of endless backbreaking work to the constant accompaniment of hunger—gnawing at the gut, clogging the mind, warping every human interaction.

The way stations of this *via dolorosa* became increasingly familiar to audiences in the 1950s. Yet when Solzhenitsyn's work appeared in the West a decade later, it was widely greeted as a revelation de novo. His oeuvre was soon supplemented by the memoirs of Nadezhda Mandelstam and Evgenia Ginsburg, the autobiographical stories of Varlam Shalamov, and other samizdat works that had migrated west, but Solzhenitsyn still remains credited as the one to illuminate a particularly dismal episode of Soviet history for western readers. During the most recent flurry of attention to the gulag, primed by the publication of Anne Applebaum's Pulitzer-winning *Gulag: A History of the Soviet Camps* in 2003, Solzhenitsyn has again been cast in the role of lamplighter, eclipsing not only other witnesses but any recollection of earlier iterations of camp consciousness. "Even the word 'Gulag' does not appear to have made its entry into our dictionaries prior to the early 1970s," Hilton Kramer proposed in 2003.[169]

As we have seen, though, the acronym GULAG featured prominently on a map distributed by the million, whether or not the word had yet found its way into *Webster's*. Bound tightly to new geopolitical exigencies, awareness of the Soviet camp system expanded during the early 1950s, encouraged by a state keen to spectacularize knowledge production through dramatic trials, witness testimony, and graphic representations. Whether referred to as "the gulags," "slave labor camps," or simply "Siberia," the camps' existence became integral to American understandings of life behind the Iron Curtain, with forced labor sparking public protests against the few Soviet products still imported in the early 1950s.[170]

With little exaggeration, one might claim that almost *all* news from or of the "slave world" in early cold war America gestured toward the gulag if it did not furnish more concrete detail. In the wake of the Kasenkina affair, editorials on the fate of Consul Lomakin and Vice-Consul Chepurnykh expressed certainty that the Kremlin would "reward" these diplomats with one-way tickets to Siberia. (Chepurnykh was indeed sentenced to fifteen years' hard labor, while Lomakin defied expectations by returning to New York as a delegate to the UN.) Anatoly Barsov, the airman who defected to the West only to change his mind, did not need U.S. commentators to engage in ominous speculation on his behalf. In forebodings confided to the diary that *Life* excerpted at length, he correctly anticipated years of "corrective labor" on return to the Soviet motherland he had betrayed.

Escapee stories also constantly conjured the camps. When two Romanian brothers who had spent seven years as "hostages" of their regime arrived in the United States to be reunited with their father in 1954, their second stop—after a handshake from President Eisenhower at the White House—was a trip to see the Dodgers play at Ebbets Field. Nineteen-year-old Constantin opened the game by tossing out the first ball, but reporters also noted another striking moment during the Georgescu brothers' introduction to the great American game. Puzzled by the expression "sent to the showers," the boys were told by their father, "It is like saying they were sent to Siberia"—a remark greeted "with the heartiness of those who no longer have to worry about that possibility," observed the *New York Times*.[171]

As this "hearty" punchline suggests, over the course of the 1950s references to the gulag became so ubiquitous as to assume casual or trivializing form. Cole Porter's opening number for *Silk Stockings,* to take one prominent example, included a throwaway couplet that rhymed "can't write that line / you'll be sent to a mine." Noting a Kremlin crackdown on parents who celebrated the five-year plans by giving their children unorthodox names like "Electrification Pavelovich Popov" and "Cracking Combineov," a wry editorial in the *Washington Post* mused whether any Soviet couple had boldly named their baby "Gulag Gogol" or "Ogpu Samarov."[172] Meanwhile, General MacArthur averred on national radio in 1956 that the present income tax law resembled "the Soviet forced labor system . . . reduc[ing] the citizen for long periods almost to involuntary servitude"—a cavalier analogy that attests the gulag's status as common knowledge, if not MacArthur's acuity.[173]

At the same time, Americans who cared to acquaint themselves more thoroughly with Soviet camp life enjoyed access to rich resources, including the memoirs of Buber-Neumann, Lipper, Herling, and John Noble—an American who had spent years in Soviet camps. Widely reviewed and critically esteemed, these firsthand accounts were commonly serialized or abridged in popular magazines like *Reader's Digest,* the *Saturday Evening Post,* and the *American Mercury.* Their authors also appeared as witnesses in hearings designed to heighten awareness of the camps, such as David Rousset's Brussels tribunal in 1951. Half a century later, their testimony continues to inform studies of the Soviet camps—which makes it all the more striking that many recent commentators should insist that almost nothing was known of the camps in the West before Solzhenitsyn.

How, then, to account for the fact that the gulag has required serial rediscovery, each generation forgetting that it had been at least partly uncovered before? More particularly, how do we explain obliviousness to the camps' early cold war exposure? The answer surely owes much to the way writers of that era typically represented the Soviet camps: as pockets of extremity engulfed by a vast empire of abjection. In other words, the terminally austere universe behind barbed wire was portrayed as differing from communist society at large by only a matter of degrees. Thus an editorial in the *Washington Post* rhetorically inquired (as early as March 1947) "whether life for the great bulk of the population in modern totalitarian states can be distinguished from actual slavery; that is to say, whether the status of the so-called free workers on collective farms and in state factories differs other than materially from the status of workers in the great Soviet penal camps."[174]

Contemporary descriptions of the Soviet bloc constantly stressed the stunted existence of ordinary citizens, not merely prisoners. Launching the Crusade for Freedom on Labor Day, 1950, Eisenhower lamented the fact that "one third of the human race works in virtual bondage." In the eastern bloc, employees were bound to the state, incapable of freely moving from city to city, or switching employment at will as an American worker could. "For his work, he is rewarded with a tiny, crowded place to live, a poverty-type diet and little more than the clothes he wears on his back," wrote Harry Schwartz in 1952. "The life of a Soviet worker today seems to be closer to the bitter phantasmagoria described in George Orwell's *1984* than to the dream world the Bolsheviks of 1917 thought they were fighting to win," Schwartz concluded.[175] Leland Stowe made the point yet more bluntly: "The communist state cannot avoid wholesale enslavement because it is enslavement, per se."[176]

With verdicts such as these typifying popular impressions of the eastern bloc, the gulag was brought into focus only to dissolve again into the larger picture of misery and immobilization, decay and deprivation that characterized the entire "brutalitarian" system (as William Henry Chamberlin dubbed it).[177] The camp provided a compelling metaphor for the constriction of life under communism, in which exile was a permanent condition of being and "Siberia" effectively stood for the whole. But the effect of this synecdoche was to minimize the gulag's character as a distinct "world apart." And though it was easy for westerners to elide the camps with the entire communist system, for inmates the chasm between the zone and what lay beyond often appeared vast, if not utterly unbridgeable.[178]

When heightened attention to forced labor lapsed in the mid-1950s, Americans retained the larger image of Soviet society as prison, without an abiding appreciation of the peculiar society of the camps themselves. Paradoxically, then, the gulag suffered from the totality and fixity with which *slave world* came to define everything east of the Iron Curtain.

First Captive in a Hot War

The Case of Robert Vogeler

A LYNCHING UNDER THE CLOAK OF LAW

When the U.S. businessman Robert Vogeler delivered a fulsome confession of guilt to a Budapest court in February 1950, the scene struck many Americans as both wholly alien and eerily familiar. Exactly a year earlier József Cardinal Mindszenty had stood trial in the same grubby courtroom on similar charges of espionage and sabotage, with the same judge presiding.[1] According to the Hungarian regime, both Vogeler and Mindszenty had confessed in custody before voicing their contrition in public. The guilty verdicts they received surprised no one: life imprisonment for the "traitor" Mindszenty; fifteen years for the "spy" Vogeler. In the Kafkaesque realm to the east of the Iron Curtain, prosecution meant certain punishment. The only question was whether either man would emerge again alive, since sentences in such cases were generally believed to bear the same fictitious relationship to punishment that punishment bore to crime.

That communist courtroom procedure was so wearily predictable heightened the outrage many Americans experienced as they contemplated first the "rape of justice" suffered by Mindszenty and then the "lynching" of Robert Vogeler.[2] Show trials of the past had typically targeted old Bolsheviks fallen from grace, which made it possible to comprehend how Stalin's inquisitors managed to extract confessions to patently trumped-up charges. In the 1940s, the scenario proposed by Arthur Koestler in *Darkness at Noon* gained widespread credence: that interrogators manipulated prisoners' residual revolutionary loyalty.[3] But the Hungarian communists' ability to break a staunchly anticommunist prince primate of the Catholic Church, "a brave and stubborn man, who at every fork in his life proudly took the dangerous, uphill way," required a different explanation.[4] Mindszenty's confession—a "sort of miracle of evil," in *Time*'s opinion—left commentators debating whether he had been drugged, tortured, hypnotized, or degraded by other means. Had the term been coined in 1949, observers would doubtless have described the cardinal as "brainwashed." As it was, many adopted a more severe term for his ordeal: martyrdom.[5]

From Brazil to Brooklyn, Catholic congregations rose in furious protest against Mindszenty's "diabolical treatment." Pope Pius XII was reportedly reduced to tears by the sentence, declaring that God himself had been "driven into exile"—the escapee of all escapees from the eastern bloc. Meanwhile, from the pulpit of Saint Patrick's Cathedral in New York City, Cardinal Spellman thunderously denounced "the world's most fiendish, ghoulish men of slaughter"—"men who as their gods know only Satan and Stalin!" Unless Americans abandoned their "ostrich-like actions and pretenses" and united "to stop the Communist floodings" of their own land, they would face "trickery, torturings, disasters and defeat."[6] Heeding the call, four thousand boys in Catholic Youth Organization uniforms paraded up Manhattan's Fifth Avenue with a fifteen-foot banner proclaiming, "CYO Boy Scouts—Pray for Cardinal Mindszenty."[7] Throughout the country, crowds massed around his crepe-draped portrait in gatherings that were at once requiem rituals and political rallies, occasions for piety and polemic.[8]

If Catholics spearheaded this grassroots mobilization to stem the tide of atheistic communism, others soon rallied to the cause. Editorial comment documented animation in parts of the country that were neither home to sizable Catholic constituencies nor generally sympathetic to "furriners." In a report surveying reaction to Pirogov and Barsov's visit, the *New York Times* found the "overwhelmingly Protestant" Upper South—Virginia, more specifically—discussing Mindszenty's case with "unusual attention." "No recent move by the Communists seems to have stirred up so fierce a reaction as the Mindszenty trial," the columnist concluded, a verdict borne out by the flood of telegrams inundating the State Department and White House.[9] Truman was beset by pleas to attend protests, say prayers, and take more stringent measures to denounce the "shocking totalitarian sacrilege" perpetrated on "the saintly person" of Mindszenty. One veteran went so far as to enclose his Purple Heart in a letter to Truman, explaining that although the medal had always "meant a lot" to him, it would lose its meaning "if Cardinal Mindszenty is murdered without the President at least knowing enough about the case."[10]

Given this ferocity of feeling, we might imagine that a secular restaging of the Mindszenty story with an unknown American businessman in the lead role would elicit a less vehement response. Yet while the arrest, confession, trial, and sentence of Robert Vogeler didn't stir religious sentiment in the same way, popular reaction was, in other regards, more bellicose. Vogeler was, after all, an American. To many fellow citizens it seemed more perplexing and outrageous that Mátyás Rákosi's

FIGURE 17. Mindszenty on trial, February 1949. The cardinal's unnatural expression convinced many observers, like Ferenc Nagy in *Life,* that communists possessed techniques "by which a man's soul can be torn apart and put together again." © The Associated Press.

henchmen had extracted a mea culpa from a vigorous thirty-eight-year-old executive for the International Telephone and Telegraph Corporation than from an ag-
ing Hungarian prelate. What had hitherto been a rather abstract puzzle—the communist "confession complex"—now seemed pressingly personal.[11]

Vogeler's captivity in Hungary thus resonated with especial intensity. But more
than posing an intellectual conundrum—how had they done that, to an *American?*—
the imprisonment of a U.S. citizen behind the Iron Curtain raised practical questions about Washington's response. Since American commentators unanimously
believed the charges against Vogeler to be concocted from thin air, his incarceration appeared nothing but a calculated insult designed to present the United States
as a "'pushover' for the Communist state apparatus."[12] A deliberate taunt of this
sort demanded a vigorous response. In the opinion of Morris Ernst (a prominent
attorney hired by IT&T to defend their assistant vice president), Vogeler was the
"first captive in a hot war" with the Soviet satellites. What, then, did the State Department propose to do to deliver this innocent victim of "legicide" from a fifteen-
year sentence many thought tantamount to an execution warrant?[13]

A clamorous segment of lawmakers, editorialists, and citizens demanded an answer with mounting impatience, their frustration exacerbated by the stalemate in
Korea. Advocates of General Douglas MacArthur's proposal to drop atomic bombs
on China tended to favor similarly drastic measures against Hungary. The Vogeler
episode thus coincided with, and kindled, an increasingly belligerent mood in the
United States.

This twitchy eagerness for a decisive showdown with the forces of communism
was not a purely spontaneous public reaction. Right-wing Republicans stoked discontent by encouraging Americans to regard Washington's failure to prevail as
symptomatic of a profound malaise in government. In short, if America was losing both the cold war in general and the hot war in Korea, the fault lay with pusil-
lanimous policy makers and insidious subversives who deliberately stymied the
prospects of victory. No one peddled this line more tirelessly than Joseph McCarthy.
Vogeler's simultaneous abuse by Hungarian Reds and betrayal by State Department
"pinks" provided the Wisconsin senator with powerful ammunition: an illustration of the constitutive character of the cold wars within and without.

A boon to McCarthy, the Vogeler case contributed to the eastern bloc's alien-
ation from the United States. The IT&T man's plight, in tandem with a handful of
similar cases, sharpened a widespread belief that the satellite states lay beyond the
ken of Americans, as politically unfathomable as they were physically inaccessible.
For John Foster Dulles (later Eisenhower's secretary of state), the "haggard persons" of Cardinal Mindszenty and Robert Vogeler offered a stark illustration of what
Soviet communism was "trying to do to the captive peoples, *en masse*"—deprive
them of "any will power or private thought or self-esteem." According to Republican congressman Jacob K. Javits, the arrest and incarceration of U.S. citizens be-

hind the Iron Curtain proved that the Soviets were "interdicting a part of the world to normal movement and . . . destroying fundamental humanities by which people live."[14] The satellite states increasingly struck U.S. observers as a "brutally archaic" zone where law served to persecute, not protect—a sphere conceived as Asiatic in its cruelty and African in its barbarism, distant in both time and space.[15] For the *New York Times,* the eastern bloc had become "what the world of Mid-Africa used to be," a "new Dark Continent in which civilized man penetrates at the risk of being captured, abused and perhaps killed by savages."[16]

With each successive captivity crisis, perceptions of the eastern bloc's extremity intensified while commerce and communication dwindled. As the first American to face trial behind the Iron Curtain, Vogeler loomed unusually large in the process of estrangement by which the eastern bloc became East, with the satellite states Orientalized as a realm of unbridgeable alterity.

THE ARREST OF AN AMERICAN REPRESENTATIVE

Had the Budapest regime deliberately sought to target a representative U.S. citizen, it could hardly have made a better selection than Robert Vogeler. Patriot, businessman, athlete, and family man, the thirty-eight-year-old IT&T executive personified "a very high type and respected citizen of his country."[17] Born of a German father and French mother who had met on the ship that delivered them both from pre–World War I Europe to the United States, Robert, in turn, met his future wife on a train traveling between Antwerp and Zurich. Within forty-eight hours, he had proposed to Lucile Eykens, a strikingly attractive Belgian "former beauty queen." A few weeks later, once the bride-to-be had broken off with an earlier fiancé, the couple married in Ghent Cathedral.[18]

Despite these exotic elements, Vogeler's personal history conformed to a familiar paradigm of first-generation mobility and assimilation. After schooling in both the United States and Europe, Robert completed his education at Peekskill Military Academy before attending the U.S. Naval Academy at Annapolis. A combination of naval retrenchment and debilitating illness led Vogeler to resign his commission in December 1931. However, as an engineering major at the Massachusetts Institute of Technology, he enrolled in the Naval Reserve before embarking on a professional career in telecommunications and the private pursuit of fatherhood. Robert and Lucile lost no more time in producing a family than they had in rushing to the altar. Vogeler accordingly found himself in 1945, barely thirty-five, the father of two young boys (Bobby Junior and Billy) and a senior manager with IT&T, overseeing its subsidiaries' operations in central Europe from an office in Vienna.

As Vogeler later described it, the Austrian capital differed little from its depiction in Carol Reed's *The Third Man* (1949): rubble strewn and chaotic, teeming with displaced persons, black marketeers, and fractious tripartite occupation forces among whom pilfering and profiteering were not unknown. In the late 1940s, despite the rapid Sovietization of Czechoslovakia and Hungary, traffic still flowed across Austria's northern and eastern borders. Writing in 1949, the popular author Joseph Harsch cautioned American readers against too literal an interpretation of the phrase *Iron Curtain,* pointing out that it was "in fact neither iron nor a tier of provinces consolidated firmly into the Soviet Russian domain." Eastern/central Europe was better understood as "a twilight zone in which many crosscurrents swirl and struggle." The epicenter of East-West tension, this region was neither lost to the West nor inaccessible to westerners—for the time being.[19]

Amidst this turbulence, Vogeler had two principal tasks. One was to prevent Red Army troops from looting IT&T's local subsidiaries and hauling their stripped assets back to the USSR. The other was to counter moves by Rákosi's pro-Soviet regime to expropriate foreign corporations' property and capital without compensation. But these weighty responsibilities didn't stop clubbable Bob Vogeler from joining the International House and the Jockey Club. He also assumed the vice-presidency of the Austro-American Society and honorary chairmanship of the Austro-American Club—networks of influence that Judge Olti, presiding over his trial, would represent as filaments of a dense espionage network.

After his arrest in November 1949, friends described Vogeler as "a skilled sportsman (fencer, marksman, skier, golfer) and a gay companion." Reporters also noted his well-groomed good looks, attested by photographs that showed a debonair, dark-haired figure, sporting a Clark Gable–style moustache and polka-dot tie: a man confident of his own charm, secure in his worldly position.[20] Personal acquaintances anticipated that Bob's detention and subjection to "the various things Communists do to some one they don't like" would "not sit well with American citizens," as a golf partner warned Secretary of State Acheson.[21] That Vogeler embodied such a robust American masculinity aggravated the insult felt by fellow citizens who didn't know the IT&T executive personally but nevertheless recognized and responded to what he represented. Unlike other Americans whose detention passed without comment, his disappearance was headline news from the moment he failed to return home from a trip to Budapest to negotiate the future of IT&T's Hungarian subsidiary, Standard Electric.[22]

At first Vogeler was simply missing, whereabouts unknown. Since other U.S. businessmen had recently been arrested in Hungary and promptly released after confessing to economic sabotage, Vogeler's absence wasn't immediately regarded as critical.[23] For two days, while the State Department pressed for clarification, Budapest claimed to "know nothing" about the IT&T executive. Then came an announcement that the Hungarian government had arrested three businessmen—Vogeler, Edgar Sanders (a Briton), and Imre Geiger (a Hungarian)—on charges of espionage and sabotage. A terse communiqué related that their conspiracy had been foiled when Geiger attempted to exit the country without proper state permission.

Under interrogation, he had revealed an extensive network of subversion that led to his coconspirators' speedy arrest. Wrong-footed by their colleague's betrayal, the others duly confessed. As in the Mindszenty case, the accused were reported to have admitted their guilt within hours of arrest.[24]

From the vantage point of the U.S. Legation in Budapest, the situation now looked grave. Other foreign detainees had been hastily ejected from the country, so Budapest had obviously assigned a different function to Vogeler and the members of his alleged espionage ring. American diplomats speculated that Rákosi's regime was planning a show trial of "spies and saboteurs" to legitimize its nationalization of foreign assets.[25] As hostage and tradable commodity, Vogeler would also provide leverage to extract concessions directly from Washington, his arrest simultaneously sending a strong signal that westerners were no longer welcome in Hungary—a state that seemed determined to immure itself from the West.

In the United States, Vogeler's champions maintained his complete innocence of charges "completely false, completely ridiculous and absolutely without any foundation in fact," as an IT&T representative put it.[26] The State Department maintained the same public line and, within a month of Vogeler's arrest, announced decisive retaliatory steps in response to the "wholly false" charges. Washington also protested Budapest's refusal to grant U.S. consular and legal representatives access to an American prisoner: a direct violation of the 1926 Treaty of Friendship, Commerce and Consular Rights between the two countries. In a sharply worded note of December 20, 1949, the State Department announced it would "until further notice" stamp all its citizens' passports "not valid for travel in Hungary"—a restriction already in place on Americans' travel to Yugoslavia, China, and Albania.[27] U.S. citizens, the note protested, could not visit "without suffering surveillance, arbitrary arrest, and other intolerable molestations at the hands of the Hungarian police authorities and other infringements of their rights"—privations with which Hungarian citizens were all too familiar.[28]

Washington's prohibition on travel did not produce the desired effect, however. On the contrary, Budapest elaborated its charges against Vogeler, Sanders, Geiger, and their alleged associates, offering a fuller public account of their multifarious crimes. These fascist adventurers had "forwarded industrial and military spy reports, technical blueprints which were state secrets, maps and other spy material . . . to their centers abroad." In addition, Vogeler was alleged to have directed economic sabotage by siphoning off profits from Standard Electric, reporting a false balance sheet, and smuggling out foreign currency.[29] These charges assumed a prominent place in the Hungarian press. But staff of the U.S. Legation in Budapest were more alarmed by the fact that the Hungarians' private negotiating position was every bit as adamant as their public posture. The communist line was fixed: Vogeler was a spy, and irrefutable proof would soon convince even U.S. diplomats about his espionage activities, if they weren't merely feigning ignorance.[30]

Confronted with this obduracy, Washington requested that Budapest expel Vogeler. A precedent existed with Ruedemann and Bannantine—two New Jersey oil executives who, on arrest earlier in 1949, had confessed to sabotage and had then been deported. Besides, since the Hungarian government had rapidly pressed ahead with its expropriation of foreign capital during the first month of Vogeler's incarceration, the American captive had surely served his purpose.[31] But Budapest proved immovable. What, then, to do? Since American trade with Hungary was already meager, its severance would hardly place Budapest under intolerable pressure to relent. Lacking an economic weapon, Washington applied diplomatic pressure, announcing the closure of Hungary's consulates in New York City and Cleveland in January 1950.[32] Hungary's consular representative in Cleveland had in fact resigned his post some eleven months earlier in protest at Mindszenty's trial—a gesture that Cardinal Spellman likened to Kasenkina's leap in its bold defiance of "the Soviet."[33] Largely symbolic, Washington's move was nevertheless announced in unusually strident language—a statement dripping with "unconcealed scorn and some sarcasm": "Apparently it has become increasingly inconvenient to the Government of Hungary that the Hungarian people should have contact with representatives of the free world. It suits its purpose, moreover, that these contacts should be severed in a manner which represents quite normal and necessary business practices as 'espionage and sabotage.' Under these circumstances in which any United States businessman or relief administrator in Hungary may be subject to arbitrary arrest and imprisonment, the United States Government has found it necessary to refuse to permit private American citizens henceforth to travel to Hungary."[34]

To show they meant business, U.S. officials refused to let the national table tennis team participate in the 1950 Budapest world championships. The State Department did, however, seek one exemption to its own ordinance, pressing that Morris Ernst be permitted to enter Hungary to defend Vogeler. Budapest flatly refused—"outdo[ing] even Nazi 'justice' in denying rights," Dean Acheson bitterly noted.[35] With diplomatic sparring at an impasse, the trial of Vogeler and his "associates" opened on February 17, 1950.

TRIAL AND TRIBULATION

Any American newspaper reader who had missed reports of a business executive's arrest and confession in Hungary in November 1949 would certainly have seen the bold print announcing Robert Vogeler's trial, just days after the first anniversary of Cardinal Mindszenty's sentence. An American on trial behind the Iron Curtain was indisputably front-page news, interest in no way diminished by the sensation of déjà vu that blinked over the proceedings. As many commentators pointed out, this courtroom drama gave every appearance of being a show—ploddingly scripted, woodenly acted—without constituting a trial.[36] The jaded tone of an observer from the U.S. Legation in Budapest typified the tenor of press coverage more broadly: "The travesty of justice which has unfolded is patently fraudulent. As in other trials in the People's Democracies the 'public' performance of the accused is drama of a quality reminiscent of a high-school play. There have been sufficient rehearsals to enable all members of the cast to handle their cues without too much prompting."[37] Despite innumerable hours of practice, the effect remained as unconvincing as an eighth-grader regurgitating a Shakespearean soliloquy.

A single widely circulated courtroom photograph accentuated the air of amateurish theatricality. Looking every inch the thespian ham, Vogeler appeared heavily made up: pancaked in white, with lips rouged into an exaggerated cupid's bow and eyebrows pointedly arched. As they had during the Mindszenty trial, commentators took physical form as a palimpsest from which traces of torture might be read. Secretary of State Acheson specifically instructed legation staff to report daily on Vogeler's "physical appearance and condition," taking care to "emphasize any aspects indicating physical or mental coercion."[38] Before Vogeler had done more than confirm his date of birth and acknowledged that he understood the charges against him (his only direct participation in the opening day's proceedings), the State Department issued a statement warning that he had likely been "subjected to coercion by intimidation, lack of food, drugging or other forms of mistreatment."[39]

Courtroom photographs of Mindszenty that showed him "terrifyingly altered"— eyes unnaturally widened, staring to the side in exaggerated alarm—had fueled speculation that he must have been drugged into making his confession.[40] Even before the trial, press reports had asserted with complete confidence that when he appeared in court it would be under the influence of actedron—a drug reputed to paralyze "psychic resistance," inducing "the urge blindly to obey the slightest orders."[41] One year later, many expected that Vogeler would appear in a similar trance. Yet over the trial's three-day duration, nothing about his demeanor seemed altogether unusual, heavy makeup aside. Only one U.S. press representative, Alexander Kendrick of CBS, gained access to the courtroom, and his efforts at decryption were inconsistent. In some reports he pronounced Vogeler pale but showing "no sign of strain," while in others he likened the accused to a "frightened rabbit."[42] Faced with such inconclusive visual evidence, reporters turned their forensic skills from dissection of the trial's photographic record to its phonographic transcripts. Audiotapes broadcast by Radio Budapest, then picked up by the BBC's monitoring service, gave American commentators an opportunity to formulate hypotheses based on Vogeler's vocal timbre and cadence.[43]

Mindszenty's courtroom responses had been mostly monosyllabic. Vogeler, by contrast, was assigned a more loquacious role in the proceedings. Day two of the trial was dominated by his testimony, which offered an elaborate account of espionage and sabotage activities orchestrated by the Office of the Director of Intelli-

FIGURE 18. Exactly one year after Mindszensky was prosecuted, Robert Vogeler's trial in the same Budapest courtroom caused alarm. This grainy Hungarian state-issued image was touched up by many U.S. newspapers to give the defendant (right) a theatrically rouged and powdered appearance. © The Associated Press.

gence in Vienna. According to these statements, Colonel Sosthenes Behn, a senior IT&T executive (and personal friend, Vogeler averred, of Truman, Acheson, Morgenthau, and Marshall), was the architect of U.S. intelligence in eastern/central Europe. Merely posing as an IT&T manager, Vogeler had undertaken a wide array of subversive activities with full support from the U.S. Legation in Budapest. Having implicated several individuals in this network, he then detailed the forms this clandestine activity took: from gathering secret data on Hungary's radio communications, radar systems, and uranium processing to encouraging atomic physicists to defect. Furthermore, Vogeler confessed that he had seen to it that Standard Electric produced defective products for dispatch to the Soviet Union and "people's democracies." These criminal acts, announced the state prosecutor, amounted to "the vilest stab in the back of the working people toiling heroically for the reconstruction of their country."[44]

Vogeler delivered his responses in an even tone, neither unmodulated nor impassioned.[45] He made only one emotional appeal: a concluding apology "for the subversive acts . . . committed towards the Hungarian People's Democracy," reprised at greater length the following day when each defendant received a final opportunity to declare their guilt and convey due contrition. More obsequious than his codefendants, Vogeler coupled expressions of sincere remorse with insistence that he had been "treated correctly and fairly" throughout the investigation and trial and that his testimony had been given "freely and openly, without coercion or maltreatment."[46]

American commentators didn't believe a word of it. They duly attuned themselves to Vogeler's hesitations, repetitions, and stumblings—his fluffed lines and peculiar locutions—for confirmation that he was in effect "reading from a script."[47] Very few columnists ventured the possibility that Vogeler might actually have engaged in espionage. Where that possibility was entertained, it was aired only to expose its flimsiness. Would an unmasked American agent, after less than two months' imprisonment, repent so radically as to brand his fellow conspirators "pro-fascist executives . . . and adventurers greedy for money"? It seemed just as unlikely that a CIA spymaster would describe his strategic objective as assisting Hungary's "reactionary elements."[48] And then there was the confession itself, "a statement so queer and unnatural as to make it wholly unconvincing," editorialized the *Nation*. "I was sent here from a big country, America, to Hungary, a small country, to interfere and undermine its efforts in rebuilding and rehabilitating itself from the effects of war," Vogeler announced.[49] If the very fact of an American businessman confessing to such charges were not improbable enough, the curious wording of Vogeler's mea culpa surely confirmed it as an act of ventriloquism—"some sort of diabolical puppet show."[50]

Vogeler's intimates found both the intonation and sentiments wholly incredible. His flat delivery and impassive courtroom demeanor were quite out of character. "Bob is a nervous, quick-moving, high-strung guy," a close friend protested. "He could no more stand calmly and confess than he could fly to the moon."[51] Before the judge, however, the formerly animated IT&T man "stood almost motionless . . . and, in a voice as monotonous as the drone of a litany, confessed to having plotted against the Red regime."[52] Vogeler's wife agreed that her husband was emphatically not himself, enumerating eighty-five instances in which "words had been put in his mouth": "Everything he said was in a colorless monotone. . . . But Bob is an excitable, warm and lively person. Maybe he was drugged, hypnotized or beaten. That wasn't normal, intelligent Robert Vogeler speaking. Nobody knows that better than I." By the same token, nobody could attest more persuasively than Lucile the confession's palpable fraudulence, couched in language Bob had never used in his whole life, "the kinds of phrases in which Communists express themselves."[53] Americans, the *New York Times* ventured on the day of the trial's conclusion, would greet this spectacle with "blank incredulity": "It simply just doesn't add up. Americans don't think that way and don't talk that way." The confession was nothing more than a "stage effect, obviously contrived and obviously rehearsed": "After the Russian purge trials, and especially after the 'confession' of Cardinal Mindszenty, we should know that we are confronted with a political and pseudo legal technique that has quite a different import than anything that exists under our law. It comes as a shock, however, to discover that this technique is apparently effective enough to be used on a person of the stature of Mr. Vogeler. Some terrible thing has taken place behind the scenes of this Budapest spectacle and we are right in feeling horror and loathing when we are confronted with it."[54]

American columnists devoted considerable energy to pondering this "terrible thing"—a U.S. businessman's surrender to communist coercion seemingly more shocking than Mindszenty's capitulation. Had the communists managed to bamboozle Vogeler into believing that he'd really committed subversive acts against a beleaguered "small country"? Or had they secured a semblance of guilt that the penitent merely performed? Either way, unimaginable pressure must have been applied.

Many, including his wife, invoked "torture" and "drugs" as the likeliest explanations for Vogeler's docility. But what form of torture—and what kind of drugs—would leave a man looking so unaltered, yet behaving so pliably in a public courtroom? Even if he had been beaten or doped in captivity, why wouldn't Vogeler use the opportunity of a public hearing to tear up the rehearsed script and repudiate whatever false confessions had been extracted earlier?[55] None of the obvious answers added up. A confidential memo by Gerald Mokma, counselor of the U.S. Legation in Budapest, ran through the various options, casting doubt on all of them.

> Fear . . . Torture and physical punishment can force most men to any extremes, but there appears to be no evidence that actual torture has been employed in former postwar Hungarian trials nor in this one. Fear for the consequences of non-cooperation as it might affect family or friends is usually present in trials of this nature, but Vogeler's family is out of reach and his former associates in Hungary suffered more from his testimony than from lack of it. . . .
>
> Drugs may be partially responsible for his cooperation. He appeared to be fatigued, his voice was subdued, his usual emotional mode of expression was replaced by a dull monotone. But, although drugs can produce fatigue, it is doubtful that they can be used so effectively as to make a strong man jeopardize his freedom and that of others by cooperating at a public hearing.
>
> Hypnosis is sometimes believed to be responsible for the docile attitude of the accused. In the present case the presiding judge, Vilmos Olti, dominated all others in the courtroom. Olti always made sure that he was the center of attention and he was interrupted only infrequently by the public prosecutor or the defense attorneys. But even assuming that Olti has unusual powers, it is inconceivable that he could so enchant Vogeler that the latter would testify to fictitious actions.
>
> Fatigue . . . is applicable in the present case because Vogeler appeared to be ex-

hausted. But in spite of long hours under bright lights, incarceration in cell-boxes so small he could not lie down, long periods of exposure to excessive noise or long periods without adequate food or drink, the question remains is any one of these enough to induce a man to refuse to take advantage of a public hearing in order to expose his captors?[56]

Mokma concluded that the Hungarian state had probably deployed all these instruments in its campaign of attrition, and further that the collapse of this resilient American offered an ominous warning that *anyone* so assaulted would surrender. Others drew the same conclusion, with public dissections of Vogeler's confession less commonly attributing it to drugs than to abusive interrogation techniques. Within a few months, Lucile Vogeler also jettisoned drugs from her account of Bob's transformation.[57] Sidelining the pharmacological explanations of Mindszenty's breakdown, this new emphasis on psychological attrition initiated a shift in popular understandings of communist mind control techniques that would soon inform responses to the treatment and behavior of U.S. prisoners of war in Korea.

Mounting evidence from both the eastern bloc and the People's Republic of China suggested that communist captors preferred less bodily invasive forms of coercion than "old-fashioned torture," targeting the mind rather than the body—but without simply drugging it into compliance. In the wake of Vogeler's trial, several Americans who had been exposed to such techniques ventured hypotheses regarding his treatment. The briefly imprisoned Standard Oil executive Paul Ruedemann related how deprivation-induced despair and long hours of relentless interrogation had led him to sign false confessions—*anything* to alleviate the prison cell's privations.[58] Likewise, Angus Ward, a former U.S. consul in Mukden who had spent thirteen months as a "virtual prisoner" of the Red Guard, informed the U.S. Overseas Press Club of "subtler methods of intimidation that 'break down the human mind.'" While still only clumsily copied by the neophyte Chinese, these strategies were irresistible when deployed by more sophisticated practitioners. "You can't blame Vogeler or anyone else," Ward insisted, "for confessing after being kept in isolation and interrogated continuously for months."[59]

Few did. In fact, as the weeks and months of Vogeler's captivity wore on, many Americans devoted more energy to lambasting the State Department than to blaming either the Hungarian communists or their defenseless American victim for his plight.

VOGELER ENSLAVED AS U.S. PUSSYFOOTS: THE STATE DEPARTMENT ASSAILED

At first blush, Americans' vitriolic condemnation of their own foreign service might seem counterintuitive. However, in the early 1950s denunciation of the State Department became increasingly common—in no small measure thanks to a junior senator from Wisconsin who, eight days before Vogeler's trial began, announced that Acheson's office was riddled with communists and that the secretary of state proposed to do precisely nothing about it.

In the course of an animatedly inarticulate speech delivered to the Women's Republican Club of Wheeling, West Virginia, McCarthy claimed to possess a list of 205 names "made known to Secretary of State as being members of the Communist party and who nevertheless are still working and shaping policy in the State Department."[60] Since his alcohol-clouded powers of recall were as muddled as his syntax, the number of "card carrying communists" reputed to make up the State Department's fifth column constantly changed, as did his targets.[61] Over the next four years McCarthy would take scattershot aim at almost every prominent American institution. But though Hollywood, labor unions, the academy, and ultimately the army attracted the senator's restless attention, the State Department's "lavender boys" remained perennially in his sights. From Wheeling onwards, McCarthy made a particular target of "striped pants diplomats with phony British accents," not only in bed with the Reds but also, so he nudgingly insinuated, with one another. As the archetypal embodiment of the East Coast candy-ass, Dean Acheson was the bull's-eye on McCarthy's dartboard.[62]

Seizing the limelight as America's preeminent Red hunter in February 1950, McCarthy found an especially piquant theme in the "loss" of China. By his account, the world's most populous country had "gone communist" thanks to the influence of a group of fellow-traveling China hands in and around the State Department. Under the sway of subversive Sinologists (Owen Lattimore and John Service in particular), Washington had abandoned Chiang Kai-shek's Nationalists, ushering Mao into power—an entirely avoidable victory for communism. Determined to milk the loss of China for all it was worth, McCarthy adopted the cause of two U.S. servicemen who had been held prisoner in the People's Republic for twenty months, Sgt. Elmer Bender and Chief Machinist's Mate William C. Smith. "The President should say tonight to the Chinese Communists, 'We want these young men out, or we're coming after them,'" McCarthy railed on May 7, 1950. "To those who say that would mean war, the time has come to put our foot down and develop some self-respect. The holding of those two men in uniform is a symbol of complete degeneration of the greatest nation on earth."[63]

By chance, Smith and Bender were released just days later. Vogeler, however, remained imprisoned—a fact that attracted an increasing volume of impassioned commentary along identical lines, less because he was America's "first captive in a hot war" (as Morris Ernst asserted) than because his captivity fit into a pattern of humiliating incarcerations.

Vogeler's confinement coincided with rising unease in the United States over communism's worldwide advance. In rapid succession, several developments dented confidence in America's postwar supremacy: the Soviets' acquisition of a nuclear bomb in 1949, Mao's consolidation of the People's Republic, and the outbreak of war in Korea in June 1950. McCarthy and his cohort both tapped and channeled popular anxiety, coupling American vulnerability abroad with a heightened risk of takeover from within. Far from being self-contained spheres, the "foreign" and "domestic" were dangerously interpenetrated, McCarthy insisted. The United States' overseas setbacks could thus be traced to domestic softness, subversion, and treason, but these corrosive forces in turn ultimately emanated from the Kremlin. Thus by McCarthy's reckoning Stalin's nuclear advances owed much to the betrayal of American "atomic secrets" by Klaus Fuchs, Julius Rosenberg, et al.; Mao's revolution had succeeded thanks to fellow travelers in the State Department; and Kim Il Sung's impunity in precipitating the Korean War had been galvanized by Dean Acheson's vacillating statements as to where America's defensive perimeter lay in Asia.

For those minded to seek it, Vogeler's imprisonment provided further evidence of Washington's inability (or unwillingness) to prevail in the cold war. Irate citizens vented their frustration in letters to local newspaper editors, congressional representatives, and the secretary of state himself. Outrage assumed many shadings, of which the most common was angry disbelief that the Reds dared do this—*to an American*. According to their mother, both young Vogeler boys shared this sense that their father's imprisonment upended the natural order of things in which Americans' inviolability formed a fix point. "They wouldn't dare do anything to my daddy—he's an American," was their common refrain, Lucile told reporters. Meanwhile, Daddy (his memoir later explained) was being rudely disabused of precisely the same notion: "The thought kept running through my mind, *You can't do this to an American*. And then I would laugh hysterically, thinking of the old chestnut about the indignant citizen saying, 'you can't do this to me,' and the gangster's stereotyped reply, 'Oh, yeah?'"[64]

Under international law, only diplomatic and consular representatives enjoy immunity from prosecution by foreign jurisdictions. Yet popular commentary tended to construe any arrest of a U.S. citizen by another state as an affront not simply to that individual but to the populace as a whole, a blow to Americans' presumption of national innocence. In this particular case, even if Vogeler *had* been spying, many Americans would doubtless have held—as contemporary press and political opinion did—that he should simply have been expelled rather than imprisoned.[65] After all, the U.S. government had magnanimously returned a Soviet agent, Vladimir Gubitchev, to the USSR in March 1950 after finding him guilty of espionage in the Judith Coplon case.[66] But since Vogeler was *not* a spy, his fellow citizens believed, Budapest appeared to be simply dressing up its crude extortion tactics with a "pseudotrial."

In many quarters, the rage provoked by this "gangsterism" was less potent than the ire animated by Washington's apparent passivity. Thanks to Hollywood movies and other cultural cues, Americans already knew that communists didn't play fair, that Red subversives favored the same methods as the criminal underworld.[67] However, it was neither customary nor conscionable that Washington would meekly acquiesce to bullying and demonstrate such impotence when confronted with the captivity of a virile American. Even before the trial, Americans expressed concern that the State Department was *permitting* Stalin's Hungarian stooges to detain Vogeler and extract a confession "by the usual Communist methods."[68] America's global prestige hung in the balance: "What has happened to our proud country that its citizens can be kicked around like that?" one enraged Manhattan couple enquired in the letters page of a local paper.[69] "No wonder the Communists consider us soft and decadent when we sit supinely by and allow our citizens to be treated in this manner," another "Indignant Citizen" opined. In more pugnacious vein, Mr. and Mrs. Walter Braun (of Beverly Hills) cabled the State Department in protest "that American citizens are allowed to be kidnapped and made Midzentys [sic] by Communistic Huns. These United States must take action to Free Vogeler."[70]

The Brauns were not alone in their conviction that securing Vogeler's release—thereby reaffirming U.S. global supremacy—was merely a matter of will. "Would to God that we had a Teddy Roosevelt in the White House. He would find a way to stop such work of the devil," fumed the writer of an anonymous letter to the *Los Angeles Times*. Self-assertion would assuredly produce results if only the State Department exhibited more of the Rough Rider spirit. "The Vogeler case demands action—drastic action—even to the extent of severing all relations, diplomatic, commercial and otherwise, with the Government of Hungary," Congressman T. Vincent Quinn urged Acheson.[71] Others took their indignation a step further, announcing that Truman's administration should *force* Budapest to release a wrongly imprisoned American even at the risk of sparking war—a posture identical to McCarthy's vis-à-vis the two U.S. airmen held in China. Vogeler's golf partner N. Raymond Clark captured the increasingly combative mood: "I think none of us wants to go to war, but I think, too, none of us is willing to have Hungary granting our citizens visas and then seizing them and maltreating them and holding them, contrary to all honest principles of international law."[72]

Segments of the press actively promoted such sentiments. On the anniversary of Vogeler's arrest, the Scripps-Howard group launched a campaign for his release with a series of articles in the *New York World-Telegram* under the provocative banner, "Vogeler Enslaved as US Pussyfoots." Yoking Acheson's ineffectual diplomacy to his etiolated masculinity, these articles dripped disdain for his failure to "flex the biceps." The secretary of state had made only "feeble protestations" and "dainty protests"—a theme taken up by various petitioners who rued his wholly un-American and unmanly posture of "wilting before every bluff."[73] While Acheson minced, Vogeler languished, not merely imprisoned but *enslaved*. Subject to enforced indolence rather than forced labor, the prisoner was hardly a human chattel of the Hungarian state, but the whisper of "white slavery" was too compelling for the Scripps-Howard press to pass up. Where the *New York Times* likened the eastern bloc to equatorial Africa—the new "dark continent"—the *New York World-Telegram* imaginatively relocated Hungary somewhat further north, along Africa's Mediterranean coast.

The Barbary motif struck a popular chord, amplified by Hollywood's concurrent rediscovery of North African corsairs and American captives in movies like Charles Lamont's *Slave Girl* (1947), Lew Landers' *Barbary Pirate* (1949), and Will Price's *Tripoli* (1950). The analogy not only accentuated Vogeler's torment at the hands of barbarians—transmuting imprisonment into slavery—but provided another stick with which to beat the State Department. In most analogists' hands, whether invoking the Tripolitan War of 1801–5 or a showdown one hundred years later, the moral remained identical: in years gone by, the White House took vigorous action when bandits enslaved Americans, demonstrating to renegades the folly of interference with American persons and property. Thus in 1804, after the crew of a grounded American frigate, the *Philadelphia,* had been taken captive by the bashaw of Tripoli, Jefferson authorized William Eaton to invade this Ottoman province and topple its ruler rather than deliver a ransom of $1.69 million that exceeded the fledgling republic's entire military budget.[74]

This piece of derring-do did not, in fact, succeed. While Eaton's band of marines straggled across the desert, an American diplomat negotiated a treaty and reduced ransom payment to the bashaw. It fell instead to Stephen Decatur to end U.S. tribute payments to the Barbary states after the War of 1812, warning the Algerian ruler, "If you insist in receiving powder as tribute, you must expect to receive balls with it."[75] However, those eager to recall Eaton's bravery on the "shores of Tripoli" as proof that national muscularity had subsequently turned to flab rarely bothered with such historical niceties. Or they seized on a later Barbary captivity for a rousing illustration of "how different things were back in 1904," when TR ruled the roost. As the *New York World-Telegram* explained,

> Then an American citizen, Ion Perdicaris, was waylaid on the road and held for ransom by a Morroccan bandit named Raisuli. John Hay, then Secretary of State, didn't sit around wringing his hands. He got quick action with a seven-word cable, "We want Perdicaris alive or Raisuli dead!" a message which thrilled all America and caused its citizens to hold their heads higher.
>
> True, Secretary Hay was dealing with a private outlaw and Secretary Acheson is confronted by an outlaw government. He cannot demand "Vogeler alive or Hungarian communism dead!" But surely American resourcefulness has not dwindled to the point when this country must take everything lying down.[76]

The columnist appreciated that some latitude was required to cast Rákosi as Raisuli and may have intuited that gunboats would prove less persuasive when aimed at a landlocked state like Hungary. It is unclear, though, whether this author realized the Perdicaris incident was a "pseudo-event," staged, scripted, and manipulated in different ways by its key protagonists.[77]

For Theodore Roosevelt's White House, the kidnapping of a U.S. citizen overseas provided serviceable stuff with which to spice up a lackluster Republican National Convention, and Hay seized it as an opportunity for theatrical bluster that would produce a ringing American victory at very little cost. The ruse seemingly worked. Hay's mantra passed into history as a refrain to be reprised whenever American puissance was impugned by a hostage crisis, as it appeared to be with Vogeler's captivity in 1950, and again during the Iranian Embassy siege of 1979–81, when critics taunted an "impotent" President Carter for allowing America itself to be "held hostage."

But the received version of Hay's ultimatum presented to Americans in 1904, in 1950, and in 1980 obfuscated several pertinent details. For one, Hay's posture was not so combative as the famously bellicose injunction suggested: the second sentence of his cable warned the consul general *not* to "land marines or seize customs without the Department's specific instructions." As it happened, neither tactic was required. Perdicaris had been released before Hay's message was even wired. Raisuli, keen to advance his own domestic political ambitions, had already achieved his objective of putting the Moroccan government's weakness on embarrassingly public display. For his part, the liberated Perdicaris proved most sycophantic toward his former captor—as well he might, since it seems he had been so eager for the limelight as to connive in his own captivity. In American publications, Perdicaris lauded Raisuli's "natural dignity" and "singular gentleness" with an ardor symptomatic of what would later be called the Stockholm Syndrome. Like its most famous sufferer, Patty Hearst, Perdicaris was exorbitantly wealthy, a millionaire with vast assets in South Carolina garnered in the gas illumination business. But one crucial difference set Perdicaris apart from Hearst: he was *not* a U.S. citizen. (He had in fact repudiated his citizenship to avoid conscription into the Confederate army and confiscation of his property.)[78]

The whole episode, then, was thoroughly bogus. Perdicaris, the American saved by Hay's saber rattling from the clutches of a Riffian ruffian, turned out to be an entrepreneurial Greek who appreciated that Barbary captivity could be lucratively commodified by selling his story. But a narrative sufficiently flexible to be refashioned by Hollywood in 1975 with Sean Connery as Raisuli and Candice Bergen as a gender-swapped *Eden* Perdicaris in John Milius's *The Wind and the Lion* (1975) was more than malleable enough for the *New York World-Telegram*'s purposes in 1950. As an emotional call to arms, the analogy seemed to have the desired effect. Taking up cudgels on Vogeler's behalf, Jacob Javits, avowedly inspired by the Scripps-Howard columns, wrote to Acheson: "The Government cannot let the matter rest . . . but must find some way of going on from there in vindication of its own dignity and determination to protect its own citizens from injustice at the hands of foreign governments. This is a doctrine in our Nation as old as freedom of the seas and as essential to national survival and security. The United States was far weaker than it is today when one of our early Presidents was prepared to commit American armed forces against Moroccan pirates when facing a similar situation."[79] A similar situation? Well, if one overlooked almost every salient detail about these two situations. Literalism, however, was scarcely the point of invoking Hay's famous bluster. Providing no obvious prescription for contemporary policy, since (as William Henry Chamberlin pointed out in the *Wall Street Journal*) "the Barbary pirates did not have the Kremlin behind them," the Perdicaris incident was less a historical glove that fit than a gauntlet to be thrown down.[80] With the chant "Perdicaris alive," Acheson was taunted by his failure to measure up to John Hays.

As for an appropriate response to Hungary's "blackmail," Vogeler's young sons had the right idea, their mother informed the *World-Telegram*. "They write me little notes which they leave around the house. They illustrated one of these notes with a cartoon of a bomb dropping on the home of Hungarian Communist boss Mátyás Rákosi."[81] Bobby Jr. and Billy were not alone in their enthusiasm for such a move.

FAMILY AFFAIRS AND AFFAIRS OF STATE

Historically, American captivity narratives have served a variety of purposes: as Puritan jeremiads, calls for religious rededication, armor for national righteousness, invitations to Indian hating, and/or titillating gothic fantasies. In each variant, though, these cautionary tales are commonly domestic dramas that accentuate the desecration of households. Framed in this way, captivity appears less an ordeal of individual liberty deprived than of kinship attenuated. With bonds of affection and allegiance stretched thin or severed altogether, captivity represents a violation not only of particular homes but of *family* itself. The pathos of sundered spouses and parentless children endows a sentimental genre with much of its affective potency, since "family" is often understood as a synecdoche for "nation."

Mindszenty's captivity clearly did not lend itself to such domestication. Felix Feist's feature *Guilty of Treason* (1950) vainly sought to inject some female interest into the cardinal's story by depicting the torture of an attractive schoolteacher who had protested his mistreatment.[82] But most other narrators emphasized Mindszenty's isolation from mortal attachments, depicting a Hungarian primate who suffered alone—or alone (his coreligionists trusted) but for God. While the latter appeared incapable of divine intervention on the cardinal's behalf, Vogeler had a compelling champion: his beautiful, platinum-haired wife, whose movie-star aura, razor-sharp cheekbones, hourglass figure, and palpably sexual presence seemed made for the cameras. Appealing to a conservative press eager for ammunition against Acheson, not least when fired by an unusually photogenic blonde, Lucile kept her husband's plight in the headlines throughout his imprisonment.

From the outset, news media cast the Vogeler story as a simultaneous assault on family and nation, allotting Lucile a starring role that became more militant as time went by. Initially, she played the tearful supplicant, begging first Truman and then Rákosi to release her beloved spouse: "I appeal to Hungary to send my husband back. It should take pity on me because I love him and my children need him. If they have hearts in Hungary they won't do this to us."[83] She also provided a domestic alibi that undermined the charge that Vogeler had been a spymaster in Illinois during the war. Bob was "too busy washing diapers and doing war work in Chicago in 1942 to get mixed up with any FBI agents," Lucile insisted.[84] Aged eight and nine in 1950, the two infants who had kept their father so busy—now brush-cut, all-American boys in matching plaid shirts—featured prominently in press stories. When Vogeler's fifteen-year sentence was announced, the younger son reportedly exclaimed, "But I'll be an old man by then!" as the implications of his father's prolonged absence sank in.[85] No less heartrending was the picture painted by the *World-Telegram* of Mr. Vogeler senior: a broken figure, clutching his bathrobe, alone with the awful news of his son's imprisonment—let down and ignored by his government, and far removed in Queens from his stricken daughter-in-law and young grandsons in Vienna.[86]

Lucile, however, was not one to take the violation of her family "lying down." Having failed in her attempts to move Rákosi (even when she seemed to offer herself up to the Hungarian state as ransom for her husband), she targeted leaders closer to home, all the while maintaining that she was "uninterested in politics." The Scripps-Howard group, however, appreciated the precise overlap between her position and theirs. Adopting her as their plucky belle, they helped enthrone her as the State Department's bête noire, for her ire (like theirs) was increasingly trained on Acheson's shortcomings and pusillanimity.

This theme took some time to develop. Lucile Vogeler initially responded positively to a May 1950 meeting with Acheson in London: "I now have certain knowledge that something is being done for my husband, and by the highest authorities," she related, noting that the secretary of state had been "most charming."[87] The mood soured, though, when rumors of her husband's impending release proved premature and negotiations over his fate lapsed into abeyance. That August, Lucile publicized her desire to meet Truman in person.[88] By November 1950, one year after Vogeler's arrest, the *New York World-Telegram* reported that she had been driven to a nervous breakdown by the shameful way in which she'd been "kidded along" by a State Department that treated her, and insisted she consider herself, as a widow.[89]

Four months later, in March 1951, the same paper ran a series of five articles ("in her own words") under the banner "I Want My Husband Back," with the ex-

156 COLD WAR CAPTIVES

plicit goal of galvanizing Washington into renewed action. Politically, the central charge was that the State Department had refused to apply economic sanctions against Hungary, despite Lucile's repeated promptings.[90]

Lucile's wrenching situation—bereft of her husband, betrayed by her state—made for a powerful human-interest hook. As *Life* magazine made clear, a single mother, no matter how valiant her attempts to master her sons' train set, was no substitute for a missing father.[91] Columnists further encouraged readers to regard Vogeler's plight as a consequence of Washington's deficient paternalism. Failing to discharge its proper protective responsibilities toward an imperiled citizen, the U.S. government forced Vogeler to replicate its own stance as neglectful, absent parent. "There are many who believe if it was one of your kin, you would have made it your business to get a release immediately," one disgruntled citizen rebuked Acheson, deploring his failure to appreciate what was owed to all members of the extended national family, and summoning *the* Father to corroborate the point. "I doubt very much that the Good Lord would condone the work done by your department in the past, judging by the results."[92]

But how justified were mounting complaints that the State Department had "done nothing" to secure Vogeler's release? Diplomats aside, did anyone know exactly what was, or was not, being done on the prisoner's behalf? Negotiations were necessarily conducted out of the public eye, since premature publication of possible terms threatened to undermine any compromise. An agreement tentatively reached in June 1950 did in fact unravel following press speculation that the price agreed for Vogeler's release was return of the Crown of Saint Stephen. (Looted from Hungary by the Nazis, this sacred object had been in the custody of U.S. military authorities in Germany since 1945.) When this rumor was circulated—*Life* devoting it a whole-page photo spread—a deal that would have freed Vogeler after four months of his fifteen-year sentence collapsed.[93]

Since the crown had *not* been under negotiation hitherto, the stakes were duly raised, leaving U.S. officials to wonder whether the Hungarian regime had purposely planted this piece of misinformation to derail Vogeler's release. But if Budapest wanted the crown, why hadn't it upped the ante more directly at an earlier stage? And why would apostles of atheism *want* an object revered by members of a church they were so keen to destroy? To prove that a "small country" could dictate whatever terms it pleased? To highlight U.S. reluctance to restore Hungarian property "looted and stolen by fascists"? Or did this new demand for the crown (formally tabled by the Hungarians in September 1950) simply stem from "a pinch of pure cussedness" that was "in the recipe for every Moscow brew," according to the U.S. minister in Budapest, Nathaniel Davis?[94]

American diplomats in Budapest struggled to understand precisely what the Hungarians were up to and what larger Soviet scheme lay behind the increasing number of westerners arrested and imprisoned in the eastern bloc.[95] Their strongest initial impression was that the Hungarians genuinely believed Vogeler to be a spy and were quite serious in trying to convince legation personnel of his guilt. But U.S. negotiators weren't persuaded that the administration of justice ("communist style") was the Hungarians' sole, or even primary, purpose. Symbolic politics seemed more significant. Domestically, "Vogeler-the-spy" would serve a useful function in fueling popular anti-Americanism, with Hungarians encouraged to believe that agents of imperialism existed everywhere in their midst, sabotaging socialist reconstruction. For western observers, the trial was surely intended to transmit a different message, akin to Budapest planting a giant "KEEP OUT" notice at the Austro-Hungarian border. On this reading, Rákosi's harassment of foreigners aimed to rigidify the Iron Curtain, terminating commerce between the blocs, a move driven more by fear of westerners importing "dangerous" information into Hungary than by paranoia about foreign agents extracting it.

Show trials generated powerful effects. But at bottom, U.S. diplomats interpreted Vogeler's imprisonment as a form of "blackmail."[96] The Hungarian regime's apparent willingness to relinquish foreign prisoners confirmed American analysts' sense that Vogeler and Sanders (his British "associate") were "no more than commodities to be exchanged for the highest acceptable price."[97] More surprising was the relatively low price Budapest initially seemed willing to accept.

The first of Budapest's demands related to Voice of America broadcasts transmitted into Hungary from Munich. Radio broadcasting was a profound irritant in East-West relations—calculatedly so on Washington's part. To Budapest, America's erosion of its monopoly over the means of communication was all the more irksome because Voice of America transmissions encroached on the frequency assigned to Hungarian state Radio Petofi. In practice this "blanketing" meant that Hungarians could hear neither Petofi nor Voice of America through a wall of white noise. Washington, while concerned about the appearance of caving in, ceded nothing material when it agreed to transfer Voice of America broadcasts to another frequency—a move American engineers favored in the interests of audibility.[98] At no point (contrary to press reports) did U.S. diplomats agree to the complete suspension of Voice of America broadcasts to Hungary, a substantive concession they would never have countenanced.

The size of the U.S. Legation in Budapest formed a second area of negotiation. Some American officials believed that this represented *the* core issue for their opposite numbers. Here too the Hungarians sought to curtail western influence, seeming particularly eager to rid themselves of American military personnel. Initially, the State Department bridled at this request to trim the size of its legation staff, fearing that any reduction not only would be branded an act of "appeasement" by Republican critics but would consign the rump of U.S. representatives to "innocuous desuetude."[99] This position soon softened, however. The State Department acknowledged that the legation was indeed overpopulated with "alien staff," some of whom were surely Hungarian counterintelligence agents. Far from damaging U.S. interests, pruning the legation staff represented a sensible precautionary move.[100]

By June 1950, a mutually satisfactory arrangement had been brokered along these lines—only to disintegrate in the face of press speculation over the crown. Frustrated by this setback, the U.S. head of mission in Budapest, Nathaniel Davis, bitterly remarked that he had been "played for a sucker." The communists, he now suspected, had been insincere all along. It was, after all, impossible to divine the intentions of dialecticians whose (il)logic was seasonally restyled by the Kremlin's ideological couturiers.[101] But if U.S. diplomats found themselves at a loss in fathoming Budapest's intentions, Vogeler scarcely struck them as an open book either. In public, they proclaimed his innocence. In private, however, legation staff expressed skepticism that Vogeler's word could be entirely trusted.

In the telegrammed back-and-forth between Budapest and Washington, State Department officials candidly addressed a question that hovered in the air during Vogeler's trial. Why did a man who looked "approximately normal" offer such an abnormal confession? Davis considered it possible that Vogeler had cut a deal with the regime, agreeing to perform the part of repentant spy in return for an early release. Collusion would explain the lack of visible markers of duress, though it begged questions as to *why* Vogeler would enter into such an arrangement. Did cowardice—or, more kindly put, desperation—offer sufficient explanation?[102] (Vogeler had reportedly remarked before his arrest that he would confess to anything rather than undergo torture.)[103] Or had the IT&T executive engaged in criminal activity—black marketeering, perhaps, or currency speculation—that left him vulnerable to blackmail? Apprehended by the Hungarian authorities, Vogeler might have agreed to assume the show trial's starring role of imperialist agent and saboteur on the understanding that he would be released soon thereafter.[104]

The other possibility was that Vogeler had been caught conducting the activity for which he was subsequently tried: spying. U.S. intelligence agencies insisted otherwise to legation staff, though the latter knew him to be on friendly terms with various intelligence personnel.[105] Having taken a fine-tooth comb to Vogeler's courtroom testimony, Davis concluded that at least some of it had a "certain basis in fact," however much was distorted or invented. For instance, not only had Vogeler informed American intelligence agents about a Hungarian contract negotiated by the Dutch firm Phillips, but he had furnished details of the Tungsram plant—an episode elucidated in the courtroom. Moreover, Davis learned that these agents had specifically *instructed* Vogeler to gather this information. Was Vogeler paid to do so, or did he regard such favors as part of the warp and weft of reciprocity that bound expatriates together?[106] Inaccuracies in his courtroom account of American espionage in eastern/central Europe inclined State Department officials against concluding that the IT&T executive was formally on any civilian or military intelligence payroll.[107] Nevertheless, whether he was rewarded for information or had volunteered it over cocktails, Vogeler had clearly operated in that twilight zone where routine local fact-finding (of the sort that both businessmen and diplomats necessarily undertake) shades into clandestine acquisition of sensitive material—or "spying."

Vogeler was not, then, as innocent of all espionage involvement as American press and governmental pronouncements on his case insisted. Yet whatever doubts it entertained, the State Department was more energetic on his behalf than its critics either appreciated or cared to admit. Neglect was reserved for errant U.S. citizens suspected of being *Soviet* agents, or of harboring procommunist attitudes, such as the Field brothers, who had gone missing in Poland and Czechoslovakia shortly before Vogeler's arrest and who remained imprisoned longer with far less diplomatic exertion on their behalf.[108]

By contrast, Vogeler's case formed "the dominant issue in US-Hungarian relations," personally handled by Nathaniel Davis, who engaged in repeated rounds of talks.[109] Options were limited, however. The threat of escalation that critics clamored for—"Vogeler alive or Rákosi dead!"—was a bluff too easily called when the U.S. government had no intention of risking war over this issue, as Budapest surely knew. Furthermore, too assertive an American stance might substantiate the communist propaganda line that Budapest had unmasked a major U.S. intelligence asset that had to be recovered at any cost. Davis thus had to tread a delicate line between assertion and "appeasement," conciliation and "collapse." Whatever he did to secure Vogeler's release, it couldn't appear to have been *bought,* since those fond of Barbary analogies were quick to brandish another slogan more rousing than historically accurate: "Not one cent of tribute."

In striking this balance, the State Department's efforts were beset—not bestirred—by those of Lucile Vogeler. A sympathetic press represented her as a righteously (and rightfully) indignant wife and mother, tenaciously battling for her husband against government indifference. But there was a more complicated backstory here too. Far from encouraging the State Department to take ever firmer action against the Hungarians, she pleaded with diplomats neither to cut off diplomatic relations nor to be "too tough on Hungary." She herself, it seemed, was no great respecter of the "Not one cent of tribute" approach to captives' redemption. Far from it, she attempted (behind the State Department's back) to bribe Hungarian Communist Party officials into freeing her husband and doubtless feared that tough talk might prejudice her chances of success. From the legation's vantage point, her increasingly antic behavior—which included scheming with dubious Viennese underworld figures to spring Vogeler from jail in return for $2 million of strategic war materiel (courtesy of IT&T)—threatened to do far more harm than good to her husband's prospects for release and U.S.-Hungarian relations alike.[110] A stern warning that she desist from "such contacts and negotiations" met the stubborn response that she had "no intention of refraining from any contacts or associations that might lead to the release of her husband."[111]

RETURN FROM CAPTIVITY:
THE HAPPIEST MAN ALIVE

When Judge Olti sentenced Vogeler to fifteen years' imprisonment on February 21, 1950, Morris Ernst (the attorney who wasn't permitted to represent him) expressed doubt that the unfortunate victim of "legicide" would ever be seen again. Others were equally pessimistic. With press reports constantly harping on State Department inaction, few Americans expected the announcement that emerged from Budapest on April 21, 1951: Vogeler was about to be released. The Scripps-Howard group claimed instant credit.[112] Making common cause with Lucile Vogeler, its reporters had blasted "the lethargy of the nation's diplomatic chiefs," finally jolting them into action. The *New York World-Telegram* went so far as to propose a direct causal relationship between its recent series of articles showcasing her plight and Vogeler's impending freedom.[113] Needless to say, from the State Department's perspective this felicitous outcome owed nothing to Lucile's public posturing or her clandestine maneuverings in central Europe's shady demimonde and everything to painstaking diplomatic efforts to broker a mutually satisfactory arrangement. Until Vogeler finally arrived back in Vienna, Nathaniel Davis professed himself "nervous as a kitten on a hot stove."[114]

In April 1951, the Hungarians proved willing to accept almost identical terms to those agreed the previous June, the Crown of Saint Stephen vanishing from discussions as unexpectedly as it had surfaced. Somewhat to American negotiators' surprise, Budapest settled instead for smaller-scale restitution of Hungarian property and claims still outstanding from the war.[115] Washington had already switched the frequency on which Voice of America broadcast and had simultaneously trimmed the legation staff. The only new condition was an agreement to permit the reopening of the Hungarian consulates in New York and Cleveland and to lift the prohibition on Americans' travel to Hungary. Anticipating criticism, State Department officials assured skeptics that these moves didn't represent substantial concessions. The consular shutdowns and travel embargo had always been temporary expedients, displays of displeasure enacted with a view to their subsequent lifting once Budapest relented.[116]

Despite this clarification, much confusion surrounded the terms of Vogeler's release. Some headlines and editorials spoke of a "ransom," even suggesting that the crown had been exchanged for the prisoner. An editorial in the *New York Times* regretfully credited Budapest with a "successful application of the highly developed Communist art of international blackmail."[117] By the State Department's own reckoning, though, the concessions they had made for Vogeler's release were remarkably inconsequential. In the end, Budapest appeared more interested in extracting symbolic capital from their captive's imprisonment than in securing material recompense for his release. By April 1951, Vogeler had obviously done his work. He was free to go home.

As soon as word of his imminent release was issued, Vogeler's return was breathlessly anticipated. Lucile injected a frisson of sexual expectation into the proceedings as she confided to reporters that she had "unpacked some beautiful nylon nighties and a pale blue negligee" for her husband's return, hinting at one very particular blessing of freedom.[118] No wonder that back on "free soil," with his wife in his arms ("Bob, oh Bob!"), Vogeler proclaimed himself the "Happiest Man in the World." "Gosh—at last!" chimed Bobby Junior, completing the tableau of blissful family reunion.[119]

But all was not well. Homecoming, the captivity narrative's climactic moment, was rarely an occasion of undiluted joy. The very event that promised to complete a sundered community also threatened to destabilize it, for the individual who returned was never quite the same person who had been taken away. Eyed warily by neighbors as a possible source of cultural contamination, the redeemed captive was just as likely to rebuke a community that had proven unequal to the challenge of barbarism.

What was true of canonical captivities was also true of Vogeler's. Haggard and overwhelmed by tumultuous emotion, Robert contrasted starkly with his radiant wife. Reporters described him as pale and sunken-eyed, his hair thinner and frame lighter than in November 1949. The man returned by the Hungarians was a "shattered, twitching wreck."[120] "I have never seen anyone in war look worse shellshocked," opined a physician who examined him.[121] Talking briefly to the press corps gathered outside the U.S. Legation in Vienna, Vogeler explained that he had not "seen or talked with a friend" in seventeen months and now felt like "a man with a bad case of jitters."[122] Struggling to appreciate that the cold war had escalated—with approximately five thousand American prisoners in Chinese and North Korean hands by April 1951—Vogeler's stunned response was "You mean there's real fighting?"[123] Asked by thronging reporters for an initial appraisal of his Hungarian captors, the newly redeemed captive managed to stutter, "Those dirty bastards . . . " before lapsing into speechlessness.[124]

That trenchant verdict made for a good headline, but reporters wanted more. After all, Vogeler emerged from the eastern bloc's terra incognita with a definitive solution to the riddle that had perplexed his fellow citizens in February 1950: how the communists had extracted his confession and what they'd done to leave him in this pitiful state. Over the course of successive public appearances, both in Vienna and on return to the United States (where he arrived at Idlewild Airport on May 1, 1951), Vogeler's demeanor caused intensifying alarm. While his sons were reportedly delighted to be free from constant worry about "the Russians"—absorbed with an as-

FIGURE 19. "Back from the dead." Robert Vogeler's haggard appearance on release in April 1951 offered a study in contrasts with Lucile's expression of ecstasy. Photo by Red Grandy. Used with permission from the *Stars and Stripes*. © 1951, 2009 *Stars and Stripes*.

tonishing new phenomenon, television!—their father was tearful, trembling, inarticulate. At several press conferences, he appeared incapable of controlling his bodily tics or of consistently marshaling language in the service of meaning.[125]

Communist captivity had left a man noted for his "erect" carriage "sagging all over," his wife related, suggesting a degenerative condition that even her sheerest negligee couldn't cure.[126] "Oh, what they must have done to him!" Lucile lamented. "He was such a strong man, and now he is weak as a baby and so nervous. He can't bear to have anyone behind him."[127] Of this inferior substitute, Mrs. Vogeler ventured, "If I had met him on the street accidentally I wouldn't have known him."[128] Unlike her erstwhile husband, this man slouched, round-shouldered and diffident, shirking his proper duties as paterfamilias. Stripped of self-confidence, Bob now asked his *wife's* advice—a reversal of gender roles that typified the perverted condition of communist marriages in which women called the shots (at least according to a report on communist psychology coauthored by attorney Morris Ernst). Having no truck with such un-American behavior, although clearly adept at issuing instructions herself, Lucile preferred things otherwise: "The day he starts ordering me around again, I'll say to him, 'Vogeler, you're yourself.' He hasn't even ordered me around once."[129]

After seventeen months' solitary confinement, Vogeler wanted to talk, however haltingly. In particular, he was anxious to exonerate himself for not (as he put it) "quite liv[ing] up to American traditions." According to U.S. Legation staff in Vienna, who debriefed Vogeler immediately after his release, he was "extremely nervous." Prompted by his Hungarian captors, Vogeler apparently believed that his fellow citizens would scorn him as a returning traitor. Prompted by his own conscience, he fretted that legation personnel would have heard, and believed, rumors that he had been engaged in black market activity. (They had, but assured him these rumors "in no way affected" their efforts on his behalf.) U.S. ambassador Donnelly in Vienna therefore recommended an early press conference to ease Vogeler's "guilt complex."[130] But his first public appearances had just the opposite effect, raising questions where previously there had been none.

For contemporary tastes, Vogeler struck the right note in his denunciation of communist methods, avoiding any hint of private remarks to Vienna Legation staff that his captors been polite, even when beating him.[131] Whether drugs had been administered, he couldn't say for sure. His mental state had been so degraded that it was impossible either to know or to subsequently recall precisely what had transpired in the prison cell. However, he did recollect interminable interrogations, bright lights and sleep deprivation, immersion in icy water: a litany of punishments and privations that gave firmer shape to the contours of duress that many had imaginatively mapped at the time of his arrest. But he did *not* repudiate his confession. On the contrary, he announced that, "like all confessions, some of it was true."[132]

This was not what people expected or wanted to hear, and Vogeler (under close surveillance by both his IT&T superiors and the State Department) was obviously alerted to the tremors this elliptical statement triggered. At subsequent appearances his refusal to elaborate on a tantalizingly cryptic remark only compounded the damage. As *Time*'s columnist put it, "Reporters took away the impression that they had not yet heard the whole story."[133] Naturally, they were keen to get to the bottom of it. Did Vogeler mean that he *had* engaged in espionage work, or did his lingering adherence to a false confession confirm that the communists had successfully "brainwashed" their American prisoner?[134]

Vogeler's second televised appearance caused yet more alarm. Beset by violent tremors that Lucile's firm pressure couldn't quell, a cigarette burning dangerously close to his knuckles, Robert mumbled through a statement and then faltered into silence. Clearly, it was time to retire. Two days after his return to America, the press reported that Vogeler would be hospitalized at the U.S. Navy Medical Center in Bethesda, Maryland, for "malnutrition."[135] When he resurfaced three weeks later to address the National Press Club on "What Freedom Means," Vogeler was fitfully assertive. Talking "in detail" about his captivity for the first time, he mustered some striking turns of phrase with which to convey an "indescribable unreality": "The mind, the spirit and the body are attacked over and over again until the will is slowly ground away. The very body is forced into league against one's personality." Any confession signed under such conditions, he now insisted, was simply "rubbish." The "true" elements earlier alluded to? "The fact is that my name, my birthplace, my employer's name and other similar facts were indeed accurately given. But little, if anything else, applied." If he had earlier suggested something different, this should be attributed to the "excruciating experience" of readjustment "to freedom."[136]

FROM RED PAWN TO
PROFESSIONAL ANTICOMMUNIST

Back in the United States, his connection with IT&T at first uncertain and then severed, Vogeler immediately embarked on a new career, putting his experience in eastern Europe to productive use.[137] He joined the ranks of a specialized, though not always highly qualified, occupation: professional anticommunist. As "one who knows what freedom means because he lost it so thoroughly," Vogeler was assured an attentive audience so long as the mood for a particularly stringent brand of anti-communism lasted.[138]

As public speaker and author, Vogeler plied a number of familiar themes. Like many earlier exponents of the captivity narrative, he endowed his experience with eschatological significance, representing his ordeal in Budapest as revelatory of a divine purpose that would test national will just as it had tried his individual mettle. In a foreshortened first television appearance the newly released prisoner advised fellow citizens that "God has given us the mission to destroy the Communist enemies of freedom." Global in scope, the campaign against communism was fundamentally domestic in intent: a fight for the right of a man "to be able to go to bed with an easy feeling, not thinking that he may be taken away in the middle of the night from his family into prison." Casting the challenge of communism as an occasion for Christian rededication, Vogeler reprised a well-worn motif, echoing George Kennan's expression of gratitude that Providence had supplied an "implacable challenge" to mobilize a spiritually lethargic community, an exhortation that would be sounded more stridently in the aftermath of the Korean War.[139]

Vogeler combined stern rebukes with apocalyptic intimations that "every last one of us is subject to constant attack by the Soviet Union and its satellites."[140] But having exposed the barbarity of his captors, he soon devoted greater energy to excoriating the rottenness within American institutions that made them vulnerable to subversion and liable to collapse. As was more or less mandatory among professional anticommunists, he reserved particular opprobrium for Truman and

Acheson.[141] Expressions of bitter betrayal became Vogeler's stock-in-trade, though they hadn't represented his feelings immediately after release from Hungary. In April 1951, Vogeler had sounded a very different note, requesting a personal meeting with Acheson and cabling both the president and secretary of state to express sincere appreciation. "It is amazing to me that with all your difficulties and troubles time was found to complete so successfully negotiations for my liberation," Vogeler informed Truman. "This is an example of the great solicitude our country has for every one of its humblest citizens."[142] Soon, however, Vogeler was eagerly contributing to the president's "difficulties and troubles."

Vogeler's attacks on Truman and Acheson weren't restricted to his speaking engagements or radio and television appearances. They were amplified by publication of his memoir, *I Was Stalin's Prisoner,* which was serialized between October and December 1951 in the *Saturday Evening Post.*[143] Even though the articles amounted to a significant proportion of the book, they apparently didn't diminish the appetite for further helpings of Vogeler's story. As rendered by Leigh White, the narrative gave a strikingly Orientalist cast to an otherwise familiar commentary on communist methods, with frequent references to their sadistic preference for "Asiatic" punishments, including bastinado and the fearful "water treatment." The memoir's other vital ingredient was an assault on the State Department so scabrous that one favorably disposed reviewer cautioned potential readers, "You may have to watch your blood pressure." This warning was not intended to chastise an apoplectic author, however. Vogeler was routinely treated with all the respect owed a redeemed captive whose claim to firsthand authority lay beyond dispute. Thus *I Was Stalin's Prisoner* was lauded as "an *American Darkness at Noon,* starker than a psychological shocker because it is truth and not fiction"—a verdict that, even Koestler's detractors might agree, erred generously in Vogeler's favor.[144]

Communist "hostage taking" remained headline news throughout 1951, not simply because Vogeler's experiences were so thoroughly chewed over but because several more Americans were arrested in rapid succession. In Czechoslovakia, William Oatis, the thirty-seven-year-old bureau chief of the Associated Press in Prague, was found guilty of gathering secret intelligence and "spreading malicious information," a category that apparently encompassed any material that didn't emanate directly from the Czech government. The American press cast the Oatis case as a rerun of Vogeler's, itself a carbon copy of Mindszenty's: "stamped with the same fraudulency," as the *Washington Post* put it.[145] For Vogeler, the message was clear. "As long as we don't take a firm stand in these gangster kidnappings, we shall have more and more and more," he warned an audience in Grand Lake, Colorado. While the American Legion clamored for the expulsion of all Czechs from U.S. soil, others called for direct retaliation against Czechoslovakia itself.[146] Senator Jenner of Indiana led the charge, angrily petitioning the State Department to "tell the government of Czechoslovakia to release Oatis or we will send an air missile to Prague and take him." With a nod to the Perdicaris incident, he added, "We know what bullies do when their bluff is called."[147]

The Barbary theme received more pertinent play with respect to another set of captivities that roiled America in December 1951.[148] Budapest had claimed four more American captives—airmen forced down after straying en route from Munich to Belgrade. The Hungarian regime alleged that they were on an illicit mission to airlift supplies to American "spies and saboteurs" in the eastern bloc, a charge timed to support Vishinsky's attack on the Kersten Amendment at the UN.[149] When Budapest announced that the prisoners had confessed to their role in clandestine warfare against the people's democracies, American commentators yawned wearily. "'Confessions' can be manufactured when needed, like a pair of shoes," observed a tart editorial in the New York Times. "They are part of the apparatus on which Communist propaganda marches." After a brief trial, the four Americans were sentenced to three months' imprisonment, a punishment Budapest proposed to waive if each man paid a $30,000 fine. This maneuver sparked a furious debate on Capitol Hill, many lawmakers vehemently opposing payment of "blood money" or a "ransom shakedown."[150] Skeptical opinion formers went so far as to suggest that the Hungarian regime would build "an up-to-date concentration camp" with the ill-gotten gains of its "gangsterism."[151]

Vogeler played a conspicuous, if inconsistent, role in this polarizing case. On December 26, 1951, the Chicago Daily Tribune reported that he personally intended to raise the $120,000 required to buy the four airmen's freedom. Concerned citizens "dug down in their pockets," just as they had when Barbary pirates had demanded tribute for Americans held captive on the North African coast and Jefferson had refused to oblige. "Even in its rising wrath," observed the New York Times, "the American public insists on freeing the captives first." Across the country, in Portland, Oregon, Wichita, Kansas, Memphis, Tennessee, and Syracuse, New York, civic groups sprang into action. With the American Highway Carriers Association offering to tender the full amount, contributions to the flyers' redemption fund rapidly exceeded what Budapest demanded.[152] But no sooner had the money been raised than Vogeler's stance changed and the donations were returned.[153] When the fine was paid, it was furnished by the U.S. government.

Repackaging himself as an opponent of blackmail, Vogeler now mooted formation of a committee for the repatriation of Oatis and other Americans held behind the Iron Curtain and in "Red China"—a group whose number he estimated at five thousand.[154] In August 1952, he launched the American Liberation Center with a view to helping liberate "all peoples enslaved by Communist tyranny." Russian airmen, Vogeler announced, should be "invited to fly to freedom" and accommodated in hostels welcoming "fugitives from Eastern Europe."[155]

That hundreds of individuals entrusted thousands of dollars to Vogeler in order to redeem captives in the eastern bloc highlights both the emotional potency

FIGURE 20. "You got any special rates for natives?" 1951 Herblock Cartoon, copyright by The Herb Block Foundation.

of this issue and his public stature as the best-known American to have "returned from death" behind the Iron Curtain. In achieving this celebrity, Vogeler was aided by a sympathetic press and the medium that had come into its own during his captivity—television. On December 23, 1951, while the four fliers spent Christmas in a Hungarian jail, American television viewers were offered "unusually grim" festive fare by NBC's Goodyear Television Playhouse: a dramatization of *I Was Stalin's Prisoner*, featuring an appearance by Vogeler himself. Indicting the Hungarian communists for having drilled him in a rote confession, he fluffed lines that had evidently been scripted for him.[156] Yet however stilted the performance, it attached a powerful meaning to his captivity. Interviewed by NBC's John Cameron Swayze, Vogeler informed viewers that his "imprisonment by the communists" had been "a personal insult to all of you, an unspeakable rebuff to every American." This "story of indignities, of torture, of the denial of human rights . . . could have happened to you," he admonished. "If you feel this is untimely, then please turn off your television." Such faintheartedness, Vogeler strongly hinted, would amount to an abnegation of patriotic duty. But there was a reward for staying tuned: the collective gratification of knowing that, while residents of the slave world went to bed dreading the midnight knock on the door, the "only invasion in the dead of the night" that Americans need expect was "that of Santa Claus"—as Swayze concluded with a chuckle.[157]

By the time of this Christmas star turn, there was no longer any pretence that the Vogelers were "uninterested in politics," as Lucile had once asserted. Having made increasingly brash denunciations of the "namby-pamby" character of U.S. foreign policy and having openly lambasted Truman, Hiss, and Acheson as "traitors," Robert and Lucile plunged headlong into the 1952 presidential election campaign.[158] With an ominous warning that the Democrats would "lead the country to socialism and communism," the couple endorsed Senator Robert Taft's bid for the Republican nomination. As president, Taft would "discourage our enemies and minimize the threat of war," Vogeler asserted. The couple thus threw their weight behind the party's most conservative wing, forging a close alliance with the individual whose political agenda and personal style they found most congenial— Senator McCarthy.[159] Together, Bob and Joe went on the stump, rallying popular support for the anti-Red crusade.

Relishing the fight, the Vogelers launched more frontal attacks on their foes. According to Congressman Melvin Price of Illinois, Mrs. Vogeler—a well-known local personality—habitually made "the most bitter and vicious castigation of the State Department, bringing it almost on a personal basis against the Secretary, making some of the foulest inferences."[160] Similar concerns reached the department from other quarters. Robert, meanwhile, was given to alleging that U.S. diplomats had threatened to revoke his wife's citizenship and remove her passport.

Scurrilous accusations made for gripping copy. They did not secure Taft's nomination, however, and with Eisenhower installed in the White House, Republican "countersubversives" found themselves in a bind. Did they abandon the Reds-in-government charge now that their party controlled the Senate, Congress, and White House, or did they continue the campaign regardless? Like McCarthy, the Vogelers chose to press on, becoming ever more bilious in their attacks. Lucile found a new role as "outstanding critic of the United Nations," campaigning in support of the Bricker Amendment. Without special legislation to keep the menace of "world government" at bay, Americans faced mortal danger, Lucile insisted. "Actually, the American citizen has more to fear from the web of international law than from the bayonet of a Red army soldier," she told an audience of five hundred "legal experts" at the Mayflower Hotel in Washington, D.C., in January 1954. "Soviet troops are still 5,000 miles away. The noose of international law is fashioned in New York and Washington."[161] In danger of being eclipsed by his more telegenic spouse, Robert continued to insist that communists still remained in key government positions under Eisenhower and that the pro-Red conspiracy extended into the realm of publishing. With presses systematically rejecting anticommunist material, it was "impossible for the average citizen to find out much about Communist activities either here or abroad," he asserted—a claim belied by the success of *I Was Stalin's Prisoner*.[162]

By 1954, the Vogelers' charges had assumed a more personal and pecuniary character. Running short of funds, Robert launched a $500,000 suit against IT&T for the damage he had sustained as their representative in central Europe. In the course of building his case, Vogeler claimed that reports written for his bosses at IT&T on conditions in eastern Europe had been "turned over to the State Department" without his knowledge. "Communists" in the department had then sent photostatic copies straight to the regime in Budapest—a succession of betrayals that had led directly to Vogeler's arrest.[163]

If Vogeler was disappointed by the $50,000 payoff his former employer tendered, larger reversals lay in store. In 1954, the political tide turned. With Eisenhower's White House less susceptible to pressure from Red-baiters than a Democratic administration on the defensive, McCarthy's star was in the descendant. The senator's critics, emboldened by his growing recklessness, now pointed to the parodic way in which the investigatory committees synonymous with McCarthyism replicated the calculated disregard for due process that prevailed east of the Iron Curtain. The HUAC hearing, like the communist show trial, was a "degradation ceremony," in the words of Elia Kazan, designed less to yield information than to abase witnesses through the act of informing.[164]

Undeterred, Robert and Lucile Vogeler stuck by the Wisconsin senator, campaigning on his behalf long after shrewder tacticians had edged away. Whether flattered by McCarthy's attention or hungry for the television cameras (or both), the Vogelers remained close at hand to the last. They attended the army-McCarthy hearings in June 1954, and on the final day of the proceedings McCarthy introduced Robert as a "loyal American" and one of his "unpaid consultants on communism."[165] But Vogeler was considerably more than a "consultant" or a theatrical prop, wheeled out as living proof of communist tyranny and State Department perfidy. The two men had become close friends. After the hearings concluded, the disgraced sena-

FIGURE 21. Outfoxed. Lucile Vogeler relaxes after the rigors of the army-McCarthy hearings with Joe and wife, Jean, vacationing in La Jolla, August 1954. © The Associated Press.

tor and his wife, Jean, spent a week vacationing with Robert and Lucile in La Jolla, where for the second year in a row McCarthy's vacation "coincidentally" overlapped with J. Edgar Hoover's annual "rest and physical check-up" at the same hotel. One of the last pictures of Lucile carried in the national press showed her, resplendent in a leopard print bikini, dabbling her toes in a pool, with Joe McCarthy at her side and Jean at his other elbow. Tellingly, Bob was nowhere in sight.[166]

HOW THE EAST BECAME THE EAST

Robert Vogeler's career as a cold war celebrity stalled with the censure of McCarthy in December 1954. Within a couple of years, the former IT&T executive had lapsed back into obscurity, struggling to keep a new business venture afloat and fending off foreclosure on a luxurious family home in Bedford Falls, New York. In the drama of McCarthyism, Vogeler had played a supporting part. His chief political contribution, however, was less as a Red-baiter, the role he enthusiastically embraced in 1951, than as a cold war captive, the fate bestowed on him by Budapest in November 1949.

As "Stalin's prisoner," Robert Vogeler helped crystallize for American audiences what was meant by "police state": the constant fear of arrest; the persecutory character of justice in a society bound by excessive legalism; the reduction of individuals to mere political pawns; and the claustrophobic sense of entrapment that stifled all residents, not just prisoners. Press reports on Vogeler's release from captivity, as he was delivered by Hungarian armed guards into the custody of U.S. diplomats at the Austrian border, accentuated the radical disjuncture between two antithetical ways of life. Freedom was regained not by leaving a Budapest prison cell but only by leaving Hungary itself. Vogeler, meanwhile, characterized his return from the eastern bloc as a form of resurrection. Telling journalists that he had been allowed to sit in the plane's cockpit as it landed at New York's Idlewild Airport, he mused: "I guess it's a privilege accorded to those back from the dead."[167]

Where Vogeler depicted Hungary as an outer circle of hell, others ventured alternative motifs and mappings. But whether they likened Hungarian communists to pirates, gangsters, or (in Morris Ernst's analogy) a lynch mob, contemporary opinion formers all located the Soviet satellites in a realm conceived as morally and temporally remote from Western civilization, backward and barbarous.[168] Twenty years earlier, Chip Bohlen had described Russians as "primitives—in the best sense of the word."[169] Now they appeared savages in the least noble sense of that term, and with "the blackness of barbarism" having descended, the *New York Times* warned that all "fruitful exchange" would surely cease between these two incommensurable worlds. The eastern bloc had become "what the old geographers called Terra Incognita, a territory unknown and unexplored."[170]

By the time this prediction appeared in February 1950, there was already scant East-West exchange, fruitful or otherwise. In the wake of Vogeler's arrest, travel across the Austro-Hungarian border became more fraught and correspondingly less frequent. To signal its displeasure, the State Department banned all travel to Hungary in December 1949, lifting the embargo in April 1951 only to reinstate it that December when the four U.S. airmen were imprisoned. William Oatis's indictment led to the imposition of an identical restriction on American travel to Czechoslovakia in June 1951. In May 1952 the State Department took the more radical step of stamping all U.S. passports "NOT valid for travel to Albania, Bulgaria, China, Czechoslovakia, Hungary, Poland, Rumania, or the Union of Soviet Socialist Republics unless specifically endorsed under authority of the Department of State as being valid for such travel." Stressing that this move was not intended to place the eastern bloc off limits altogether, U.S. officials stated that their goal was to curb "sneak visits" to forbidden areas "by persons who might not really understand the hazards to Americans in the Iron Curtain countries."[171] In the wake of the Vogeler and Oatis cases, however, few Americans could have been unmindful of the risks posed by a trip to the "Communist jungle world." The *New York Times* even printed a sardonic inducement it imagined the Budapest government might issue to lure travelers: "Spend your vacation in beautiful Hungary*** Visit our courts and our jails*** Never a dull moment—midnight arrests and secret trials . . . *** All sports, including solitaire and forced labor*** No cover charge at any time for signed confessions."[172]

As travel and trade between the United States and eastern Europe dwindled, diplomats in the satellite states found their lives increasingly constrained and experienced many of the same curtailments that their colleagues in Moscow had chafed against for some time. In his private journal, Nathaniel Davis tracked the progress of Hungarian anti-Americanism, waking on Stalin's birthday in December 1949 (days after Vogeler's arrest) to the strains of a catchy marching song— "We are going to hang Tito and we will hang Truman too." Social ostracism quickly followed, since very few Hungarians cared to be seen in the company of an American diplomat in this climate.[173] To add to the discomfort of life in the legation, Budapest imposed a travel restriction on U.S. personnel, a measure hastily imposed on Hungarian representatives in America, whose movement was likewise limited to within an eighteen-mile radius of Washington, D.C.[174]

These developments punched more bolts into the heavy sheet metal partition that American cartoonists imagined as the "Iron Curtain." Eastern Europe—a region to which millions of Americans traced their ancestry—had come to seem impossibly distant and menacingly impenetrable. The communist takeover of Czechoslovakia in 1948 and Mindszenty's trial in 1949 left a deep imprint on American opinion. But it was Vogeler's imprisonment that really brought home the Sovietization of eastern Europe.

Depending on how the kaleidoscope was rotated, his captivity appeared as spy thriller, romantic melodrama, or family story. However, the most common framing of Vogeler's predicament was as an emblem of America's postwar enfeeblement, a demonstration that the United States could no longer hope to protect its citizens— or "civilized values"—in a bifurcated world, a growing portion of which was presided over by "primitive men who have not yet outgrown the swaddling clothes of savagery." Confronted with communist barbarism, what was Washington to do? "We cannot get down in the mud with the Communists and seize innocent Hungarians, to be held in durance as hostages," noted the *New York Times* with regret. "In these encounters, civilized man is always at a disadvantage."[175] Cold war liberals regarded the curse of civility as a condition without easy remedy. But for others the cure was as obvious as it was appealing. When one impatient citizen from Ohio cabled Truman requesting that he "please take action" against Russia and its satellites because they "only understand when hit," he voiced a widely shared sentiment.[176]

Across Asia, western Europe, the Middle East, and South America, U.S. influence was expanding rapidly in the years after World War II. Many Americans, however, had no sense that they were witnessing their state's "rise to globalism." Quite the reverse. Convinced that Washington was losing the global battle with communism, a substantial segment of opinion maintained that America lacked the muscle, ingenuity, and ruthlessness to score a decisive victory, whatever its apparent advantages in economic strength and atomic weaponry. "The Reds are doing the pitching and we keep popping fouls into the bleachers until they toss a fast one at us when we are called out on the strikes," noted a rueful editorial on Vogeler's imprisonment in the *New York World-Telegram*.[177] That captivity was so widely understood as a testament to U.S. vulnerability—a shameful sign of impotence—goes some way to explaining this apparent paradox.

If it was intolerable that eastern bloc states should have imprisoned a handful of American citizens with apparent impunity, a yet more alarming scenario soon compounded this beleaguered sense of victimization. Over the winter of 1950–51, thousands of American soldiers surrendered to, or were captured by, the forces of communist China and North Korea. Their fate occasioned shudders of dread at home. "Multiply the suffering of Vogeler by 10,000 and add the well known brutality of the oriental Communists and Americans will have some notion of the misery and human suffering of American boys being held prisoner in North Korea and Manchuria." Thus three Republican lawmakers entreated fellow citizens in July 1951, offering instruction in cold war Orientalism that many Americans scarcely required.[178]

Prisoners of Pavlov

Korean War Captivity and the Brainwashing Scare

THE SORRIEST BUNCH

For soldiers, war is all about getting home—or so civilians often say. It is an article of faith that men in uniform want nothing more than to return with all possible speed when hostilities end. This notion received a powerful boost when GIs stationed in occupied Europe and Japan staged massive demonstrations to demand immediate demobilization in early 1946. When the Korean War ended in July 1953, after months of fitful armistice talks, contemporary commentators imagined that soldiers would be similarly eager for home—none more so than the 4,400 men who had spent almost three years in communist-run POW camps. To the astonishment of many fellow citizens, however, twenty-three American prisoners refused to accept repatriation. Rather than returning home to "the highest standard of living the earth had ever seen," as journalist Edward Hunter put it, these men were heading for Red China, "an extremely backward, dreadfully impoverished country, supposedly out of preference for its way of life."[1]

That POWs could opt against repatriation wasn't itself a revelation. For more than a year, the question of whether prisoners had a right to choose their postwar destinations had dominated the armistice talks. Any attentive American would have known that negotiations had foundered on precisely this issue, with China insisting that prisoners should automatically be repatriated and Washington asserting their right to decline. But of course Truman's administration hadn't espoused the cause of voluntary repatriation on behalf of *American* prisoners. And though CIA director Allen Dulles had tried to prepare domestic opinion for this eventuality by overplaying the likely scale of desertion from U.S. ranks, his efforts made little im-

pression on media treatment of the POW story.[2] News of the "turncoats'" repudiation of their country was thus as unexpected as it was shocking. "The defection of
even one . . . would have been enough to sadden the heart of any loyal American,"
lamented an editorial in *America* magazine. Desertion by twenty-three was "almost
like a blow in the face to the rest of us," *Commonweal* chimed.[3]

Throughout that fall Americans had ample opportunity to contemplate this
bruise to national pride. Under the armistice terms, all prisoners who refused repatriation were required to spend ninety days at Panmunjom under Indian army custody while officers of their own nationality made the case for going home. During
this three-month interlude for "explanations," U.S. commentators obsessively
probed the motives of these men, their psychological peculiarities, and the family
backgrounds generative of such sorry specimens of American manhood.[4]

The "balky GIs" were forthright in explaining their position, issuing a press statement that pointedly referenced the "murder of the Rosenbergs" and the "legal lynching [of] dozens of Negroes" in defense of their desire to work for peace in China,
a country where "there is no contradiction between what is preached and what is
practiced." Such sentiments were "pure communist jargon," one columnist remarked. But it remained unclear whether these young men had possessed deviant
leanings before captivity or only as a result of it. While it was conceivable that the
U.S. military contained a handful of communists—since "what we have at home,
we have in our Army," George Sokolsky reminded readers of the *New York Journal-
American*—most commentators suspected that the twenty-three had been indoctrinated during their long incarceration.[5] Despite disagreements over how a
brain was washed and whether it could subsequently be relaundered, many insisted
that these men had fallen foul of diabolical techniques hitherto applied to Cardinal Mindszenty and Robert Vogeler. The nonrepatriates offered "living proof that
Communist brainwashing does work on some persons," announced an unequiv-
ocal editorial in the *New York Times*.[6]

As sufferers of an "artificially imposed mental illness," they were to be gently
encouraged back into the fold, counseled the *Times*. Thousands of civilians rose to
the challenge, with Sunday schools, civic groups, and old people's homes organizing letter-writing drives. According to the Indian officer in command at Panmunjom, children played the most prominent role in this epistolary campaign to
cajole the unredeemed captives. "The number of letters, containing the most cloy-
ing sentiments, and written in pathetically childish scrawls, was truly amazing," he
later reminisced.[7] Several prominent figures volunteered more lucrative entice-
ments. Myron Wilson, president of the Cleveland Indians, wrote to offer each of the
twenty-three a job "either in baseball or in private industry," a signal that fellow
citizens understood that "a man might choose communism to a horrible death."[8]
Meanwhile, Harry Myers, director of the American Legion's Los Angeles branch,
floated a plan—vigorously backed by the Hearst press—to fly the nonrepatriates'

mothers to Korea so they could personally participate in the "explaining" process at Panmunjom.[9]

The Defense Department, which had considered flying out persuasive person-alities like Arthur Godfrey, Jackie Robinson, Edward R. Murrow, and Bishop Ful-ton Sheen to reanimate faith in the democratic way, hastily squelched this scheme as "neither practical nor desirable," imagining the chaos that would ensue if twenty-two thousand Chinese and Korean mothers demanded equivalent access to *their* sons.[10] Nevertheless, one mother (Mrs. Portia Howe of Alden, Minnesota) flew to Tokyo, protesting that she had been called by God to do so—with the finan-cial assistance of her church and sale of her son's defense bonds.[11] Despite a curt rebuke from her twenty-two-year-old son, who insisted that whatever she had heard about his having been "forced, doped or brainwashed" was "horse manure that they use to slander and defile people like myself who will stand up for his own rights," Mrs. Howe still maintained that he was "a victim of brainwashing."[12] Several other relatives, lacking access to the same spiritual and material resources, relied on lo-cal radio stations to record appeals to sons and brothers who couldn't truly prefer the privations of communist China to the comforts of home. Whatever "spell" these boys languished under would surely be "pierced" if they could just hear their moth-ers' loving voices, claimed Mrs. Gladys Peoples, whose son Clarence Adams was one of three African Americans in the group.[13]

But not everyone accepted that the recalcitrants were laboring under a malign spell or that they deserved compassionate consideration. Military sources signaled that several members of the group were "such thoroughgoing collaborators" that they feared coming home to "face the music." The men weren't necessarily com-munist converts, just self-seekers who had curried favor with their captors and ratted—or worse—on their buddies.[14] A long *Newsweek* report emphasized the judgment of Lt. General K. S. Thimayya (the Indian officer commanding the Neu-tral Nations Repatriation Commission) that these Americans were "about the sor-riest, most shifty-eyed and groveling bunch of chaps he had ever seen."[15]

Among the "rats" too cowardly to face the wrath of their peers or the judgment of courts-martial, *Newsweek* ventured that some had fallen in love with Chinese girls. Worse yet, others had allegedly fallen for fellow American boys. In reporting rumors "started by persons who had been inside the camps" that "about half the Americans were bound together more by homosexualism than Communism," the magazine mooted a convergence of "deviances" common in early cold war dis-course: a conflation of the Red Scare with a "lavender menace" promulgated not only by McCarthy but by many contemporary epidemiologists of communist pathology. Embroidering the same motif, the *Washington Post* announced that per-haps four of the non-repats were "homosexuals who have taken to letting their hair grow long," and used "language so foul as to repel the regular soldiers of the India Army who are their guards." Two men, it was reported, had been seen "dressed in women's clothes." Curtain crossing and cross-dressing were, it seemed, all of a piece.[16]

If sexual "perversion" didn't suffice as an explanation for treachery, other observers hypothesized that an array of material rewards must have been held out to lure these gullible dupes. Each of the "pro-Red POWs" had reportedly been promised "$5000, a fancy car, and a college education, plus a commissar's job when the Reds took over America," moonshine pledges that would soon evaporate along with whatever down payments of "cigarettes, liquor, women and hashish" had secured the men's defections.[17] "Pathetic men" who'd hoped to get "something for nothing," they would soon pay a heavy price for succumbing to the cheap lure of ego gratification when they ended up in Chinese labor camps, many editorialists predicted.

A similar shudder of distaste rippled through official responses to the nonrepatriates. At Panmunjom, U.S. officers made little secret of their growing repugnance for the men who wouldn't come home. Had the twenty-three appeared emaciated, bewildered, or obviously cowed, empathy might have been sustained. As it was, these "bronzed young men, obviously well-fed and seemingly in the best of physical condition," soon exhausted lenient inclinations, taunting American reporters as "Yankee Imperialists" and evidently relishing their performance of defiance. "If I had my way they would be told they had five minutes to make up their minds and let it go at that," one unnamed "high ranking officer" informed the *New York Times*. "If we got them back I'm afraid they would all be constant security risks."[18]

As the deadline for the termination of "explanations" approached, a U.S. military spokesman broadcast one five-minute appeal, affirming that the twenty-two remaining recalcitrants would be fairly treated should they undergo an eleventh-hour change of heart. Corporal Edward Dickenson, who had already decided to return to the United States, was reported to be enjoying a thirty-day furlough and honeymoon. But during the military's halfhearted exercise, the rest of the group maintained their intransigent posture. Linking arms with fellow South Korean resisters, the Americans stamped, banged cymbals, sang, and joined in a "wild folk dance," posing for photographers with their mascot, a dog whose coat was emblazoned with the defiant slogan "Unexplained To." A final press statement reiterated that "McCarthyism, McCarranism and KKKism" at home disinclined them to return.[19]

On January 28, 1954, after a further member of the group, Claude Batchelor, changed his mind, the twenty-one remaining American nonrepatriates set off for China. However uncertain their future, one thing was clear: they were no longer members of the U.S. military. Three days earlier, Secretary of Defense Charles E. Wilson had announced their dishonorable discharge. Meanwhile, at the very moment that word of Edward Dickenson's lenient treatment was being broadcast to his former comrades as an assurance of the army's understanding attitude, the twenty-three-year-old corporal was arrested at Walter Reed Hospital. Having ear-

FIGURE 22. Four of the "nonrepats" prepare for their journey to China, wearing their politics on their truck. From left to right, Albert C. Belhomme, Clarence C. Adams, Andrew Condon (the "lone Briton"), and John R. Dunn. © The Associated Press.

lier been led to believe that his unconsummated flirtation with communism would go unpunished, Dickenson now faced charges of "unlawful intercourse" with the enemy.[20]

In the wake of this episode, many U.S. opinion formers reassured a perturbed populace that twenty-one "lost souls" didn't amount to such a shameful tally when compared with twenty-two thousand defections from North Korea and China— or with the "ratio of treachery" found among the Twelve Apostles, as the *Washington Post* noted.[21] Few seemed quite so sanguine, however. Judas might have accepted thirty pieces of silver, but at least he hadn't sung the Internationale while doing so. Americans simply didn't reject the free world for a "slave civilization." And since earlier defections of U.S. citizens in the USSR and GIs who had gone AWOL in East Germany had barely dented public consciousness, the decision of the twenty-one prodigals seemed utterly unprecedented. Overlooking a long history of unredeemed captives refusing to rejoin their Euro-American communities, commentators in the 1950s repeatedly stressed that *never before in history* had

Americans elected to remain with their captors. No wonder, then, that a story burdened with such radical implications sustained attention throughout the 1950s and beyond, inspiring press reports, scholarly analysis, novels, teleplays, and movies.

Yet the rapid gyrations of judgment that saw these men deemed successively (or simultaneously) victims, invalids, dupes, "rats," and "cheese-eaters" also track larger anxieties generated by America's first mass experience of communist captivity. What the unredeemed captives experienced with particular force, three thousand other returning prisoners would encounter with varying degrees of intensity as their individual records were appraised, then collectively reevaluated. Their captivity came to function as something akin to a Rorschach test for social commentators in the fifties. The shapes Americans discerned there mapped an intricate set of cold war anxieties over gender roles, sexuality, parenting, class, and race, concerns anticipated in constructions of the nonrepatriates' characterological deficiencies. From schooling to segregation, "momism" to McCarthyism, affluence to anomie, every ailment believed to afflict the body politic as a whole could apparently be diagnosed by dissecting the infirm bodies and fragile psyches of America's POWs.

SLAUGHTER OR SLAVERY:
THE POLITICS OF REPATRIATION

In the furor surrounding the twenty-one "turncoats," far less attention was paid to the twenty-two thousand Korean and Chinese prisoners who opted against repatriation, men so happy to be free that (according to *Time*) they wept tears of joy and "sang songs of what they would do to the women" when they reached Taiwan.[22] Since their repudiation of communist regimes represented the UN's most tangible gain from a war that left Korea divided much as it had been in June 1950, Eisenhower's psychological strategists worked hard to stress what amounted to "victory of a kind" after an unpopular war that had claimed in excess of thirty thousand American lives, left another ninety-eight thousand wounded, and cost taxpayers $15 billion—to say nothing of the human and environmental devastation wrought on the Korean peninsula.[23]

With many disgruntled U.S. citizens inclined to accentuate the negative, government officials assiduously emphasized that thousands of valiant Chinese and North Korean freedom lovers had been saved from totalitarian slavery. More than that, Washington's role in championing their right to defect would embolden communist troops in any future war to surrender at the earliest opportunity, secure in the knowledge that they wouldn't be sent back to a miserable fate. Fear of wholesale desertion would make the Kremlin think twice about launching future wars. "From now on, the Red Armies will be less dependable as tools of aggression. We have increased the prospect of peace and added to the security of our nation," announced an ebullient John Foster Dulles in September 1953.[24] Washington had thus found a way to win the cold war without fighting—or without fighting very much.

Triumphalism of this sort aimed to reassure Americans that the principle of non-forcible repatriation—staunchly asserted by Truman on May 7, 1952, and then embraced by his successor—had merited fifteen additional months of war. On this question, psychological strategists were warranted in suspecting that popular conviction could be stronger. Opinion sampled during the war revealed public support for the administration's POW policy to be less than resolute. Surveys conducted in March, April, and June 1952 (while White House policy on repatriation was hardening) showed that although a growing number of respondents favored refusal to return reluctant communist prisoners a majority assented to this proposition only if it wouldn't jeopardize the return of American POWs.[25] Clearly, though, the impasse on this issue *did* delay the signing of an armistice, and in its absence GIs remained encamped along the Yalu—not without some murmurings of discontent. In May 1952, Walter Judd (R-MN) read into the congressional record the complaint of three women who charged that "the lives of enemy POWs were being put before those of our own men." Was the United States really so hard up that it must "stoop to purloining prisoners of war for prospective converts to our way of life," demanded a disgruntled veteran of his congressman.[26]

Why, then, did the White House commit itself so implacably to the principle of nonforcible repatriation? As the historian Barton J. Bernstein points out, the president could have made a strong case for compromise on the POW question had he been so minded.[27] A prisoner's right to refuse repatriation was not mandated by international conventions, and until the summer of 1951, when armistice negotiations were about to begin, U.S. officials had given little hint that they planned to stake out an unorthodox new position of questionable legality. Truman's stance, by contrast, placed U.S. prisoners in danger of reprisals, extended their captivity, and "for month after weary month . . . constituted a gigantic monkey wrench thrown into the truce-negotiating machinery"—this at a time when public opinion was increasingly polarized between those who believed U.S. troops should quit Korea altogether and those impatient to drop atomic bombs on China and be done with it.[28]

On the face of it, prisoner repatriation shouldn't have occasioned controversy. Article 118 of the Geneva Convention of August 12, 1949, for the Protection of War Victims appears unambiguous: "Prisoners of War shall be released and repatriated without delay after the cessation of hostilities." Although neither Beijing nor Pyongyang had signed the 1949 Convention, and Washington hadn't ratified it, the war's chief protagonists all announced within weeks that they intended to observe it. Within months, both sides held significant numbers of prisoners—and there the problems began.[29]

Most prisoners were captured in 1950. Only 465 American prisoners (of 6,656) were taken during the second and third years of the war. By the time truce talks

began in July 1951, the UN Command had detained 97 percent of the eventual total of 150,000 Korean prisoners and 85 percent of its Chinese prisoners—a POW
population that ultimately rose to 21,000.[30] That the UN Command detained far
more prisoners than its opponents represented a major complication, inclining U.S.
negotiators against an all-for-all exchange of prisoners, since this arrangement
would mean delivering to the enemy a much larger supply of military manpower
than the UN Command would receive in return. But the greatest problem arose
not from the discrepancy in numbers held by the two sides but from the hetero-
geneity of prisoners confined in UN-run camps and the vigor with which they made
their political preferences known.

Ostensibly members of the Chinese People's Liberation Army or soldiers of the
Democratic People's Republic of Korea, many POWs held by the UN Command
were neither. Referred to as "communist prisoners," only a minority comfortably
fit or readily embraced that description. Of the Chinese prisoners, almost two-thirds
had served with Chiang Kai-shek's Nationalist forces during the civil war. Having
been imprisoned, reeducated, and maneuvered into the People's Liberation Army,
many were hardly volunteers, and their loyalty to China's new regime was at best
uncertain.[31] The Koreans, meanwhile, were "probably the most motley crew ever
classified as prisoners of war," noted Demaree Bess in the *Saturday Evening Post*.[32]
Their number included forty thousand civilians who had been either impressed into
service with Kim Il Sung's forces or mistakenly taken prisoner by UN forces during the early months of the war, when chaotic reversals of military fortune uprooted
almost the entire Korean population. Some forty-nine thousand of the UN Command's Korean POWs originated from the South.[33] In the circumstances, it is un-
derstandable that thousands of prisoners—both Korean and Chinese—should
have objected to "repatriation" to North Korea or China, destinations alien by
either birth or inclination.

Object they assuredly did, with anticommunist POWs going so far as to present
their captors with petitions signed in blood. Hyperbolic gestures of this kind, underscored by violent riots in the camps, made clear that large numbers of prisoners would resist delivery into communist custody at pain of death. Their vehemence
pushed Truman toward the increasingly intractable position he enunciated in May
1952: that he would not "buy an armistice by turning over human beings for slaughter or slavery."[34]

This inflexible stance had its critics. Although Secretary of State Acheson came
to support it, he initially argued against voluntary repatriation on the grounds that
it conflicted with the Geneva Convention, threatening to jeopardize the safety and
timely return of American POWs.[35] Others in the State Department made the case
yet more forcefully that Washington couldn't espouse a position on repatriation
at variance with international law. Having championed the 1949 Geneva Convention to shame Moscow over its ongoing detention of Axis prisoners, it would hardly

do for U.S. forces to retain thousands of prisoners after the Korean War ended. As one State Department official heatedly argued in October 1951: "The United States would be put in a very embarrassing position if they did what the Russians did after World War II. . . . We would not accept from the North Koreans, the Chinese, or the Russians the explanation that they were not returning prisoners of war because they did not want to come home." Nor would the North Koreans and Chinese accept it from the United States, as subsequent events confirmed.[36]

For supporters of voluntary repatriation, however, fear of behaving like Russia after World War II wasn't the largest concern. More worrisome was the prospect that U.S. troops might end up replicating *American* postwar actions. With thousands of Korean and Chinese prisoners insisting that they would kill themselves rather than submit to forcible repatriation, many of Truman's advisers foresaw a replay of scenes like those at Fort Dix in June 1945. There Soviet prisoners (captured in German uniforms) had tried to provoke their GI custodians into killing them because they preferred death to whatever fate awaited them in the USSR. While this episode in New Jersey was uncomfortably close to home, there had been numerous "unpleasant incidents" of a similar sort in Europe. As Psychological Strategy Board personnel vigorously pointed out, U.S. participation in the forced repatriation of millions of reluctant Soviet citizens had caused—and continued to occasion—"widespread despair" in the eastern bloc. It had also occasioned much embittered comment from conservative critics of the Yalta agreement and those State Department staff responsible for enacting its noxious provisions. Truman's position in Korea was thus contrived "to a great extent in an effort to retrieve—or at least not add to—the damage done in 1945–47 by this forced repatriation policy."[37]

Truman's attempt to erase the stain of the past was fashioned with an eye firmly on the future. "Repetition of our previous mistake would discourage defection by Chinese communist forces in any future conflict," advised Wallace Carroll, prefiguring the line later endorsed by Dulles. "It would therefore in the long run cost us more American lives than are involved in the exchange of prisoners problem."[38] U.S. prisoners might experience hardship or loss of life during their long captivity, but their sacrifices were a price worth paying—and their suffering constituted its own rationale for continuing the war until Washington's terms had been met.

Although some historians have construed Truman's position as a largely ad hoc piece of opportunism, it was entirely congruent with the administration's broader commitment to defection as a lodestone of cold war strategy. Just two months before Truman made his assurance that no POW would be sent to "slaughter or slavery," he had unveiled the United States Escapee Program, underscoring his administration's commitment to a new "Fifth Freedom"—freedom of movement. White House policy on prisoner repatriation emerged from the same tangled web of symbolic and strategic aspirations spun around the escapee, that exemplary anticommunist whose salvation would demonstrate Washington's absolute commitment to the worth of the individual, thereby encouraging a steady flow of defectors to the West. In view of this very public promotion of flight from the "slave world," Truman could hardly have adopted any other position on the fate of reluctant POWs in Korea.

Like other escapee projections, however, repatriation policy was marked by substantial slippage between rhetoric and practice. Naturally, Truman and his successor presented the dispute between the UN Command and its communist opponents as expressive of the central dichotomy between freedom and slavery: individual choice versus mass compulsion. Yet the POW camps run by the UN Command for the prisoners at the center of this contest were assuredly not places that suggested a high regard for the "dignity and worth of the human person."

In these grim sites of material scarcity and brutal excess, "freedom of choice" was simply not a meaningful possibility. When one British journalist visited the camp on Koje Island in May 1952, he found inmates in "sensationally appalling condition": "puppets of skin with sinews for strings—their faces . . . a terrible, translucent grey," cringing "like dogs."[39] Lacking food and medicine, they consumed a daily ration of violence. Running battles occurred between prisoners and guards, who made liberal use of lethal force. In addition to strife between captors and captives, the camps were also staging grounds for two unfinished civil wars, Korean and Chinese. But since pro- and anticommunist prisoners were quickly screened and segregated, most of the camp's brutality arose not from clashes between ideological antagonists but from compound leaders' attempts to enforce *internal* discipline. Chinese Nationalist strongmen practiced extreme intimidation to ensure that none who found themselves in the anticommunist camp could subsequently switch sides.

The State Department knew that prisoners' attitudes toward repatriation were canvassed against a backdrop of "physical terror including organized murders, beatings, threats, before and even during the polling process" and that American officers themselves had done more to foster than to suppress this "police-state type of rule" in the camps.[40] Early in the war, U.S. personnel empowered Nationalist "trusties" among the prisoners to impose order. When General MacArthur supplemented his South Korean staff with recruits from Taiwan, Nationalist "patriotic organizations" not only were actively encouraged in the camps but became a dominant source of authority. Chinese prisoners thus experienced intense pressure to resist repatriation and were scarcely in a position to make an "uncoerced, unintimidated, informed choice." One ill-starred attempt to screen prisoners in February 1952 left 69 dead and 142 wounded.[41]

Conscious that a "reign of terror" governed camp life, U.S. personnel were nevertheless taken aback by the sheer volume of Chinese and Korean POWs who objected to repatriation.[42] American negotiators, estimating in early 1952 that 10 to 25 percent of POWs might resist, had already told the Chinese and North Koreans that they could expect 116,000 prisoners back. This figure was high enough that Beijing signaled willingness to explore a deal, asking U.S. officials to conduct a screening to confirm the numbers. When the Far Eastern Command duly did so, they were perturbed to find that only about 70,000 prisoners agreed to accept repatriation: 5,000 of 21,000 Chinese; 54,000 of 96,000 North Koreans; 4,000 of 15,000 South Koreans; and 7,500 of 38,000 civilian detainees.[43]

Understandably, Beijing refused to accept that less than a quarter of the People's Volunteers would be returned. Instead they accused American negotiators of a breach of faith and of using "force and cruel mistreatment" to deliver prisoners to its friends in South Korea and Taiwan.[44] Keen to settle terms, Washington responded to this setback by trying to *reduce* the number of nonrepatriates. When a further screening was held in late April–May 1952, American officials posed leading questions that emphasized the desirability of returning home, while stressing that the UN Command would accept no responsibility for those who refused repatriation.[45] The category of "nonrepatriate" was simultaneously narrowed to exclude those who merely *preferred* not to return, including only the prisoner who "would cut his throat, drown himself, [or] be prodded with a bayonet" before returning to the communist side.[46] Still, the total remained higher than Beijing could possibly accept.

As these hasty but ineffectual side steps suggest, Washington's chief concern lay neither in offering prisoners real freedom of choice nor in securing the largest possible number of "converts." Rather, U.S. policy makers sought to tap the symbolic potential of defection while averting the calamitous blow to U.S. prestige that would ensue if UN Command forces ended up repatriating anticommunist prisoners at gunpoint. When U.S. personnel began indoctrination efforts in the camps in 1951, they aimed (like the Chinese and North Koreans) to win ideological *converts* among their prisoners, not to engineer a mass defection. The prospect of fervent admirers of capitalist democracy returning home to undermine their state's social cohesion and political legitimacy initially held more appeal for U.S. strategists (and for their Chinese communist antagonists) than finding homes and occupations for myriad deserters. But Nationalist "patriotic organizations" and some zealous American Civilian Information and Education officers had other ideas, and once thousands of Chinese and Koreans announced their resistance to repatriation in unmistakable terms, even Foggy Bottom's skeptics warmed to the cause.[47]

Even then, though, American tacticians balked at the prospect of "too many" prisoners refusing repatriation. Since this war was clearly not going to be settled on the battlefield, a deal on the POW question would ultimately have to be struck: hence U.S. officials' attempts to shrink the number of nonrepatriates in April–May 1952. In the end, it took Stalin's death, intensive bombing of North Korea, and Eisenhower's threats of retaliation against the People's Republic to break the deadlock. Finally, in March 1953, Zhou En-lai proposed that all prisoners who rejected repatriation be delivered into neutral custody, pending a final adjudication of their fate. The following month, a limited exchange ("Little Switch") of sick and wounded prisoners was agreed upon, while those who consented to repatriation were subsequently released in the "Big Switch" of August–September 1953.

At last, the haggling was over. But the price of disagreement was exorbitant. Forty-five percent of the Korean War's casualties were incurred in the fifteen months during which repatriation formed the sole impediment to an armistice. On the UN side, approximately 125,000 were injured or killed, and as many as a quarter million on the North Korean and Chinese side: physical victims of Washington's "psychological" investment in the symbology of escape.

NO HARD FEELINGS: THE CAPTIVES RETURN

Little hard news about conditions in Chinese-run prison camps filtered back to America during the war. But when snippets of information were glued together with copious amounts of speculation a bleak picture emerged. The discrepancy between the number of prisoners the Chinese acknowledged holding and the figure the U.S. military believed had been taken prisoner lent itself to various readings, none of them encouraging. Had thousands of men perished en route to camps along the banks of the Yalu River? It was easy to imagine that hundreds had succumbed to frostbite, disease, or untreated battle injuries during these grueling forced marches, and just as easy for many Americans to suspect that North Korean guards would treat invalids and stragglers with utter ruthlessness. Perhaps some of these missing GIs had been smuggled across the border into Manchuria, or even transported to the Soviet Union. No one really knew.

It was no secret, though, that Beijing was making considerable use of their POWs for propaganda purposes. In 1952 and 1953 several U.S. airmen made radio broadcasts confirming Chinese claims that the United States had waged bacteriological warfare in Korea. From these disturbing "confessions," many concluded that American prisoners were being brutalized and brainwashed by captors whose ideological fanaticism was supplemented by an "Oriental" propensity for cruelty and "indifference to suffering"—or a more sadistic relish for inflicting pain. As the psychologist Raymond Bauer bitingly noted after the war, many Americans seemed to believe that "nothing less than a combination of the theories of I. P. Pavlov and the wiles of Fu Manchu could produce such results."[48]

Pilots like Marine Colonel Frank Schwable and Lieutenants Floyd O'Neal and John S. Quinn formed the prize exhibits in Beijing's germ warfare campaign.[49] However, when hundreds of families and local newspapers began receiving letters from prisoners full of peculiarly phrased pleas for peace, indictments of U.S. imperialism, and barbs about Wall Street warmongers, suspicions grew that the Chinese had launched a full-scale indoctrination campaign. "My brother couldn't have written those letters," announced Myrtle Wilson of her sibling, Aaron (one of the non-repatriates). "He was too dumb to write like that. Why, when he went in the Army he was seventeen and still in the eighth grade."[50]

Widely circulated "expert opinion" encouraged Americans to believe not only that their fellow citizens had been subjected to mental coercion but that brainwashing was an irresistible process. Every man was ultimately defenseless when confronted with communists trained in "mind murder," claimed Edward Hunter, the journalist who popularized the term *brainwashing*. In his opinion, this hijacking of free will represented the ultimate form of captivity. "The aim is to create a mechanism in flesh and blood, with new beliefs and new thought processes inserted into a captive body," Hunter claimed. "What that amounts to is the search for a slave race that, unlike the slaves of olden times, can be trusted never to revolt, always to be amenable to orders, like an insect to its instincts."[51] Similarly, Joost Meerloo insisted that "menticide" was a crime against humanity analogous with—or even worse than—genocide. Unless the victim died first, "capitulation [was] inevitable."[52]

Such notions carried ambiguous implications for the reception of homecoming POWs in 1953. If no one could withstand the insidious pressure Chinese cadres applied to the fragile human psyche, it stood to reason that returning prisoners should receive compassionate consideration. They had endured coercion of a kind no American POW had hitherto confronted, and most press columnists duly urged that returning prisoners who showed signs of duress be judged "not as traitors but as sick men."[53] Yet to conceive these men as brainwashed was also to acknowledge that they'd been "infected" with a poisonous ideology. If minds could be emptied "like overturned, corkless bottles and then refilled with Communist dogma," returning POWs were vessels containing a toxic substance that threatened to contaminate those with whom they came into contact.[54] Why would the Chinese devote so much manpower to the time-consuming business of brainwashing if not to send home men programmed to act under their captors' implanted instruction? The long-range objective was surely to create a network of saboteurs working like termites to hollow out and topple the American state from within, or sleeper cells awaiting activation during some future crisis. Writing in the *Saturday Evening Post*, Rear Admiral D. V. Gallery speculated that the Chinese had sown mental seeds that they anticipated would "take root and sprout" in ten or twenty years, should another depression grip America. "This may seem farfetched to us who live from year to year," he cautioned. "But it isn't to Asiatics, who look at centuries as we do months."[55]

Oscillations between sympathy and suspicion characterized popular commentary and official policy alike. Convinced that U.S. citizens still failed to grasp the enemy's true colors, the Psychological Strategy Board regarded servicemen's ordeal in captivity as a vehicle for popular enlightenment, an education in communism's inhumanity that would reinforce collective commitment to long-range cold war objectives. It was imperative, then, that Americans regard their homecoming prisoners as "victims of communist mental aggression"—a position the Psychological Strategy Board adopted before the first prisoner exchange of April 1953. Again in July, the board affirmed that returnees who had succumbed to psychological pressure were "not held to be traitors to their country, nor are they to be blamed for having adopted a practice of limited cooperation." To ensure this message hit home, the board's personnel cultivated press assistance to explain the POW issue in its "true magnitude and perspective" to the American people. Chinese "indoctrination efforts" were inseparable from "the global conspiratorial drive of International Communism. The one is simply a part of the greater whole."[56]

For their part, Defense officials, preoccupied by the apparent breakdown of military discipline among POWs, were much less inclined to write off the germ warfare "confessions," peace petitions, and other forms of prisoner cooperation as evidence of irresistible communist pressure. Fighting men were supposed to maintain discipline in captivity, not simply cave in to their captors' demands. On the long journey back from Asia, returnees would accordingly be interrogated about the still-hazy specifics of their treatment and behavior. Collaboration required investigation and punishment—whatever the appropriate penalty might be. On this matter, opinion differed, as it did over the delicate question of how to "deindoctrinate" those who'd been brainwashed, both for the psychological health of those "infected" and the well-being of the body politic as a whole.

Fears of contagion shaped the army's decision to quarantine twenty-three prisoners released in the "Little Switch" exchange of April 1953. On the basis of initial screening reports, intelligence officers concluded that 66 percent of all 149 American POWs in this group had been "politically reindoctrinated" by their captors, some to a "post-graduate level." The segregated men constituted the hard core, a "security risk" to the country at large.[57] Flown back to the United States under the guard of armed MPs, they were conveyed to Valley Forge Army Hospital at Phoenixville, Pennsylvania, for psychiatric evaluation, curative treatment, and further interrogation. But while the army regarded these contaminated men as a grave threat to national security, press commentators adopted a more compassionate position.

Editorial opinion uniformly condemned the army for stigmatizing these returnees as "Red-tinged," a charge sufficiently toxic at the height of the blacklisting era that some of those so labeled complained they'd be incapable of securing civilian employment and would be compelled to reenlist. Interviews with the Valley Forge internees, including an eight-page photo story in *Life*, accentuated the barbarity they had suffered at communist hands.[58] Their subsequent mistreatment by the U.S. military was thus all the more distressing. "A profound apology to these men is obviously in order," editorialized the *New York Times*. "They should have, in addition, the knowledge that their fellow-countrymen are profoundly sympathetic toward them and outraged over this misrepresentation of them."[59] Taking

FIGURE 23. Lichty takes aim at the U.S. military's program to "de-brainwash" returning POWs in a cartoon from June 1, 1953. Grin and Bear It © North America Syndicate.

their cue from staff at the hospital who insisted that they weren't "running a damned Laundromat here," press commentators also rubbished the notion of "de-brainwashing" as another manifestation of the Eisenhower administration's overweening obsession with "psychological warfare."[60] "The idea is as repugnant to us as it was to the GIs who came to Valley Forge," announced the *Philadelphia Inquirer.* "We don't believe any elaborate cure is needed for the minds of these men who went to war as Americans, endured prison as Americans and came back as Americans."[61]

Press opinion diverged sharply from the private judgment of prominent military and administration officials. The colonel in charge of evaluating the twenty-three men detained at Valley Forge speculated, with evident approbation, that the army would "probably hang" prisoners who had voluntarily collaborated with the enemy. Henry Cabot Lodge viewed prisoners who had accepted communist "re-arrangement of thought" as "intellectual eunuchs," while C. D. Jackson (Eisen-hower's PR impresario) disparaged the "hard-shelled commies" among the re-turnees as "goons" whom the FBI would continue to tail.[62] But lessons were learned from what *Newsweek* dubbed the "snafu at Valley Forge."[63] At least in pub-lic, the tone softened. Defense Department spokesmen announced that, when the major prisoner exchange occurred, there would be no further segregation. All would receive the same hands-off treatment. "In the future, the aim will be to counter Com-munist indoctrination of prisoners by 'letting the American way of life speak for itself,'" the *Washington Post* reported.[64]

Brigadier General Rawley Chambers, the army's chief psychiatrist, counseled civilians that "the wisest, kindest thing to do" was treat returning prisoners with casual nonchalance, as though they'd "just been around the corner to the drug-store." Press columnists replicated this advice, warning readers to resist the ten-dency to ask too many "nagging questions."[65] *Life* cited the opinion of a "top Army psychiatrist" whose visit to Valley Forge led him to conclude that there was no quicker way to drive men exposed to communist indoctrination "over the line . . . than a hostile attitude at home."[66] The president himself, touting his newfound re-ligiosity, preached a gospel of forgiveness and understanding. Asked to comment on the case of Corporal Dickenson—the first of the twenty-three "turncoats" to recant—Eisenhower encouraged fellow citizens to refamiliarize themselves with the parable of the Prodigal Son (Luke 15:11–32).[67] Americans were thus primed to em-brace returning prisoners warmly, including those who had wavered under pres-sure or whose attitudes seemed altered. "There's nothing to this brainwashing that a good steak and an ice-cream cone won't cure," one official confidently asserted, which translated into GI vernacular as "There's nothing the matter with our minds that can't be cured by a beer, a blonde, and a hometown newspaper."[68]

News media narrated the "return of the captives" in a variety of registers but typically staged homecoming as a celebration of down-home values as thousands of "nice little towns" across America experienced their "stirring moment of high emotion and high purpose."[69] Community spirit, godliness, and neighborly cheer formed a heartwarming contrast to the cruelties of communist captivity, though affirmations of homespun virtue in the pages of *Time, Life,* and *Newsweek* rarely avoided class condescension.

Edward Dickenson's return to Virginia in November 1953 provided a field day for reportage of this sort. The very name of his remote Appalachian hamlet, Crack-ers Neck, hinted at the types found residing there: a community largely untouched by twentieth-century technology and untutored in world affairs. Pop, a fragile sev-enty-two, announced himself "all tore up" over his son's mystifying initial decision in favor of Red China. Why, he'd "never heard the Communist name until this war started. Us mountain folks don't understand things and don't pay much attention

FIGURE 24. "Ain't no hard feelings." Members of the Dickenson family prepare to welcome a prodigal son home to Crackers Neck, Virginia, in December 1953. © The Associated Press.

to the papers and things," Pop told reporters. "They say my boy is a Communist, but he ain't. . . . Why, I'll bet if they had the President over there, they'd make him do anything they wanted." His wife, Bessie, a forty-four-year-old mother of thirteen, was "shore happy" her "purty boy" would soon be back.[70] "We done some shouting, but nothing like we are going to do when Ed gets home," she related, asking reporters to tell her son that "hereabouts nobody thinks hard of him for what he done and we will give him a big welcome home. Ain't no hard feelings."[71]

Sure enough, the conclusion of Ed's seven-thousand-mile odyssey occasioned "Joy in Crackers Neck." Scores of people crowded into the family's four-room cabin to offer an "almost hysterical welcome" to a local hero whose reappearance was little short of miraculous. A returnee from the slave world, the twenty-three-year-old corporal was greeted not only as a restored family member but as a voyager from the great unknown who had been farther, and seen more, than anyone else for miles around.[72]

Many homecoming stories similarly stressed the collision of worlds wrought by the return of men burdened with experience beyond their years and beyond the ken of their isolated communities. The very presence of former communist captives in these sleepy towns and villages was instructive, press commentators repeatedly stressed. "Through these young men the devious, ominous nature of the global war of ideas will be brought home to many Americans who have had little realistic contact with this intangible struggle," noted Malvina Lindsay in the *Washington Post*. Far from contaminating society, these men's debilitated bodies and vacant expressions lifted "the domestic quarantine from knowledge of communism."[73]

TELL US ABOUT THE BRUTALITY: REPRESENTATIONS OF COMMUNIST ATROCITY

"Everybody grabbed you," complained one newly returned former prisoner. "TV, radio, everybody." *Life* conjured scenes of GIs disembarking at San Francisco to the insistent call, "Tell us about the brutality!" But if the magazine intended to scold these overly intrusive hacks, it proved no less keen than competitors to deliver the goods.[74] Homecoming soldiers faced ceaseless entreaties to elucidate communist brutality, the more gruesome their stories—or emaciated their bodies—the better. "The tales being told by the prisoners returned by Communists in Korea are of a kind to make the heart sick," noted the *Washington Post* with evident relish.[75] While a few prisoners quietly attested that they had been fairly treated, experiencing no "rough stuff" and a diet only as poor as their captors', the "horrors of red slavery" monopolized attention in the fall of 1953.[76]

No phase or dimension of POW experience went undocumented, from the shock of capture to the euphoria of release. For most prisoners, captivity began—and for several hundred it also ended—with a long march north through austere, snow-covered terrain to the overhead accompaniment of strafing by U.S. bombers: "as bloody an experience as the Bataan Death March," noted *Time*.[77] Without adequate food, clothing, shelter, or medical attention, numerous prisoners succumbed to illness, chronic fatigue, and frostbite long before they reached encampments by the banks of the Yalu River. The *New Yorker* vividly relayed the story of one twenty-five-year-old sergeant who, after eighteen days of marching, "had nothing left of his toes but the bones. He kept walking anyway, urged along by an occasional prod of a rifle butt or bayonet, and goaded on even more forcefully by the realization that each time someone in the group dropped out, the sound of a single shot was quickly heard to the rear."[78] Later, to avoid an improvised amputation without anesthetic, the prisoner dug into his rotted joints with his fingernails and snapped off the bones himself.[79]

Descriptions of camp conditions enumerated myriad denials, shortages, and privations, particularly the meager rations on which men were forced to subsist. Food loomed correspondingly large in the moral economy of camp life and prisoners' imaginative projections.[80] Like inmates of the Soviet gulag, these prisoners dreamed of food, talked about food, and sometimes did whatever it took to acquire more of it. On an unfamiliar diet of millet, sorghum, and soybeans, supplemented rarely by vegetables or meat, many inmates developed beriberi, dysentery, and night blindness. But if food and medicine were in short supply, soap and hot water were altogether lacking. Journalistic accounts spoke euphemistically of the "filth" prisoners endured, but readers required little imagination to deduce that latrines in POW camps where many inmates suffered from dysentery would leave much to be desired. Imprisonment meant extended exposure to "excremental assault," not simply an olfactory affront but a blow to dignity and morale. Just as camp personnel manipulated rations to reward cooperation and punish disobedience, denial of "sanitation privileges" served to coerce as well as degrade.[81]

That every dimension of camp life was contrived to modify prisoners' behavior formed a common denominator of press reports. More than merely seeking compliance, however, the Chinese had set out to reengineer these GIs as "new communist men." Never before had a captor attempted a "systematic attack on the mind," asserted *US News and World Report*.[82] Much ink was spilled pondering the precise ways in which prisoners' psyches were assaulted: the relationship between bodily pain and mental pressure, indoctrination and suggestion, volition and subconscious. However mysterious the mechanics of brainwashing, the mastermind ultimately responsible for this "systematic attack" was commonly agreed to be Ivan P. Pavlov. In *Life*'s judgment, American POWs in North Korea were less pawns of Mao or Kim Il Sung than "prisoners of Pavlov."[83] For those convinced that the Soviets secretly controlled every aspect of the Korean War, the Russian psychologist did more than furnish an explanation of how reflexes could be conditioned to respond to external stimuli. His spectral influence in North Korea seemed to corroborate the Soviets' shadowy direction of the war itself. "A new, devilish technique evolved by the Chinese Communists," brainwashing was nevertheless "adapted from Russian methods," announced Richard Wilson in *Look* magazine.[84]

But what did this "devilish technique" entail? Rear Admiral Gallery explained to *Saturday Evening Post* readers how "red Brainwashers"—through a combination of physical torture and psychological manipulation—reduced men to "borderline case[s] between a human being and a rat struggling to stay alive." In the end, "natural instincts" were "replaced, like the rat's, by conditioned reflexes."[85] Often in less alarmist language returning prisoners told how they'd been forced to sit through haranguing monologues on topics such as the "decaying of capitalism" and U.S. imperialist aggression, then made to recapitulate these lectures with perfect fidelity. Information in the camps—and from the world beyond—was tightly controlled to permit prisoners access only to material that corroborated the Chinese line. Camp libraries contained copies of the *Daily Worker,* canonical works of Marx and Lenin, approved realist American fiction from Dreiser to Sinclair, and "specially prepared history books, 'all fixed up,' as one P. W. put it, 'about how bad we treated the Indians and the Spanish.'"[86] But indoctrination of this kind struck many contemporaries as the least insidious—and also least effective—form of brainwashing. Had the Reds relied on rote instruction alone, they'd surely have failed, encountering obdurate resistance from GIs skeptical of BS in general and communist "horseshit" in particular. According to *Time*, only 30 POWs of 3,500 proved "really susceptible to enemy propaganda."[87]

Since most critics similarly discounted the possibility that any number of prisoners found their captors' position *genuinely* persuasive, brainwashing necessarily appeared all the more sinister because it bypassed reason, turning men into automata despite themselves. How was this done? Where Admiral Gallery envisaged the individual prisoner reengineered in tormented isolation—like Robert Vogeler or Winston Smith—others saw the essence of brainwashing as manipulation of group dynamics and social milieu. To this end, the Chinese disrupted military command structures, organizing prisoners according to the degree of pliability they exhibited, while cultivating the tensions, suspicions, and resentments that camp life encouraged.

African American prisoners formed a particular target of attention. In 1952, they were segregated from their white peers and subjected to an intensive campaign to nurture disaffection with racist America. As one returnee later told the *Chicago Defender*, "The Chinese ignored the fact that segregation had been abolished in the American army . . . playing instead on any sensational news item or propaganda bit that could infer inequality." According to most mainstream American columnists, black and white, this indoctrination effort was an unmitigated failure. "The Negro retained a far greater capacity than the white man to keep his mind focused on fundamentals," wrote Edward Hunter, while a *Reader's Digest* story entitled "US Negroes Make Reds See Red" typified the tenor of much press reportage.[88]

Chinese cadres may have focused particular attention on African American prisoners, but many reports stressed the tenacity with which they sought *all* prisoners' psychological weak spots. "Self-criticism," a process derived from Maoist reeducation practice, provided a key. Under the watchful scrutiny of their peers and captors, POWs were required to review their life histories through the corrective lens of class consciousness. Written autobiographical statements had to be amended and finessed until all vestigial deviations had been ironed out, a wearisome process that not only sapped prisoners' stamina but helped interrogators pinpoint sources of hidden guilt, weakness, or fear of exploitation.[89]

Some commentators depicted the relationship between captor and captive as a sinister perversion of that between analyst and analysand.[90] But for a newfangled psychological process, mind control apparently relied on a good deal of "old-fashioned torture" applied to those who failed to submit to more subtle psychic pressures. Accounts of camp life spared their readers no detail—with sleep deprivation and solitary confinement ranking among the communists' milder abuses. More severe punishments saw recalcitrants immured in dank pits dug five feet or so into the ground or locked in wooden boxes too cramped to allow the occupant either to stand or to sit. Other techniques, like the "water treatment" ("waterboarding" in today's parlance), were typically described as unique "Oriental" inventions. "They would bend my head back, put a towel over my face and pour water over the towel," one former POW related. "I could not breathe. This went on hour after hour, day by day. It was freezing cold. When I would pass out they would shake me and begin again. They would leave me tied to the chair with the water freezing on and around me."[91]

Chinese interrogators also favored techniques that turned the tortured into their own torturers, forcing prisoners to adopt stress positions—sitting or standing to attention—that caused excruciating pain when sustained for hours. Leaving little or no trace of rough handling on prisoners' bodies, these self-administered punishments appealed to the Chinese, U.S. government spokesmen maintained, because they enabled Beijing to deny that it practiced torture. In reality, the Chinese not only employed multiple forms of torture but also softened prisoners up with constant reminders of death's proximity. Mock executions and real ones, coupled with the camps' high fatality rates, left prisoners in no doubt about the value their captors placed on preservation of human life.

Harrowing details of this sort were supplemented in the U.S. press by uplifting stories of resistance: tales of prisoners defying and outsmarting their captors, whether through humor, guile, or Christian faith. "If anything is surprising to me," announced Dr. Charles Mayo (a widely cited expert on the psychology of returning POWs), "it is that so many of our soldiers . . . although for months they were treated like animals or worse, somehow continued to act like men."[92] Captivity, it seemed, was an ordeal American prisoners had heroically survived—or even transcended.

SQUEALERS, CHINK-LOVERS, AND CHEESE-EATERS: RECKONING WITH COLLABORATION

Tales of communist "savagery and sadism," "terror and torture" laid powerful claim to readers' emotions, "almost too much horror for the public to comprehend," in *Newsweek*'s estimation.[93] Yet the accent on communist atrocity did not preclude publication of other "ugly stories" from the POW camps in which ugliness was predominantly an *American* attribute. Confronted with cruel and calculating captors, some prisoners had collapsed, and the specter of "collaboration" cast an ominous shadow over the reception of homecoming prisoners.

Discussion of collaboration drew on an idiom imported from Korea, where Chinese camp personnel dubbed receptive prisoners "Progressives" and resisters "Reactionaries." GIs reversed the valence of these appropriated labels, turning *Reactionary* into a badge of honor to be worn with pride. *Progressive,* meanwhile, was a dirty word, as the array of synonyms used in its place made abundantly clear: *chink-lover, squealer, rat.* "Progressives" were traitors who'd turned on their buddies, tattling to their captors and even betraying fellow captives' escape attempts.[94]

Former prisoners offered various explanations for these acts. Some attributed collaboration to venality. "It's not pretty to see your GI buddies go over to the Communists—this one for a warm room, that one for a few cigarettes, someone else for rice instead of millet," wrote Lt. Col. Thomas D. Harrison in *Collier's.*[95] Others suggested that progressives were "garden-variety quitters who found it easier to live by playing the Commie game," "just spineless men who didn't have the gumption to kill the lice in their shirts."[96] But many conflated collaboration with conversion. The lowest of the low, the "chink-lovers," were men who freely—even eagerly—embraced communism.[97]

Whatever impulses they ascribed to collapse, several former POWs stressed that men in captivity weren't completely stripped of agency. They had choices. Some had bravely resisted and paid the price, while others opted to make their lives easier by collaborating, often at fellow prisoners' expense. Maybe it didn't really matter whether a prisoner had "gone communist" or had just responded to the promptings of an empty stomach? The result looked the same, and self-styled "Reactionaries" made no secret of their desire for vengeance. "'Reactionaries' have come out of prison with an angry hatred," noted *US News and World Report.* "More than one has spotted a 'progressive' and asserted that, 'If I get a chance, I'll kill him.'" Similarly, a returning corporal from Boone, Iowa, told a *Newsweek* reporter that any "Pros" found on board the transports conveying servicemen back from Korea would be "shark bait." "Chink lovers," he insisted, were "hated worse than the Chinese."[98]

These venomous warnings weren't empty threats. Violent confrontations, including attempted homicides, did occur on the long oceanic voyage home, just as they had in the camps. Adopting the Klan as the model for their vigilantism, some "Reactionaries" summarily dealt with alleged "Progressives." Rarely, however, did these episodes make it into the press.[99] Stories of collaboration were so discomforting, motives and circumstances so murky, that many columnists derived reassurance from their conviction that "Reactionaries" were straightforwardly the "good guys." From the whole confused saga of captivity in Korea, their resistance appeared to offer something stable and affirmative. Reactionaries were soldiers who had "stuck steadfastly to all their patriotic beliefs through months of prison life," announced one press report.[100]

Girded with the assumption that "Pros" were all "commie lovers" or "stool pigeons" just as surely as "Reactionaries" were heroes and patriots, conservative civic leaders were apt to cold-shoulder men who returned under the malign star of "Progressivism." In Benham, Kentucky, homecoming celebrations that had drawn a crowd of ten thousand to a town of 3,500 soured when rumors began circulating that the twenty-one-year-old honoree, Army Staff Sergeant Jack Flannery, was a "Progressive." Veterans of Foreign Wars and American Legion officials abruptly stalked off the platform, leaving the smeared sergeant to insist that he "had just done a lot of reading in the camp library to better his vocabulary." Appreciating that this defense might not suffice, Flannery added that he "believed in capitalism, not Communism, and wanted to be a good American citizen."[101] Another alleged "Progressive," Bennie Smith, received "terroristic warnings" by phone and mail after the *Commercial Appeal* ran a series of derogatory stories about him, charging that the former POW had come home with "new, un-American ideas." The grounds for this claim? He had told a local businessmen's club in Mississippi that he "believed capitalism was not perfect."[102]

"To distinguish the converts to Communism from the victims of Communism" was, as *Newsweek* averred, no easy task.[103] But many nevertheless tried to map the contours of collaboration, to discern who had "turned," why, and what it might mean. Hardly had the last POWs disembarked before fictionalized representations of camp life began to appear on television and cinema screens, all preoccupied with this issue and eager to redeem prisoners' reputations by locating responsibility for "collapse" squarely with the captors or by erasing the taint of collaboration altogether.[104]

In September 1953, NBC's Fireside Theatre presented a POW drama entitled *The Traitor*. Based on a story by a Korean War combat veteran, Forrest Kleinman, it features as protagonist a stool pigeon assigned to betray his fellow prisoners' escape attempt but ultimately incapable of "justifying the means with the ends."[105] Broadcast one month later, U.S. Steel Hour's *POW* focused more squarely on the psychic repercussions of captivity. Set in a U.S. military hospital, David Davidson's teleplay depicts the strained dynamics among a group of newly returned POWs as they wrestle with feelings of guilt, inadequacy, and betrayal. Flashbacks to North Korea keep the traumatic past dangerously present. But the prospect of idolization by families and civic dignitaries makes the future hardly more appealing for men who fear their behavior in captivity was far from heroic. These anxieties take acute form in the central character, "Lucky" Dover (Richard Kiley). Beloved by his fellow comrades-at-arms—bar one, the self-styled Reactionary "Iron Man" Bonsell— Lucky carries a crippling psychological burden. Ashamed of having been captured, he is also tormented by the specter of having confessed under duress, a lapse so unspeakable he can't bring himself to disclose it to the hospital's "head doctor," Major Mead (Gary Merrill).

Like many social critics at the time of Big Switch, the playwright adopted a sympathetic position toward returning POWs, using the psychiatrist, Mead, to issue reassuring bromides. Throughout *POW*, he reminds the tormented former prisoners that the army expects captured soldiers to be only the "best men" they can, not martyrs. Mead assures Lucky that "every man has his breaking point" and that this particular enemy won't rest until he has located and exploited each man's Achilles' heel. Why, even Cardinal Mindszenty—"You've heard of him, Lucky?" "Everybody's heard of him!"—was finally broken by the communists. Should American prisoners, ordinary mortals, really demand more of themselves than a "Prince of the Church"? Mead thus absolves Lucky, whose guilt turns out not merely to be excessive but altogether misplaced. A third-act plot twist reveals that Dover hadn't confessed at all. It was Bonsell, the ostensible "Reactionary," who betrayed an escape attempt to the Chinese, with Lucky framed as the stool pigeon. Yet even Bonsell finds absolution. As the final credits roll, a voice-of-God narrator gravely cautions viewers to remember that it was the "nature of the enemy" to *force* prisoners into submission.

POW clearly struck a receptive chord. The "greatest play ever done on television," as the *Hollywood Reporter* gushed, it was appreciatively received by the Pentagon, which acquired its own kinescopes for private screenings.[106] Television viewers' responses were no less avid. When *POW*'s transmission was disrupted in Detroit by a blown condenser at WXYZ-TV, public reaction was stronger than anything the station had ever experienced. Callers jammed the switchboard, sending thousands of letters and petitions protesting that their viewing had been interrupted—just as the Chinese began torturing the American POWs. "Immediate reaction was a cry of 'sabotage!'" related *Variety*, with many viewers "believing that some Communist had purposely cut off the video at that point." The episode became a front-page cause célèbre as Detroit viewers demanded a complete rebroadcast.[107] Primed by *POW*'s characterization of a foe for whom no tactic was too devious and by ubiquitous depictions of communists as shady fifth columnists, viewers made the obvious imaginative leap: that Red saboteurs had engineered the blackout at WXYZ-TV.

Hollywood also proved keen to tap the vein of impassioned anticommunism exhibited by Detroit's clamorous viewers, though the studios proved less willing than television dramatists to concede that any American prisoners had in fact collapsed. Eager to shake off MGM's reputation for "buying a story when it's topical and releasing it when it's typical," Dore Schary assigned a writer to his POW project on August 22, three days after the army signaled its approbation. Two days later, when the first transport docked in San Francisco with a consignment of 328 former prisoners, the screenwriter Allen Rivkin was waiting on the dock to conduct interviews.[108] On release in May 1954—with *Prisoner of War* touted by the studio as the "Film of the Year"—MGM bragged that it had set a "speed record for the development from original screenplay to actual filming of a motion picture," four months and two days.[109]

Promotional material made substantial claims on behalf of a feature that purported to depict "the factual, unbelievable story of the hell behind enemy lines."

Rivkin's sixty interviews with newly returned prisoners meant that all "incidents and dialog" were "for real"—or so publicists announced. But MGM tiptoed with extreme caution around the issue of collaboration, hinging its plot on a "pseudo-Progressive," an army intelligence officer, Captain Web Sloane (Ronald Reagan), parachuted into North Korea to gather "proof and documentation" of communist violations of the Geneva Conventions. To gain closer access, Sloane assumes the identity of an eager "Pro," even suggesting that the Reds force American prisoners to make propaganda broadcasts. The camp commandant, a familiar screen Russian (played, as ever, by Oscar Homolka), expatiates on the "conditioned reflex of the rat," but his Chinese underlings display less psychological acuity and more a sadistic relish for torture. Over the course of the film's eighty-four-minute running time, American prisoners are stretched out on wooden poles; given a "water cure" in which the victim's head freezes in an icy death mask; made to lie "in their own filth" for days in shallow graves; and subjected to mock executions. Confronted with unswerving resistance from the camp's arch-Reactionary, Corporal Stanton (Steve Forrest), the communists deploy their ultimate weapon—bludgeoning the American's puppy to death. "An old Chinese custom," Sloane remarks knowingly.

No tactic is too dastardly for the communists. Yet nothing breaks the indestructible Stanton, whose powers of endurance stand in stark contrast to the craven behavior of fellow prisoner Jesse Treadman (Dewey Martin). "One percent brain and ninety-nine percent stomach," as a disgusted POW puts it, Treadman has been bought by his captors and is now "playing footsie with Stalin." "Just a little mouse," this "cheese-eater" doesn't even need shock therapy to make him squeal. But Treadman's treachery turns out to be a tease. Having taunted audiences with the noxious presence of a rat in the POW camp, MGM offers a final reel reprieve. Treadman is revealed as another undercover military operative merely *posing*, like Reagan's character Sloan, as a "Pro" to gather intelligence. With the cloud of collaboration lifted, cinema audiences could breathe easy, assured that American prisoners were uniformly as valorous as their captors were monstrous.

Few, however, seemed to want this kind of comic book comfort. Far from claiming its mantle as "movie of the year," *Prisoner of War* offended just about everybody. The army distanced itself from an "unhelpful" production it had initially supported with gusto. Movie critics, meanwhile, passed harsh judgment on a feature that handled a sensitive topic so crudely: "unbelievable" but not in the way MGM publicity intended to denote. The Soviets and Chinese were cartoonish grotesques whose repertoire of cruel and unusual punishments—as crude as the film's politics—strained credulity beyond breaking point. *Prisoner of War* "only rings faintly of the horrible truth," lamented *Variety*. The torture scenes, like those in Felix Feist's Mindszenty melodrama, *Guilty of Treason*, offered viewers "a series of oversimplifications of what could have been a serious and visually impressive indictment."[110]

FIGURE 25. "An old Chinese custom." Not content with physical torture, the Reds prepare to bludgeon an American prisoner's puppy to death in MGM's *Prisoner of War* (1954). Courtesy of Photofest.

"Laudable" in purpose, the picture's emphasis on "commie blandishments . . . would seem to limit the audience appeal," echoed the *Hollywood Reporter*.[111]

Columbia Pictures' *The Bamboo Prison*, released seven months later in December 1954, was even less serious and just as unsuccessful. Whereas *Prisoner of War* aspired to verisimilitude, its successor played captivity for laughs—a "poor man's *Stalag 17*," one trade critic opined.[112] Everything MGM's picture lacked *The Bamboo Prison* strove to provide. Romance and comedy topped the list of bankable ingredients not typically found in a prisoner-of-war camp and nowhere visible in *Prisoner of War*. Unencumbered by pretensions to documentary realism, director Lewis Seiler equipped the camp's "brainwashing chief from Moscow," a Communist Party USA defector, with a ballerina bride, Tanya (Dianne Foster), thus introducing some "feminine appeal." As the comely brunette arrives at the camp, the American prisoners jostle behind the barbed wire to get a better view. "Boy, could I use a brainwash!" one joker exclaims. Indoctrination lectures provide an opportunity for fun at the communists' expense, while allowing the camp's one African American inmate (a middle-class professional who has volunteered for service in Korea) to refute communist slurs about discrimination in the United States. The "problem of the Negro in America will one day be ended," he intones solemnly, in terms redolent of Edith Sampson. "I would rather be black than Red!"

More breezily pitched than its predecessor, *The Bamboo Prison* nevertheless shares a central plot device with *Prisoner of War*. Its two key protagonists are also U.S. military intelligence agents who feign communist sympathies to amass evidence about atrocities—a covert mission that involves Sergeant Bill Rand (Robert Francis) "climbing under the covers of the Proletariat" with the alluring Tanya. ("Horrible, ain't it, the sacrifices a guy's gotta make for his country," quips Rand's sidekick, Corporal Brady.) The dancer quickly overcomes her scruples about stealing incriminating documents from under her husband's nose. Communism, she ruefully announces, has "emasculated" Russian men, though it doesn't appear to have altogether debilitated her husband. Discovering Tanya's perfidy, he subjects her to a "charming game called Russian roulette"—a dice with death from which she's saved by Rand and Brady, who arrange her passage to America along with the repatriated POWs.

The Bamboo Prison met no greater critical acclaim or commercial success than had *Prisoner of War*, offending for some of the same reasons while adding new sources of affront. Above all, it outraged Catholic sentiment by making its one real traitor the camp padre: an American communist cloaked in a cassock whose imposture is rumbled when it becomes clear that he neither knows the meaning of mea culpa nor feels any remorse for his own egregious trespasses. Catholic organizations were outraged that a vodka-drinking Red would pass himself off as a man of the cloth and that Columbia Pictures would expose cinemagoers to such blasphemy, even though the sin hardly goes unpunished. (After exposing the interloper,

Brady strangles the phony priest to death with his bare hands.) In response to church pressure, several state censorship boards moved to ban the picture's exhibition— a testament not only to Catholic primacy over the cinema screen but also to the volatility of feeling that surrounded the "POW story."[113]

PITY OR PUNISHMENT?

If sympathy provided the initial leitmotif of homecoming, compassion was complicated by less forgiving judgments of prisoners' record in captivity. Within months of Operation Big Switch, empathy had ebbed. By mid-decade, social critics overwhelmingly construed U.S. prisoners' record in captivity as a source of alarm, less a testament to communist brutality than an index of national collapse— and, as such, a source of shame that required vigorous remedial action if a disastrous repeat performance were to be avoided. The speed with which this volte-face occurred owed much to promptings from the army. For homecoming prisoners press columnists had contemplated "Pity or Punishment?" After the Valley Forge "de-brainwashing" snafu, the military's softer tone suggested an inclination toward clemency, a verdict mandated by civilian sentiment. Soon, though, it became clear that a dim view of collaborators—hitherto largely confined to private discussion— would govern military policy. Punishment, not pity, was the order of the day.[114]

The military response to *Prisoner of War* serves as a barometer of this shift. At first, Defense officials endorsed Schary's project as a marvelous instructional tool, appointing a liaison officer—himself a former POW who had spent thirty-three months in captivity—to improve the "overall accuracy and authenticity" of Rivkin's screenplay. But by May 1954, when the film opened, the army publicly distanced itself from the feature, even refusing to permit military bands to play at theaters where *Prisoner of War* was premiering. Where had the studio gone wrong? According to an army spokesman, the movie's central failing was that the incidents depicted "were just contrary to the facts as we know them."[115] More to the point, MGM's contribution was no longer helpful. In the army's estimation, the implication that *no* U.S. prisoners had collaborated—except those tasked to do so by Military Intelligence—was problematic. For one thing, *Prisoner of War* threatened to confirm Chinese charges that uniformed Americans were all spies, and since the People's Republic continued to detain several U.S. airmen this wasn't an inconsequential matter.[116] For another, while the feature was in production the army had begun court-martial proceedings against former prisoners accused of violating the 1951 Uniform Code of Military Justice: a policy that rearranged imperatives for home-front opinion management.[117]

No longer were portraits of communist cruelty and unbelievable feats of soldierly endurance so germane to military purposes. On the contrary, *Prisoner of War*'s depiction of staunch resistance unto death displeased an army struggling to quell public unease over the courts-martial. A very different message was now required: that captivity did *not* automatically render every POW a hero. Some captured soldiers had in fact dishonored their uniform and their country. Echoing this line, the *New York Times*'s military correspondent, Hanson Baldwin, urged that Americans "learn to distinguish between villains and heroes. They must rid themselves of sentimentality . . . and they must strive to see the prisoner-of-war issue whole." In other words, civilians must accept that some "weak, maladjusted, dissatisfied and immature young men"—traitors and cowards—deserved punishment.[118] The "organs of public information," Baldwin continued, had been derelict. "We drew up a simple equation . . . the Communists were wicked, conditions in the prison camp were terrible, many prisoners were tortured, this American was a prisoner of the wicked and the cruel, and therefore he must be good and brave."[119] Perpetuating this pattern, *Prisoner of War* was deemed most regrettable. Army Motion Picture Section personnel fretted that "all men who were progressives or who were considered in that category might use the story to further their own end."[120]

Prisoner of War was released in May 1954—in tandem with the first court-martial of a former POW. The accused: Corporal Edward Dickenson, the "turncoat" who had quickly changed his mind in October 1953, claiming (among other things) that he had remained behind to gather more dirt on the Chinese, like Reagan's screen character. Army statements took pains to stress, however, that Dickenson's offense was not that he initially refused to come home. Since U.S. negotiators had fought for months to instantiate the principle of voluntary repatriation, military authorities could hardly arraign a soldier who had chosen to exercise this right. Instead, the corporal was charged under Article 104 of the Uniform Code of Military Justice with "unlawful intercourse" and currying favor with his captors "to the detriment of fellow prisoners."[121]

His trial was the first of fourteen conducted by the army, and it attracted front-page press coverage. The fresh-faced boy from Crackers Neck had achieved national celebrity, returning to a hero's welcome and, within days, marrying a local girl to whom he had proposed in a letter from Korea—months before their first date. Yet even if Dickenson hadn't been feted in *Life* or likened to the Prodigal Son by President Eisenhower, the first army court-martial of a former POW would surely have generated intense interest as a highly charged moment of reckoning. If it was true that every man had his breaking point, did duress constitute a legally acceptable defense for every act of capitulation, or was it a "crime to crack up," as *US News and World Report* inquired?[122]

Adjudication of soldiers' actions in captivity posed vexing evidentiary questions—in Dickenson's court-martial as in those that followed. How credible were witnesses recently returned from a long, arduous, and disorienting experience?[123] The journey home was, in different ways, little less demanding. With Intelligence questionnaires running to eighty pages, some former prisoners ended up with files "close to two feet thick."[124] No one emerged from camp free from suspicion, and on the ship-bound voyage back, former POWs fresh from extended "self-criticism" sessions were required to make detailed statements about their own and others' behavior to military interrogators and psychiatrists. This febrile situation—in which guilt feelings were exacerbated by superiors' evident mistrust and a pervasive mood of vengefulness—produced a frenzy of recriminatory accusations. POW stories naturally tended toward the self-justificatory. Not surprisingly, then, the witnesses in Dickenson's court-martial, including the defendant himself, proved of questionable reliability.[125]

During the court-martial a succession of former prisoners testified. Dickenson was alleged to have informed camp authorities about four fellow POWs' escape plans, causing one man (himself a witness) to be "beaten brutally by Chinese Communists."[126] Accusers also claimed that the corporal had tried to convert camp inmates to communism, solicited signatures for an "Asiatic peace pact," and pushed an ailing prisoner down some stairs after the sick man had asked for food. During a heated discussion about the Rosenbergs in the summer of 1953, Dickenson was said to have "asked why, if there was freedom in the United States, the nation would execute people who were 'fighting for peace.'" He himself had announced over the loudspeaker system at Pyoktong, Camp #5, that he intended to fight for peace. Worse yet, he had been seen entering the quarters of a Chinese communist known as "Screaming Skull" three or four times a day, proof positive that he'd been snitching.[127] But while the accusations mounted, the accusers' credibility waned. One week into the trial, a star witness for the prosecution—the only man to claim that he had *personally* overheard Dickenson informing on fellow POWs—swore that he was so uncertain about the events in question that he wanted all his previous testimony thrown out: "I was mistaken—I think so—I am still confused on it."[128] Despite this befuddled protestation, his earlier statements remained extant.

Dickenson's lawyer unsuccessfully attempted to have the case dismissed on the grounds that the army had implied, if not directly promised, that Dickenson would enjoy immunity from prosecution on returning to the United States. The remaining nonrepatriates had, after all, been encouraged to recant in January 1954 with reference to the good treatment Dickenson received on return, and assurances that "no harm" would come to them or their families if they accepted repatriation. Throughout the court-martial, Dickenson opted to remain silent, claiming in a written statement that he had been subjected to "cruel and brutal treatment." Intensively indoctrinated, he had been promised "a home, a job and any woman in China" if he refused repatriation. Chinese camp officials had further assured the corporal that, since revolution was imminent in the United States, he would soon be able to select any job "from President on down."[129]

When the presiding legal officer, Colonel Richard Scarsborough, remained unmoved by pleas of duress, Dickenson's lawyer argued—as did defense teams in later courts-martial—that the defendant's mental balance had been impaired during his captivity.[130] Three psychiatrists testified that he was the kind of "emotionally un-stable" young man who could be "intimidated easily." One described Dickenson as a "passive-aggressive personality"—a term glossed by the *Washington Post* as "the sort of person who after a brief and ineffectual struggle against environment tends to follow the line of least resistance." With a background of "insecurity, deprivation and a feeling that nobody really cared for him," Dickenson had capitulated much more readily to "Communist bullying" than "more stable individuals."[131]

That Dickenson was "easily led" was hardly the kind of mitigating factor liable to sway an army intent on disciplining deviance. The defendant was duly pro-nounced guilty. Dishonorably discharged, with forfeiture of all pay and allowances, the twenty-three-year-old corporal was sentenced to ten years' imprisonment with hard labor: the first soldier to be convicted under a code not yet promulgated when he enlisted.[132] With a few virulent exceptions, like George Sokolsky of the *New York Journal-American,* who had long argued that the military should court-martial those "rats" that Reactionaries hadn't already strung up on the journey home, opinion sided with Dickenson, not the army.[133] The verdict "deeply disturbed" Representa-tive Frances Bolton (R-OH). "Let's be human in these things," she urged. Another Republican member of Congress, William C. Wampler of Virginia, described Dick-enson as a "mere country boy victimized by a shrewd propaganda technique."[134] Many wondered what had happened to the army's intimations of clemency. "The boys was promised to have a big welcome if they would come home," Dickenson's sister, Rose Helen, reminded the president. "Now look what they have done to him. I know you (IKE) have all power to stop it."[135] But Eisenhower didn't intercede, and more than one draft board member resigned in disgust over this breach of faith. "The Army lied to him and if it will lie to one it will lie to another," announced Al-bert L. White of Hattiesburg, Mississippi.[136]

Despite these signs of restiveness, the army's judgmental turn was decisive. Claude Batchelor, the second of the twenty-three nonrepatriates to change his mind, was found guilty of "aiding the enemy" in September 1954. Many voices were again raised in protest—Robert Vogeler condemning the former POW's life sentence to hard labor as the "most unjust thing" he had "ever heard." All told, Batchelor served four and a half years, one year longer than Ed Dickenson, who emerged in November 1957—divorced, embittered, but saved—to pursue his ec-clesiastical calling at a Baptist ministerial college in Nashville.[137] "The only differ-ence between me and a lot of others," Dickenson told reporters as he left the dis-ciplinary barracks at Fort Leavenworth, "is the others have not been caught."[138] Or, at any rate, not court-martialed.

The army had, in fact, made vigorous efforts to catch every case of collaboration, investigating 426 men—11 percent of repatriated prisoners. Of all the services, it adopted the least yielding line.[139] The air force, by contrast, examined eighty-three men suspected of misconduct before announcing that it wouldn't court-martial any of them. Twelve were honorably discharged, with an opportunity to demonstrate why they should not be disciplined.[140] For its part, the marine corps launched an investigatory hearing into the conduct of Colonel Frank Schwable in February 1954. This two-month-long investigation ended in his partial exoneration. The colonel would not face court-martial, but his germ warfare confession was deemed to have "seriously impaired" his "military usefulness." General Lemuel Shepherd, who made no secret of his disgust with this subordinate, advised that Schwable would hence-forth be assigned duties that would make "minimum demands" on his leadership capacity. The colonel was consigned, in *Time*'s plangent phraseology, to "some kind of military limbo . . . compelled to wander, unpunished but unloved" for the rest of his life.[141] Draconian though this fate appeared, it could have been considerably worse. "There isn't any question but that Colonel Schwable is a coward and a trai-tor and the Marines will probably hang him," crowed Walter Bedell Smith during a private telephone conversation with Dulles.[142]

Neither Schwable nor any other former POW was in fact hanged for crimes committed in captivity. Only one, Sgt. James Gallagher, was sentenced to life im-prisonment, found guilty of murdering two fellow prisoners.[143] Still, both in the Pentagon and beyond, the view gained ground that something had gone terribly awry in Korea—that the American fighting man was not what he once had been or ought to be.

SELF-CRITICISM

By the late 1950s Americans of almost every political stripe had come to believe that their soldiers' record in captivity during the Korean War was uniquely shame-ful. Journalist Eugene Kinkead crystallized this verdict in a book entitled *In Every War but One* (based on an extended essay written for the *New Yorker* in 1957), in which he argued that never before in history had U.S. prisoners behaved so dis-gracefully. Their lapses extended beyond "wholesale collaboration" and a perplex-ing collective failure to escape to brutal—or murderous—behavior toward fellow prisoners. Most damningly of all, 38 percent of American POWs (2,730 of a total of 7,190) had died in captivity: a "calamity that might not, on the face of it, seem to point to any moral or disciplinary weakness among the prisoners."[144]

Kinkead sought to disabuse his readers of any such sanguinity. Rates of collab-oration, acquiescence to captivity, and the high number of fatalities all pointed to-ward an alarming attrition of martial manhood. In his opinion, these various forms of surrender owed nothing to brainwashing, a notion he forcefully refuted. If POWs had been neither politically reoriented, psychologically rewired, nor physically tor-tured by their captors, then their "sad and singular record" must be the result of personal inadequacies and, by extrapolation, national deficiencies. In droves, these pathetic captives had voluntarily—even willfully—lapsed into inertia, exhibiting something approximating a collective death wish, a syndrome Kinkead termed "give-up-itis." Instead of maintaining discipline and sustaining their esprit de corps as captured Turkish and British soldiers had, American prisoners turned on one another, adopting an "each to his own" mentality or opting out of this Hobbesian war for individual survival altogether. Many had simply refused to struggle through the monotonous days of captivity—hence the unprecedented death toll.

That Americans had *only themselves to blame* for dying in such large numbers as prisoners of Chinese and North Korean communists might seem an unlikely message for cold war America to embrace. As the military sociologist Albert Biderman noted, Kinkead painted a "strangely white portrait of the Reds"—a snapshot of camp life that consigned its privations, pressures, and underlying brutality to the background.[145] Together with Edgar Schein, Raymond Bauer, Robert Lifton, and other psychologists, Biderman made a systematic effort to expose Kinkead's fallacies, contending that POWs behaved no differently—hence no worse—in Korea than in any previous war. That they died in greater numbers was due not to terminal apathy but to "malnutrition, disease, exposure, and wounds which were not treated."[146] Yet clinical correctives did little to mitigate popular perceptions that American behavior in captivity constituted a national disgrace. The "collapse thesis" soon dominated interpretations of POW experience, and even those drawn to more outré conceptions of brainwashing accepted Kinkead's questionable indices of "give-up-itis." Thus John Frankenheimer—whose 1962 feature *The Manchurian Candidate* memorably depicted POWs whose minds had been "not only washed but dry-cleaned"—credited *In Every War but One* as a particular influence. In an interview with Gerald Pratley, the director recalled how he had been struck that "not one prisoner ever attempted to escape"—an exaggerated restatement of Kinkead's erroneous assertion.[147]

The "collapse thesis" was, in Biderman's analogy, a millipede that grew back legs as fast as they could be hacked off. But what gave a *New Yorker* article and its spin-off that sold no more than fifteen thousand copies such traction? Clearly, the "something-new-in-history" line required more than one proponent, and sure enough, Kinkead said little that the army sources on whom he relied hadn't been saying for years—privately and publicly. The 1955 Department of Defense report *POW: The Fight Continues after Battle* articulated a more mangled version from which Kinkead subsequently ironed the wrinkles. Asserting that the prisoners' record had been "fine indeed," the report nevertheless insisted that a similar episode "must never be permitted to happen again."[148] To this end, President Eisenhower unveiled a new Code of Conduct for captured service personnel in August 1955. After much interservice disagreement over whether in the age of "brain-warfare" it was reasonable to expect prisoners to remain uncooperative, the code reaffirmed that POWs should divulge no more than their name, rank, date of birth, and serial number—information that a captor was lawfully permitted to request.[149]

The code underscored the message transmitted by the army courts-martial: that soldierly conduct in Korea had been reprehensible and could not go unchallenged. Military-sponsored reports on communist interrogation and indoctrination techniques also concluded that brainwashing—"the voluntary submission of people to an unthinking discipline and robot-like enslavement"—did not explain prisoners' lapses in the camps of North Korea.[150] Kinkead popularized these conclusions in such a way as to imply that no serious pressure at all had been applied to the prisoners, enunciating a gospel of collapse also fervently preached by Colonel William Erwin Mayer. An army psychiatrist, Mayer toured the country during the late 1950s and early 1960s, making a handsome livelihood from delivering the same talk approximately twice a week on the POWs' traitorous conduct and what it indicated about the "rottenness of American character."[151]

These social critics alighted on symptoms of national malaise with unalloyed greed—the appeal of their message attesting a mania for morbid introspection by a generation of "cultural hypochondriacs."[152] Captivity was accordingly less compelling for what it revealed of men in extremis than what it implied about the "weakness" of American society as a whole. Thanks to the diligent efforts of Kinkead, Mayer, and others of their ilk, the much-prodded and probed Korean War prisoners became "the subjects of another type of propaganda—propaganda by Americans, about Americans, directed to Americans."[153] Construed as a referendum on national character, the POWs' parlous record prompted a vote of no confidence in the entire postwar generation.

According to the Cassandras of decline, those susceptible to give-up-itis were "people without strong religious or family ties—in other words, persons who are spiritually and emotionally adrift." These "dependent personalities," "more than normally eager for affection and social approval," often tried to please their captors by giving them the right answers. In their passivity, anomie, and "other-directedness," the prisoners resembled their gray flannel–suited peers who had never been drafted to fight in Korea but had floated adrift in the lonely crowd. Somehow the younger siblings of the "greatest generation" weren't valiant warriors but sluggish conformists with a tendency toward "emotional constriction."[154] Somewhere along American history's onward march, these characterological defects had supplanted the "barbarian virtues" of a vigorously expansionist population. Prone to depression and increasingly addicted to tranquillizers, midcentury man was, as Arthur Schlesinger put it, "tense, uncertain, adrift"—descriptors that arguably fit midcentury American woman even better. This was certainly the view advanced by Betty Friedan. In *The Feminine Mystique* she proposed that the symptoms in question were quintessentially those of a *female* malady, even if psychologists took note only when "the apathetic, dependent, infantile, purposeless being, who seems so shockingly non-human" happened to be male. Citing Kinkead's litany of POW lapses, Friedan concluded that the "new American man" was "strangely reminiscent of the familiar 'feminine' personality."[155]

For many critics, passivity wasn't simply an affliction of the spirit. Psychic lassitude assumed a corporeal form every bit as alarming. As fiber frayed, so American bodies became soft, pudgy, and prone to "muscular deterioration," a condition that many agencies, including the White House, sought to address. "What's Wrong with American Youths?" inquired US News and World Report nervously in 1954, and answered that they were "not as strong as Europeans," who "enjoyed fewer of the advantages of modern civilization."[156]

If the symptoms of demise were everywhere apparent, social clinicians were in no doubt as to their ultimate source: affluence. Success hadn't spoiled just Rock Hunter; the privilege of existence "under the highest standard of living that the earth had ever seen" had corroded national character.[157] In support of this thesis, Meerloo cited experimental tests on overfed laboratory rats that demonstrated that "luxury negatively influences man's capacity to endure."[158] Prosperity had plumped the flesh and sapped the spirit. Like Richter's lethargic lab rats, the children of plenty no longer toughened their bodies through constant motion and vigorous play. Instead, they munched and slouched in front of the television—a pacifying device that worked its own form of brainwashing on young and old alike.

Affluence had also apparently produced a different kind of parent: one inclined to pamper, coddle, and cosset the child. "Are unusually permissive, indulgent parents more numerous today—and are they weakening the character of our children?" Dr. Spock inquired in 1960.[159] Many thought so, typically locating responsibility for this troubling development with America's mothers. The presumptive primary caregiver, "mom" was an unstable neurotic liable to smother her offspring with excessive maternal love. "Momism" had become a menace. This, at any rate, was the position aggressively staked by Philip Wylie in Generation of Vipers, a wartime polemic that continued to reverberate through the 1950s and beyond. According to Mayer, "A boy who has been brought up largely by his mother alone, a boy who has become what in psychiatry we refer to as a dependent character, something like the result of 'momism' as described by Philip Wylie . . . did not withstand the stresses of captivity at all well."[160]

Critics of maternal excess weren't all fueled by Wylie's misogyny. Friedan, for example, offered a lamentation for the children of frustrated middle-class mothers who devoted themselves "almost exclusively to the cult of the child from cradle to kindergarten," lacking other creative, professional, and emotional outlets. For such women, the relationship with their children "became a love affair, or a kind of symbiosis," Friedan suggested. Mothers of this sort spawned sons uniquely prone to "give-up-itis"—a proposition that The Manchurian Candidate (released the

"I'd Have Said To Those Reds, 'Now, See Here! . . . .'"

FIGURE 26. "I'd have said to those Reds, 'Now, see here! . . .'" 1954 Herblock Cartoon, copyright by The Herb Block Foundation.

same year as *The Feminine Mystique*) vividly affirmed in Angela Lansbury's portrayal of "Mother." An incestuously inclined monster, she raises an emotionally stunted son whose reflexes are ripe for conditioning.[161]

Like other forms of social criticism inspired by or extrapolating from the POWs' "sorry record," critiques of deficient parenting pulled in different directions. No style of childrearing lay beyond reproach. While indulgent stay-at-home mothers produced suggestible "momma's boys," independent working women were suspected of sapping their sons' manliness—as though a zero-sum Oedipal equation precluded the possibility that strong women might raise strong sons. Thus when the no-nonsense mother of Claude Batchelor appeared on television in November 1953 to discuss her son's refusal to return home, one critic noted, "Looking at the stern old-American features of Mrs. Batchelor, it was hard indeed to imagine her son a Communist—unless her very strength had weakened him."[162]

Authoritarian parents, male or female, were perhaps the most culpable of all. "Any POWs who accepted Communist propaganda as a result of Soviet 'mind washing' techniques were men who, as children, gave up the struggle to be themselves and abandoned themselves to the dictates of father or mother," announced Dr. James Clark Moloney at the American Psychoanalytic Association convention in 1953. By way of corroboration, Moloney cited Robert Vogeler. Anyone wondering why the IT&T executive had confessed to ludicrous charges in a Budapest courtroom need look no further than his German father, whose dictatorial habits could be taken as read.[163] Similarly, in MGM's court-martial drama *The Rack* (1956), it is a harshly disciplinarian father—an army colonel incapable of exhibiting affection—who appears most responsible for his son's collapse in captivity. This critique of fatherhood was by no means restricted to Laven's film alone.[164]

What could be done to fortify national character? The military quickly devised an array of responses to Americans' unfitness for the rigors of waging cold war. One innovation was the inauguration of military "torture schools" in which roleplaying soldiers prepared for "the abrupt transition from American life to Commie prisoner life."[165] The idea was purportedly to alert soldiers and airmen to the physical privations and interrogation techniques they might confront in captivity: an amulet against mysterious Red methods, born of a belief that (as General Jacob L. Devers put it) "the American boy can take most anything if he knows what he's up against."[166] "We must do everything we can psychologically to prepare our soldiers for the torments of these heathen Red foes," insisted General Matthew B. Ridgway, who had commanded the UN forces in Korea.[167] At Stead Air Force Base in Lemmons Valley, Nevada, airmen encountered a regime in which "hunger, pain and fatigue" were part of the training. So too was being "forced to strip, to hear lies and insults about their personality, race, religion, national origin or physical characteristics."[168]

When *Newsweek* broke the story about Americans confining one another in 120-degree temperatures in sweatboxes, instigating mock "death marches," and administering live electric shocks to their peers, many commentators were more alarmed than reassured to hear that twenty-nine thousand servicemen had "safely withstood" the seventeen-day program at this "survival school" outside Reno. Its director, Colonel Burton McKenzie, insisted that the harsh treatment—merely "stress" and "minor pain" introduced when men were tired and confused—stopped short of "any real torment," but his semantic sleight of hand left several editorial-

FIGURE 27. In the sweatbox. "There is ample time to decide which is worst—the pain that comes with crouching almost motionless in a space too small to sit, lie or stand, or the heat, or the ear-ringing produced by guards pounding the box with rifle butts," *Newsweek* explained, breaking the story of the U.S. Air Force "survival school" in Nevada, September 1955. Photo by Joseph Scherschel/Time Life Pictures/Getty Images.

ists unconvinced. Conceding that the "line between mere 'ruggedness' and outright cruelty [was] not always easy to draw," the *Washington Post* protested that this boundary had been definitively breached in the Sierra Nevada sand. In less equivocal terms, the *Saturday Review* lambasted this "school for sadists," noting: "Brutality is like a bullet; you don't shoot a man to prepare him for war. And when you degrade a man and humiliate and damage him the end result is measured in the damage it does to him, not in the supposed 'training' he receives."[169]

In the face of rising protest, the Pentagon backpedaled swiftly. A week after

Newsweek's initial exposé, the air force announced that airmen would "undergo 'torture' techniques only if they volunteer."[170] Three months later, it was announced that students would merely "watch instructors using Communist interrogation techniques on one another"—following a suggestion made by Senator Lyndon B. Johnson.

Clearly, not all citizens endorsed "ruggedness" air force–style, but most agreed that military recruits required better education in Americanism, if not preemptive shock therapy. The Defense Department Advisory Committee on POWs concluded that captured soldiers "weakened because they lacked sufficient knowledge of US democracy"—a common conviction. "The uninformed POWs were up against it," the 1955 Department of Defense Report announced. Faced with clever Chinese dialecticians, at least some of whom had been educated in the United States, American POWs "couldn't answer arguments in favor of communism with arguments in favor of Americanism, because they knew very little about their America."[171] Ignorant about the United States, they were even less knowledgeable about Marxism. Not infrequently, returning prisoners bemoaned their impoverished education in political philosophy, an ignorance that putatively made some men easy prey to enemy propagandists.[172]

Conservatives blamed liberals and liberals blamed conservatives for educational deficiencies understood in contradictory ways. In Mayer's estimation, America's "rapid moral decay" derived from "the change of ideology that since the Second World War has been inculcated into innocent minds by radical politicians and teachers."[173] Liberal critics, on the other hand, maintained that it was precisely the *absence* of exposure to radical ideas—a function of McCarthyism—that had fostered such damaging ignorance. With educators living in terror of the blacklist, communism had become a taboo topic. Even to mention Marx—or to use Russian dressing (in Herblock's satirical view)—was to invite the unwelcome attention of investigatory committees and zealous school boards. The result: an unworldly generation vulnerable to the "superficial allure" of an egalitarian message. "We must not let fear of Communism keep us from being fully informed about it," advised Virginia Pasley, concluding her study of why twenty-one Americans had resisted repatriation. With superior education, future generations would not be "taken in when they find out that Communists don't beat their grandmothers."[174]

Where totalitarian states possessed a concrete, all-encompassing political philosophy, insistently drummed into their populations, America merely had an inchoate "way of life"—or so many midcentury commentators maintained. This deficiency constituted yet another way in which the United States was presumed to lag dangerously behind its communist challengers. Hence, while some psychologists counseled that the American soldier be taught to "make up his own answers and to criticize his teachers," others believed just the opposite. NSC 68 had cautioned in 1950 against the "excesses of a permanently open mind," and by the mid-1950s many espoused the view that an independently minded citizenry wasn't nearly so desirable as a population thoroughly versed in the *right* answers—convinced of American rectitude and primed to refute the false promises of communism with the catechism of free market democracy.[175]

Mindful of this perceived "ideology gap," the Code of Conduct for POWs included the galvanizing motto "I will never forget that I am an American fighting man, responsible for my actions, and dedicated to the principles which made my country free. I will trust in my God and in the United States of America."[176] Since such an entreaty would be meaningless unless GIs appreciated what those principles were, superior training in "Americanism" assumed the status of a national priority—a task not only for the military but schools, churches, communities, and, above all, mothers. "I realize that I must instill in my child a deep understanding of American politics and American history to serve as a bulwark against enemy political indoctrination," ran the "Code of an American Mother" issued by the AmVets auxiliary in 1956. "This I shall do in my home and by urging our churches and our schools to inaugurate study groups wherein my child will be given the knowledge which will enable him to determine the rightness of the American doctrine as compared to the belief advocated by the Communist or the Marxian teachings."[177]

By becoming more like the cold war adversary—more cohesive, better regimented, more thoroughly indoctrinated in right-think—the United States would improve the odds on victory. That, at any rate, formed the gist of many recommendations for remedial action.

LACUNAE

Fifties' diagnoses of national decline, and their accompanying calls for moral, martial, and maternal rearmament, for "searching and renewal before God," bore a distinctive cold war cast.[178] Such stringent self-criticism, however, hardly represented something new in history. The corrupting properties attributed to affluence—the triumph of materialism over godliness, greed over parsimony, sloth over industry—have triggered recurrent spasms of alarm from Puritan times onward. The authors and editors of Indian captivity narratives often framed their stories as admonitory warnings that indolent bodies and impious souls were no match for heathen captors. In the Protestant imaginary, captivity served as a stimulus to spiritual regeneration: a welcome test of mettle, and opportunity for the elect to reaffirm their divine covenant—in the late 1600s and mid-1950s alike.

Early cold war America was indeed increasingly affluent, but amidst the "people of plenty" millions still lived in poverty. Certainly the young men taken to exemplify the deleterious effects of affluence on both moral fiber and national character were not well placed to corroborate a connection between coddling and collaboration.[179] Eager to fathom the twenty-one "turncoat GIs," reporters dredged up biographical details, pursuing their quarry down unpaved rural lanes and dim urban alleys in search of more salacious or squalid tidbits. One unnamed man's family was traced to an "eastern US city," where he had been raised by a hard-drinking mother who "openly went about with other men" before she vanished into skid row's "warren of flophouses." A younger brother was in jail, while a sixteen-year-old sister languished in an institution for homeless girls, "going blind from syphilis."[180] While this story was extreme, nearly all the nonrepatriates had grown up poor, some in utter destitution. One, whose home life did not furnish "the habit of breakfast," was reported to have survived by foraging for food in garbage cans.[181] Only two had attended college, neither completing a degree. Ten had attended high school, but only three had graduated. Several had never made it beyond the eighth grade; a few not even that far. Most had joined up when they were seventeen or eighteen, and some had enlisted when they were only sixteen years old.

Gothic flourishes aside, these stories of broken homes, impoverished childhoods, and truncated educations failed to mark the twenty-one as distinct from their military peers. On average, the American GI who served in Korea possessed eight and a half years of schooling. Forty-four percent had only a grade-school education, and among both captives and casualties in the Korean War African Americans were disproportionately represented.[182]

Was it altogether surprising, then, that some POWs did not regard the country that dispatched them to Korea, still in their teens or early twenties, as a bastion of high ideals and higher living standards? That some struggled to grasp what they were doing caught up in a civil war some six thousand miles from home and felt bitter toward a government that had apparently condemned them to a prolonged imprisonment? Or that twenty-one, seven of whom were teenagers when captured, should initially have chosen not to come back? "The reason for the Negro boys wanting to remain is not too hard to explain," Alonzo M. Mercer, MD, wrote in a letter to the *Chicago Defender*. "These three have had their brains washed every day from the date they were born under the American way of life as it applies to Negroes." Or as a columnist in the same paper put it, where Jim Crow prevailed, freedom had "a peculiar Southern flavor which is totalitarianism of another kind."[183] These voices aside, however, few contemporaries conceived "collaboration" as anything other than a manifestation of suggestibility at best and psychopathology at worst.

That Chinese peace appeals might have genuinely attracted some U.S. prisoners, an inadmissible proposition, wasn't the only lacuna of the Korean War. Greater than the obfuscation that surrounded America's "Progressive" prisoners was the veil drawn over the circumstances under which twenty-two thousand Korean and Chinese prisoners were "saved" for the free world. Boosters touted Washington's position on repatriation as a glittering instance of high moralism in international politics. "In the final test, free world ideas and ideals worsted communist brainwashing by a score of one thousand to one," enthused the popular author Kenneth Hansen. Citing General Mark W. Clark, he avowed that voluntary repatriation had become "a beacon to guide others now suffering under Communist tyranny to the sanctuary of freedom and human dignity"—like Kasenkina's leap multiplied by thousands.[184] But the conditions under which these prisoners had "worsted communism" miserably failed to instantiate "free world ideas and ideals." Respect for "human dignity" was in such short supply at Koje that even the UN troops dispatched there as guards considered it a place of punitive exile—the "Siberia" of American fighting forces in the Far East, according to one former commanding officer.[185] Comparisons with Nazi and Soviet camps typified internal U.S. descriptions of Koje. Where U.S. ambassador John Muccio likened the Nationalist Chinese compound leaders to "Gestapos," Frank Stelle (of the Policy Planning Staff) advised Paul Nitze that the United States should not be blind "to the fact that our prison camps for Chinese in Korea are violently totalitarian" and that "the thugs who run them" are "the actual objects of our concern in the POW policy."[186]

As for the prisoners who "chose freedom," General K. S. Thimayya (the Indian officer who presided over the process of "explanations" at Panmunjom) noted the scant resemblance between these "unfortunate people" and the "picture given to the Western world . . . of brave and noble warriors who, through experience and by an intellectual process, had learned that communism was Evil and that capitalism was Good and who were prepared to sacrifice their lives rather than be exposed again to the evil of communism." In reality, the majority were "motivated by fear, not of communism as such but of going home," having been told repeatedly that, on return, they'd be beheaded for having allowed themselves to be captured.[187]

If coercion in the U.S.-run camps made it impossible to gauge how many Korean and Chinese prisoners really wished to reject repatriation, conditions at Panmunjom—supposedly a forum in which POWs could listen to "explanations" from officers of their own nationality and then express unconstrained choices—were little freer. With U.S. military sanction, the Nationalist grip over Chinese prisoners remained so intense that most compounds violently rebelled against the explanation process.[188] Thimayya, together with the Czech and Polish representatives of the Neutral Nations Repatriation Commission, protested that these terror tactics "negate[d] all assumptions or assertions about Freedom of Choice": "any prisoner who desired repatriation had to do so clandestinely and in fear of his life."[189] By the end of the ninety-day term prescribed for explanations, only 3,362 Chinese and North Korean nonrepatriates had been screened. Of these, 628 subsequently accepted repatriation.[190] We might imagine, then, that had the other twenty-two thousand prisoners undergone the same process, a sizable number might also have changed course. In practice, what "freedom" meant for many of these former prisoners was often a period of "reeducation" before involuntary conscription into Taiwan's Nationalist army or the forces of South Korea.[191]

After the war, Eisenhower lauded the U.S. stance on repatriation as "a new principle of freedom," one that might "weigh more than any battle of our time." Bold claims abounded that communist troops would lose no time in throwing down their arms in any future conflict. But as the Vietnam War attested, fantasies of mass surrender were exactly that—projections divorced from any credible account of how and why twenty-two thousand North Korean and Chinese prisoners had come to "choose freedom" in 1953.[192]

Did Washington's championship of voluntary repatriation redeem the stain of Yalta and U.S. participation in forced repatriation? It certainly didn't hasten the westward flow of escapees from the eastern bloc. As many internal reports attested, the rate of defection from the "slave world" owed less to any actions undertaken by the United States than to permissive local conditions. Did promotion of prisoners' right to asylum bolster America's claim to free world leadership? Up to a point, perhaps. But ultimately what most Americans would recall about the Korean War wasn't Washington's stand on repatriation but their prisoners' wholesale collapse in captivity. And for this sorry state of affairs they blamed not Pavlov, Mao, or Kim Il Sung so much as mom, dad, and Uncle Sam.

Epilogue

Returns and Repercussions

THE "RETURNCOATS"

In August 1955, the *Washington Post* published a lengthy illustrated article, "A Turncoat Glories in the Trade He Made," documenting the life of Lowell D. Skinner, one of twenty-one American prisoners who chose not to accept repatriation after the Korean War. Nearly two years later, Skinner was working in Jinan, the capital of Shandong Province, as an apprentice mechanic at a factory producing ultralight paper for cigarettes and typewriters. The twenty-four-year-old from Akron, Ohio, expressed "absolutely no regrets" about a choice that had mystified and enraged many Americans in 1953.[1]

The moral of this story was clear: that there was little to choose between working-class life in Akron and Jinan. Although the two cities looked entirely different, the rhythms and preoccupations of everyday life were remarkably similar. Skinner and his friends lived, worked, and socialized together. When they weren't at the factory, they frequented neighborhood cafes, chatting and drinking beer. Sometimes they went on dates, or they talked about the motorcycles they were saving up to buy. Rarely did they discuss politics. "The only thing that matters to them is to do their job and put a little money away on the side. The rest just doesn't interest them," Skinner insisted. Most Chinese weren't, and didn't aspire to be, members of the Chinese Communist Party. "It's a big lesson for a modest American like myself, you know, to find out, little by little, that behind the regimes, beyond the governments, there are people and that at heart nothing separates us except distance."

Skinner anticipated coming back to America one day, "with a trade, rich in human experience." But not yet. The United States, he complained, was "becoming more and more reactionary and totalitarian." Was Skinner merely voicing sentiments his Chinese hosts obliged him to utter? Had he been brainwashed into finding a factory worker's life in Jinan equivalent to blue-collar existence in Ohio? Questions relentlessly pressed two years earlier found no place in the *Post*'s two-page feature. The young man from Akron appeared to lack "any bravado or mysticism," noted the reporter Jacques Locquin. "He seems to have thought it over carefully. He decided to stay in China . . . as somebody else in the United States might take a course in night school. He wanted to learn something. The dramatic part about it is that in this case his 'night school' is that of Communist China."

Times were changing. When Skinner and twenty other nonrepatriates refused repatriation at the end of the Korean War, no one suggested that curiosity, ambition, and a desire for expanded opportunities—all good American virtues—might explain behavior attributed instead to cupidity, cowardice, or conversion to communism. And certainly no one expected that the "turncoats" would ever return. To cross the Bamboo Curtain in the wrong direction was surely to seal one's fate forever. Yet within little more than a decade, most had returned to the United States. By 1966 only two still remained in the People's Republic.[2]

The first three to reverse their decision came back in July 1955, prompting so much press commentary that 88 percent of respondents to a Gallup poll that month claimed to have heard or read about these returnees.[3] Otho Bell, Lewis Griggs, and William Cowart had been "release[d] from the Marxian hell" in which millions of Chinese remained helplessly trapped, cheered the *Chicago Daily Tribune,* noting how very few Americans, including members of the Communist Party USA, had ever been foolish enough to transport themselves to a communist country. "Perhaps they know instinctively what the three men who have returned from communism now know so well—that this hateful system stifles the brain and soul and reduces life to a disciplined and terror ridden routine that can hardly be called living."[4] Yet despite some crowing of this kind, the homecoming of these three men—"returncoats," as reporters quickly dubbed them—proved anticlimactic. Those hoping for an elaborate performance of anticommunist penance were to be disappointed, as were those eager to punish the apostates for their earlier transgression.[5]

On disembarkation at San Francisco, Cowart, Griggs, and Bell were peremptorily arrested after a ninety-minute reunion with relatives. The army intended to court-martial these three just as it had Edward Dickenson and Claude Batchelor, the POWs who had changed their minds about heading to China at the eleventh hour. According to military sources, at least two of the newly returned trio had urged an American officer to desert, "one of the most serious crimes in the book."[6] Fearful of the death penalty, Cowart, Griggs, and Bell attempted to secure exemption from court-martial by stressing their utility to U.S. intelligence. What they could reveal about Chinese methods would render the military's torture schools obsolescent, the men's attorneys claimed.[7] The trio also made public statements of contrition, couched in assertively patriotic terms: "We came out because we feel we now are true Americans. Being true Americans, we'll take whatever punishment is coming to us," Cowart declared.[8]

But genuflections toward "true Americanism" weren't what spared these three men from trial. Rather, the army had bungled. Eager to signal its contempt for those who "chose China," it had dishonorably discharged all twenty-one nonrepatriates in January 1954, as soon as it became clear that their decisions were fixed. When Cowart, Griggs, and Bell returned to the United States eighteen months later, they duly did so as civilians. The army intended to court-martial them all the same—only to find itself thwarted by a Supreme Court ruling in November 1955 that former servicemen could not be subjected to military trial for crimes committed while in the service.[9] At the behest of U.S. district judge Louis E. Goodman, the three men were released the day after the Supreme Court decision. The returnees then turned the tables, suing for unpaid wages and allowances that had accrued between their capture in 1950 and dishonorable discharge in 1954.[10] They won, and the army was obliged to remunerate men it had tried and failed to court-martial.

After this fiasco, the appearance of a succession of "returncoats" occasioned neither elaborate rejoicing nor virulent recrimination. Later returnees proved less eager than Griggs, Cowart, and Bell to mouth anticommunist platitudes, stressing homesickness rather than ideological antipathy to Mao's China as the explanation for decisions made and then reversed. When Richard Tenneson returned in December 1955, he told the press, "I am not fighting for communism, nor am I against it," adding somewhat cryptically that he had "not got along with the Chinese people 'as a whole.'"[11] Arlie Pate and Aaron Wilson followed a year later, complaining of homesickness but stressing that life in China "wasn't too bad"—especially the frequent visits to dancehalls with Chinese girls.[12] Similarly, when Andrew Fortuna sailed back to America in June 1957, he informed reporters that "just plain homesickness" had impelled him west. Asked how he felt about communism, he bridled: "That's a loaded question. . . . I'd rather not answer that." His years in China had been "pleasant and interesting," he insisted.[13]

Where these cagey returnees hedged, others were downright unapologetic in defense of the country that had provided them a temporary home. In March 1958, LaRance Sullivan, first of the three African American nonrepatriates to return and reportedly the "bitterest US turncoat," insisted that he'd been "very happy among a soul-stirring people—a peaceful people" but that he had "thought it was time to come home."[14] And when Richard Corden (the group's supposed ringleader) came back nine months after Sullivan, he defiantly proclaimed that there was "more democracy in China than the US": "I've got nothing to be ashamed of. I learned a lot." Though not a communist, he remained "impressed" with socialism.[15]

A few years later, in August 1963, Lowell Skinner—the subject of the *Washing-*

ton Post's profile—headed home, obliged to travel without his ailing Chinese spouse and expressing "disillusion," a *New York Times* headline related.[16] Within the next three years, Clarence Adams, William White, and Morris Wills also returned, all with Chinese wives. The burgeoning Cultural Revolution had made China considerably less hospitable than in 1954, though coming back to the United States wasn't necessarily easy either—least of all for Adams, who had made a broadcast for Radio Hanoi in 1965 urging African American GIs to stop fighting "supposedly . . . for the freedom of the Vietnamese" and return home to struggle for their own rights. This exhortation ensured that a subpoena from the House Committee on Un-American Activities was among Adams's earliest welcome-home offerings.[17]

Soon, however, Adams, Skinner, and others whose choices had once been so thoroughly scrutinized lapsed into anonymity, as had earlier feted escapees.[18] After the riptide of celebrity receded, Oksana Kasenkina spent her days painting in oils, improving her English, and writing a novel, *The Red Devil*. ("Of course, the Red Devil is Stalin. Who else?" she rebuked a dull-witted reporter.) But the manuscript remained unpublished, and on journalists' dwindling anniversary visits she expressed dissatisfaction with being forever sought as a figurehead by some fractious émigré group or other. "Persons pleading special causes 'trouble' her," related the *New York Times* on the fifth anniversary of her feted "leap for freedom." "Nobody is interested in helping me to do something . . . but so many people are interested in pushing me into a political party," she complained. Too long and too insistently spoken for, she wanted merely to be left alone. In 1957, she became a U.S. citizen at a "heavily guarded ceremony" in Boston before moving to Florida, where she spent her final year under the assumed name Mary Kamita at a "hotel for the elderly." She died of a heart condition in 1960, at the age of sixty-three.[19]

Victor Kravchenko, meanwhile, fearing lethal retribution from Soviet agents for having "chosen freedom," stocked his apartment with anesthetizing supplies of alcohol and a loaded gun. Much in the limelight during the late 1940s, the Russian defector again claimed the headlines in 1956 when he shot a twenty-one-year-old Puerto Rican piano student who had knocked, in error, at the door of his Upper East Side apartment.[20] By now Kravchenko was living under the assumed name Peter Martin. "I so wanted Kravchenko to be dead—I have a new life, I am an American," he explained to journalists. But killing Kravchenko in name turned out to be insufficient. A decade later, Peter Martin also wanted to be dead, and in 1966, at the age of sixty-one, he used the .38 caliber revolver again, this time to put a bullet in his head. A "rambling" suicide note, signed in the names of both Kravchenko and Martin, alluded to financial problems but more explicitly referenced the author's deep unhappiness with U.S. involvement in the Vietnam War and "the nation's treatment of nonwhite people."[21]

Of the celebrated escapees, only Peter Pirogov—the Russian pilot who "took Virginia" in February 1949—appeared to achieve a measure of contentment, though not without surmounting some obstacles. In 1955, his application for U.S. citizenship was rejected, falling foul of the McCarran Act's stipulation that individuals who had once belonged to a communist organization were ineligible for naturalization until they had spent a ten-year quarantine period in America. An act of Congress granted Pirogov permanent residence, but his onetime membership in the Komsomol was deemed by the Alexandria federal court judge Albert V. Bryan to constitute an insuperable barrier to early naturalization.[22] As a result, Pirogov lost his position at the Library of Congress, where he had been employed as an air information specialist. He then picked up work as opportunities arose: driving taxis around Washington, D.C., writing scripts for Radio Liberty, and assisting an anticommunist refugee organization. In 1956, the *Washington Post* reported that the former flier had "caught the real estate fervor" and was building an eight-room, split-level brick house near Annandale, Virginia. "There is an old Russian proverb that a man is not a man who in his life not write a book, not build a house and not have a son," Pirogov told the *Post*'s reporter ("with a slight accent" that the latter strove to reproduce). "Look at the house. Pretty nice, don't you think? Now all I need is to have a son. But with my luck, I will have triplets. All girls."[23] In fact, he already had three daughters: three-year-old twins and a nine-year-old adopted when he had married a Russian refugee in New York in 1951. Since no male offspring subsequently materialized, Pirogov attained only two markers of Russian manhood. In December 1958 he did, however, secure U.S. citizenship, a "priceless Christmas gift" that may or may not have compensated for the lack of a son and heir.[24]

THE TIDE EBBS

The disappointments and frustrations experienced by once-celebrated captives, defectors, and escapees attracted little public comment. Nothing merited such attention as the moment of decision when individuals chose—or rejected—"freedom." For these fleetingly lionized individuals, both the brevity and the selectivity of public attention were themselves sources of embitterment. Numerous individuals and organizations pounced with alacrity on stories of communist captivity and escape, stamping them with ideologically congenial meanings. But few tried to help their human subjects wrestle with difficult life adjustments or narrate their experiences in ways that might complicate the crude anticommunism that passed as the moral of these stories. While these cold war captivities diffused into America's cultural bloodstream, the individuals themselves sank into what was often a troubled obscurity. Eagerly appropriated, they were just as quickly abandoned. Thus Pirogov attributed his copilot Barsov's redefection in part to the "bitter realization . . . that Americans are not really interested in hearing our stories. . . . They are a little tired of all those Russians who tell us of slave labor camps, the NKVD [secret police] and such."[25]

When the "returncoats" arrived back in America, the notice most received was inversely proportionate to the clamor that had greeted news of their defections in 1953. Deciding to come home again wasn't, after all, nearly as remarkable as refusing repatriation. But the more restrained press coverage devoted to these men's extraordinary "double-crossings" attests something more than celebrity's abbreviated shelf life. By the mid-1950s, a certain phase of the cold war had ebbed. Jacques Locquin's dispassionate portrait of Skinner as a young man who had decided to sample life in China in the same spirit that drew others to night school signaled a broader attitudinal shift: a softening of antipathy toward the "slave world," uneven but unmistakable. Skinner's vaunted epiphany—that only twelve thousand miles separated Ohio from Shantung—represented a remarkable discursive volte-face. It may have been fashionable after World War II, as Kurt Vonnegut noted in *Slaughterhouse-Five,* for anthropologists to claim that "there was absolutely no difference between anybody," but conceptions of universal kinship tended to halt abruptly at the Iron Curtain.[26]

At the height of the early cold war, the "jungle world of communism" had been typically rendered as a hellish realm where "ownlife" (Orwell's term for an inner life free from state scrutiny) had been eliminated and civilized man ventured at his peril. Whether the "captive peoples" shared the same attributes as those born in liberty remained a moot point. Rear Admiral L. C. Stevens cautioned an audience at the Naval War College in January 1951 that Russia's peoples were "more alien to us than those of any European country, full of dualities and contradictions, with a natural talent for deviousness and cunning," as anyone who had "read that appalling book *1984*" would recognize.[27]

As the 1950s wore on, however, the nightmarish vision of totalitarianism as supreme in its subjugation of every human impulse eased its grip on American imaginations. With the "paranoid style"—an admixture of "heated exaggeration, suspiciousness and conspiratorial fantasy"—no longer so modish, anticommunism shed some of its hysterical excess.[28] This normalization owed much to the demise of McCarthy, who never recovered from the blow delivered in December 1954, when the Senate voted by 67 to 22 to condemn him. "I don't feel like I've been lynched," McCarthy quipped with jarring bravado on learning the news. Yet within three years he was dead, and already so thoroughly marginalized that his terminal illness passed with little comment. The obituaries had already been written.

McCarthy's demise was both a symptom and a catalyst of relaxation. When he impugned the army as yet another hornets' nest of subversion, he overstepped the bounds of acceptable Red-hunting, alienating many members of his own party. But his downfall was due to more than this miscalculation. By 1954, the "-ism" to which McCarthy had given a name was widely regarded as doing more to damage U.S. security than to fortify it against subversion. Critics charged that the senator's licentious abuse of power had generated an atmosphere of fear akin to the dread that enveloped communist societies: a species of domestic totalitarianism that alienated potential foreign friends and succored confirmed foes. "Were the Junior Senator from Wisconsin in the pay of the Communists he could not have done a better job for them," claimed Ralph E. Flanders, Republican senator for Vermont, in June 1954.[29] Escapades such as the trip around Europe made by McCarthy's aides Roy Cohn and G. David Schine in April 1953—pulling subversive books, like the novels of Mark Twain and Theodore Dreiser, from the shelves of U.S. Information Service reading rooms—fueled mounting antipathy toward countersubversive excess, both within and beyond the United States.[30] Such antics, together with the rituals of self-incrimination and name-naming that were McCarthy's stock in trade, undermined America's claim to embody "freedom" at its purest. And if the leader of the "free world" were no longer credible in that role, how could Washington hope to win a global battle for allegiance?

As the likelihood of a third world war receded with Stalin's death in 1953, criticism of American pugnacity and paranoia grew in western Europe and elsewhere. To those convinced that a rapprochement with the Soviet bloc lay within reach, fervid anticommunism appeared as unnecessary as it was unedifying. The Kremlin wanted peace. Or at any rate, Stalin's successor had launched a vigorous peace offensive that many Europeans took at face value, hoping that the Geneva Summit of July 1955 would consolidate a genuine and lasting abatement of East-West tension.

Eisenhower mistrusted the Kremlin's pacific turn as mere sham. For two years he resisted Soviet calls for a four-power conference. But he couldn't ignore the new mood, adopting the same language for his own propaganda initiatives, such as an "Atoms for Peace" campaign that sold "the friendly atom" to those less convinced of nuclear fission's life-enhancing properties. Presidential skepticism notwithstanding, the great power gathering at Geneva—the first meeting of Soviet, U.S., British, and French heads of state since 1945—did result in greater exchange between the two blocs. After three years of stasis, Washington and Moscow agreed to permit some movement across the Iron Curtain. Shortly after the summit, the State Department lifted the embargo on American travel to the eastern bloc imposed in May 1952, enabling a few intrepid voyagers to venture east in late 1955.[31]

Americans who expected to risk life and limb crossing a ferociously guarded border were encouraged to moderate their image of the Iron Curtain. The *New York Times* duly cautioned, "lest movie-minded sight-seers should be disappointed," that "the Iron Curtain is nothing to look at. It consists of a few wooden observation towers, a restricted area that looks like any non-restricted area, and minefields that look like any other fields."[32] Having printed numerous descriptions of the Iron Curtain as a lethal, ferociously guarded perimeter, the *Times* was hardly exempt from tendencies ascribed to Hollywood. Tales of escapee heroism—conveyed by the press, movies, and government publications, then reenacted in public pageantry— had worked to fix exactly this perception of the cold war frontier, with no little success. But now that the curtain was lifted, or at least somewhat parted, journalists adopted a jauntier tone in discussing the eastern bloc, offering American travelers advice on how to negotiate its idiosyncrasies. "Don't ask to see a slave labor camp. It seems to annoy them," the *Times* sardonically advised in November 1955.[33]

In 1956, some three thousand Americans journeyed to the USSR. The first trail-blazers, a doughty couple from Florida, returned in February "with cold feet but warm memories of five days in the Soviet Union," full of praise for the "excellent service and facilities" they had enjoyed.[34] The following year, it was estimated that ten thousand Americans would flock to the eastern bloc: a drop in the bucket compared with the number visiting western Europe (six hundred thousand to eight hundred thousand) but nevertheless a significant departure from the closure that had characterized East-West relations during the early cold war.[35] Strikingly, the volume of Americans touring the USSR far outstripped the number of Soviet citizens entering the United States. Fewer than one hundred received visas in 1956. Stringent controls against communist entry into the United States remained in place, together with new deterrents such as mandatory fingerprinting of eastern bloc visitors, a criminalizing move Moscow lambasted as both an affront to human dignity and further evidence that the Iron Curtain was an *American* construction designed to exclude visitors from the socialist world.[36] In the estimation of one former State Department employee, this "apparent reversal of roles as between Moscow and Washington since the death of Stalin" was "a factor in the decline of American prestige in many parts of the world."[37]

In the United States, persistent suspicion about the motives and bona fides of Soviet visitors validated these precautionary measures. Leo Cherne, chair of the International Rescue Committee, warned in June 1956 that "those who travel to the United States from the Soviet Union are trained, skillful observers, propagandists and, in certain instances, spies."[38] The cold war was clearly not over. But by mid-decade it had entered a markedly different phase, with 1956 offering a dramatic illustration of the precarious new equilibrium within and between the blocs.

In November 1956, Red Army tanks rumbled into Budapest to quell an uprising against Rákosi's communist regime. This popular eruption had been dynamized by the ostensibly new spirit of heterodoxy prevailing in Moscow and by Radio Free Europe broadcasts that had encouraged the "captive peoples" to shake off their Stalinist shackles. Hungary's rebellion was not the first to roil the eastern bloc since Stalin's death. A revolt in East Germany in 1953 had also been repressed, but with considerably less bloodshed. Leaving approximately 2,500 fatalities, Hungary's crushed revolt announced in the most emphatic terms that Soviet talk of "peaceful coexistence" was not an open invitation to dissidence in the satellite states.

While the Red Army's incursion into Hungary instantly aged Moscow's vaunted new look, Washington's response simultaneously exposed the limitations of Eisenhower's commitment to liberating the "captive peoples." In 1952, Ike had campaigned against Truman with the bold promise to roll back communism rather than merely contain it. When the moment of reckoning came four years later, however, it was clear that his White House had no desire to precipitate an all-out confrontation with the Soviet Union by sending troops to defend the Hungarian revolution. The rebels could be forgiven if they expected otherwise. Radio Free Europe broadcasts had done nothing to tamp down insurrectionary sentiment. Arguably they had done just the opposite—creating an expectation that Washington would support the "captives peoples" when they rose up. A CIA enquiry into the role of U.S. broadcasting in Hungary's revolt later exonerated Voice of America and Radio Free Europe from charges of reckless incitement. But the taint of bad faith remained. The CIA's conclusion that American broadcasters had done nothing to instigate an organic revolt, incubated entirely within Hungary, smacked strongly of self-exculpation.[39]

Exposing the limits of Eisenhower's commitment to liberation, the crushed Hungarian revolt did have one more positive effect on Capitol Hill. It expanded congressional willingness to admit eastern bloc refugees into the United States. After years of mixed signals, the hollowness of one set of claims about rollback was recuperated by making good on another set of declaratory promises—to eastern bloc escapees. After its refusal to intervene in Hungary, the White House hesitated to damage its emancipatory credentials further by denying refuge to Hungarian refugees, thousands of whom had left the country as Soviet troops entered. The International Rescue Committee immediately set about rallying American opinion to their cause.[40] Within sixty days, the committee's appeal—boosted by the *Ed Sullivan Show,* a mass rally at Madison Square Garden, and proceeds from a special edition of *Life*—had raised $2,500,000.[41]

From a total of almost two hundred thousand, about thirty-five thousand Hungarian refugees were eventually admitted into the United States.[42] Not all were active participants in the revolt, some simply seizing the opportunity of a temporary rupture in the Austro-Hungarian border to head west. But Republican lawmakers hesitated to question (as they had in the past) whether these escapees were bona fide anticommunists or mere opportunists hungrily grasping at higher standards of living in the free world. Eager to valorize these refugees, Vice President Nixon insisted that most had fled "only when the choice was death or deportation . . . or temporary flight to a foreign land." With the Hungarian "freedom fighter" hailed as *Time*'s "man of the year" in January 1957, it seemed that the escapee's moment had finally arrived.

Or had it? In practice, the Hungarian refugee episode remained as lacking in resolution as other cold war captivity dramas. A year after "Russian tanks smashed their bid for liberty," the fate of fifty thousand Hungarians tenuously encamped in Europe remained uncertain. In *Life* magazine's doleful phraseology, these unfortunates were "stalled—and unwanted."[43] Those who gained admittance to the

United States weren't necessarily wanted there either, despite the International Rescue Committee's best efforts to raise consciousness as well as contributions for refugee assistance.

One emblematic instance of American hostility offers an ironic coda to two intertwined stories, one of Hungarian refugees in the United States and the other of an American who had been a prisoner in Hungary. In June 1957, a small notice in the *New York Times* drew attention to the plight of Robert and Lucile Vogeler, both of whom were currently looking for work. Owing $3,000 in back taxes, they were the victims of foreclosure. Robert's small electronics plant was facing bankruptcy, while Lucile's plans for a career in television had foundered. She was too "controversial," she suggested, for the cold war's coolest medium. As for her husband's business misfortune, Lucile attributed it to the recent influx of Hungarian refugees—cheap laborers who had poached Americans' jobs.[44] Would Vogeler (the founder of an organization that promoted escape from the eastern bloc) have shown greater generosity had these refugees not imperiled *his* livelihood or had they not been *Hungarian?* We'll never know. But Vogeler was certainly not alone in failing to practice what he preached with regard to the "captive peoples."

AROUSED AND INFLAMED:
CAPTIVITY AND POPULAR MOBILIZATION

Americans have long figured the entire course of their history as a "predestined rescue operation," proposes the historian Anders Stephanson.[45] Quick to conceive themselves as liberators to captive others, they have often regarded America as a victim of its own virtue—beset by barbarism but constrained by civility. Early cold war America's fascination with captivity thus fits within a national tradition that stretches back to the Puritans and forward to the present. But for all the durability of this trope, it would be misleading to imagine, as some cultural commentators have, that Americans are held in perpetual thrall to a timeless and unchanging "captivity cult." Linda Colley's notion of a "captivity panic" better captures the way in which encounters with "captivating others" achieve prominence at moments of external crisis and internal convulsion, heightening perceptions of foreign threat while sharpening national self-criticism.[46] These periods of intense busywork have discernible durations.

In the cold war's inaugural phase, captivity struck many policy makers and opinion shapers as a clarifying prism through which Americans might apprehend the true character of their antagonist. For Hanson Baldwin, military correspondent of the *New York Times,* incarceration at communist hands was "the essential tragedy of our times," an ordeal then being endured by American POWs in North Korea, U.S. airmen in Hungary, and the journalist William Oatis in Czechoslovakia: "The situation of our prisoners, if understood, can serve to illustrate most forcibly to the

American people the nature of the enemy. The tears and sudden hopes, the swift surge of relief, the fear and sorrow, the bright flow of human emotions, the anxiety of man for man—out of all these may grow an understanding that the struggle of two worlds is not merely power politics, not only national rivalries, but a conflict of man against absolutism, of man against savagery, of man against power and evil, of man for his soul."[47] Like many contemporaries, Baldwin rendered the cold war as a Manichean contest between good against evil—not so much a confrontation between rival power blocs or incompatible ideologies as a spiritual struggle for salvation waged against the forces of damnation.

For cold war opinion formers, captivity promised to jolt Americans into the proper state of alertness that a condition of permanent mobilization and ideological vigilance required. Each episode explored in this book was billed as the key to popular enlightenment. No sooner had Oksana Kasenkina been hailed for bringing home the Soviets' utter disregard for individual rights than eastern bloc escapees were seized on as the most powerful illustration of what the Iron Curtain meant and what its existence disclosed of conditions behind it. Forced labor also received star billing. State Department officials were convinced that publicizing the Soviet gulag would trigger an epiphany as people around the world realized that, in the communist bloc, workers had won nothing from revolution but their chains. Captivity was indeed an emotional stimulus, at various times bringing Americans onto the streets in protest and prayer, commemoration, and celebration. Nothing, however, animated such strong feeling in the United States as communist incarceration of American citizens, whether in isolation or en masse. Above all, it was their plight that undammed the "bright flow of human emotions."

Strikingly, those "psychological warriors" most heavily invested in putting captivity to productive use remained least convinced of their own success. In the late 1940s, cold war strategists tended to conceive the postwar U.S. electorate as stubbornly isolationist and "basically unstable," "too prone to volatile oscillations between complacency and hysteria, withdrawal and engagement."[48] Loath to embrace the challenges and costs of global leadership, and lacking the stamina that a posture of perpetual alertness required, Americans needed to be whipped into a state of existential dread or otherwise invigorated by the thrill of "properly directed hatred."[49]

Within and beyond government, those keen to mold public attitudes construed the object of their endeavors in strikingly sexualized terms. Just as *Time*, reflecting on the reverberations of Oksana Kasenkina's leap, had conjured a "free nation's decision" as the "slow swelling of resolve," the masseurs of cold war sentiment regarded popular will as an unpredictable entity with a mind of its own—prone to the full panoply of erectile dysfunctions. Sluggish in stiffening, opinion was given to premature outbursts followed by precipitous subsidences. The task, Truman's psywarriors came to appreciate, was more delicate than merely *arousing* the citizenry. Since excessive "inflammation" risked uncontrollable results, channeling these volatile responses required an assured touch and a trusted aphrodisiac, but also (Acheson advised) "restraint and self-discipline." Escapee testimony and accounts of communist enslavement would, it was hoped, gird American loins for prolonged confrontation with totalitarian expansionism, a menace George Kennan described as "unceasing pressure for penetration."[50]

Replete with intimations of bondage, submission, and violation, captivity functioned as a stimulant. Midcentury commentators often construed both bodily confinement and mental coercion in terms of sexual subjugation; hence the trials of both Mindszenty and Vogeler were described as "rapes of justice," while Joost Meerloo explained that his coinage *menticide* denoted "the rape of the mind." Such metaphors sprang readily from Americans' propensity to elide communism with an array of psychosexual "deviations." Empowering women, Marxism emasculated men. According to Morris Ernst and David Loth, Julius Rosenberg was Ethel's "slave," in a relationship typical of the inverted pattern of communist couplings. Underground communist cells, meanwhile, were depicted as incubators for "introverted" urges.[51] In Arthur Schlesinger Jr.'s estimation, communism "pervert[ed] politics into something secret, sweaty, and furtive, like nothing so much . . . as homosexuality in a boys' school." The *Washington Post* insinuated something similar when it noted that GIs in communist-run POW camps in North Korea divided into "furtive coteries," making the connection unmistakable when it related that the twenty-one "turncoats" favored long hair and women's clothes.[52]

Early cold war figurations of captivity enabled a wide array of emotional responses: an invitation to empathy, pity, and fury toward those whose insults—to humanity in general or Americans in particular—could not be allowed to go unpunished. Quickening the pulse of anticommunism, captivity contributed to the consolidation of what is often referred to as a "cold war consensus" in the United States. However, we should take care not to flatten the variegated work of captivity or to overstate the uniformity and totality of a consensus often conceived as the inert product of bludgeoned acquiescence. Some Americans resisted conscription, like the hundreds of protesters who gathered outside Manhattan's Roxy Theater on May 12, 1948, chanting, "One, two, three, four; we don't want another war!" in protest against *The Iron Curtain*—the movie Kasenkina would later credit as the catalyst for her leap from the Soviet consulate. Others, like those POWs' families who claimed never to have "heard the communist name" before the war in Korea, remained oblivious to eddying geopolitical currents. However, amid those turned off by, or tone-deaf to, the era's strident anticommunism were many passionate subscribers to the cold war cause whose ardor is barely captured by the homogenized catchall "consensus." Millions eagerly enlisted in a holy war against the "great anti-Christian movement" that was, according to Billy Graham, masterminded not by the "red devil" Stalin but by Satan himself.[53]

At times, popular zeal for exterminating communism strained the bounds within

FIGURE 28. A hanging offense. Residents of Mosinee offer a chilling demonstration of how they propose to deal with any communist who dares tamper with the Stars and Stripes during the 1950 May Day "Red takeover." © The Associated Press.

which cold warriors hoped to encircle consent. The most fervent crusaders advocated an array of extraconstitutional measures that included the death penalty, removal of citizenship, deportation, and internment of those whose atheistic creed negated their claim to inclusion within the national community. Such attitudes weren't hard to find. Opinion polls routinely recorded evidence of more punitive sentiment among the public than in the administration.[54] And since some citizens clearly regarded the federal government as pussyfooting around the Red menace, never going far enough to annihilate the scourge with which it too was infected, acts of vigilantism were not unknown. On October 26, 1947, for example, a mob of some four thousand gathered in what one witness termed a "festive spirit of revelry"—punctuated by "racist mutterings" and cries of "Where's the rope, boys?"—to prevent communist leader Gerhart Eisler from addressing a public meeting in Trenton, New Jersey.[55]

A similar impulse, if more attenuated, animated advocates of bombing China, Hungary, or any other state that presumed to detain American captives. Frustration over the stalemate in Korea and unease over communist abuse of POWs lent revenge fantasies an atomic edge. As one Seattle housewife told *Newsweek* in August 1953: "The whole thing's made me supermad. Why don't we just A-bomb them? We should either pull out of Korea or have all-out war. I see no reason to delay it." Just as the character Harry "Rabbit" Angstrom in John Updike's *Rabbit at Rest* saw no point in being an American without the cold war, many Americans saw no point in nuclear weapons if they couldn't be dropped on the communists.[56]

CAPTIVE MINDS

Eisenhower's administration, having fashioned its self-image around the captive peoples' liberation, didn't lightly abandon this mantle, despite its hesitancy in Hungary and evidence of flagging public interest. In July 1959, Dulles proclaimed a Captive Nations Week to be celebrated annually as an occasion for U.S. citizens to rededicate themselves to the captive peoples' liberation.[57] (As George Kennan tartly observed, the accompanying resolution committed the United States to the liberation of twenty-two "nations," "two of which had never had any real existence, and the name of one of which appears to have been invented by the Nazi propaganda ministry during the recent war.")[58] Timed by accident or design to coincide with Richard Nixon's historic visit to the Soviet Union, the inaugural Captive Nations Week animated predictable Soviet ire. Throughout the tour, Premier Khrushchev ribbed Nixon by asking whether he had encountered sufficient slaves to satisfy his curiosity, pointing at ordinary Muscovites and asking if the vice president believed them enslaved.[59] More felicitously for the administration, Khrushchev's clowning breathed life into an initiative that had otherwise done little to inspire Americans to "recommit themselves to the support of the just aspirations of the peoples of those captive nations." "Until Premier Nikita S. Krushchev heard of it," observed the *New York Times,* "Captive Nations Week was causing less of a stir in the United States press than the concurrent observance of National Hot Dog month."[60]

By 1959, communist captivity had been a detumescent trope for some time. Pondering Americans' apparent susceptibility to psychological pressure in the aftermath of the Korean War, many commentators lost interest (at least temporarily) in incarceration at its most literal. As many as nine hundred U.S. prisoners remained unaccounted for at the end of the war, some of whom the military believed still alive and hidden away in North Korea or Manchuria—possibly to be sent back to America later, with false identities stolen from GIs who had perished in the camps. Yet the fate of these men failed to animate popular passion in the way some officials, worried about the emergence of a "Frankenstein" pressing for revenge or turning furiously on the administration, feared it might in 1953. Only when the POW/MIA issue became a lightning rod for discontent over America's failure to prevail in Vietnam (or Washington's refusal to do so, as many alleged) did the unaccounted missing of the Korean War become an emotional rallying point, twenty years after the event.[61]

In the mid-fifties, social critics were instead preoccupied with the multiple ways in which modern mass society corroded individual autonomy. Captivity became a condition associated as much with *consumerism* as communism. Cut loose from its Chinese antecedents, "brainwashing" now encompassed any and every manifestation of browbeating, coercion, indoctrination, or persuasion. Stories abounded in American magazines and newspapers concerning henpecked husbands brainwashed by their wives, students brainwashed by their school texts, and felons claiming to have been brainwashed into making false confessions by police interrogators.

Amid these proliferating usages, few Americans probably disagreed with Walter Cronkite when he informed television viewers in 1957 that brainwashing—a phenomenon that jeopardized "our preservation as human beings"—was "one of the underlying themes" of the twentieth century. As such, it merited an hour-long episode in a CBS documentary series dedicated to exploring the burning issues of a century barely beyond its halfway point. Driving home the same message, bestselling author Vance Packard informed Americans that they were "the most manipulated people outside the Iron Curtain." This malaise he attributed not to communist infiltration of national thought-waves but to Madison Avenue's slick "hidden persuaders"—"depth boys" who deployed insights gleaned from Freudian psychology to persuade insecure Americans that the key to personal fulfillment lay in buying particular products or electing certain politicians.[62]

Two movies of the era neatly illustrate how residual anxiety over brainwashing in Korea dovetailed with concern over domestic species of opinion manipulation. Both Jacques Tourneur's *The Fearmakers* (1958) and John Frankenheimer's *The Manchurian Candidate* (1962) open in Korea, where U.S. prisoners are brutalized and, in the latter, whisked over the border to Manchuria for systematic brainwashing, a process attributed to Pavlov but seemingly reliant on posthypnotic suggestion.[63] On return to the United States, the movies' former POW protagonists find themselves plunged into conspiracies to subvert American democracy. In *The Fearmakers,* the hero, Alan Eaton (Dana Andrews), returns home to discover that his opinion-polling business has been taken over by a power-hungry maniac, later revealed as the murderer of Eaton's erstwhile business partner. The scam? To use phony opinion data for further malign purposes like "promoting peace at any price," lobbying Congress, or getting candidates elected to high office. ("You mean, they could use this to get a television program cancelled?" asks the incredulous secretary when Eaton clues her in to the myriad alarming implications of slanted sampling.)

The stakes are considerably higher in *The Manchurian Candidate,* where the ultimate Sino-Soviet objective is to install in the White House a countersubversive demagogue, Senator Johnny Iselin (James Gregory), whose sozzled incapacity to remember precisely how many communists are in government leaves no doubt about this character's real-world counterpart. Conjuring anticommunist populism as a Red conspiracy, Frankenheimer made literal Senator Flanders's charge that if the communists had invented a device to discredit the United States they could have done no better than Joseph McCarthy. But if the film at once vindicates cold war paranoia (there really *is* a communist plot to subvert American democracy from within!) while excoriating McCarthyism, it also delivers a blistering critique of television as a thoroughly untrustworthy box of tricks. "I think that our society is brainwashed by television commercials, by advertising, by politicians, by a censored press," Frankenheimer asserted. "More and more I think that our society is becoming manipulated and controlled," he added, echoing Packard's assertion that hucksters treated American voters "more and more . . . like Pavlov's conditioned dog."[64] That the Sino-Soviet conspirators come so close to realizing their ambitions in *The Manchurian Candidate* owes as much to their shrewd media manipulation as to the brainwashing of a susceptible POW. Like Elia Kazan's *A Face in the Crowd* (1957), Frankenheimer's film portrays television as an insidious enemy within, spawning monstrous celebrities whose mesmeric screen presence stuns and stunts an audience of slack-jawed dupes.

That the prospect of rigged opinion polls, televised "pseudoevents," and phony personalities should have inspired filmmakers' nightmarish projections fifty years ago seems quaintly antiquated in an era when flagrant political corruption scarcely raises an eyebrow and "reality" TV dominates the schedules. Perhaps more remarkable, though, is the quality of astonished innocence that surrounds midcentury Americans' discovery of the modern self's fragility—or, in the theologically inflected argot of the day, the soul's flimsy sovereignty. "Of course the public is often being manipulated," wrote a phlegmatic Scottish psychologist in 1963, doubting whether the communists had "devised any method which is half as efficient in 'brainwashing' (or with results which are half as permanent) as the English public school." The "only surprising thing," he added, with a pointed nod across the Atlantic, "is that it has taken so long to find this out."[65]

But find out Americans assuredly did, and having made the discovery they kept pushing at its edges. Susceptibility to manipulation—a regression in man's "long struggle to become a rational and self-guiding being"—became a national preoccupation, coinciding with the onset of what *Life* magazine termed the "age of psychology."[66] Between 1940 and 1950, membership of the American Psychological Association grew from three thousand to sixteen thousand, prompting *Newsweek* to claim in 1955 that the United States was "without doubt the most psychologically oriented, or psychiatrically oriented nation in the world."[67] Whether this preeminence was something to brag about, however, was less clear.

REVISITATIONS

Since September 11, 2001, traces of the early cold war have been everywhere apparent. With the inauguration of a "global war on terror," Americans have again been mobilized for a worldwide struggle against a nebulous enemy cast as the epitome of evil: a war without limits—geographical, ethical, or temporal—that may be fought anywhere, with any weapon, for all time. To galvanize popular sentiment, this war's advocates have deployed a succession of historical analogies, many seeking to draw legitimacy and luster from the "good war." It was only to be expected that al-Qaeda's assault on the Twin Towers would immediately be likened in infamy to the Japanese "sneak attack" on Pearl Harbor—no matter how imprecise the parallel. Thereafter, President Bush repeatedly presented the extirpation of "Islamofascism" as a contemporary calling analogous with the destiny proudly discharged by the "greatest generation." But despite constant invocations of World War II, aspects of this new campaign much more closely replicate the early cold war. Opinion shapers employ the same tropes to inscribe civilizational threat and the same explanation—"brainwashing"—to pathologize seemingly aberrant political behavior, whether with reference to John Walker Lyndh (the "American Taliban") or suicide bombers in Iraq.

But the early cold war's most tangible contribution to the "war on terror" is less to discursive constructions of enmity than to those practices deemed necessary to combat a deadly and implacable foe. The "harsh interrogation" techniques employed at Guantánamo Bay, Cuba, Bagram Air Base in Afghanistan, Abu Ghraib in Iraq, and the nameless destinations of "extraordinary rendition" are a direct outgrowth of America's encounter with communist captivity in the late 1940s and early 1950s.[68]

In the wake of the Korean War, administration officials insisted that Chinese communist success in eliciting compliant behavior from U.S. prisoners demanded close scrutiny. Whatever "diabolically ingenious pressures" had been brought to bear in North Korean camps required thorough scientific analysis. Only then would GIs stand a chance of resisting such techniques in the future—a point on which government agencies and editorial opinion concurred. When Defense Secretary Wilson announced a special interservice committee to study communist brainwashing techniques in August 1954, it was widely welcomed—with one important caveat. "Naturally, 'brainwashing' will not be studied with a view to emulating its techniques, which we hold to be an abominable contradiction of what we regarded as a proper code of moral behavior," the *New York Times* urged. "It is all very well to fight fire with fire when the need arises but we cannot burn down the edifice of our own morality to do so."[69]

Out of public view, however, the touch-paper had been ignited, and the fuse kept burning even when Wilson's committee later announced that drugs, hypnosis, electric shocks, sensory deprivation, and torture—"brainwashing," in short—had *not* been routinely used on American POWs. But the CIA had already authorized experimentation to refine these precise techniques. And if the Soviets and Chinese had not yet cracked this particular code, that was no reason to halt America's race to manufacture a "Manchurian candidate" of its own.[70]

Determined to ascertain how Cardinal Mindszenty's confession had been induced, U.S. military and intelligence agencies began to fund research into communist interrogation techniques in 1949. Behavioral scientists, in a range of disciplines and institutions, set out to discover the most effective means of producing a perfectly compliant human subject, an individual who under interrogation would divulge everything, confess to anything, but remember nothing. The Soviets, Chinese, and North Koreans could no more be conceded an advantage in the neurological domain than they could be permitted to sustain a bomber gap, a missile gap, or (in the parodic world of *Dr. Strangelove*) a "mineshaft gap." "We must . . . learn to subvert, sabotage, and destroy our enemies by more clear, more sophisticated and more effective methods than those used against us," advised Herbert Hoover in 1954.[71] Through secret programs like MKUltra, the CIA kindled the expertise that would enable U.S. agents to break captives with superior skill and speed—borrowing some techniques, such as the water treatment (or "waterboarding") that had been employed in North Korea, while adding new refinements of their own.

All this came to light in 1977, when a Senate select committee exposed MKUltra—a "Manhattan Project of the mind"—to public scrutiny.[72] In the course of its inquiry, the committee investigated what had been done in the name of behavior modification research and to whom. Over ten years, from 1953 to 1963, behavioral scientists had apparently located unsuspecting subjects in many places, from partygoers in New York to psychiatric patients in Canada. These individuals had been variously given massive quantities of LSD; subjected to electric shocks; confined in padded cells; and deprived of the ability to see or feel their surroundings—induced into temporary psychotic states or damaged yet more irrevocably. For "terminal experiments" (those that knowingly risked their subjects' lives) American agents had scoured Europe for what one historian terms "dubious defectors or double agents deemed 'expendable.'"[73] The CIA thus found a novel use for eastern bloc escapees. If they could not be entirely trusted in any other capacity, these individuals could at least perform one valuable service for the free world—as "captive minds" in the most literal sense.

Lethal experimentation was presumably not what Senator Lodge had in mind when he lauded escapees' potential as the "biggest, single, constructive, creative element" in U.S. foreign policy. But the possibility that research into interrogation techniques would exceed acceptable parameters was not unforeseen by contemporaries. When the U.S. military authorized "torture schools" in the wake of the Korean War, ostensibly to improve American troops' resistance in captivity, some opinion formers predicted where this might lead and sounded the alarm. In a September 1955 editorial, the *Washington Post* anticipated a crisis in which the U.S. military, seeking "to determine the farthest limits of physical and mental endurance," would authorize experiments "on some despised and expendable portion of the population disqualified for service, such as the inmates of penitentiaries." While this editorial overlooked the possibility of yet more expendable bodies being located overseas, it derived a stark warning from recent European history. Reminding readers that the "rigorous training of the Afrika Korps was based on findings from physiological experiments conducted in a cold and compassionless scientific spirit on the inmates of the Nazi concentration camps," the *Post* ventured an unusually stark analogy. Nazi camps were routinely likened to the Soviet gulag, but to broach a comparison between the U.S. military and the SS was unprecedented.[74]

The *Washington Post*'s intimations as to where necessitarian logic would lead proved prescient. With Amnesty International referring to the U.S.-run prison at Guantánamo Bay as "the gulag of our times," the circle has been closed.[75] As for the gulag of *previous* times, it is now possible for visitors to stay at former Soviet camps as paying guests: "extreme tourism," in the words of Igor L. Shpektor, mayor of Vorkuta. Once the center of the Arctic mining industry, this city built on forced labor offers accommodation to tourists in wooden barracks surrounded by barbed wire and patrolled by soldiers armed with guns and dogs. "Americans can stay here," Shpektor announced in 2005, perhaps inspired by Iron Curtain theme parks already operating in eastern Germany.[76] "We will give them a chance to escape. The guards will shoot them"—but "only with paintballs." If this prospect does not entice the fainthearted, today's tourist can choose from a steadily lengthening menu of cold war options: from museums dedicated to spy craft and the Stasi's surveillance methods to tours of atomic test sites or the more lighthearted attractions of Lithuania's "Stalin World," whose owner strives to combine "the charms of Disneyland with the worst of the Soviet gulag."[77]

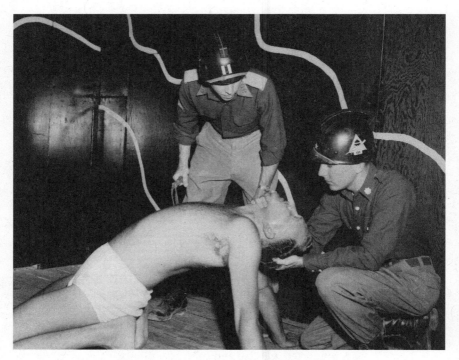

FIGURE 29. "Torture Hardens GIs to Brainwashing," ran the original caption to this picture. "Soon pain becomes unbearable," added *Newsweek* below a cropped version of the image that appeared in its issue of September 12, 1955. © Bettmann/CORBIS.

What impulses does this packaging of the cold war as adventure-amusement gratify? Enterprises like Vorkuta's gulag holiday camp attest the spine-tingling charge of imagining oneself captive, but atrocity tourism of this sort is also a token of, and an invitation to, historical amnesia. For many twenty-first-century travelers, what may be most pleasurable to revisit about this seemingly vanished era isn't so much its thrilling dangerousness as its ostensible *security*. With growing wistfulness, commentators in the West have taken to lamenting the passing of a golden age: a fifty-year lull when the enemy's identity was clear, threats were stable, and confrontation was bloodless. Back then, insecurity had a comfortingly familiar feel—and, most reassuringly of all, the cold war was a confrontation from which "freedom" emerged victorious.

Informed by equal quantities of nostalgia and triumphalism, hindsight of this sort is grossly distorting. To Americans who lived through it, the cold war looked anything but placid and predictable. Then as now, U.S. citizens were constantly reminded that they confronted an elusive enemy—unseen yet ubiquitous, relentless in its bid to destroy everything they held dear. At times during the cold war's first decade, opinion polls found that more than 70 percent of Americans expected to live through another major war. Although they were spared this catastrophe, others assuredly were not.[78] To envision the cold war as a casualty-free battle of nerves requires us to overlook the millions of lives lost—in Korea, Vietnam, Afghanistan, central America, southern Africa, and elsewhere—as competition between the first and second worlds was played out in the third.

Cold war atrocity tourism surely does more to efface than to memorialize the suffering of those who were once imprisoned in the gulag or who died in unsuccessful attempts to cross the Iron Curtain. In this commodification of the past, it is easy to lose sight of the cold war's immense destructiveness and thus to ignore legacies that continue to shape the present. Will tourists of the future similarly pay to stay in razor wire compounds at Guantánamo, donning orange jumpsuits and posing for pictures with friendly dogs and guards? Time will tell. But for now that troubling prospect might give us pause about the desire to restage captivity for pleasure and for profit.

ABBREVIATIONS

CDT	*Chicago Daily Tribune*
DDEL	Dwight D. Eisenhower Presidential Library, Abilene, Kansas
ECOSOC	Economic and Social Council of the United Nations
ESS	Edith Spurlock Sampson Papers, Arthur and Elizabeth Schlesinger Library on the History of Women in America, Radcliffe Institute for Advanced Study, Harvard University
FRUS	U.S. Department of State, *Foreign Relations of the United States* (series)
HSTL	Harry S. Truman Presidential Library, Independence, Missouri
LAT	*Los Angeles Times*
NACP	National Archives, College Park, Maryland
NAUK	National Archives of the United Kingdom, Kew, Surrey
NSC	National Security Council
NYT	*New York Times*
OCB	Operations Coordinating Board
PPS	Policy Planning Staff
PSB	Psychological Strategy Board
RG 59	Record Group 59: General Records of the Department of State
RG 84	Record Group 84: General Records of the Foreign Service Posts of the Department of State
RG 200	Record Group 200: UN Universal Newsreel Catalog
SMOF: PSB	Staff Member and Office Files: Psychological Strategy Board Files
WP	*Washington Post*

NOTES

INTRODUCTION

1. On U.S. cold war historiography, see Anders Stephanson, "The United States," in *The Origins of the Cold War in Europe: International Perspectives,* ed. David Reynolds (New Haven: Yale University Press, 1994), 23–52. The vast literature on the cold war devotes surprisingly little attention to the origins of the phrase. Many histories cite Walter Lippmann as its progenitor, but in *The Global Cold War: Third World Interventions and the Makings of Our Times* (Cambridge: Cambridge University Press, 2005) Odd Arne Westad attributes the coinage to George Orwell, who used it in "You and the Atomic Bomb," an essay published in the UK *Tribune*'s issue of October, 19, 1945.

2. "Cold War: Something People Can Understand," *Newsweek,* August 23, 1948, 17–20.

3. Sam Tanenhaus, *Whittaker Chambers: A Biography* (New York: Random House, 1997), 203–78.

4. "Cold War," 17.

5. "Mrs. Kasenkina Leaps into High Income Bracket," *CDT,* May 24, 1949, 12.

6. Laurence Burd, "Reject Red Demand on US," *CDT,* August 15, 1948, 1.

7. The United Press annual worldwide survey of "ten biggest" news stories in fact ranked Kasenkina's leap at number four, after Truman's election, the Berlin airlift, and the high cost of living; "Election Tops 10 Biggest News Stories," *LAT,* December 10, 1948, 6; "Big News of 1948," *NYT,* December 10, 1948, 24; "1948: The Year in Review," *CDT,* January 2, 1949, C2.

8. "The Nation: Fighter in a Fighting Year," *Time,* January 3, 1949, 9–10.

9. Lynn Boyd Hinds and Theodore Otto Windt, *The Cold War as Rhetoric: The Beginnings, 1945–1950* (Westport, CT: Praeger, 1991), 129–61; Martin J. Medhurst et al., *Cold War Rhetoric: Strategy, Metaphor and Ideology* (New York: Greenwood Press, 1990);

Michael Leigh, *Mobilizing Consent: Public Opinion and American Foreign Policy, 1937–1947* (Westport, CT: Greenwood Press, 1976).

10. Harry S. Truman, "Aid to Greece and Turkey," speech delivered to Congress, March 12, 1947, *Vital Speeches of the Day*, March 15, 1947, 322–24.

11. "Here We Go Again," *CDT*, March 13, 1947, 18.

12. Daniel T. Rodgers, *Contested Truths: Keywords in American Politics since Independence* (New York: Basic Books, 1987), 215.

13. Eric Foner, *The Story of American Freedom* (New York: W. W. Norton, 1998), xvi, 249–73.

14. "The House of Fear," *NYT*, August 15, 1948, E8.

15. "Thriller Diller," *WP*, August 10, 1948, 10.

16. Tellingly, when John Adams, Benjamin Franklin, and Thomas Jefferson gathered in 1776 to select a design for the national seal, the latter two both proposed images derived from the story of Exodus; Anders Stephanson, *Manifest Destiny: American Expansionism and the Empire of Right* (New York: Hill and Wang, 1995), 5.

17. Pauline Turner Strong, *Captive Selves, Captivating Others: The Politics and Poetics of Colonial American Captivity Narratives* (Boulder, CO: Westview Press, 1999), 4–5.

18. Richard Slotkin, *Regeneration through Violence: The Mythology of the American Frontier, 1600–1860* (Middletown, CT: Wesleyan University Press, 1973), 95.

19. The classic analysis of the "cultural uses" of the captivity narrative appeared at the start of the cold war; Roy Harvey Pearce, "The Significances of the Captivity Narrative," *American Literature* 19 (1947): 1–20.

20. See, for example, Christopher Castiglia, *Bound and Determined: Captivity, Culture-Crossing, and White Womanhood from Mary Rowlandson to Patty Hearst* (Chicago: University of Chicago Press, 1996); Melani McAlister, *Epic Encounters: Culture, Media, and U.S. Interests in the Middle East since 1945* (Berkeley: University of California Press, 2005), 199–200, 296–97; Tom Engelhardt, *The End of Victory Culture: Cold War America and the Disillusioning of a Generation* (Amherst: University of Massachusetts Press, 1998), 22–25, 215–16.

21. Dean Acheson, speech at the Army War College, August 27, 1951, Dean G. Acheson Papers, Secretary of State File, 1945–1972, Classified Speech File, Box 74, Folder, Classified Off the Record Speeches, Pre-Edited Copies, 1947–52, HSTL.

22. Leland Stowe, "Conquest by Terror," *Reader's Digest*, June 1952, 137.

23. Don Whitehead, "Dope Slave World Perils US Youth," *LAT*, January 23, 1952, 24.

24. Joost Meerloo, *The Rape of the Mind: The Psychology of Thought Control, Menticide, and Brainwashing* (Cleveland: World Publishing, 1956); John Foster Dulles, *War or Peace* (New York: Macmillan, 1950), 248.

25. Anders Stephanson, "Liberty or Death: The Cold War as US Ideology," in *Reviewing the Cold War: Approaches, Interpretations, Theory*, ed. Odd Arne Westad (London: Frank Cass, 2000), 81–100.

26. Henry R. Luce, "The American Century," *Life*, February 17, 1941, 61–65; Anne O'Hare McCormick, "First Specifications for the Post-War Order," *NYT*, June 1, 1942, 12.

27. "US Is Acclaimed for Its Generosity," *NYT*, August 4, 1952, 18; Anne O'Hare McCormick, "The Grim Century of the Homeless Man," *NYT*, August 6, 1952, 20.

28. Heinrich Böll, "The Imprisoned World of Solzhenitsyn's *The First Circle*," in *Aleksandr Solzhenitsyn: Critical Essays and Documentary Materials*, ed. John B. Dunlop, Richard Haugh, and Alexis Klimoff (Belmont, MA: Nordland, 1973), 227.

29. Frank Biess, *Homecomings: Returning POWs and the Legacies of Defeat in Postwar Germany* (Princeton: Princeton University Press, 2006), 3.

30. Niall Ferguson, "Prisoner Taking and Prisoner Killing: The Dynamics of Defeat, Surrender and Barbarity in the Age of Total War," in *The Barbarization of Warfare*, ed. George Kassimeris (New York: New York University Press, 2006), 137.

31. Ibid., 140.

32. Richard Drinnon, *Keeper of the Concentration Camps: Dillon S. Myer and American Racism* (Berkeley: University of California Press, 1987), 31–32.

33. By 1945, one in eight soldiers in German uniform was a Soviet citizen; Frank Costigliola, "'Like Animals or Worse': Narratives of Culture and Emotion by US and British POWs and Airmen behind Soviet Lines, 1944–45," *Diplomatic History* 28, no. 5 (2004): 759. On the Soviet attitude toward repatriation, see George Ginsburgs, "The Soviet Union and the Problem of Refugees and Displaced Persons, 1917–1956," *American Journal of International Law* 51, no. 2 (1957): 325–61.

34. Tony Judt, *Postwar: A History of Europe since 1945* (New York: Penguin Books, 2005), 27.

35. Ibid., 28–29; Harold Marcuse, *Legacies of Dachau: The Uses and Abuses of a Concentration Camp, 1933–2001* (Cambridge: Cambridge University Press, 2001), 160–70; Liisa H. Malkki, "Refugees and Exile: From 'Refugee Studies' to the National Order of Things," *Annual Review of Anthropology* 24 (1995): 495–523.

36. Director of the Office of War Mobilization and Reconversion, quoted in Robert McMahon, *The Cold War: A Very Short Introduction* (Oxford: Oxford University Press, 2003), 6; Michael R. Marrus, *The Unwanted: European Refugees in the Twentieth Century* (New York: Oxford University Press, 1985), 297.

37. Anne O'Hare McCormick, "Abroad: Europe Is the Laboratory of Allied Policies," *NYT*, June 23, 1945, 12.

38. Dean Acheson, *Present at the Creation: My Years in the State Department* (New York: W. W. Norton, 1969), 726.

39. John Deane, quoted in Frank Costigliola, "'I Had Come as a Friend': Emotion, Culture, and Ambiguity in the Formation of the Cold War, 1943–45," *Cold War History* 1, no. 1 (2000): 117.

40. Costigliola, "'I Had Come as a Friend'" and "'Like Animals or Worse'"; Cathal J. Nolan, "Americans in the Gulag: Detention of US Citizens by Russia and the Onset of the Cold War, 1944–49," *Journal of Contemporary History* 25 (1990): 523–45; Jason Kendall Moore, "Between Expediency and Principle: US Repatriation Policy toward Russian Nationals, 1944–1949," *Diplomatic History* 24, no. 3 (2000): 381–404.

41. "Freedom to Move," *Life*, August 30, 1948, 18.

42. Dulles, *War or Peace*, 242. On his inaugural television appearance, see John Lewis Gaddis, *Strategies of Containment: A Critical Appraisal of Postwar American National Security Policy* (Oxford: Oxford University Press, 1982), 135.

43. General Dwight Eisenhower, launching the "Crusade for Freedom" in September

1950, announced that one-third of the human race languished in "virtual bondage"; "Eisenhower Says Conflict Is Not Limited," *WP*, September 5, 1950, 1. Spellman's remark was made in a sermon denouncing the Hungarian communists' treatment of Cardinal Mindszenty; "Spellman Warns US to Halt Reds; Lauds Mindszenty," *NYT*, February 7, 1949, 1.

44. Harlow Robinson, *Russians in Hollywood, Hollywood's Russians* (Lebanon, NH: Northeastern University Press, 2007), 115–45. On the OWI's role in burnishing the image of the USSR, see Benjamin L. Alpers, *Dictators, Democracy, and American Public Opinion: Envisioning the Totalitarian Enemy, 1920s–1950s* (Chapel Hill: University of North Carolina Press, 2003), 224–34; Todd Bennett, "Culture, Power, and *Mission to Moscow*: Film and Soviet-American Relations during World War II," *Journal of American History* 88, no. 2 (2001): 489–518.

45. Drew Middleton, "First Pages from a Russian Notebook," *NYT*, July 7, 1946, 83; George Kennan, *Memoirs, 1950–1963* (London: Hutchinson, 1973), 90.

46. McCormick, "Grim Century."

47. Abbott Gleason, *Totalitarianism: The Inner History of the Cold War* (New York: Oxford University Press, 1995), 3.

48. J. Edgar Hoover, "Red Fascism in the United States Today," *American Magazine*, February 1947, 24; Les K. Adler and Thomas G. Paterson, "Red Fascism: The Merger of Nazi Germany and Soviet Russia in the American Image of Totalitarianism, 1930s-1950s," *American Historical Review* 75 (April 1970): 1046–64.

49. Hannah Arendt, *The Origins of Totalitarianism* (1951; repr., New York: Harcourt, Brace, 1973), 437, 441–42, 455. In her characterization of camp inmates' utter passivity, Arendt was clearly influenced by the work of Bruno Bettelheim, whose article "Individual and Mass Behavior in Extreme Situations" did much to shape early discussions of subjectivity in the camps; *Journal of Abnormal and Social Psychology* 38 (1943): 417–52. See Alpers, *Dictators, Democracy*, 250–302.

50. Barbie Zelizer, *Remembering to Forget: Holocaust Memory through the Camera's Eye* (Chicago: Chicago University Press, 1998).

51. George Kennan, "Totalitarianism in the Modern World," in *Totalitarianism: Proceedings of a Conference Held at the American Academy of Arts and Sciences, March 1953*, ed. Carl J. Friedrich (Cambridge, MA: Harvard University Press, 1954), 19.

52. The Chargé in the Soviet Union (Kennan) to the Secretary of State, secret telegram, February 22, 1946, FRUS, *1946*, vol. 6, *Eastern Europe; the Soviet Union* (Washington, DC: Government Printing Office, 1969), 699, 706. On the trope of penetration, see Frank Costigliola, "'Unceasing Pressure for Penetration': Gender, Pathology and Emotion in George Kennan's Formation of the Cold War," *Journal of American History* 83, no. 4 (1997): 1309–39.

53. X [George Kennan], "The Sources of Soviet Conduct," *Life*, July 28, 1947, 56.

54. The text of NSC 68, endorsed in April 1950, is reproduced in *Containment: Documents on American Policy and Strategy, 1945–50*, ed. Thomas H. Etzold and John Lewis Gaddis (New York: Columbia University Press, 1978), 386, 387, 388.

55. Ibid., 388. Like Arendt, the authors of NSC 68 regarded the concentration camp as the prototype of "a society in which the personality of the individual is so broken and perverted that he participates affirmatively in his own degradation" (396).

56. Nitze, quoted in David Callaghan, *Dangerous Capabilities: Paul Nitze and the Cold War* (New York: Harper Collins, 1990), 106.

57. As O'Brien puts it, "We bring him over to our side, not in appearance but genuinely, heart and soul. . . . It is intolerable to us that an erroneous thought should exist anywhere in the world, however secret and powerless it may be"; George Orwell, *1984, a Novel* (New York: Harcourt, Brace, 1949), 205.

58. Eric Fromm, *Escape from Freedom* (New York: Rinehart, 1941); Stanley Elkins, *Slavery: A Problem in American Institutional and Intellectual Life* (Chicago: University of Chicago Press, 1959); Bettelheim, "Individual and Mass Behavior." Similarly, Arthur M. Schlesinger Jr. stressed that the concentration camp was "the culmination of dominance and surrender, of sadism and of masochism; it is the climax of the system which keeps totalitarianism taut and triumphant." Arthur M. Schlesinger Jr., *The Vital Center: The Politics of Freedom* (Boston: Houghton Mifflin, 1949), 88.

59. Corey Robin, "Why Do Opposites Attract? Fear and Freedom in the Modern Political Imagination," in *Fear Itself: Enemies Real and Imagined in American Culture,* ed. Nancy Lusignan Schultz (West Lafayette: Purdue University Press, 1999), 15. On Schlesinger's *Vital Center* and cold war masculinity, see K. A. Cuordileone, *Manhood and American Political Culture in the Cold War* (New York: Routledge, 2005), 1–36.

60. Schlesinger, *Vital Center,* 243; *Invasion of the Body Snatchers* (dir. Don Siegel, Walter Wanger Productions, 1956).

61. Betty Friedan, *The Feminine Mystique* (New York: W. W. Norton, 1963), ch. 12.

62. Harriet Beecher Stowe, paraphrasing Laurence Sterne, quoted in Michelle Burnham, *Captivity and Sentiment: Cultural Exchange in American Literature, 1682–1861* (Hanover: University Press of New England, 1997), 123.

63. Chen Jian, "The Ward Case and the Emergence of Sino-American Confrontation, 1948–1950," *Australian Journal of Chinese Affairs* 30 (1993): 149–70.

64. "Red China's Captive Americans," *Life,* May 19, 1952, 51.

65. "M'Carthy Asserts a File Was 'Raped,'" *NYT,* May 8, 1950, 3.

66. This phrase was used by Morris Ernst, the attorney hired by IT&T to defend Vogeler but denied entry into Hungary; "Record on Vogeler Spurs Doubts Here," *NYT,* February 23, 1950, 2. One year earlier, Mayor O'Dwyer of New York had referred to the "lynching" of Cardinal Mindszenty, tried in the same courtroom in February 1949; "Protests Rising in Primate's Case," *NYT,* February 8, 1949, 2. Mindszenty's trial was also referred to as a "rape of justice" by various parties, including Rev. Dr. Daniel A. Poling, president of the World Christian Endeavor Union; "Spellman Warns US," 1.

67. "The New Barbary Pirates," *NYT,* December 26, 1951, 24; C. L. Sulzberger, " 'Incidents' Show How Diplomacy Has Fallen," *NYT,* December 9, 1951, 169.

68. "U.S. Again Bows to Demands of Red Hungary," *CDT,* July 8, 1951, 2.

69. Gladwin Hill, "Brain-Washing: Time for a Policy," *Atlantic Monthly,* April 1955, 58.

70. The term *give-up-itis* was coined by journalist Eugene Kinkead to describe the apathy that, in his account, led many U.S. prisoners in Korea to abandon the will to live in captivity; "A Reporter at Large: The Study of Something New in History," *New Yorker,* October 26, 1957, 102–53. The term *brainwashing* (ostensibly from the Chinese *hsi-nao*) was introduced to American readers by Edward Hunter in 1950 with reference to thought re-

form in the People's Republic of China; Edward Hunter, "Brain-Washing in 'New' China," *New Leader,* October 7, 1950, 6–7. For two early debunkings, see Raymond A. Bauer, "Brainwashing: Psychology or Demonology?" *Journal of Social Issues* 13 (1957): 41–47, and Albert Biderman, "The Image of 'Brainwashing,'" *Public Opinion Quarterly* 26, no. 4 (1962): 547–63.

71. I draw here on Burnham's discussion of sentimentality in *Captivity and Sentiment* and on Slotkin's *Regeneration through Violence.*

72. X [Kennan], "Sources of Soviet Conduct," 63; Stephanson, "Liberty or Death," 88.

73. "Town to Simulate Communist Rule for Day as Lesson," *WP,* April 14, 1950, 28. For more extended discussion of the "takeover," see Richard M. Fried, *The Russians Are Coming! The Russians Are Coming! Pageantry and Patriotism in Cold War America* (New York: Oxford University Press, 1998), 67–86; Michael J. Hogan, *A Cross of Iron: Harry S. Truman and the Origins of the National Security State, 1945–1954* (Cambridge: Cambridge University Press, 1998), 440–44.

74. "Daily Workers DTs," *WP,* May 1, 1950, 10. For Kronenwetter's pajamas, see "Town Deserts US for Day in Soviet," *NYT,* May 2, 1950, 6.

75. "Legion Would Try All Reds as Spies," *NYT,* October 12, 1950, 17.

76. "Their Sheltered Honeymoon," *Life,* August 10, 1959, 51–52, quoted in Elaine Tyler May, *Homeward Bound: American Families in the Cold War Era* (New York: Basic Books, 1988), 4–5.

77. Alan Nadel, *Containment Culture: American Narrative, Postmodernism and the Atomic Age* (Durham: Duke University Press, 1995); Douglas Field, ed., *American Cold War Culture* (Edinburgh: Edinburgh University Press, 2005); David K. Johnson, *The Lavender Scare: The Cold War Persecution of Gays and Lesbians in the Federal Government* (Chicago: University of Chicago Press, 2004).

78. Draft Resolution on Enslavement of Peoples, February 13, 1953, John Foster Dulles Papers, Box 72, Liberation Policy file, Seeley G. Mudd Manuscript Library, Princeton University.

1. UPPER EAST SIDE STORY

1. "Heat Wave," *Time,* September 6, 1948, 14.

2. "Mrs. Kosenkina Leaps from 3D Floor of Soviet Consulate Here, but Lives; Samarin Heard; Molotov Accuses US," *NYT,* August 13, 1948, 1, 3.

3. "The House on 61st Street," *Time,* August 23, 1948, 13.

4. "Cop Defies Red 'Iron Curtain' to Save Teacher," *CDT,* August 14, 1948, 3.

5. "Mrs. Kosenkina Leaps," 3.

6. "Cold War: Something People Can Understand," *Newsweek,* August 23, 18.

7. "Another 'Diplomatic Incident'?" *Atlanta Constitution,* August 11, 1948, 6.

8. "Farewell to Mr. Lomakin," *NYT,* August 21, 1948, 14.

9. "Voice of America Told Russia 41 Minutes after Teacher's Leap," *New York Herald Tribune,* August 14, 1; "Kosenkina Case Is Major News on 'Voice' Broadcast to Russia," *NYT,* August 14, 1948, 1.

10. Joseph Alsop and Stewart Alsop, "The Kosenkina Case Is One of Thousands," *LAT*, August 18, 1948, A4.

11. When Washington requested that Lomakin be recalled, the explanation offered Moscow by the State Department was that the government could not "permit the exercise within the United States of the police power of any foreign government"; "Better Late Than Never," *CDT*, August 21, 1948, 8.

12. Alsop and Alsop, "Kosenkina Case."

13. "Grandstand Play," *Time*, September 6, 1948, 15. Readers also had to adjust to two different spellings of her name, initially rendered as Kosenkina and then corrected to Kasenkina.

14. "The Mystery of the Kidnaped Russian," *Life*, August 23, 1948, 23–27.

15. "Russian Factions Here War over 'Kidnapping' of Woman," *NYT*, August 8, 1948, 1.

16. "NY Russian Thriller," *New York Herald Tribune*, August 8, 1948, 1, 29.

17. "Russian Factions," 1.

18. "Teacher, Reported Fleeing Russians, Surrendered in New York Subway," *WP*, August 9, 1948, 3.

19. "Reds 'Kidnap' or 'Rescue' Russian Woman," *LAT*, August 8, 1948, 48.

20. On August 9, Soviet Ambassador Panyushkin visited the State Department, lodging his complaints with Undersecretary of State Lovett, Chip Bohlen, and Ernest Gross, the State Department's legal advisor; Memorandum of Conversation by the Counselor of the Department of State (Bohlen), August 9, 1948, FRUS, *1948*, vol. 4, *Eastern Europe; the Soviet Union* (Washington, DC: Government Printing Office, 1974), 1030–32.

21. The Embassy of the Soviet Union to the Department of State, August 12, 1948, FRUS, *1948*, 4:1037.

22. According to J. Edgar Hoover, Mundt had been put on the trail of the three teachers by Victor Kravchenko, who was in touch with Alexandra Tolstoy; the Director of the Federal Bureau of Investigation (Hoover) to the Chief of the Division of Foreign Activity Correlation (Neal), August 9, 1948, FRUS, *1948*, 4:1028.

23. Walter Goodman, *The Committee: The Extraordinary Career of the House Committee on Un-American Activities* (London: Secker and Warburg, 1969), 226–71; on Elizabeth Bentley, see Lauren Kessler, *Clever Girl: Elizabeth Bentley, the Spy Who Ushered in the McCarthy Era* (New York: Perennial, 2003); and Kathryn S. Olmsted, *Red Spy Queen: A Biography of Elizabeth Bentley* (Chapel Hill: University of North Carolina Press, 2002).

24. "Red Fugitive Seeks FBI Aid," *CDT*, August 9, 1948, 7.

25. Lomakin insisted to reporters that Kasenkina was, in fact, allowed out and had even gone to the movies (he thought); " 'Rescued' Teacher Well, Says Consul," *NYT*, August 11, 1948, 2. On the immunity issue, see Lawrence Preuss, "Consular Immunities: The Kasenkina Case (US-USSR)," *American Journal of International Law* 43 (1949): 37–56.

26. Smith to Secretary of State, telegram, August 11, 1948, 311.60N3/1–148–311.615/12–3149, State Department Decimal File, 1945–49, Box 1642, RG 59, NACP; Walter Bedell Smith, *My Three Years in Moscow* (Philadelphia: J. B. Lippincott, 1950), 74–75.

27. The writ referred to the teacher's "imprisonment"—exercised by "power, deceit and

terror"—ascribing to Soviet officials an intention to transport the teacher "to slavery and death" in the USSR; New York Supreme Court, Special Term, Part II, *The People of the State of New York on the Relation of Christopher Emmet, vs. Jacob Lomakin, Consul-General of the Union of Soviet Socialist Republics, Respondent,* August 12, 1948, Stenographic Record, 702.6111/8–1248, State Department Decimal File, 1945–49, Box 3069, RG 59, NACP.

28. "Document Served on Soviet Consul for Appearance of Mrs. Kosenkina," *WP,* August 12, 1948, 1. Materials on the involvement of Common Cause, Inc., in the Kasenkina case can be found in the Emmet (Christopher T., Jr.) Papers, Hoover Institution Archives, Stanford University.

29. State Department, Chief of Detectives, George P. Mitchell, "Memorandum for Police Commissioner, City of New York Police Department," August 16, 1948, 702.6111 State Department Decimal File, 1945–49, Box 3069, RG 59, NACP.

30. Commanding Officer, Borough Manhattan Detective Bureau East to Commanding Officer, Detective Division, "Injuries Sustained by Mrs. Kosenkina at 7 East 61st Street," August 12, 1948, 702.6111/8–1348, State Department Decimal File, 1945–49, Box 3069, RG 59, NACP.

31. John Gunther, *Behind the Curtain* (New York: Harper and Brothers, 1949), 225; Joseph C. Harsch, *The Curtain Isn't Iron* (New York: Doubleday, 1950), 17.

32. "Text of Tass Dispatch on the Kosenkina Case," *NYT,* August 15, 1948, 3.

33. "Statement by Consulate," *NYT,* August 17, 1948, 3; "City Police Reject Russians' Version in Kosenkina Case," *NYT,* August 17, 1948, 1, 3; "Teachers Sought Death to Avoid US, Russ Say," *LAT,* August 17, 1948, 1.

34. "Woman Teacher Escapes Soviet Consulate by Leap Out of Window," *LAT,* August 13, 1948, 1.

35. "House on 61st Street," 12–13.

36. Helen Iswolsky, "The School-Teacher and the Commissar," *Commonweal,* September 10, 1948, 513.

37. "Mrs. Kasenkina Rejects Consul's Offer of 'Help,' Accuses Him," *WP,* August 14, 1948, 1.

38. Embassy of the Soviet Union to the Department of State, August 14, 1948, FRUS, *1948,* 4:1043–44.

39. Truman's announcement came after vociferous criticism of the State Department for its insufficiently muscular response to the Soviets; Lewis Wood, "Strong Note Sent to Soviet by US on Teachers' Case," *NYT,* August 20, 1948, 1.

40. The State Department publicized both Soviet protests and U.S. responses; "US Rejects Soviet Charges Concerning Refusal of Two Russian Teachers to Return to Soviet Union," *Department of State Bulletin,* August 29, 1948, 251–62.

41. "Telling Off Moscow," *Newsweek,* August 30, 1948, 16–17; "An Unusual Step," *NYT,* August 21, 1948, 1.

42. Marshall to Embassy, Moscow, telegram, August 24, 1948, 702.6111/8–2448, State Department Decimal File, 1945–49, Box 3069, RG 59, NACP.

43. "Git—US to Red Consul," *Atlanta Constitution,* August 21, 1948, 1; "Fugitive Russians," *New Republic,* August 23, 1948, 7.

44. Alsop and Alsop, "Kosenkina Case," A4; "Thousands of Russians Dare Death to Escape," *LAT*, September 7, 1948, A4.

45. Precisely who was a Soviet citizen was an ongoing source of dispute between the USSR and the western allies, with the United Kingdom and United States refusing in May 1945 to recognize as citizens the populations of countries or areas (namely, the Baltic states and parts of Poland and Ukraine) annexed by the Soviet Union since 1939, unless individuals "affirmatively" announced themselves as such. Malcolm Proudfoot states that more than 250,000 nationals of these annexed territories resisted repatriation in 1945; *European Refugees, 1939–52: A Study in Forced Population Movement* (London: Faber and Faber, 1957), 214.

46. Mark Elliott, "The United States and Forced Repatriation of Soviet Citizens, 1944–47," *Political Science Quarterly* 88 (1973): 255.

47. During the war, some 8.7 million Soviet citizens were deported from the USSR by the Nazis, including 3.2 million prisoners of war; Pavel Polian, "The Internment of Returning Soviet Prisoners of War after 1945," in *Prisoners of War, Prisoners of Peace*, ed. Bob Moore and Barbara Hately-Broad (Oxford: Berg, 2005), 123.

48. Estimates of the number of Soviet citizens who served in the Wehrmacht vary significantly. George Fischer estimated the total at half a million in 1952, while German sources put the figure at one million; George Ginsburgs, "The Soviet Union and the Problem of Refugees and Displaced Persons, 1917–1956," *American Journal of International Law* 51, no. 2 (1957): 355. On the phenomenon of Vlasov and the Vlasovites, see George Fischer, *Soviet Opposition to Stalin: A Case Study in World War II* (Cambridge, MA: Harvard University Press, 1952); Mark Elliott, "Andrei Vlasov: Red Army General in Hitler's Service," *Military Affairs* 46, no. 2 (1982): 84–87; Alexander Dallin and Ralph S. Mavrogordato, "The Soviet Reaction to Vlasov," *World Politics* 8, no. 3 (1956): 307–22.

49. Elliott, "United States," 255–57.

50. Liisa H. Malkki, "Refugees and Exile: From 'Refugee Studies' to the National Order of Things," *Annual Review of Anthropology* 24 (1995): 495–523, and "National Geographic: The Rooting of Peoples and the Territorialization of National Identity among Scholars and Refugees," *Cultural Anthropology* 7 (1992): 24–44; Nevzat Soguk, *States and Strangers: Refugees and Displacements of Statecraft* (Minneapolis: University of Minnesota Press, 1999).

51. Whether or not the loosely worded agreement at Yalta sanctioned *forced* repatriation remained a moot point, with many critics arguing that it did not; Julius Epstein, *Operation Keelhaul: The Story of Forced Repatriation from 1944 to the Present* (Old Greenwich, CT: Devin Adair, 1973); Nikolai Tolstoy, *The Secret Betrayal* (New York: Charles Scribner's Sons, 1977); Mark R. Elliott, *Pawns of Yalta: Soviet Refugees and America's Role in Their Repatriation* (Urbana: University of Illinois Press, 1982).

52. Rüdiger Overmans, "The Repatriation of Prisoners of War Once Hostilities Are Over: A Matter of Course?" in *Prisoners of War*, 11–22.

53. Michael R. Marrus, *Unwanted: European Refugees in the Twentieth Century* (New York: Oxford University Press, 1985), 296–345.

54. "Kosenkina Case Is One," A4; Elliott, "United States," 258; Eugene Lyons, *Our Secret Allies: The Peoples of Russia* (London: Arco Publications, 1954), 254–77; Ginsburgs, "Soviet Union," 354–56.

55. Murphy, quoted in Cathal J. Nolan, "Americans in the Gulag: Detention of US Citizens by Russia and the Onset of the Cold War, 1944–49," *Journal of Contemporary History* 25 (1990): 533.

56. There were some exceptions, however, including the Alsops. See also Cleaves Jones, "When We Drove Fugitives Back to the Slave Masters," *LAT*, September 8, 1948, A5.

57. Wood, "Strong Note," 1. As early as August 14, State Department press officers announced that Kasenkina and Samarin would be granted asylum; "2 Russ Teachers Given Right to Remain in US," *CDT*, August 14, 1948, 3.

58. David J. Dallin, "The Kravchenko Case," *Modern Age* 6 (1962): 267–76; Robert J. Lamphere, untitled ms., detailing Dallin's role in Kravchenko's defection, Robert J. Lamphere Papers, Box 1, folder 49.5, Lauinger Library, Georgetown University, Washington, DC; FRUS, *1944*, vol. 4, *Europe* (Washington, DC: Government Printing Office, 1966), 1224–41; FRUS, *1945*, vol. 5, *The Soviet Union* (Washington, DC: Government Printing Office, 1968), 1131–38.

59. "Russians Captured with Nazis Riot at Fort Dix; 3 Commit Suicide," *NYT*, June 30, 1945, 1; Nicholas Bethell, *The Last Secret: The Delivery to Stalin of Over Two Million Russians by Britain and the United States* (New York: Basic Books, 1974), 166–70.

60. "US Halts Return of 150 to Russia," *NYT*, July 1, 1945, 4.

61. Bethell, *Last Secret*, 169.

62. "International Convention Relative to the Treatment of Prisoners of War," signed at Geneva, 27 July 1929, FRUS, *1929*, vol. 3 (Washington, DC: Government Printing Office, 1944), 336–63.

63. The State Department claimed that it *did* treat the men as German POWs, and hence was repatriating them to Germany—a move that delivered them straight to the Soviets; Jason Kendall Moore, "Between Expediency and Principle: US Repatriation Policy toward Russian Nationals, 1944–1949," *Diplomatic History* 24, no. 3 (2000): 396–97.

64. "America and the DPs," *NYT*, August 18, 1948, 24.

65. Timothy K. Nenninger, "United States Prisoners of War and the Red Army, 1944–45: Myths and Realities," *Journal of Military History* 66 (2002): 761–82.

66. Lt. Col. James D. Wilmeth, writing after a visit to Lublin in February–March 1945, quoted in Costigliola, "'Like Animals or Worse,'" 757.

67. Pavel Polian, *Against Their Will: The History and Geography of Forced Migrations in the USSR* (Budapest: Central European University Press, 2004).

68. Moore, "Between Expediency and Principle," 400.

69. Joseph Alsop and Stewart Alsop, "Concerning Human Sacrifice in Korea," *WP*, January 23, 1953, 13.

70. "Refugees from Communism: We Have a Miserably Neglected Duty to Fulfill toward Them: Let's Do It," *Life*, September 29, 1947, 38.

71. Anders Stephanson, *Manifest Destiny: American Expansionism and the Empire of Right* (New York: Hill and Wang, 1995), 122, and "Fourteen Notes on the Very Concept of the Cold War," in *Rethinking Geopolitics*, ed. Gearóid Ó Tuathail and Simon Dalby (London: Routledge, 1998), 62–85.

72. "The Ambassador and the Law," *WP*, August 16, 1948, 6.

73. Kasenkina's memoir also repeatedly drew attention to the disjuncture between the

opulence of life in the consulate and ordinary citizens' deprivation in the USSR; Oksana Kasenkina, *Leap to Freedom* (Philadelphia: J. B. Lippincott, 1949).

74. Kennan, quoted and critiqued in Frank Costigliola, "'Unceasing Pressure for Penetration': Gender, Pathology and Emotion in George Kennan's Formation of the Cold War," *Journal of American History* 83, no. 4 (1997):1309–39.

75. On Soviet screen stereotypes, see Siegfried Kracauer, "National Types as Hollywood Presents Them," *Public Opinion Quarterly* 13 (1949): 66–70.

76. "Personae Non Grata," *Daily Mirror*, August 10, 1948; Ralph McGill, "The Significance of Window Leaping," *Atlanta Constitution*, August 24, 1948, 6.

77. "Grandstand Play," 14–15.

78. "Protection for Spies," *CDT*, August 14, 1948, 8. Such arguments drew strength from the arrest of Valentin Gubitchev (an engineer with the Soviet UN delegation) on espionage charges—the conduit via which Judith Coplon, a Department of Justice employee, allegedly passed U.S. secrets to the Kremlin; "Soviet UN Aide and US Girl Seized by FBI Here as Spies," *NYT*, March 6, 1949, 1.

79. Memorandum from Department of State to Embassy of USSR, July 16, 1946, 702.6111/7–1646, State Department Decimal File, 1945–49, Box 3069, RG 59, NACP; "Teacher Barring Russian Visitors, Lomakin Is Told," *NYT*, August 22, 1948, 12.

80. More than 130 listening devices were discovered between 1949 and 1964 in U.S. embassies in eastern bloc countries; Clifton E. Wilson, *Cold War Diplomacy* (Tucson: University of Arizona Press, 1966), 21.

81. David Mayers, *The Ambassadors and America's Soviet Policy* (New York: Oxford University Press, 1995), 165.

82. Thayer to "Muzzy," October 23, 1934, Papers of Charles W. Thayer, Correspondence with "Muzzy" (Mrs. George C. Thayer), Box 5, HSTL.

83. Thayer to Sissy, June 2, 1934, Papers of Charles W. Thayer, Box 5, HSTL. The ballerina and "fervent Communist" in question was Irena Charnodskaya. According to Thayer, who denied that there was any sexual impulse at work, "We [Thayer, Bohlen, and Bullitt] simply cannot keep our hands off her. She has become an acquisition of the Embassy and . . . sleep[s] in some vacant room which the three of us carefully lock together and then fight violently as to who will keep the key"; Diary, April 14–May 20, 1934, Papers of Charles W. Thayer, Diaries, Box 6, HSTL. Bohlen nurtured similarly fond memories; Charles Bohlen, *Witness to History: 1929–69* (New York: W. W. Norton, 1973), 21. See also Will Brownell and Richard N. Billings, *So Close to Greatness: A Biography of William C. Bullitt* (New York: Macmillan, 1987), 157; Costigliola, "Unceasing Pressure," 1316–17.

84. Thayer, Diary, April 14–May 20, 1934, Papers of Charles W. Thayer, Diaries, Box 6, HSTL.

85. Travel restrictions on U.S. diplomats in the USSR were tightened in response to the Kasenkina affair; "USSR Travel Restrictions for Diplomatic Personnel," *Department of State Bulletin*, October 24, 1948, 525.

86. Kennan, quoted in Costigliola, "Unceasing Pressure," 1321.

87. Reeling from the rebuff, "they felt Stalin's efforts to isolate the Soviet people as a kind of aggression against them," hypothesizes Costigliola, "and this sentiment contributed to their visceral anticommunism"; "Unceasing Pressure," 1317.

88. Kennan, quoted in Mayers, *Ambassadors*, 184. This remark brought his ambassadorship to a swift conclusion as the Soviet government declared him persona non grata—which was perhaps exactly what Kennan intended.

89. "Soviet Harassment of Foreign Diplomats," *Department of State Bulletin*, November 17, 1952, 786.

90. U.S. Embassy officials in January 1949 counted twenty-one children in this position; Chargé in the Soviet Union (Kohler) to the Secretary of State, January 12, 1949, FRUS, *1949*, vol. 5, *Eastern Europe; the Soviet Union* (Washington, DC: Government Printing Office, 1976), 550.

91. Edmund Stevens, *This Is Russia: Uncensored* (New York: Didier, 1950), 84–86.

92. In 1948, Chile took the lead in international protests after Moscow refused an exit visa to the Russian wife of the Chilean ambassador's son; "Russian Wife Ban under Fire in UN," *NYT*, December 3, 1948, 7; "UN Again Beats Head in Vain on Kremlin Wall," *CDT*, April 26, 1949, 5; "United Nations Action on Human Rights in 1948," *Department of State Bulletin*, January 2, 1949, 22.

93. "UN Finds Russians Violating Charter by Curb on Wives," *NYT*, April 26, 1949, 1.

94. "Soviet Wives Held for State Security," *NYT*, August 21, 1948, 5.

95. "UN Finds Russians," 14.

96. "Leap Survivor Calls Russian Life 'Misery,'" *WP*, March 24, 1949, 2. Kasenkina's points were elaborated in a column by Malvina Lindsay, who also drew attention to high rates of miscarriage and abortion in the USSR; "Nation's Test—Women's Place," *WP*, March 26, 1949, 8.

97. In February 1950, the pro-Soviet governments of Hungary and Czechoslovakia introduced legislation prohibiting citizens from marrying foreigners and adopted an equally obstructive stance on exit visas; "Soviet Group Curbs Foreign Marriages," *NYT*, February 9, 1950, 8.

98. "Truman Proposes Moscow Lift Bars," *NYT*, August 10, 1950; "US Bids Soviet Let Russian Wives Join American Husbands Abroad," *NYT*, May 14, 1953, 1.

99. "A Soviet Opportunity," *NYT*, May 15, 1953, 22. Bohlen's efforts secured an exit visa for the Russian wife of an AP correspondent in Moscow; "Two US Wives Get Exit Visas in Soviet," *NYT*, June 10, 1953, 1.

100. *Never Let Me Go* (dir. Delmer Daves, MGM, 1953); "Never Let Me Go," *Variety*, March 25, 1953; "Never Let Me Go," *Newsweek*, June 29, 1953, 90.

101. Bosley Crowther, "Clark Gable Outwits Russians Again, Wins a Ballerina in *Never Let Me Go*," Screen in Review, *NYT*, June 11, 1953, 37.

102. "The Current Cinema: Clark Parts the Curtain," *New Yorker*, June 20, 1953, 89–90.

103. Chargé in the Soviet Union (Kohler) to the Secretary of State, January 12, 1949, FRUS, *1949*, 5:550.

104. Ibid., 554.

105. Smith, *My Three Years*, 186.

106. Annabelle Bucar, *The Truth about American Diplomats* (Moscow: Literaturnaya Gazeta, 1949).

107. Chargé in the Soviet Union (Kohler) to the Secretary of State, March 4, 1949, FRUS, *1949*, 5:581–83; "US Embassy Aide Quits in Moscow," *NYT*, February 28, 1948, 3.

108. Smith, *My Three Years,* 186.

109. "Smith Proposes Exchange," *NYT,* February 29, 1948, 4. Bucar had, in fact, been married thirteen months—and had a child—before she resigned. Whatever her legal status vis-à-vis the USSR, she had broken embassy rules, which required staff to resign if they married a foreign national; "US Embassy Aide Quits," 3.

110. Joseph B. Phillips, "Memoir of a Disillusioned Agent," *Newsweek,* March 7, 1949, 46.

111. "Father Disowns Clerk in US Embassy Who Renounced Native Land for Russia," *NYT,* February 29, 1949, 4.

112. For the U.S. Embassy, this defection raised the possibility that encryption codes had been compromised. For twenty-one-year-old McMillin the future looked bleak indeed. Soon dissatisfied with his lot as a Soviet intelligence asset/propaganda pawn, and estranged from the reportedly pregnant Galina, he was too fearful of punishment to throw himself on the U.S. Embassy's mercy, realizing (too late) the irrevocable consequences of his impetuosity—or so informants reported to the embassy; State Department Decimal File 1945–49, 121.5461/1–145–121.5465/12–3149, Box 554, RG 59, NACP.

113. Durbrow to Secretary of State, May 15, 1948; 121.5461/5–1548, State Department Decimal File, 1945–49, Box 554, RG 59, NACP; "Russ Launch Sex Campaign against US," *LAT,* June 15, 1948, 1.

114. "Flight to Freedom," *NYT,* August 17, 1948, 20.

115. Kohler to Marshall, March 4, 1949, FRUS, *1949,* 5:582–83.

116. "Anti-US Film Planned," *NYT,* December 6, 1950, 55.

117. Kohler to Marshall, March 4, 1949, FRUS, *1949,* 5:583. U.S. diplomats speculated that the Soviets were going to town on the Bucar case to distract attention from the Kravchenko libel trial (discussed in chapter 3).

118. "Mundt Says Soviet Story Is Twisted," *WP,* August 8, 1948, M1; Yakov Lomakin to Commissioner Arthur Wallander, August 7, 1948, 702.6111/8–948, State Department Decimal File, 1945–49, Box 3069, RG 59, NACP; "Kremlin Attacked by Mrs. Kasenkina," *NYT,* November 20, 1948, 6.

119. "Teacher Changes Mind on Interview," *NYT,* August 25, 1948, 3.

120. "Mrs. Kasenkina Says Leap Was to Avoid Return Home," *NYT,* August 26, 1948, 3.

121. Isaac Don Levine, "Mrs. Kasenkina to Tell Own Story in Journal," *New York Journal-American,* September 21, 1948, 1.

122. So claimed the Prologue to her memoir, *Leap to Freedom,* 9.

123. Fulton Oursler, "Whose Business Was It?" *Reader's Digest,* May 1949, 1–7.

124. Charles Grutzner, "Kravchenko Aided Samarin in Flight from Soviet Agents," *NYT,* August 20, 1948, 10.

125. Levine, "Mrs. Kasenkina to Tell," 9.

126. Kathryn H. Stone, "Kasenkina 'Melodrama' Explained," *WP,* November 13, 1949, B5.

127. "Farewell to Mr. Lomakin," 14. Messages to the president can be found in the Papers of Harry S. Truman, General File, Box 1345, HSTL.

128. This judgment was expressed in August 1948 but continued to be the way in which her leap was memorialized, as for example, six years later, with reference to the defection of a Soviet diplomat's wife, Mrs. Petrov, in Australia; "Drama at Darwin," *NYT,* April 21, 1954, 28.

129. "The Text of Dewey's Campaign Address in Des Moines," *NYT*, September 21, 1948, 20.

130. "Mrs. Kasenkina and the Bomb," *CDT*, August 28, 1948, 8.

131. Kasenkina, *Leap to Freedom*, 9.

132. Universal Newsreel, vol. 23, no. 173, August 26, 1948, "Mrs Kasenkina Blasts Reds," RG 200, NACP.

133. E. A. Gross to Bohlen, September 13, 1948, and Bohlen to Kennan, September 14, 1948, and translations of this letter and another found in the consulate on August 12, 702.6111/9–748, State Department Decimal File, 1945–49, Box 39, RG 59, NACP.

134. Robert G. Hooker to Mr. Amshey, September 20, 1948, 702.6111/9–2048, State Department Decimal File, 1945–49, Box 3069, RG 59, NACP.

135. Transcript of interview between Inspector Ledden and Kasenkina, September 9, 1948, and Thomas F. Mulligan (Acting Police Commissioner) to Ernest Gross, September 10, 1948, both in 702.6111/9–1048, State Department Decimal File, 1945–49, Box 3069, RG 59, NACP.

136. State Department translators hesitated over the best rendition of this last sentence—an earlier translation phrasing it as "I have lost my own power to make decisions," from the more literal "I have been divested of my mind." At the August 7 press conference, Lomakin rendered the final sentence as "I was deprived of freedom," giving Kasenkina's words a rather more sinister implication.

137. Soviet protest delivered to Bedell Smith by Molotov on August 12, FRUS, *1948*, 4:1035.

138. This abduction narrative continued to be recirculated by the *Chicago Daily Tribune* throughout the 1950s and beyond. Protesting the resumption of consular relations in 1964, an editorial in that paper invoked the "kidnapped" schoolteacher as evidence that a Soviet consular presence was most unwelcome; "The Consular Treaty with Russia," *CDT*, June 1, 1964, 20.

139. In this interview she claimed that she had been confined to a room in the consulate, but also said that she had been allowed to move about freely and that she had never attempted to open the door and walk out; "Statement Taken from Kasenkina Oksana Stepanova at Roosevelt Hospital—August 12, 1948, 10.45 pm," 702.6111/8–1348, State Department Decimal File, 1945–49, Box 3069, RG 59, NACP.

140. Kasenkina, *Leap to Freedom*, 228. In August 1948, at her first hospital press conference, Kasenkina explained the letter—somewhat tendentiously—as a vain attempt to "speak to them as human beings in order to see that proper arrangements [for staying in the United States] could be made"; "Grandstand Play," 15.

141. "The Line on 'The Curtain,'" *Newsweek*, May 24, 1948, 31, 8–9; "Police on Guard at Film Picketing," *NYT*, May 13, 1948, 21; "Red Show," *Motion Picture Herald*, May 15, 1948, 9; "The Iron Curtain Creates a Furor," *Life*, May 17, 1948, 59.

142. "Randan at the Roxy," *Time*, May 24, 1948, 27.

143. *The Iron Curtain* (dir. William Wellman, Twentieth Century-Fox, 1948). This "opening salvo" characterization was offered by Bosley Crowther; "The Screen," *New York Times*, May 13, 1948, 31. See also Daniel J. Leab, "*The Iron Curtain* (1948): Hollywood's First Cold War Movie," *Historical Journal of Film, Radio and Television* 8 (1988): 153–88.

144. John McCarten, "The Current Cinema," *New Yorker*, May 22, 1948, 103.

145. Robert Hatch, "Fait Accompli," *New Republic*, May 24, 1948, 31. See also the correspondence between Rev. William Howard Melish, chairman of the National Council of American-Soviet Friendship, and the American Civil Liberties Union (ACLU), whose support he unsuccessfully attempted to enlist in suppressing the film on the grounds that it was "war propaganda"; American Civil Liberties Union Records, Series 3, Censorship, Box 755, folder 28, *The Iron Curtain*, Seeley G. Mudd Manuscript Library, Princeton University.

146. Kasenkina, *Leap to Freedom*, 228–30.

147. Igor Gouzenko, *The Iron Curtain* (New York: E. P. Dutton, 1948) and *Fall of a Titan* (New York: W. W. Norton, 1954); "Gouzenko Novel Sold," *NYT*, July 1, 1954, 21.

148. "Kasenkina Lawyer Will Speak Here Tomorrow," *LAT*, July 28, 1949, 19.

149. "Mrs. Kasenkina Nets $45,000 on Writings," *LAT*, May 25, 1949, 12; "Mrs. Kasenkina to Leave Hospital," *NYT*, November 18, 1948, 1.

150. These letters were in addition to the seven thousand or more she received while in the Roosevelt Hospital; "Mrs. Kasenkina Sees Soviet Doom, Possibly after the Death of Stalin," *NYT*, August 12, 1949, 19.

151. Julian Bach, "From Hitler to Stalin," review of *Under Two Dictators*, by Margarete Buber-Neumann, *Saturday Review of Books*, February 17, 1951, 21. On the phenomenon of the "ex-communist anticommunist," see Herbert L. Packer, *Ex-Communist Witnesses: Four Studies in Fact-Finding* (Stanford: Stanford University Press, 1962); David Seed, "The Ex-Communist Memoirs of Howard Fast and His Contemporaries," *Prospects* 24 (1999): 605–24; Hannah Arendt, "The Ex-Communists," in *Essays in Understanding, 1930–1954: Formation, Exile, and Totalitarianism* (New York: Schocken Books, 2005), 391–400.

152. Whittaker Chambers, *Witness* (New York: Random House, 1952); Stephen J. Whitfield, *The Culture of the Cold War* (Baltimore: Johns Hopkins University Press, 1996), 18.

153. The canonical work is Richard Crossman's edited collection *The God That Failed* (New York: Harper, 1950). See also Elizabeth Bentley, *Out of Bondage: The Story of Elizabeth Bentley* (New York: Devin Adair, 1951); Angela Calomiris, *Red Masquerade: Undercover for the FBI* (Philadelphia: J. B. Lippincott, 1950). The quote here is from Bentley's *Out of Bondage*, as cited in Ellen Schrecker, *Many Are the Crimes: McCarthyism in America* (Boston: Little, Brown, 1998), 133.

154. At the March 1949 meeting, Kasenkina was reported "too weak to speak," and her statement was read by Christopher Emmet of Common Cause, Inc.; "Soviet Is Attacked at Counter Rally," *NYT*, March 27, 1949, 1, 46; "Freedom Sunday Observed in City," *NYT*, October 9, 1950, 11; Oksana Kasenkina, "We Worship GOD Again," *Collier's*, October 27, 1951, 33–34.

155. Kasenkina was hired as Russian-language tutor to Helen Hayes for the Tsarist-era costume drama *Anastasia*; Hedda Hopper, "Looking at Hollywood," *CDT*, May 25, 1956, A8.

156. *The Red Danube* (dir. George Sidney, MGM, 1949); "At the Capitol," *NYT*, December 9, 1949, 37.

157. Bruce Marshall, *Vespers in Vienna* (Boston: Houghton Mifflin, 1947); Robert Hatch, "Gott Mit Uns," *New Republic*, December 26, 1949, 22–23.

158. "Thriller-Diller," *WP*, August 10, 1948, 10.

159. "Sofia," *Variety,* August 18, 1948, 11.

160. Richard English, "What Makes a Hollywood Communist?" *Saturday Evening Post,* May 19, 1951, 149.

161. "The Nation: Fighter in a Fighting Year," *Time,* January 3, 1949, 9–10.

2. BLOC-BUSTERS

1. "I Is Russian Pilot," *Time,* November 1, 1948, 30; "Escaped Soviet Fliers 'Take' Richmond, Va.," *LAT,* February 6, 1949, 34; "Flight to Freedom," *Newsweek,* November 1, 1948, 39; "2 Russian Fliers Stress Discontent," *NYT,* October, 22, 1948, 2.

2. "Flight to Freedom," 39; "Most Russians Dislike Soviet Rule, Red Air Force Deserters Assert," *LAT,* October 22, 1948, 1.

3. "Anatoly and Piotr Are Carried to Old Virginny," *Life,* February 21, 1949, 36–37.

4. "Tale of a US Bungle," *Newsweek,* September 12, 1949, 23–25.

5. "2 Who Fled Russia Seek Home in US," *CDT,* October 22, 1948, 1.

6. "They Had to See Virginia," *NYT,* February 5, 1949, 14.

7. "Russian Rubbernecks," *Time,* February 14, 1949, 22. Gargantua died later that year; "Gargantua, Circus Gorilla, Dies; Awed 40,000,000 in 12 Years," *NYT,* November 26, 1949, 28.

8. William Henry Chamberlin, review of *Why I Escaped,* by Peter Pirogov, *CDT,* March 12, 1950, H3.

9. "Escaped Soviet Fliers," 34; "Russians Amazed by US Abundance," *NYT,* February 6, 1948, 44. On Pirogov as an exemplar of the genus, see Ada Siegel, "The New Soviet Man," *American Mercury* 171 (November 1950): 524–32. (Siegel translated Pirogov's subsequent memoir.)

10. "Russian Rubbernecks," 22–23.

11. "Escaped Soviet Fliers Spend Busy Day on Virginia Tour," *WP,* February 6, 1948, M3.

12. "Russian Rubbernecks," 22–23.

13. "2 Russians Marvel at Assembly Line," *NYT,* February 19, 1948, 6.

14. "Red Fliers' Tour Stirs Controversy," *WP,* February 10, 1949, 7.

15. "Ex-Red Flier on Tour Charges 'Mistreatment' at Press Talk," *WP,* February 11, 1949, 1, 8; "Russian Flier Balks Queries on Secrets," *NYT,* February 11, 1949, 10.

16. "Flying High," *WP,* February 12, 1948, 8. On Pirogov's pecuniary tendencies, see also Siegel, "New Soviet Man," 528.

17. "Tale of a US Bungle"; "US Returns Pilot-Deserter to Russians," *WP,* September 1, 1949, 1.

18. "Flight from Freedom," *Time,* September 12, 1949, 19–20. *Newsweek* reported that Barsov, piqued that Pirogov had sold his story to *Life* for $3,000, killed the deal by selling an "as told to" article to *True;* "Tale of a US Bungle," 24. Pirogov's memoir was published the following year; *Why I Escaped: The Story of Peter Pirogov* (New York: Duell, Sloane and Pearce, 1950). In a gushing review, Sterling North described it as "one of the most overwhelming social documents of our time"; "A Russian Pens a New 'Inferno,'" *WP,* February 26, 1950, B6.

19. "Tale of a US Bungle," 23–25; "The Barsov Case," *WP,* September 3, 1949, 6; "US

Deports Flier Who Fled Russia; His Views in Doubt," *NYT,* August 31, 1949, 1; "Barsov Reported Seized at Parley," *NYT,* September 2, 1949, 8.

20. "Flight from Freedom"; "The Gloomy Diary of a Russian Deserter," *Life,* September 12, 1949, 57–60.

21. "Gloomy Diary," 57. These documents attracted much press commentary as various commentators attempted to deduce Barsov's motives and mental state; "Barsov Diary Arouses US Suspicions," *WP,* September 3, 1949, 1.

22. "The Slavic Soul," *NYT,* September 2, 1949, 16.

23. "The Upper South: Tour by Two Soviet Ex-Pilots Evokes a Mixed Reaction," *NYT,* February 13, 1949, E6.

24. PPS 22, "Utilization of Refugees from the Soviet Union in the US National Interest," February 5, 1948, Records of the Policy Planning Staff, Microfiche 1171, card 23, RG 59, NACP.

25. "Athletes of Red Nations Seek Escape," *CDT,* August 16, 1948, 1.

26. George V. Allen, "The Russians Are Listening," *LAT,* December 12, 1948, H7; "Reds Rebuffed Elsewhere," *LAT,* August 19, 1948, 1; "Turks Report Red Attempt at Kidnapping," *WP,* May 29, 1949, M2.

27. PPS 54, "Policy Relating to Defection and Defectors from Soviet Power," June 28, 1949, Records of the Policy Planning Staff, Microfiche 1171, card 62, RG 59, NACP.

28. This aim was enshrined in the still classified NSC 86/1; Gregory Mitrovich, *Undermining the Kremlin: America's Strategy to Subvert the Soviet Bloc* (Ithaca: Cornell University Press, 2000). NSC 86/1 clearly evinced considerable unease among those who thought that reception facilities were inadequate to cope with a mass exodus, or those who maintained—and continued to argue—that it would better serve U.S. purposes to encourage dissatisfied eastern bloc residents to stay put and engage in active resistance.

29. On Hitler's failure to make full use of Vlasov, see George Fischer, "Vlasov and Hitler," *Journal of Modern History* 23, no. 1 (1951): 58–71. On schemes to "roll back" Soviet power during both the Truman and Eisenhower presidencies, see Scott Lucas, *Freedom's War: The US Crusade against the Soviet Union* (Manchester: Manchester University Press, 1999); Bennett Kovrig, *Of Walls and Bridges: The United States and Eastern Europe* (New York: New York University Press, 1991); Peter Grose, *Operation Rollback: America's Secret War behind the Iron Curtain* (Boston: Houghton Mifflin, 2000); Jim Marchio, "Resistance Potential and Rollback: US Intelligence and the Eisenhower Administration's Policies toward Eastern Europe, 1953–56," *Intelligence and National Security* 10, no. 2 (1995): 219–41; László Borhi, "Rollback, Liberation, Containment, or Inaction?" *Journal of Cold War Studies* 1, no. 3 (1999): 67–110.

30. Charles Bohlen to Mr. Lovett, August 18, 1948, 702.6111/8–1848, State Department Decimal File, 1945–49, Box 3069, RG 59, NACP.

31. Jack D. Neal, Division of Foreign Activity Correlation, to J. Edgar Hoover, Director, FBI, August 19, 1948, 702.6111/8–1848, State Department Decimal File, 1945–49, Box 3069, RG 59, NACP.

32. PPS 54, "Policy Relating to Defection."

33. Ralph McGill, "The Significance of Window Leaping," *Atlanta Constitution,* Au-

gust 24, 1948, 6; "Next Stop Siberia," *WP*, August 14, 1948, B10; "Chepurnykh Put in Soviet Prison," *NYT*, February 14, 1954, 7.

34. Gil Loescher and John A. Scanlan, *Calculated Kindness: Refugees and America's Half-Open Door, 1945 to the Present* (New York: Free Press, 1986), 1–24.

35. "Underground Railway: How and Why Thousands of Russians Slip beneath the Iron Curtain to Find Haven in the West," *Newsweek*, October 25, 1948, 46–47.

36. T. Alexander Aleinikoff, "State-Centered Refugee Law: From Resettlement to Containment," in *Mistrusting Refugees*, ed. E. Valentine Daniel and John Chr. Knudsen (Berkeley: University of California Press, 1995), 260.

37. PPS 22, "Utilization of Refugees."

38. The U.S. Displaced Persons Commission estimated that between September 1950 and March 1951 in excess of one hundred thousand people were "adversely affected by the Attorney General's interpretation" of this act; Loescher and Scanlan, *Calculated Kindness*, 29.

39. "Red Pilot Loses Plea for US Citizenship," *WP*, November 3, 1955, 10.

40. PPS 22, "Utilization of Refugees."

41. Rates of departure from East to West Berlin fluctuated in the late 1940s and 1950s but were never fewer than several thousand each month, running to fifteen thousand a month in 1953; George L. Warren, "The Escapee Program," *Journal of International Affairs* 7, no. 1 (1953): 83.

42. "Underground Railway," 46–47. In February 1948, the Alsops estimated that five thousand Soviet military personnel had deserted from East Germany in the past two years; "US 'Wasting' 5000 Desertions," *WP*, February 15, 1948, B5.

43. H. W. Brands, "A Cold War Foreign Legion? The Eisenhower Administration and the Volunteer Freedom Corps," *Military Affairs* 52 (1988): 7–11; James Jay Carafano, "Mobilizing Europe's Stateless: America's Plans for a Cold War Army," *Journal of Cold War Studies* 1, no. 2 (1999): 61–85.

44. Henry Cabot Lodge, "An Army of the Free," *Life*, October 2, 1950, 38; "An American Foreign Legion?" *Look*, September 14, 1948, 100.

45. "Memorandum by the President to the Executive Secretary of the National Security Council," February 14, 1953, FRUS, *1952–54*, vol. 8, *Eastern Europe; the Soviet Union; Eastern Mediterranean* (Washington, DC: Government Printing Office, 1988), 181.

46. Alien Enlistment Act of 1950, P.L. 81–597 (64 Stat. 316), June 30, 1950; PSB D-18a, "Psychological Operations Plan for Soviet Orbit Escapees," December 20, 1951, PSB Working File, 1951–53, Lot File 62D 333, Box 2, RG 59, NACP.

47. Section 101(a)(1) of the Mutual Security Act of 1951; Godel to Cutler, October 19, 1951, Harry S. Truman Papers, SMOF: PSB, 383.7 Educational Programs for Iron Curtain Escapees, Project ENGROSS, File #1, Box 33, HSTL.

48. "Liberation of Poland and Other Captive Nations of the Communists Should Be Keystone of New American Foreign Policy," *Congressional Record*, vol. 98, part 6, 82nd Cong., 2nd sess., June 20, 1952, 7768.

49. Record of Meeting of the Ad Hoc Committee on NSC 143, March 30, 1953, FRUS, *1952–54*, 8:209–10.

50. Arthur M. Cox to Mr. Morgan, "Report of Richard Brown on Escapee Program,"

December 31, 1952, SMOF: PSB, 383.7 Report of Richard Brown on Escapee Program File #2, Box 33, HSTL.

51. Only about 30 percent of eastern bloc refugees in western European camps were "single men of military age"; ibid.

52. Charles B. Marshall to Lt. Gen. Willis D. Crittenberger, memo, "Department of State Comments on Volunteer Freedom Corps," April 13, 1953, Records Relating to State Department Participation in OCB and NSC, Lot File 63D351, Box 70, RG 59, NACP.

53. Record of Meeting of the Ad Hoc Committee on NSC 143, March 27, 1953, FRUS, 1952–54, 8:199–204.

54. "Statement of Policy by the National Security Council on a Proposal for a Volunteer Freedom Corps," April 15, 1953, Records Relating to State Department Participation in OCB and NSC, Lot File 63D351, Box 70, RG 59, NACP.

55. Statement by Mike J. Mansfield, U.S. Delegate to the General Assembly, made on December 19, 1951, *Department of State Bulletin,* January 7, 1952, 28–35.

56. Quoted in Bennett Kovrig, *The Myth of Liberation: East-Central Europe in U.S. Diplomacy and Politics since 1941* (Baltimore: Johns Hopkins University Press, 1973), 103.

57. An attempt to "liberate" Albania by parachuting armed defectors back into the country was a particularly striking disaster; Grose, *Operation Rollback,* 160–62; Michael W. Dravis, "Storming Fortress Albania: American Covert Operations in Microcosm," *Intelligence and National Security* 7, no. 4 (1992): 425–42.

58. Serious planning for the Volunteer Freedom Corps lapsed after 1955, but NSC 143/2 was not rescinded altogether until three weeks after Eisenhower departed office in 1960; Carafano, "Mobilizing Europe's Stateless," 84.

59. This hostility to escapees' admission into the United States was certainly true of Wiley, an opponent of the 1953 Refugee Relief Act (discussed below), but not of Kersten, who urged the government to grant asylum to all satellite refugees; Kovrig, *Of Walls and Bridges,* 103.

60. Michael Hoffmann, "West Bitter Haven for Red Refugees," *NYT,* September 19, 1951, 15. Hoffman's claims were confirmed in a long memorandum; William Godel to Robert Cutler, "The Question of the Role of PSB in the use of the 'Defector Funds' Authorized in the Mutual Security Act, 1951," October 19, 1951, SMOF: PSB, 383.7 Educational Programs for Iron Curtain Escapees, Project ENGROSS—File #1, Box 33, HSTL.

61. "US Bars Exiles' Return to Soviet under New Policy of Maximum Aid," *NYT,* April 25, 1951, 14.

62. That U.S. authorities had contemplated handing the pilots back wasn't absent from initial press reports; *Time*'s original "I Is Russian Pilot" story related that the State Department had been minded to turn the men over to the Red Army. U.S. authorities allowed Soviet personnel extensive access to the pilots before granting them a right to remain; Pirogov, *Why I Escaped,* 3–16.

63. This was the judgment of a top-secret report, entitled Project TROY, commissioned by the U.S. government in 1950 to assess ways in which the Iron Curtain might be "perforated"; "Report of Project TROY," Annex 12, February 1951, PPS Working Papers, 1947–63, Lot File 64D 563, Box 70, RG59, NACP. On Project TROY, see Allan Needell, " 'Truth Is Our Weapon': Project TROY, Political Warfare, and Government-Academic Relations in

the National Security State," *Diplomatic History* 17, no. 3 (1993): 399–420. Similar verdicts also appeared in the press; Drew Pearson, "Iron Curtain Refugees Neglected," *Washington Post*, October 15, 1951, B11; Isaac Don Levine, "A Weapon for the West: Here Is a Way to Induce Soviet Occupation Troops to Desert," *Life*, March 23, 1953, 91–92.

64. Siegel, "New Soviet Man," 532.

65. Joseph Alsop, "Men without Countries," *International Herald Tribune*, March 21, 1951.

66. Anne O'Hare McCormick, "Abroad: The Human Factor Will Count Most in the End," *NYT*, March 17, 1951, 11.

67. "D.P. Head Asks Aid to Eastern Exiles," *NYT*, December 22, 1951, 4.

68. "Report of Project TROY," 3–4.

69. "1951 Convention Relating to the Status of Refugees," July 28, 1951, www.ufsia.ac.be/~dvanheul/genconv.html.

70. Aristide Zolberg, "Contemporary Transnational Migrations in Historical Perspective: Patterns and Dilemmas," in *U.S. Immigration and Refugee Policy. Global and Domestic Issues*, ed. Mary M. Kritz (Lexington, MA: D. C. Heath, 1983), 31. On the racialized binary between the "political refugee" and the "economic migrant," see Rachel Buff, *Immigration and the Political Economy of Home: West Indian Brooklyn and American Indian Minneapolis, 1945–1992* (Berkeley: University of California Press, 2001), 58–59.

71. Elfan Rees, "The Refugee and the United Nations," *International Conciliation* 492 (June 1953): 295–96; Nevzat Soguk, *States and Strangers: Refugees and Displacements of Statecraft* (Minneapolis: University of Minnesota Press, 1999), 172–73; Loescher and Scanlan, *Calculated Kindness*, 40–41. Washington's refusal to fund the UN High Commission for Refugees left it with a paltry annual budget of $300,000, supplemented by the Ford Foundation.

72. "Legislation Requested to Handle Overpopulation Problem in Western Europe: Message of the President to the Congress (H. doc. 400, transmitted March 24)," *Department of State Bulletin*, April 7, 1952, 551–55.

73. Frank C. Nash, Office of the Secretary of Defense, to Mr. Lincoln Gordon, Assistant Director for Mutual Security, memo, "Recommendations of the PSB with respect to a Program for Escapees from the Soviet Orbit which would utilize funds provided by Section 101(a) (1) of the Mutual Security Act of 1951," SMOF: PSB, 383.7 Escapee Program—Section 2, Box 33, HSTL; Mr. Cox to the Director, memo, "Meeting with Kersten, 22 January 1952," 383.7, Report of Richard Brown on Escapee Program, File #2, Box 33, HSTL. The Escapee Program's commitment to refugee care and resettlement constituted "Phase A" of a dual-track "Psychological Operations Plan for Soviet Orbit Escapees." A covert second track (code-named Operation ENGROSS) included plans to train refugees for future political leadership roles and to form guerrilla units and other outfits tasked with pursuing "unconventional war." Endorsed by the PSB in December 1951, this plan aimed to accelerate and augment human traffic west with a view to eroding Soviet power "by application of affirmative psychological pressures upon segments of the enslaved populations"; PSB D-18a/1, "A National Psychological Program with Respect to Escapees from the Soviet Orbit: Phase B," December 5, 1952, Lot File 62 D 333, PSB Working File, 1951–53, Box 2, RG 59, NACP.

74. "Message of the President," 552.

75. "Meeting, 12/14 [December 12, 1951] on Defector Problem," SMOF: PSB, 383.7 Escapee Program—Section 1, Box 33, HSTL.

76. PSB D-18a, "Psychological Operations Plan for Soviet Orbit Escapees," December 20, 1951, PSB Working File, 1951–53, Lot File 62D 333, Box 2, RG 59, NACP, n. 1. This list of countries from which escapees might emanate is shorter than that covered by the Kersten Amendment. For a more detailed account of the escapee's fabrication as a legal category, see Susan L. Carruthers, "Between Blocs: Eastern Bloc 'Escapees' and Cold War Borderlands," *American Quarterly* 57, no. 3 (2005): 911–42.

77. PSB D-18, Meeting, September 18, 1952, SMOF: PSB, 383.7 Escapee Program—Section 2, Box 33, HSTL.

78. Joseph B. Phillips, Department of State, to Mr. Charles Johnson, PSB, memo, "Secret. Progress Report on the Escapee Program," July 2, 1952, SMOF: PSB, 383.7 Escapee Program—Section 2, Box 33, HSTL.

79. Several key State Department advisers urged that Truman not link escapee provision—a potentially popular move, closely tied to foreign policy objectives—with assistance to displaced persons in general, an unpopular measure without such a clear cold war mandate; Cox to Sherman, "Meeting on Legislative Strategy to Support Administration's Bill on Immigration and Escapees from Communism," May 12, 1952, SMOF: PSB, 383.7 Report of Richard Brown on Escape Program, File #2, Box 33, HSTL; Loescher and Scanlan, *Calculated Kindness*, 39–46.

80. Walter, quoted in Cabell Phillips, "That Phony Refugee Law," *Harper's Magazine*, April 1955, 71.

81. James Burnham, quoted in David S. Foglesong, "Roots of 'Liberation': American Images of the Future of Russia in the Early Cold War," *International History Review* 21, no. 1 (1999): 60.

82. Walter Bedell Smith, introduction to *Journey for Our Time: The Journals of the Marquis de Custine*, by Astolphe de Custine, ed. and trans. Phyllis Penn Kohler (London: Arthur Baker, 1953), 12–13. On Custine's "Chinese wall" as a prefiguration of Churchill's Iron Curtain, see Larry Wolff, *Inventing Eastern Europe: The Map of Civilization on the Mind of the Enlightenment* (Stanford: Stanford University Press, 1994), 365.

83. George Kennan, *Memoirs, 1950–1963* (London: Hutchinson, 1973), 97.

84. E. P. Hutchinson, *Legislative History of American Immigration Policy, 1798–1965* (Philadelphia: University of Pennsylvania Press, 1981), 290.

85. These sentiments appear as the minority view dissenting from Eisenhower's proposed Emergency Immigration legislation of 1953. 83rd Cong., 1st sess., House of Representatives, Report #974, Emergency Immigration Program, July 27, 1953, Minority Views, 19–20, Senate Research Files of William B. Welsh, File 17, Herbert H. Lehman Collections, Butler Library, Columbia University.

86. "Report of Project TROY," 3. The possibility of "dumping" was discussed during planning for Phase B of Operation ENGROSS, though members of the PSB considered that any such act of Soviet desperation would afford the U.S. government "a major propaganda victory"; Working Draft, Phase B, PSB D-18a/1, November 5, 1952, SMOF: PSB 383.7, Report of Richard Brown on Escapee Program, File #2, Box 33, HSTL.

87. Loescher and Scanlan, *Calculated Kindness*, 29.

88. Alona E. Evans, "Political Refugees and the United States Immigration Laws: A Case Note," *American Journal of International Law* 62, no. 4 (1968): 921; Otto Kirchheimer, "Asylum," *American Political Science Review* 53, no. 4 (1959): 992.

89. Statement by Philip B. Perlman of Maryland, Former Solicitor General of the United States and Chairman of President Truman's Commission on Immigration and Naturalization, to the Subcommittee on Escapees and Refugees of the Senate Committee on the Judiciary, June 16, 1955, Senate Research Files of William B. Welsh, D 362, folder 13. Not only did U.S. sponsors have to guarantee admissible entrants documented employment and accommodation in advance, but they further had to affirm that U.S. citizens would not thereby be "displaced." Individual sponsors then had to preserve these exacting assurances indefinitely, as cumbersome screening procedures ensured that it took months for eligible applicants to reach the United States.

90. "New York Democratic Delegation Points Out Utter Failure of the Operation of the Refugee Relief Act of 1953," press release, May 16, 1955, Senate Research Files of William B. Welsh, D 362, folder 13, Herbert H. Lehman Papers, Herbert H. Lehman Collections, Butler Library, Columbia University.

91. Phillips, "That Phony Refugee Law," 69.

92. "Increase in Escapees to US Seen," *LAT*, December 5, 1954, A1; Phillips, "That Phony Refugee Law," 72.

93. PSB D-18a, "Psychological Operations Plan for Soviet Orbit Escapees," December 20, 1951, PSB Working File, 1951–53, Lot File 62D 333, Box 2, RG 59, NACP; PSB D-18a/5, "Escapee Program Submission FY 1954," October 23, 1952, SMOF: PSB, 383.7 Educational Programs for Iron Curtain Escapees, Project ENGROSS, File #1, Box 33, HSTL.

94. Poll conducted by the Gallup Organization, November 11–16, 1951, based on the question: "Will you tell me what is meant by the term, 'the iron curtain'?"; retrieved April 30, 2008, from the iPOLL Databank, Roper Center for Public Opinion Research, University of Connecticut, www.ropercenter.uconn.edu/ipoll.html.

95. Anne O'Hare McCormick, "Abroad: A Close-Up View of the Iron Curtain," *NYT*, August 17, 1953, 14; Joseph Wechsberg, "No Game for Sissies," *Saturday Evening Post*, June 9, 1951, 36–37, 49, 51–52, 56.

96. Memo by Marshall D. Shulman, March 15, 1951, Records of the Policy Planning Staff, 1947–53, Subject Files, Box 11a, RG 59, NACP.

97. Georgia Carvellas to Mr. Cox, Draft Material for Inclusion in Paper "Program for Soviet Orbit Escapees," December 11, 1951, SMOF: PSB, 383.7 Escapee Program—Section 1, Box 33, HSTL. In 1950, this discussion overlapped with plans for promoting NSC 68; Steven Casey, "Selling NSC-68: The Truman Administration, Public Opinion, and the Politics of Mobilization, 1950–51," *Diplomatic History* 29 (2005): 655–90.

98. "Crusade for Freedom," *WP*, August 13, 1950, B4.

99. "Trends Favoring Communism and Possible Remedial Action," Records of the Policy Planning Staff, 1947–53, Box 8, RG 59, NACP.

100. "The Freedom Crusade," *NYT*, September 4, 1950, 10. On the National Committee for a Free Europe's connection to escapee planning and CIA funding, see Loescher and Scanlan, *Calculated Kindness*, 32–33; Lucas, *Freedom's War*, 67–68.

101. "Enlist in the Crusade for Freedom," *LAT*, August 23, 1950, A4.

102. Loescher and Scanlan, *Calculated Kindness,* 38–39; Aaron Levenstein, *Escape to Freedom: The Story of the International Rescue Committee* (Westport, CT: Greenwood Press, 1983), 36.

103. Pirogov appeared at one such event in August 1950; "Russians' Pay Cut to Aid US 'Jobless,'" *NYT,* August 23, 1950, 3. In March 1950, he had also appeared alongside Whittaker Chambers on a DuMont network documentary, *Casebook on Treason,* "Variety Marathon," *NYT,* March 5, 1950, 107.

104. *Iron Petticoat* (dir. Ralph Thomas, London Film Productions/MGM, 1956); *Jet Pilot* (dir. Josef von Sternberg, Universal Pictures, 1957); *Man on a Tightrope* (dir. Elia Kazan, Twentieth Century Fox, 1953). On "love and defection" as a cinematic trope, see Tony Shaw, *Hollywood's Cold War* (Amherst: University of Massachusetts Press, 2007), 9–41.

105. Richard L. Coe, "'Man on Tightrope' Is Absorbing Tale," *WP,* May 23, 1953, 15. According to Coe, Kazan's feature was based on the "real-life escape of the Czech Brumbach circus into the free world."

106. Eleanor Harris, "Too Smart for the Reds," *LAT,* December 20, 1953, H7.

107. Foreign Operations Administration, *Escape to Freedom* (Washington, DC, 1954).

108. On Konvalinka's defection by air with 108 passengers and the broadcasting of this story behind the Iron Curtain, see Walter Hixson, *Parting the Curtain: Propaganda, Culture, and the Cold War, 1945–1961* (Basingstoke: Macmillan, 1997), 66; Lt. Gen. Izydor Modelski, "I Saw Red Spies at Work in Washington," *Look,* May 10, 1949, 10, 49–57.

109. On Mrs. Kapus, see Foreign Operations Administration, *Escape to Freedom,* 18–20; on the MiG pilot, see "A MiG from a Red Renegade," *Life,* March 16, 1953, and Franciszek Jarecki, "Flights for Freedom Pierce Iron Curtain," *Life,* April 6, 1953, 32–34. On the Freedom Train, see Loescher and Scanlan, *Calculated Kindness,* 34.

110. Progress Report on NSC 174, "US Policy toward the Soviet Satellites in Eastern Europe," May 26, 1954, Records Relating to State Department Participation in NSC and OCB, Box 31, RG 59, NACP; Escapee Program Report to the OCB, August 17, 1954, Records Relating to State Department Participation in NSC and OCB, Box 38, RG 59, NACP.

111. "Mobilization for Freedom Crusade Due," *LAT,* September 3, 1950, A2. On the 1947 Freedom Train, see Eric Foner, *Story of American Freedom* (New York: W. W. Norton, 1998), 249–52; Stuart J. Little, "The Freedom Train: Citizenship and Postwar Political Culture, 1946–1949," *American Studies* 34 (1993): 35–67; Michael J. Hogan, *A Cross of Iron: Harry S. Truman and the Origins of the National Security State, 1945–1954* (Cambridge: Cambridge University Press, 1998), 426–36.

112. Richard M. Fried, *The Russians Are Coming! The Russians Are Coming! Pageantry and Patriotism in Cold War America* (New York: Oxford University Press, 1998), 48. In August 1953, the *Hollywood Reporter* announced that the story of this "home made tank" used by Czech refugees would be incorporated into a feature entitled *The Lost Woman,* to be produced by Eagle Lion studios; "Freed, Woods Plan Czech Escape Film," *Hollywood Reporter,* August 12, 1953.

113. Thomas Caldecott Chubb, "The Ingenuity of Freedom," *Saturday Review,* February 20, 1954, 26–27.

114. "US Citizen Smuggles Kin from German Reds," *NYT,* March 12, 1954, 9; "Grimes Children, Smuggled from Reds, Lack US Visas," *NYT,* March 13, 1954, 3.

115. Foreign Operations Administration, *Escape to Freedom*, 22.

116. Record of Meeting of the Ad Hoc Committee on NSC 143, March 27, 1953, FRUS, *1952–54*, 8:199–200.

117. "Freedom to Move," *Life*, August 30, 1948, 18.

118. "Freedom's Exiles," *NYT*, March 21, 1950, 28.

119. Kirchheimer, "Asylum," 992.

120. "Immigration and Nationality Act—Message from the President of the United States" (H. Doc. No. 520), 82nd Cong., 2nd sess., *Congressional Record* 98, pt. 6 (June 25, 1952): 8082–85.

121. "Fact Sheet on the Paul Robeson Passport Case," issued by the Robeson Passport Case Committee, Records of the ACLU, MC #001, Box 832, folder 17, Robeson, Paul, 1955, Seeley G. Mudd Manuscript Library, Princeton University.

122. "The Choolokian Case," *Christian Century*, March 29, 1950, 391–93. For further details on the case, see Records of the ACLU, MC#001, Series 4, Legal Cases, Box 1297, Seeley G. Mudd Manuscript Library, Princeton University.

123. Department of State to the Embassy of the Soviet Union, note, May 28, 1947, FRUS, *1947*, vol. 4, *Eastern Europe; the Soviet Union* (Washington, DC: Government Printing Office, 1972), 728–29.

124. Samuel M. Blinken, "The Shoemaker's Children," *Nation*, May 14, 1949, 551–54.

125. "Mission Here Opposes Plan to Send 2 Boys to Join Their Parents in Soviet Armenia," *NYT*, December 4, 1947, 21.

126. Blinken, "Shoemaker's Children," 553.

127. "People ex rel. Choolokian v. Mission of Immaculate Virgin. 509," *American Journal of International Law* 42, no. 2 (1948): 507–8.

128. Ibid.

129. "Repatriate Fights Ruling," *NYT*, January 27, 1948, 27.

130. "Choolokian Case," 392.

131. Once the children had been denied permission to join the family in Armenia, Choolokian's next legal bid was to remove them from the care of Catholic institutions that had forcibly made them assume that faith as a condition of admission, despite their prior baptism in the Armenian Apostolic Orthodox Church. In this matter, he was also turned down; "City Asked to Shift 3 to Protestant Care," *NYT*, June 5, 1948, 16; "Denial of 3 Children to Armenian Upheld," *NYT*, October 21, 1949, 26.

132. "The Choolokian Case—More of the Same," *Christian Century*, July 5, 1950, 812.

133. "Choolokian Case" (March), 393.

134. "US-Born Trio Demanded by Soviet Union in a Note," *NYT*, January 4, 1955, 3.

135. "Communism and Children," *Newsweek*, August 9, 1948, 21.

136. "Search Ship for Russ Dad and US Baby," *CDT*, October 4, 1956, 1; "Mother Hopes for Return of Baby by Reds," *CDT*, October 5, 1956, 7. As an emotionally rousing case of contested international custody and citizenship, the Chwastow story could be read as prefiguring the saga of Elián González in 1999—except that in 1956 the U.S. state intervened to *retrieve* the infant and return her to the United States. See Sarah Banet-Weiser, "Elián González and 'The Purpose of America': Nation, Family, and the Child-Citizen," *American Quarterly* 55 (June 2003): 149–78; Lillian Guerra, "Elián González and the 'Real

Cuba' of Miami: Visions of Identity, Exceptionality, and Divinity," *Cuban Studies* 38 (2007): 1–25.

137. "Ship Line Accused in Girl's Sailing," *NYT*, October 25, 1956, 68.

138. "Father Hides US-Born Girl, 2½, on Queen Mary for Trip to Soviet," *NYT*, October 4, 1956, 1. The *Times* reported that, according to the World Church Service's immigration service director, Chwastow had recently received a letter from his ninety-one-year-old mother, urging him to return, passage paid by the Soviet government.

139. "Kidnaped: A Citizen," *US News and World Report*, November 2, 1956, 8.

140. "International Hide and Seek," *Life*, October 22, 1956, 56; "US Child Taken Off Soviet Ship in Britain," *NYT*, October 13, 1956, 1.

141. "2 Soviet Aides Accused of Kidnaping Tanya," *WP*, October 24, 1956, A3; "Dockers Here Refuse to Handle Luggage of Ousted Russian as He Sails for Home," *NYT*, December 1, 1956, 13; "Longshoremen Snub Ousted Russ Envoy," *LAT*, December 2, 1956, 16.

142. Statement by Mike J. Mansfield, December 19, 1951, *Department of State Bulletin*, January 7, 1952, 28–35.

143. Psychological strategists privately discussed the need to develop "techniques for the preservation of non-Soviet Eastern European cultures" to be practiced by diasporic communities. To this end, they mooted the creation of a "Free University in Exile," imagining that the émigré population would have "a salutary effect on the communistically-inclined indigenous student." Discussion of these schemes is contained in SMOF: PSB, 383.7 Educational Programs for Iron Curtain Escapees, Project ENGROSS—File #1, Box 33, HSTL.

144. Report of Project TROY," 11.

145. Levine, "Weapon for the West," 98.

146. Operations Coordinating Board, "Report on Assistance Programs in Behalf of Refugees and Escapees of Interest under NSC 86/1," December 2, 1955, General Records of the State Department, Records Relating to Participation in the OCB and the NSC, Box 37, RG 59, NACP.

147. Liberia represented the fullest realization of such schemes, but Nova Scotia was also salient to emigrationist designs, first as a site of refuge for black loyalists after the War of Independence and then as the point of embarkation from which many set sail for Liberia; Michelle Burnham, *Captivity and Sentiment: Cultural Exchange in American Literature, 1682–1861* (Hanover: University Press of New England, 1997), 124–25.

148. "Summary of Report of the Examination of the Effectiveness of the Escapee Program in Meeting Objectives under NSC 86/1," February 2, 1954, Records of the State Department in cooperation with OCB/NSC, Box 38, RG 59, NACP; John Stoessinger, *The Refugee and the World Community* (Minneapolis: University of Minnesota Press, 1956), 176.

149. "USIA Progress Report on US Escapee Program," October 13, 1954, General Records of the State Department, Records Relating to Participation in the OCB and the NSC, Box 38, RG 59, NACP.

150. US Mission to the UN, Memorandum of Conversation, "Soviet Approaches to High Commissioner for Refugees," September 28, 1955, Records of the United States Mission to the UN, Box 36, Folder, International Organisations: ECOSOC, RG 84, NACP; Elmer B. Staats, Memorandum for the Operations Coordinating Board, "Program under NSC 86/1

to Counter Soviet Efforts to Demoralize Emigration," April 15, 1955, General Records of the State Department, Records Relating to Participation in the OCB and the NSC, Box 37, RG 59, NACP. See also Frank R. Barnett, "America's Strategic Weakness—Redefection," *Russian Review* 15, no. 1 (1956): 29–36.

151. Mr. Kotschnig, OES, to Mr. J. Barry, USUN, memo, "Summary of Facts Relating to the Soviet Redefection Campaign," November 19, 1956, Records of the United States Mission to the UN, Box 36, Folder, International Organisations: ECOSOC, RG 84, NACP.

152. "Baiting the Trap," *Newsweek*, March 12, 1956, 14, 49; "A Diplomatic Kidnapping on US Soil," *Newsweek*, April 23, 1956, 22–23.

153. "Soviet 'Come Home' Campaign Hit," *LAT*, December 26, 1956, B4.

154. Barsov's execution was ostensibly corroborated by Vladimir Petrov (a defecting diplomat) in 1954; "Reds Produce 'Slain Airman' for Interview," *CDT*, May 16, 1957, 5.

155. Mr. Kotschnig, OES, to Mr. J. Barry, USUN, memo, "Summary of Facts Relating to the Soviet Redefection Campaign," November 19, 1956, Records of the United States Mission to the UN, Box 36, Folder, International Organisations: ECOSOC, RG 84, NACP.

156. The IRC organized an emergency commission, headed by William Donovan, to publicize the "new Communist tactics of terror and blackmail in the US"; Levenstein, *Escape to Freedom*, 46–47.

157. Harrison Salisbury, "Refugees in US Shun Red Pleas," *NYT*, May 13, 1956, 1.

158. In 1952, the number of escapees (approximately 250 "bona fide" cases per month) represented half the total anticipated in the PSB plan adopted in December 1951; Cox to Morgan, December 31, 1952, SMOF: PSB, 383.7; Report of Richard Brown on Escapee Program File #2, Box 33, HSTL. During the first half of 1953, the Foreign Operations Administration/United States Escapee Program tallied a monthly average of two hundred escaping, mostly from Czechoslovakia; "Summary of Report of the Examination of the Effectiveness of the Escapee Program in Meeting Objectives under NSC 86/1," February 2, 1954, Records of the State Department in cooperation with OCB/NSC, Box 38, RG 59, NACP.

159. In April 1953, William Truehart noted that "propaganda, and encouragement efforts in general, have only a slight effect at best on the rate of defection," observing that "Soviet defections have declined to near-zero concurrently with an all-out propaganda and inducement campaign." Whether this was a regrettable state of affairs was a moot point, however, since escapees as actual persons represented more a problem than an asset; Truehart to Mr. Connors, "*Life* Article by Isaac Don Levine," April 9, 1953, 761.00/4, State Department Decimal File, Box 3807, NACP.

3. STALIN'S SLAVES

1. "Japan Gets New Kind of Peace Treaty," *Life*, September 17, 1951, 29.

2. "Dulles' Conference," *NYT*, September 9, 1951, B4.

3. The phrase is borrowed from John Dower, *Embracing Defeat: Japan in the Wake of World War II* (New York: W. W. Norton, 1999).

4. After Gromyko's car was involved in a road accident, the San Francisco police department revealed that they had received a tip-off that a beer truck would attempt to ram his limousine en route to the conference. Whether or not the collision was indeed a bun-

gled assassination attempt was never subsequently established; "Moscow Scores 'Plot,'" *NYT,* September 10, 1951, 4.

5. In reproducing the map, *Time* cropped material from the edges, including the offer of a reward for information disproving its representation; "Gulag—Slavery, Inc.," *Time,* September 17, 1951, 28–29; "Gromyko Given Russ Map with Slave Camps," *LAT,* September 7, 1951, 2.

6. "Gromyko Gets Answer on Map of Slave Camps," *NYT,* September 9, 1951, 34.

7. On the State Department's involvement in the map, see correspondence in the State Department Decimal File, 1950–54, 861.064, Box 5157, RG 59, NACP.

8. William R. Young, "GULAG—Slavery, Inc.: The Use of an Illustrated Map in Printed Propaganda," in *A Psychological Warfare Casebook,* ed. William E. Daugherty (Baltimore: Operations Research Office / Johns Hopkins University Press, 1958), 597–602.

9. "Moscow Finds an Answer," *NYT,* October 23, 1951, 28; "Soviet Map Seizure in Vienna Protested," *NYT,* October 20, 1951, 5; "Soviets Seize Map of Labor, Call It Filthy," *WP,* October 22, 1951, 3.

10. NSC 68, reproduced in Thomas H. Etzold and John Lewis Gaddis, *Containment: Documents on American Policy and Strategy, 1945–50* (New York: Columbia University Press, 1978), 396; Orville Prescott, review of *Forced Labor in Soviet Russia,* by David J. Dallin and Boris I. Nicolaevsky (New Haven: Yale University Press, 1947), *NYT,* August 26, 1947, 21; Brooks Atkinson, "Penal Servitude, Russian Model," *NYT,* August 31, 1947, BR3.

11. Bertram Wolfe, International Broadcasting Division, to Walter Kotschnig, UNE, memo, "Research on Forced Labor from the Propaganda Point of View," November 29, 1951, US Mission to the UN, NYC, Box 18, Folder "Labor: Compulsory," RG 84, NACP.

12. This editorial comment was made with reference to an earlier appearance of the map on the back cover of the UK *Tribune,* based on one prepared by the anticommunist publication *Plain Talk,* edited by Isaac Don Levine; "Slavery in Russia," *CDT,* November 14, 1947, 20. *Plain Talk*'s "Gulag—Slavery, Inc." map appeared in the May 1947 issue, under the heading "First Comprehensive Map of Slave Camps in USSR," 24–25.

13. Anne Applebaum, *Gulag: A History of the Soviet Camps* (New York: Penguin, 2003), 5; Hilton Kramer, "Remembering the Gulag," *New Criterion,* May 2003, 71. On Solzhenitsyn, the classic statement is Tom Wolfe's 1976 aperçu: "Another troublesome fact has cropped up, gravely complicating the longtime dream of socialism. That troublesome fact may be best summed up in a name: Solzhenitsyn"; "The Intelligent Coed's Guide to America," in *Mauve Gloves and Madmen, Clutter and Vine* (New York: Farrar, Straus and Giroux, 1976), 122.

14. "It was this map," noted Howland Sargeant (assistant secretary of state for public affairs, 1952–53), "that played the role of matchmaker in the unusual mating of the great Russian novelist Solzhenitsyn with the leadership of the American Federation of Labor." Solzhenitsyn referred to the map in an address delivered on June 30, 1975. Sargeant's comments are contained in a memorial tribute to Isaac Don Levine, "Day of Remembrance at the National Press Club, Washington, DC, May 2, 1981," Papers of Howland Sargeant, Box 4, General File / Correspondence File, folder Isaac Levine, 1981, HSTL.

15. "NGO and United States Government Cooperation on Collection and Presentation

of Forced Labor Materials," Memorandum of Conversation, November 14, 1951, Records of the US Mission to the UN, Box 18, Folder "Labor: Compulsory," RG 84, NACP.

16. "UN Group Avoids Irritating Soviet," *NYT*, July 1, 1953, 6.

17. "Cerise Curtain," *Newsweek*, May 7, 1951, 37.

18. Victor Kravchenko, *I Chose Freedom* (New York: Charles Scribner's Sons, 1946). For contemporary economists' estimates, see Naum Jasny, "Labor and Output in Soviet Concentration Camps," *Journal of Political Economy* 59, no. 5 (1951): 405–19; A. David Redding, "Reliability of Estimates of Unfree Labor in the USSR," *Journal of Political Economy* 60, no. 4 (1952): 337–40; and on the numbers debate, André Liebich, "Mensheviks Wage the Cold War," *Journal of Contemporary History* 30 (1995): 247–64.

19. "Slavery in Russia," 20; Max Eastman, "The Truth about Soviet Russia's 14,000,000 Slaves," *Reader's Digest*, April 1947, 139–46.

20. "Slavery in Russia"; Dewey's breach of etiquette was condemned by most editorialists; "Question of Manners," *WP*, September 23, 1950, 8; *CDT*, September 26, 1950, 20.

21. Catherine Merridale, *Night of Stone: Death and Memory in Twentieth-Century Russia* (New York: Penguin, 2000), 185–86.

22. Thomas F. Magner, review of *One Day in the Life of Ivan Denisovich*, by Alexander Solzhenitsyn, *Slavic and East European Journal* 7, no. 4 (1963): 418–19.

23. These essays were published in book form in 1891, reissued in 1958; George Kennan, *Siberia and the Exile System* (Chicago: University of Chicago Press, 1958).

24. Victor Serge, *Russia Twenty Years After* (New York: Pioneer Publishers, 1937), 70. According to Les K. Adler and Thomas G. Paterson, the 1934 edition of *Webster's New International Dictionary* contained no reference to the term *concentration camp*. In 1944, it appeared listed in the "New Words" section; "Red Fascism: The Merger of Nazi Germany and Soviet Russia in the American Image of Totalitarianism, 1930s-1950s," *American Historical Review* 75 (April 1970): 1053 n. 44.

25. Vladimir Tchernavin, *I Speak for the Silent* (Boston: Hale, Cushman and Flint, 1935); George Kitchin, *Prisoner of the OGPU* (London: Longmans, Green, 1935). See also John D. Littlepage, *In Search of Soviet Gold* (New York: Harcourt, Brace, 1938); Tatiana Tchernavin, *Escape from the Soviets* (New York: E. P. Dutton, 1934).

26. *Red Gaols: A Woman's Experiences in Russian Prisons* (London: Burns Oates and Washbourne, 1935), 37.

27. V. Tchernavin, *I Speak*, 282–83.

28. André Gide, *Return from the USSR*, trans. Dorothy Bussy (New York: McGraw-Hill, 1964), xi; Lewis S. Feuer, "American Travelers to the Soviet Union, 1917–32: The Formation of a Component of New Deal Ideology," *American Quarterly* 14 (1962): 119–49.

29. Louis Fischer, *Soviet Journey* (New York: Harrison Smith and Robert Haas, 1935), 97–106; Sidney and Beatrice Webb, *Soviet Communism: A New Civilization?* vol. 2 (New York: Charles Scribner's Sons, 1936), 587. The Webbs parenthetically admitted a lack of firsthand observation but endorsed two effusive accounts by writers who also had not witnessed the gulag at close quarters: Mary Stevenson Callcott's *Russian Justice* (New York: Macmillan, 1935) and Lenka Von Koerber's *Soviet Russia Fights Crime* (London: George Routledge and Sons, 1934).

30. Jerzy Gliksman, *Tell the West: An Account of His Experiences as a Slave Laborer in the Union of Soviet Socialist Republics* (New York: Gresham Press, 1948), 11.

31. *Red Gaols*, 24–25.

32. Kitchin, *Prisoner of the OGPU*, 267.

33. According to Kitchin, the evacuation of Archangel and Uftug cost 1,370 lives; *Prisoner of the OGPU*, 268–89.

34. See, for example, the Webbs' extensive quotation from a column by Gorky in the *Moscow Daily News*, August 14, 1933; *Soviet Communism*, 590–92.

35. K. R. M. Short, "Washington's Information Manual for Hollywood," *Historical Journal of Film, Radio and Television* 3, no. 1 (1983): 171–80.

36. William L. O'Neill, *A Better World: The Great Schism: Stalinism and the American Intellectuals* (New York: Simon and Schuster, 1982), 60–63; Benjamin L. Alpers, *Dictators, Democracy, and American Public Opinion: Envisioning the Totalitarian Enemy, 1920s–1950s* (Chapel Hill: University of North Carolina Press, 2003), 224–34; Todd Bennett, "Culture, Power, and *Mission to Moscow*: Film and Soviet-American Relations during World War II," *Journal of American History* 88, no. 2 (2001): 489–518.

37. Edwin Bacon, *The Gulag at War: Stalin's Forced Labour System in the Light of the Archives* (New York: New York University Press, 1999).

38. David J. Dallin and Boris I. Nicolaevsky, *Forced Labor in the Soviet Union* (New Haven: Yale University Press, 1947), 104, 263; Applebaum, *Gulag*, 383.

39. Soviet authorities issued a statistic of 356,687 deaths among the German POWs, while five hundred thousand to one million may have died before being registered at Soviet camps; Frank Biess, *Homecomings: Returning POWs and the Legacies of Defeat in Postwar Germany* (Princeton: Princeton University Press, 2006) 4.

40. Dallin and Nicolaevsky, *Forced Labor*, 277–78; Applebaum, *Gulag*, 391.

41. Pavel Polian, *Against Their Will: The History and Geography of Forced Migrations in the USSR* (Budapest: Central European University Press, 2004), 256.

42. A. Yugow, "Shall German Labor Rebuild Europe?" *New Republic*, May 7, 1945, 638–39.

43. Harry S. Truman Papers, White House Central File, Official File, OF 190-S Prisoners of War (1945–Jan. 1946), and OF 190-W Civilian War Benefits, Box 816, HSTL.

44. Robert Moeller, *War Stories: The Search for a Usable Past in the Federal Republic of Germany* (Berkeley: University of California Press, 2001), 29.

45. Polian, *Against Their Will*, 246–47.

46. Yugow, "Shall German Labor Rebuild Europe?" 639.

47. Luce, quoted in Adler and Paterson, "Red Fascism," 1053.

48. On the Mensheviks' contribution to exposing the gulag, see André Liebich, *From the Other Shore: Russian Social Democracy after 1921* (Cambridge, MA: Harvard University Press, 1997), 271–325; Hugh Wilford, *The CIA, the British Left and the Cold War: Calling the Tune?* (London: Frank Cass, 2003).

49. William van Narvig, *East of the Iron Curtain* (Chicago: Ziff Davis, 1946), 126–36; Henry Wallace, quoted in Dallin and Nicolaevsky, *Forced Labor*, xiii–xiv.

50. *The Dark Side of the Moon* (New York: Charles Scribner's Sons, 1947). More con-

troversially, Dallin and Nicolaevsky also employed records compiled by the Nazis from interrogation data derived from Soviet POWs.

51. Orville Prescott, review of *I Chose Freedom*, by Victor Kravchenko, *NYT*, May 22, 1950, 30.

52. Richard J. Aldrich, *The Hidden Hand: Britain, America and Cold War Secret Intelligence* (London: John Murray, 2001), 107; David Drake, *Intellectuals and Politics in Postwar France* (New York: Palgrave, 2002), 65. In the United States, *I Chose Freedom* sold seventy-five thousand copies in 1946 alone; "The Year in Books," *Time*, December 16, 1946, 108.

53. Liebich, *From the Other Shore*, 298; "Stalin Called Pawn of Soviet Politburo," *LAT*, January 25, 1949, 7.

54. Martin Malia, *Russia under Western Eyes: From the Bronze Horseman to the Lenin Mausoleum* (Cambridge, MA: Belknap Press, 1999), 364–65.

55. Anton Ciliga, *The Russian Enigma* (London: G. Routledge and Sons, 1940); Alexandre Barmine, *One Who Survived: The Life Story of a Russian under the Soviets* (New York: G. P. Putnam's Sons, 1945); Walter Krivitsky, *In Stalin's Secret Service: An Expose of Russia's Secret Policies by the Former Chief of the Soviet Intelligence in Western Europe* (New York: Harper and Brothers, 1939).

56. Elizabeth Simon, "An Ex-Communist Speaks His Mind," *NYT*, April 21, 1946, 126.

57. Irwin M. Wall, *The United States and the Making of Postwar France* (Cambridge: Cambridge University Press, 1991), 151.

58. Liebich, *From the Other Shore*, 289–90.

59. Shaplen had also translated Dallin's first book, one chapter of which was devoted to forced labor; *The Real Soviet Russia* (New Haven: Yale University Press, 1947). With Kravchenko he crafted a public statement to explain a defection that raised many eyebrows at a time when the Soviet Union remained a crucial wartime ally; Robert J. Lamphere, untitled ms., 13–16, Robert J. Lamphere Papers, Box 1, folder 49.5, Lauinger Library, Georgetown University, Washington, DC.

60. According to Liebich, the FBI's substantial file on Dallin identified him as Kravchenko's "literary agent"; *From the Other Shore*, 298.

61. Lamphere, untitled ms., 44.

62. Wall, *United States*, 151.

63. Untitled anonymous review, *Current History*, July 1946, 48.

64. Dorothy Thompson, "The Disjunction of Freedom," *Saturday Review*, April 20, 1946, 7, 51; Simon, "Ex-Communist"; "This Is Ed Sullivan Speaking" (reprinted from January 1947), *CDT*, January 17, 1953, 13.

65. Frederick L. Schuman, "Horrors of Bolshevism, Inc.," *New Republic*, May 6, 1946, 667–69.

66. Homer Metz, "One Russian's Concept of Russia," *Christian Science Monitor*, May 6, 1946, 14.

67. Kravchenko, *I Chose Freedom*, 481.

68. See Tony Judt, *Past Imperfect: French Intellectuals, 1944–1956* (Berkeley: University of California Press, 1992); Michel Winock, *Le siècle des intellectuals* (Paris: Éditions du Seuil, 1997), 460–70; Robert Desjardins, *The Soviet Union through French Eyes, 1945–85* (Bas-

ingstoke: Macmillan, 1988); Etienne Jaudel, *L'aveuglement: L'affaire Kravchenko* (Paris: Michel Houdiard Éditeur, 2003); Pierre Rigoulot, *Les paupieres lourdes: Les Français face au goulag* (Paris: Editions universitaires, 1991).

69. Judt, *Past Imperfect,* 113.

70. "Kravchenko Reveals Attempts on His Life," *NYT,* January 12, 1949, 3. *Les lettres* had announced that the book was "pure fiction" written by the "American secret service"; "3 Russians Uphold Kravchenko Book," *NYT,* 1 February, 1949, 18; "Kravchenko Wins Paris Libel Suit," *NYT,* April 5, 1949, 1. On January 19, *Le Soir* published an article implying that Kravchenko was the author of a virulently anti-Soviet book, *I Was a Prisoner of Stalin,* published in Nazi Germany in 1941 under the name of R. Krawtchenko. In response, Kravchenko threatened a further suit; "Kravchenko to Sue Second Paris Paper," *NYT,* January 20, 1949, 25.

71. *Kravchenko versus Moscow: The Report of the Famous Paris Case with an Introduction by the Rt. Hon. Sir Travers Humphreys, P.C.* (London: Wingate, 1950), 15, 24.

72. "Deputy Makes Issue of Kravchenko Visa," *NYT,* February 19, 1949, 5; Madeleine Jacob, "*L'Affaire* Kravchenko," *Nation,* February 19, 1949, 205–6.

73. Konstantin Simonov, "Ignominious Downfall of the Managers of Judas," *Pravda,* February 24, 1949, translated by the British Foreign Office, Foreign Office: Political Departments: General Correspondence, FO 371/77674, NAUK.

74. "Vishinsky's 'Slander' Brings Authors' Suit," *NYT,* November 2, 1947, 26.

75. Wall, *United States,* 152.

76. Jacob, "*L'Affaire* Kravchenko"; "Trial by Confusion," *Newsweek,* February 14, 1949, 32.

77. "Kravchenko's Suit Up for Trial Today," *NYT,* January 24, 1949, 4.

78. Michael James, "Hot Session Opens Kravchenko Case," *NYT,* January 25, 1949, 18.

79. Henry Wales, "Paris Leftists Hoot, Heckle, Harass Ex-Red," *CDT,* January 12, 1949, 14.

80. "On the Vodka Circuit," *Newsweek,* February 21, 1949, 32.

81. Jacob, "*L'Affaire* Kravchenko."

82. Michael James, "Paris Spectacle—Kravchenko Trial," *NYT,* February 13, 1949, E5.

83. Together with Kasenkina's leap for freedom, Dmytryk cast this episode as one of the epiphanies that disabused him of his communist proclivities, describing it as "definite proof that communists place the party above any country except Russia, and that no communist can ever possibly be a loyal citizen"; Richard English, "What Makes a Hollywood Communist?" *Saturday Evening Post,* May 19, 1951, 149.

84. According to Wall, *United States,* 152, the American military government in West Germany assisted Kravchenko's search for witnesses in the displaced persons camps, expediting visas for their travel to France.

85. Simonov, "Ignominious Downfall."

86. "3 Russians Uphold Kravchenko Book," 18; "4 Ex-Citizens at Libel Trial Tell of Soviet Camp Torture," *WP,* February 2, 1949, 3.

87. Margarete Buber-Neumann, *Freiheit, du bist wieder mein . . .* (Munich: Langen Mueller, 1978), 245.

88. Her memoir of camp experiences in the USSR and Germany was published under the name Margarete Buber in the United Kingdom by Victor Gollancz in 1949, and two years

later in the United States as Margarete Buber-Neumann, *Under Two Dictators* (New York: Dodd, Mead, 1951). In French, the memoir appeared shorn of its account of Ravensbrück as *Deportée en Sibérie,* trans. Anise Poster-Vinay (Neuchâtel: Baconnière, 1949). In a later autobiographical volume she related how—at a meeting with Kravchenko before the trial—he had forbidden her from mentioning her memoir, lest it appear that her testimony aimed to generate publicity for her own book (a charge that, with greater justification, could have been leveled at Kravchenko himself); Buber-Neumann, *Freiheit,* 242–43. For her testimony at the trial, see the abridged English translation in *Kravchenko versus Moscow,* 200–207; or for a full transcription in French, *Le procès Kravchenko contre Les Lettres Françaises. Compte rendu des audiences d'après la sténographie suivi d'un index des noms cités* (Paris: La Jeune Parque, 1949), 550–65. Kravchenko published a lengthy account of the trial in which he devoted just two of 458 pages to Buber-Neumann's testimony; *I Chose Justice* (New York: Charles Scribner's Sons, 1950), 386–87.

89. Oliver Harvey (British Embassy, Paris) to Ernest Bevin (Foreign Secretary), May 30, 1949, FO 371/77674, NAUK.

90. Simone de Beauvoir, *La force des choses* (Paris: Éditions Gallimard, 1963), 191–92. Another communist intellectual, the journalist Dominique Desanti, expressed identical views, finding Buber-Neumann, alone among Kravchenko's witnesses, "très évidemment sincère": "Le témoinage de Margarete fut bouleversant et j'en sortis tourmentée" ("Margarete's testimony was shattering, and I left [the courtroom] in turmoil"); *Les Staliniens (1944–1956): Une expérience politique* (Paris: Librairie Arthème Fayard, 1975), 169.

91. "Kravchenko Wins," 1.

92. Judt, *Past Imperfect,* 113.

93. Henry Wales, "Shower Kisses on Kravchenko as He Wins Suit," *CDT,* April 5, 1949, 5.

94. "The Big Red Team Loses a Road Game," *CDT,* April 7, 1949, NW22.

95. Wall, *United States,* 153.

96. Atkinson, "Penal Servitude," BR3.

97. "Investigation of Forced Labor Conditions in USSR and Satellites Urged," Statement by Walter Kotschnig, Deputy US Representative to ECOSOC, *Department of State Bulletin,* April 2, 1951, 545.

98. A *Washington Post* editorial in November 1947 related that twenty-six months after V-J Day, 2.5 million POWs had still not returned home. Of these, 73 percent were held by the Soviets, an estimated 1,656,532 German and Japanese prisoners. The *Post* expressed particular dismay that the British and French governments were so tenaciously clinging to their POW laborers—a practice "not essentially different from Hitler's." For its part, Westminster agreed to release all remaining POWs by October 1948; "Slave Labor," *WP,* November 26, 1947, 12.

99. "Truman Commends Slave Labor Book," *NYT,* September 19, 1952, 3.

100. Liebich, *From the Other Shore,* 306.

101. Orville Prescott, review of *Forced Labor in Soviet Russia,* 21.

102. Liebich, "Mensheviks," 257; Harold Karan Jacobson, "Labor, the UN and the Cold War," *International Organization* 11, no. 1 (1957): 55–67; David J. Dallin, "American Labor's Anti-Cominform," *American Mercury,* October 1951, 14–23.

103. Dallin's close involvement with the State Department as a member of the Ad-Hoc

Committee on Forced Labor is evident from documents contained in the State Department Decimal File at 861.064 (1950–54), Box 5157, RG 59, NACP.

104. The Information Research Department's interest in this issue is documented in FO 1110/179, NAUK.

105. Charles E. Egan, "Briton in UN Lays Slavery to Soviet," *NYT,* October 16, 1948, 1.

106. George Barrett, "Soviet Denies Slave Charge; Bars UN Inquiry in Camps," *NYT,* February 16, 1949; American Federation of Labor, *Slave Labor in Russia: The Case Presented by the American Federation of Labor to the United Nations* (Washington, DC: American Federation of Labor, 1949).

107. ECOSOC, *Official Records,* 8th Session (7 Feb.–18 March 1949), 471.

108. ECOSOC, *Official Records,* 8th Session (7 Feb.–18 March 1949), remarks by Mayhew, 111–12.

109. Michael L. Hoffman, "U.S. Urges Inquiry into Forced Labor," *NYT,* August 4, 1949, 1.

110. The Soviets and their allies in ECOSOC, meanwhile, made an alternative proposal that labor conditions in general be investigated—in countries that had not yet eliminated unemployment—by a committee composed entirely of trade union representatives; ECOSOC, *Official Records,* 8th Session (7 Feb.–18 March 1949), Proposal by Mr. Tsarapin (USSR), 347–48.

111. The other two members of this ad hoc committee were Pall Berg, former president of Norway's Supreme Court, and Enrique Garcia Sayan, former foreign minister of Peru.

112. "Gulag Fodder," *WP,* August 9, 1949, 10.

113. ECOSOC, *Official Records,* 8th Session, 105.

114. Ibid. These arguments were raised each time forced labor was discussed at ECOSOC. See *Official Records,* 9th Session (5 July–15 Aug. 1949); *Official Records,* 10th Session (7 Feb.–6 March 1950); *Official Records,* 11th Session (3 July–16 Aug. 1950); *Official Records,* 12th Session (20 Feb.–21 March 1951).

115. This claim was made by Georgi Arkadyev at ECOSOC on July 16, 1952, picking up stories in the *Daily Worker* on the camp at Tulelake, California (a former wartime internment camp for Japanese Americans); Kathleen Teltsch, "US Inventiveness Put on Soviet Griddle," *NYT,* July 17, 1952, 1. The U.S. Bureau of Prisons was in fact constructing what it preferred to term "standby detention camps" in California for this purpose; Charles Norberg (PSB) to Dr. Wilson Compton, Chair, Psychological Operations Coordinating Committee, memo, July 28, 1952, SMOF: PSB, Box 21, 254 Communist Propaganda re US Concentration Camps, HSTL.

116. "United States Comments and Observations to Summary of Allegation Presented to the Ad Hoc Committee on Forced Labor," March 31, 1953, 2, US Mission to the UN, Folder, Labor: Compulsory (1949–53), Box 18, RG 84, NACP.

117. Memorandum, "Soviet Rebuttal of Forced Labor Charges," n/d, 861.03/1–750, State Department Decimal File, 1950–54, Box 5157, RG 59, NACP.

118. "US Details Charges of Soviet Slavery," *NYT,* June 30, 1952, 4.

119. B. Wolfe, "Research on Forced Labor," 1–4.

120. Foy Kohler (International Broadcasting Division) to Kotschnig, memo, "Research on Forced Labor from the Propaganda Point of View," November 29, 1951, US Mission to

the UN, Folder, Labor: Compulsory, Box 18, RG 84, NACP; "Truman Commends Slave Labor Book," 3.

121. "The U.N. and the New Slavery," *Life,* July 27, 1953, 28; *Report of the Ad Hoc Committee on Forced Labor,* UN E/2431 (Geneva: International Labour Office, 1953).

122. Lodge, "Forced Labor Item," memo, August 25, 1953, US Mission to the UN, Folder, Labor: Compulsory, Box 18, RG 84, NACP.

123. Gladwin Hill, "Million a Year Flee Mexico Only to Find Peonage Here," *NYT,* March 25, 1951, 1, 41; "Peons Net Farmer a Fabulous Profit," *NYT,* March 26, 1951, 25, 41; "Peons in the West Lowering Culture," *NYT,* March 27, 1951, 31, 33; "Southwest Winks at 'Wetback' Jobs," *NYT,* March 28, 1951, 31, 34; "Interests Conflict on 'Wetback' Cure," *NYT,* March 29, 1951, 27, 30.

124. Memo by Walter Kotschnig, "Forced Labor Rebuttal Statements," November 4, 1953, US Mission to the UN, Folder, Labor: Compulsory, Box 18, RG 84, NACP.

125. William E. Bohn in the *New Leader,* quoted with approval in *Time,* "United Nations: Objectivity," March 27, 1950, 28–29.

126. Henry Cabot Lodge to John C. Baker, US Representative to ECOSOC, July 15, 1953, US Mission to the UN, Folder, Labor: Compulsory, Box 18, RG 84, NACP.

127. Memorandum from Kotschnig to Mr. Lubin (US UN Department), "Final Meeting of Ad Hoc Committee on Forced Labor," 2 September 1952, US Mission to the UN, Folder, Labor: Compulsory, Box 18, RG 84, NACP.

128. Applebaum, *Gulag,* 454.

129. Memorandum, "Forced Labor," August 7, 1953, US Mission to the UN, Folder, Labor: Compulsory, Box 18, RG 84, NACP. In private conversation with Forrest Murden of the State Department's UN office, Mudaliar confided that behind the scenes "influence" had been applied to him—by the Secretariat and the International Labour Office—who, seeking "the easing of the cold war," had urged him to "let the Soviets off lightly"; Memorandum of Conversation, "Indian Attitude on Forced Labor Report," August 18, 1953, US Mission to the UN, Folder, Labor: Compulsory, Box 18, RG 84, NACP.

130. "UN and the New Slavery," 28.

131. Carol Anderson, *Eyes off the Prize: The United Nations and the African American Struggle for Human Rights, 1944–1955* (Cambridge: Cambridge University Press, 2003), 210–70.

132. International Labour Conference, *Report VI* (2), 39th Session, Geneva, 1956, Sixth Item on the Agenda: Forced Labour (Geneva: International Labour Office, 1956); International Labour Conference, *Report IV* (1), 40th Session, Geneva, 1957, Fourth Item on the Agenda: Forced Labour (Geneva: International Labour Office, 1956); "US Bars Accord on Forced Labor," *NYT,* January 28, 1956, 4.

133. "US Details Charge of Soviet Slavery," *NYT,* June 30, 1952, 4.

134. Eugene Lyons, *Our Secret Allies: The Peoples of Russia* (London: Arco Publications, 1954), 175.

135. "UN and the New Slavery," 28.

136. Thomas Doherty, *Projections of War: Hollywood, American Culture, and World War II* (New York: Columbia University Press, 1993), 247.

137. Barbie Zelizer, *Remembering to Forget: Holocaust Memory through the Camera's Eye* (Chicago: Chicago University Press, 1998), 146.

138. Murray to Ralph, Information Dept. Paris, October 7, 1949, FO 1110/228, NAUK.

139. "Soviet Prison Camps," *Life,* September 27, 1948, 53–55. See also the drawings of Sergei Korolkov accompanying an article by John Scott, "Russia through Russian Eyes," *Life,* September 26, 1949, 114–16, 119–20, 125–26, 128, 130.

140. Daniel J. Leab, "*The Iron Curtain* (1948): Hollywood's First Cold War Movie," *Historical Journal of Film, Radio and Television* 8 (1988): 158.

141. ECOSOC, *Official Records,* 8th Session (February 7–March 18, 1949), Continuation of the Discussion on the Survey of Forced Labour and Measures for its Abolition, Mr. Tsarapkin (USSR), 110.

142. "Nazi Camp Termed Soviet Slave Unit," *NYT,* August 6, 1949, 6.

143. Hannah Arendt, *The Origins of Totalitarianism* (1951; repr., New York: Harcourt, Brace, 1973), 437. Commending Arendt's brilliant analysis, Arthur Schlesinger Jr. chimed that "only in the concentration camp does this process [of degradation] achieve its evil perfection"; Arthur M. Schlesinger Jr., *The Vital Center: The Politics of Freedom* (Boston: Houghton Mifflin, 1949), 87.

144. The other classic early cold war work is Carl J. Friedrich, ed., *Totalitarianism* (New York: Universal Library, 1954). For critiques of totalitarianism's cold war career, see Abbott Gleason, *Totalitarianism: The Inner History of the Cold War* (New York: Oxford University Press, 1995); Michael Halberstam, *Totalitarianism and the Modern Conception of Politics* (New Haven: Yale University Press, 1999).

145. William Henry Chamberlin, "Are Communism, Fascism Alike?" *Wall Street Journal,* October 20, 1947, 4. For Dallin's camel analogy, see "Empire within the Soviet Empire," *NYT,* October 14, 1951, 15, 36, 38, 40.

146. Michael Clark, "Nazi Victims Join Slave-Labor Fight," *NYT,* March 26, 1950, 143. The State Department took an initial interest in assisting Rousset's tribunal, only to back away, suspecting that his politics were not concordant with the administration's. Avowedly anti-Soviet, Rousset was also keen to investigate camps in Franco's Spain and monarchist Greece, two allies that Washington preferred to omit from the concentrationary calculus; Department of State, Division of Biographic Information, "Rousset, David," February 21, 1950, US Mission to the UN, Box 18, Folder, Labor: Compulsory, RG 84, NACP. Rousset turned instead to Britain for support, which the Foreign Office was happy to provide, remarking that their U.S. counterparts were "too emotional" on the subject of the Soviet camps. See correspondence between the IRD and British Embassy, Paris on Rousset, FO 1110/179, NAUK.

147. "Buchenwald to Kolyma," *Time,* June 11, 1951, 30–31; "Russian Prisoners Form a New Class," *NYT,* May 23, 1951, 32.

148. Peter Novick, *The Holocaust in American Life* (Boston: Houghton Mifflin, 1999), 87, 86.

149. These figures are based on opinion polls undertaken by *Fortune* magazine, cited by Warren B. Walsh, "What the American People Think of Russia," *Public Opinion Quarterly* 8, no. 4 (1944–45): 515.

150. Van Narvig, *East of the Iron Curtain,* 126.

151. Lyons, *Our Secret Allies,* 173.

152. Peter Blake, "Brown Terror—and Red," review of *Under Two Dictators,* by Margarete Buber-Neumann, *NYT,* January 7, 1951, 171.

153. C. L. Sulzberger quoted Buber-Neumann to the effect that "Karaganda was worse"; "Prisoner Who Escaped Compares Nazi and Russian Labor Camps," *NYT,* March 12, 1949, 7. By contrast, the *Times Literary Supplement* pointed out that to juxtapose Nazi and Soviet camps was "misleading and, in a way, a dangerous comparison"; "Prisoner of Two Regimes," July 22, 1949, 468. In an *American Mercury* article Buber-Neumann pointed to the obscenity of being asked to make such a choice; Margaret Buber-Neumann, "Hitler or Stalin: Which Was the Worst?" *American Mercury,* April 1952, 74–82.

154. Moeller, *War Stories,* 38–39. On the POWs' reception in—and contribution to the remaking of—both East and West Germany, see Biess, *Homecomings.*

155. Moeller, *War Stories,* 21.

156. Ward P. Allen to Area Advisers, memo, "Prisoner of War Case in Committee III," December 8, 1950, US Mission to the UN, Box 5, Folder US/A/C.3/251–343, RG 84, NACP.

157. Memorandum of Conversation with Herr Federer, German Observer on Prisoners of War, and Henry Villard, US UN Delegation, "Prisoners of War," November 7, 1950, US Mission to the UN, Memorandums of Conversations, 1950, Box 5, Folder US/A/c 3/251–343, RG 84, NACP.

158. Doris Fleeson, "Chicagoan May Get UN Post," *Chicago Daily News,* August 18, 1950. In at least one respect, though, her appointment proved a "backfire" in a slightly different sense. Originally, the State Department had proposed Sampson as a full delegate, not merely an alternate, but this suggestion met with such fierce opposition from the segregationist Senator John Sparkman (D-AL) that the appointment was downgraded to alternate status; P. L. Prattis, "Truman By-passes Negro in UN Deal," *Courier,* September 2, 1950, Edith Sampson papers, Box 10, ESS.

159. "Help America," *Des Moines Tribune,* August 23, 1950.

160. Sampson, quoted in J. D. Ratcliff, "Edith Sampson . . . Thorn in Russia's Side," *United Nations World,* March 1951, 22–25, and in *Jet,* February 7, 1952. A press release issued by the U.S. delegation to the General Assembly cited remarks made by Sampson in New Delhi that referred to Robeson belonging to a "lunatic fringe in America," Press Release #945, September 18, 1950, Box 10, folder 214, ESS.

161. Address given by Edith Sampson at the UN Pageant, Washington University, St. Louis, October 26, 1952, Box 10, folder 200, ESS.

162. Edith Sampson, "I Like America," *Negro Digest,* December 1950, 3–8.

163. Extract from the *Congressional Record,* "Peace with Freedom," Extension of Remarks of Hon. Hubert H. Humphrey. Humphrey read into the record a speech delivered by Sampson on October 1, 1950, at the UN General Assembly, to commemorate Gandhi's birthday, October 20, 1950, A7589. That Sampson's choice was ironic—given Nazi attitudes toward people of color—was pointed out in an article in *UN World* (later condensed in *Reader's Digest*), one of very few commentaries to remind readers that the POWs in question were in fact "a million men who once followed Hitler's banners"; Ratcliff, "Edith Sampson," 25.

164. Jean Kinnaird, "The Prize Package: Freedom," *High Commissioner of Germany In-*

formation Bulletin, March 1952, 29–30; "Prisoners of War," draft statement by Edith Sampson, n.d., Box 6, folder 134, ESS. Papers relating to Sampson's performance at the UN can be found in the Records of the US Mission to the UN, General Subject Files, Prisoners of War (1945—Sept. 1952), RG 84, NACP.

165. On one occasion she insisted that she would "link arms with the worst Dixicrat *[sic]* on foreign policy" to save the country—because "16 million Negroes [would] be put back into slavery if the Soviets ever win"; "Mrs Edith Sampson's Record of Performance at the Fifth General Assembly," Box 10, folder 210, ESS.

166. "Back after Eight Years," *Life,* April 6, 1953, 30–31; "Life in Soviet Slave Labor Camps: Stories of Returned West German Victims," *CDT,* January 3, 1954, 12; "A Stern Face on a Mission," *Life,* September 19, 1955, 46–47; "Smiling Steps toward a Hard Bargain," *Life,* September 26, 1955, 42–44; "Amid Anguish, Homecomings," *Life,* October 24, 1955, 51–52.

167. Biess, *Homecomings,* 97–152.

168. John Dille, "The Russia Only a Few Know," *Life,* November 9, 1953, 155.

169. Kramer, "Remembering the Gulag," 71.

170. In 1950, New York longshoremen refused to unload "products of slave labor" imported from the USSR, an embargo that related predominantly to cans of crabmeat; "Longshoremen Aid Propaganda Fight," *NYT,* August 27, 1950, E4; "US Policy Sought on Soviet Cargoes," *NYT,* September 3, 1950, 63. In 1951, the U.S. government announced the first formal import ban on a Soviet product—crabmeat processed by "forced, convict and indentured labor"—since the United States and USSR had established diplomatic relations in 1933; "Soviet Crabmeat Barred as Slave Labor Product," *NYT,* January 27, 1951, 8.

171. "2 Georgescu Boys Dazed by Dodgers," *NYT,* April 22, 1954, 20.

172. *Silk Stockings* (dir. Rouben Mamoulian, MGM, 1957); "On Calling Names," *WP,* August 31, 1952, B4.

173. He backed up his argument with recourse to a quotation attributed to Lenin, that taxation was "the vital weapon to displace the system of free enterprise"; "M'Arthur Hits Tax Laws," *NYT,* September 23, 1957, 50.

174. "Revival of Slavery," *WP,* March 6, 1947, 6. In the same vein, when Arthur Schlesinger Jr. described "totalitarian man"—the representative eastern bloc citizen—as "tight-lipped, cold-eyed, unfeeling, uncommunicative … as if badly carved from wood, without humor, without tenderness, without spontaneity, without nerves," he conjured a figure also familiar as an inmate of the gulag; *Vital Center,* 57; cf. Kravchenko's description of a group of forced laborers whose "unsmiling silence was more terrible than their raggedness, filth and physical degradation"; Kravchenko, *I Chose Freedom,* 198.

175. "Eisenhower Says Conflict Is Not Limited," *WP,* September 5, 1950, 1; Harry Schwartz, "A Worker's Life in a 'Worker's State,'" *NYT Magazine,* October 19, 1952, 16, 65, 66, 67, 68.

176. Leland Stowe, "Conquest by Terror," *WP,* August 4, 1952.

177. William Henry Chamberlin, "Two Who Survived the Terrors of Soviet Brutalitarian State," *CDT,* August 10, 1952, B3.

178. This is not to say that survivors' accounts whitewashed oppressive conditions in the USSR or that there weren't situations in which "the zone" did indeed bleed into the so-

ciety beyond. But many inmates stressed, not without reason, that their situation was not simply that of citizens as a whole and that many prisoners (unlike these memoirists) could never cross back. See, for example, Elinor Lipper, *Eleven Years in Soviet Prison Camps* (Chicago: Regnery, 1951), viii. On the complex constitutive relationship between the camps and Soviet society, see Kate Brown, "Out of Solitary Confinement: The History of the Gulag," *Kritika: Explorations in Russian and Eurasian History* 8, no. 1 (2007): 67–103.

4. FIRST CAPTIVE IN A HOT WAR

1. "Communists: Frightened Face," *Time,* February 27, 1950, 27–28. On Mindszenty, see Bela Fábián, *Cardinal Mindszenty: The Story of a Modern Martyr* (New York: Charles Scribner's Sons, 1949); George N. Shuster, *In Silence I Speak: The Story of Cardinal Mindszenty Today and of Hungary's "New Order"* (New York: Farrar, Straus and Cudahy, 1956); and for the Hungarian state's account, *The Trial of Jozsef Mindszenty* (Budapest: Hungarian State Publishing House, 1949).

2. The Rev. Dr. Daniel A. Poling, president of the World Christian Endeavor Union, used the phrase "rape of justice" to describe Mindszenty's trial; "Spellman Warns US to Halt Reds; Lauds Mindszenty," *NYT,* February 7, 1949, 1. Morris Ernst, the attorney hired by IT&T to defend Vogeler, referred to Vogeler's trial as "legicide" or "just a lynching under the cloak of law"; "Record on Vogeler Spurs Doubts Here," *NYT,* February 23, 1950, 2.

3. On Koestler's contribution to wartime discussions of totalitarianism, see Abbott Gleason, *Totalitarianism: The Inner History of the Cold War* (New York: Oxford University Press, 1995), 55–56.

4. "Hungary: Their Tongues Cut Off," *Time,* February 14, 1949, 28.

5. See, for example, "Communists Make Martyr of Cardinal," *Life,* February 21, 1949, 27.

6. Pope Pius XII, "The Mindszenty Trial," speech delivered to the College of Cardinals, Vatican City, February 14, 1949, *Vital Speeches of the Day,* February 15, 1949, 265; "Text of Spellman Plea on Mindszenty," *NYT,* February 7, 1950, 3.

7. "4000 Scouts Pray for the Cardinal," *NYT,* February 7, 1949, 3.

8. John Cooney, *The American Pope: The Life and Times of Francis Cardinal Spellman* (New York: Times Books, 1984), 163.

9. "The Upper South," *NYT,* February 13, 1949, E6; and in the same issue, "New England: Mindszenty Case Stirs Strong Protest among All Faiths," E6. See also George Dugan, "Mindszenty Trial Called Eye-Opener," *NYT,* February 12, 1949, 6.

10. Astoria Civic Association, Long Island City, Astoria, Queens, NY, to President Truman, telegram, February 8, 1949, and Richard J. Nolan, Philadelphia, to President Truman, February 6, 1949, both in Papers of Harry S. Truman, General File, Box 1653, Folder: Mindszenty, Joseph, HSTL.

11. David Seed, *Brainwashing: The Fictions of Mind Control, a Study of Novels and Films since World War I* (Kent: Kent State University Press, 2004), 20–21; Albert Biderman, "The Image of 'Brainwashing,'" *Public Opinion Quarterly* 26, no. 4 (1962): 553.

12. "Dungeon of Fear," *WP,* July 5, 1951, 10.

13. According to Ernst, "legicide" was "the destruction of the rule of law by cloaking

justice *[sic]* in the forms of law"; "Vogeler's Wife Pleads: Free Him; I Love Him!" *CDT,* February 22, 1950, 10; "Ernst Calls Vogeler Captive in New War," *NYT,* February 26, 1950, 3.

14. John Foster Dulles, *War or Peace* (New York: Macmillan, 1950), 247. Jacob K. Javits to Dean Acheson, November 28, 1950, 264.1111 Vogeler, Robert A./11–2850, State Department Decimal File, 1950–54, Box 1090, RG 59, NACP.

15. "Back to God's Country," *NYT,* December 30, 1951, E8.

16. "The New Dark Continent," *NYT,* February 24, 1950, 22.

17. R. H. Gage, La Grange, IL, to Acheson, January 6, 1950, 264.1111 Vogeler, Robert A./1–1650, State Department Decimal File, 1950–54, Box 1090, RG 59, NACP.

18. Robert Vogeler, with Leigh White, *I Was Stalin's Prisoner* (New York: Harcourt, Brace, 1951), 16.

19. Joseph C. Harsch, *The Curtain Isn't Iron* (New York: Doubleday, 1950), 10.

20. See the photographs in *Time,* February 27, 1950, 27, and a casual shot of Vogeler with his friend and Annapolis classmate Captain Eugene S. Karpe in their swimming trunks, printed in *Life,* July 3, 1950, 61.

21. N. Raymond Clark, La Grange, IL, to Acheson, January 10, 1950, 264.1111 Vogeler, Robert A./1–1050, State Department Decimal File, 1950–54, Box 1090, RG 59, NACP.

22. Vogeler's positive treatment by the U.S. press contrasted starkly with the inattentiveness and suspicion that greeted the disappearance of Noel and Hermann Field. Noel, a former State Department official recently named as a Soviet agent in the Hiss circle by Whittaker Chambers, disappeared mysteriously in Prague in May 1949. Three months later Hermann vanished in transit between Warsaw and Prague while attempting to uncover his sibling's whereabouts. Both were detained incommunicado for several years, ignorant of one another's location. Those outside the eastern bloc were little better informed, for the satellite governments repeatedly denied knowledge or disclaimed responsibility for the Fields— though Noel's name would surface in the early 1950s as an American spymaster in several purge trials. U.S. commentators, by contrast, rumored that Noel had engineered his own disappearance to evade bothersome complications in the West or that he was really a *Soviet* agent accused of being an American spy in a typically cunning communist double bluff. For an intimate account of the case, see Hermann Field and Kate Field, *Trapped in the Cold War: The Ordeal of an American Family* (Stanford: Stanford University Press, 1999).

23. Paul Ruedemann and George Bannantine of the Standard Oil Company were expelled from Hungary after a week's detention once they signed confessions that they had sabotaged Hungarian oil production; "American Feared Jailed in Hungary," *NYT,* November 21, 1949, 7.

24. "Hungary Arrests US Phone Official," *NYT,* November 23, 1949, 1, 7.

25. For State Department correspondence on the Vogeler case before the trial, see FRUS, *1949,* vol. 5, *Eastern Europe; the Soviet Union* (Washington, DC: Government Printing Office, 1976), 483–98; FRUS, *1950,* vol. 4, *Central and Eastern Europe; Soviet Union* (Washington, DC: Government Printing Office, 1981), 980–88.

26. "IT&T Denies Charges," *NYT,* December 25, 1949, 11.

27. "US Asks Hungary Release American; Bars Travel There," *NYT,* December 21, 1949, 1, 11.

280 NOTES TO PAGES 142-144

28. "US Demands Hungary Release American Citizen," note from American Minister in Budapest, Nathaniel Davis, to the Hungarian Minister for Foreign Affairs, released to the press December 20, 1949, *Department of State Bulletin,* January 2, 1950, 21–22.

29. "Budapest Rejects Protests by US; Says American Confessed Spying," *NYT,* December 25, 1949, 1.

30. Memorandum of a conversation at Foreign Office, December 30, 1949, re Robert A. Vogeler. Participants Undersecretary Berei, Minister Davis, and Mr. Gerald A. Mokma, Counselor of Legation, 264.1111 Vogeler, Robert A. 1–150, State Department Decimal File, 1950–54, Box 1090, RG 59, NACP. The same point was put again forcefully by Berei on January 3, 1950, when he proposed that Davis was simply unaware of Vogeler's work for U.S. intelligence; Memorandum of conversation at Foreign Office, January 3, 1950, 264.1111 Vogeler, Robert A. 1–450, State Department Decimal File, 1950–54, Box 1090, RG 59, NACP.

31. László Borhi, *Hungary in the Cold War, 1945–56* (Budapest: Central European University Press, 2004), 183–84.

32. "US Tells Hungary to Close Offices," *NYT,* January 4, 1950, 1, 20.

33. Charles Grutzner, "Spellman Asks Drive to Free Mindszenty," *NYT,* February 10, 1949, 1.

34. The Minister in Hungary (Davis) to the Hungarian Foreign Minister (Kallai), January 3, 1950, FRUS, *1950,* 4:980–82. This portion of the message was also reproduced verbatim in the *New York Times,* which drew attention to the note's undiplomatic "scorn and sarcasm"; "US Tells Hungary," 20.

35. "Acheson Affirms Vogeler's Defense," *NYT,* February 16, 1950, 18.

36. For the Hungarian state transcript of the trial, see *R. Vogeler, E. Sanders and Their Accomplices before the Criminal Court* (Budapest: Hungarian State Publishing House, 1950).

37. Mokma, Hungarian Press Summary #35, February 22, 1950, 264.1111 Vogeler, Robert A./2–2250, State Department Decimal File, 1950–54, Box 1090, RG 59, NACP.

38. Acheson to American Legation Budapest, secret telegram, February 15, 1950, 264.1111 Vogeler, Robert A./2–1550, State Department Decimal File, 1950–54, Box 1090, RG 59, NACP.

39. "Briton in Hungary Pleads Spy 'Guilt,'" *NYT,* February 18, 1950, 4.

40. According to Bela Fábián, former president of the Hungarian Independent Democratic Party, the communists' release of these courtroom photographs was "one of the greatest mistakes of Soviet propaganda"; "Mindszenty Trial Held Soviet Farce," *NYT,* February 10, 1949, 5.

41. The effects of actedron were first aired in the *Tablet,* a British Catholic publication, and then widely circulated elsewhere in advance of the trial; "Drugging Feared in Cardinal's Case," *NYT,* January 22, 1949, 4. After the trial it was ubiquitously asserted that Mindszenty was (as Spellman announced) "the victim of torture and druggings that put him beyond the reach or realm of human help"; "Spellman Warns US," 1.

42. "3 Plead Guilty as Spy Trial of Vogeler Opens," *New York World-Telegram and The Sun,* February 17, 1950, 1; "Vogeler's Look of Fright Impresses US Reporter," *NYT,* February 19, 1950, 41. Nathaniel Davis described Vogeler's appearance as "approximately normal"; Budapest to Acheson, telegram, #119, February 19, 1950, 264.1111 Vogeler, Robert A./2–1950, State Department Decimal File, 1950–54, Box 1090, RG 59, NACP.

43. These tape recordings of the trial, originating from the BBC, are held at the National Archives; "Hungarian Trial of Sanders and Vogeler," Parts 1–6, 03/15/1950, Sound Recordings, CSBU 45240, RG 59, NACP.

44. Indictment from the Office of the State Prosecutor, Dr Gyula Alapi, Budapest, February 7, 1950, in *R. Vogeler, E. Sanders*, 19.

45. Although many reports characterize his voice as a "dull monotone," the tapes record speech not lacking in inflection, and certainly not stupefied. U.S. Legation staff noted that there was "nothing unusual in voice or diction"; Budapest to Acheson, telegram, #119, February 19, 1950, 264.1111 Vogeler, Robert A./2–1950, State Department Decimal File, 1950–54, Box 1090, RG 59, NACP.

46. *R. Vogeler, E. Sanders*, 279.

47. "Record on Vogeler," 2. Scrutinizing the transcripts, U.S. Legation staff in Budapest identified "at least two occasions during testimony [when] Vogeler forgot lines in such a way as to indicate clearly he had memorized his testimony word-for-word, as if playing a part in a play." On one occasion, during a moment of absentmindedness, he offered an identical response to two consecutive questions before recovering himself; Budapest to Acheson, telegram, #124, February 20, 1950, 264.1111 Vogeler, Robert A./2–2050, State Department Decimal File, 1950–54, Box 1090, RG 59, NACP.

48. *R. Vogeler, E. Sanders*, 13, 118.

49. "May Have Been a Spy," *Nation*, March 4, 1950, 193. For the full text of Vogeler's confession, see *R. Vogeler, E. Sanders*, 279.

50. "Confession in Hungary," *NYT*, February 19, 1950, E8.

51. "Vogeler's Recital Stirs Skepticism," *NYT*, February 19, 1950, 41.

52. "Communists: Frightened Face," 27.

53. "Words Put in Vogeler's Mouth," *LAT*, February 23, 1950, 26; Alan Keiler, "Vogeler Tortured by Reds, Wife Says," *New York World-Telegram*, November 22, 1950, 1.

54. "Confession in Hungary," E8.

55. In eastern Europe's show trials, there had been one (but only one) instance in which a defendant repudiated a prior forced confession in the courtroom itself. This was Traicho Kostov, one of the founders of the Bulgarian Communist Party, tried with his "treacherous espionage and wrecking group" in December 1949 and hanged two days later; Tony Judt, *Postwar: A History of Europe since 1945* (New York: Penguin Books, 2005), 178–79.

56. Mokma, Hungarian Press Summary, #35, February 22, 1950, 264.1111 Vogeler, Robert A./2–2250, State Department Decimal File, 1950–54, Box 1090, RG 59, NACP.

57. "Bob looked awfully haggard in the pictures we saw of the trial. He had a terrible haircut. But I don't think he was drugged"; Lucile Vogeler, "I Want My Husband Back," *New York World-Telegram*, March 7, 1951, 29.

58. "US Oil Man Who 'Confessed' in Hungary Holds Torture Forced Vogeler Statement," *NYT*, February 21, 1950, 14.

59. "Record on Vogeler," 2.

60. McCarthy's speech at Wheeling, February 9, 1950, quoted in Richard Gid Powers, *Not without Honor: The History of American Anti-Communism* (New Haven: Yale University Press, 1998), 235.

61. In the version of the speech he inserted into the *Congressional Record*, McCarthy

amended the number to fifty-seven; reprinted in Ellen Schrecker, ed., *The Age of Mc-Carthyism: A Brief History with Documents* (New York: Bedford Books, 1994), 211–14.

62. On the strategic deployment of homophobia as a tactic of McCarthyism, see David K. Johnson, *The Lavender Scare: The Cold War Persecution of Gays and Lesbians in the Federal Government* (Chicago: University of Chicago Press, 2004); Thomas Doherty, *Cold War, Cool Medium: Television, McCarthyism, and American Culture* (New York: Columbia University Press, 2003), 215–30; K. A. Cuordileone, *Manhood and American Political Culture in the Cold War* (New York: Routledge, 2005), 37–96.

63. "McCarthy Asserts a File Was 'Raped,'" *NYT*, May 8, 1950, 3; "Chinese Release William C. Smith and Elmer Bender," Statement by Acting Secretary Webb, released to press May 19, 1950; *Department of State Bulletin*, May 29, 1950, 868–69.

64. Vogeler, *I Was Stalin's Prisoner*, 140.

65. "May Have Been a Spy," 193.

66. On the Gubitchev case, see FRUS, *1949*, 5:776–803. Segments of the press lambasted the State Department for relinquishing Gubitchev (who was a spy) without managing to secure the release of Vogeler (who was not). In fact, U.S. diplomats did try to raise this precedent with the Hungarian government, but to no avail; FRUS, *1950*, 4:998–1002.

67. This theme was crudely underscored in many of Hollywood's most didactic anticommunist movies of the era, such as *Woman on Pier 13 / I Married a Communist* (dir. Robert Stevenson, RKO, 1951); *Big Jim McLain* (dir. Edward Ludwig, Warner Bros., 1952), and *Walk East on Beacon* (dir. Alfred Werker, Columbia Pictures, 1952).

68. R. H. Gage to Acheson, Box 1090, RG 59, NACP.

69. Robert E. and Barbara Dietz to the *New York World-Telegram*, February 24, 1950, 30.

70. "Protection Abroad," letter by Indignant Citizen, *LAT*, February 25, 1950, A4; Mr. and Mrs. Walter Braun, Beverly Hills, CA, to Acheson, telegram, February 24, 1950, 264.1111 Vogeler, Robert A., State Department Decimal File, 1950–54, Box 1090, RG 59, NACP.

71. "Work of the Devil," letter by S. M. W., *LAT*, March 10, 1950, A4; T. Vincent Quinn, House of Representatives, 5th Dist. NY, to Acheson, February 10, 1950, 264.1111 Vogeler, Robert A., State Department Decimal File, 1950–54, Box 1090, RG 59, NACP.

72. N. Raymond Clark, La Grange, IL, to Acheson, January 10, 1950, 264.1111 Vogeler, Robert A./1–1050, State Department Decimal File, 1950–54, Box 1090, RG 59, NACP.

73. Allan Keller, "Vogeler Enslaved as US Pussyfoots," *New York World-Telegram*, November 21, 1950, 1, 2. Keller's articles were followed by a series of feature articles, entitled "I Want My Husband Back," by Lucile Vogeler, March 5, 6, 7, and 9, 1951.

74. Robert J. Allison, *The Crescent Obscured: The United States and the Muslim World, 1776–1815* (Chicago: University of Chicago Press, 1995), 3–34.

75. Decatur quoted in Michael B. Oren, *Power, Faith, and Fantasy: America in the Middle East, 1776 to the Present* (New York: W. W. Norton, 2007), 74.

76. "The Vogeler Outrage," *New York World-Telegram*, November 21, 1950, 28.

77. Paul Baepler, *White Slaves, African Masters: An Anthology of Barbary Captivity Narratives* (Chicago: University of Chicago Press, 1999), 50–51, 285–97, and "Rewriting the Barbary Captivity Narrative: The Perdicaris Affair and the Last Barbary Pirate," *Prospects: An*

Annual of American Cultural Studies 24 (1999): 177–211; Russell D. Buhite, *Lives at Risk: Hostages and Victims in American Foreign Policy* (Wilmington, DE: Scholarly Resources, 1995), 72–81.

78. Perdicaris sold his tale, "In Raissuli's Hands: The Story of My Captivity and Deliverance May 18 to June 26, 1904," to *Leslie's Magazine*, September 1904, and two years later to *National Geographic*. The former is reproduced in Baepler, *White Slaves, African Masters*, 288–301. On the issue of his citizenship, Harold E. Davis, "The Citizenship of John Perdicaris," *Journal of Modern History* 13, no. 4 (1941): 517–26.

79. Javits to Acheson, November 28, 1950, 264.1111 Vogeler, Robert A./11–2850, State Department Decimal File, 1950–54, Box 1090, RG 59, NACP.

80. William Henry Chamberlin, "Year of Indecision," *Wall Street Journal*, January 2, 1952, 8.

81. Lucile Vogeler, "I Want My Husband Back," *New York World-Telegram*, March 6, 1951, 25.

82. *Guilty of Treason* (dir. Felix Feist, Eagle Lion, 1950). These scenes not only served a titillating function but also imply a degree of unease on Feist's part (shared by many Catholics in 1949) that Mindszenty *had* confessed, irrespective of whatever pressure had been brought to bear. By refusing to depict the cardinal's collapse, the feature shied away—as *Variety*'s reviewer noted—from "the haunted and tragic figure of his final newspaper photographs"; *Variety*, January 4, 1950.

83. "Action on Vogeler Denounced by US," *NYT*, February 22, 1950, 6.

84. "Vogeler's Recital Stirs Skepticism," 41.

85. "Plans to Appeal to Free Her Husband," *NYT*, February 22, 1950, 7; "Son, 8, Weeps on Learning Vogeler's Fate," *New York World-Telegram*, February 22, 1950, 12.

86. "'Just Couldn't Sleep,' Says Vogeler's Father," *New York World-Telegram*, February 22, 1950, 12.

87. "US in New Talks to Free Vogeler," *NYT*, June 19, 1950, 3; "The Scars," *Time*, May 22, 1950, 29.

88. "Mrs Vogeler to Appeal," *NYT*, August 11, 1950, 11.

89. "Vogeler's Wife Spurns Political-Widow Role," *New York World-Telegram*, November 6, 1950, 28; and in the same paper, "Vogeler, in Red Jail a Year, Is Forgotten by State Dept.," November 20, 1950, 1, 2; Keller, "Vogeler Enslaved," 1, 2; "Vogeler Outrage," 28; "Mrs. Vogeler's Story," March 9, 1951, 28.

90. "I Want My Husband Back," *New York World-Telegram*, March 8, 1951, 29.

91. In its issue of March 6, 1950, *Life* carried a photograph of Lucile—in a daringly cut black dress, with a crucifix hovering over her décolletage—captioned "Lucille Vogeler tries to substitute for her husband as a model railroad engineer while the older of her two sons, Robert Jr., 9, watches skeptically"; "Vogeler Confesses," *Life*, March 6, 1950, 40.

92. L. M. Henning, Mt. Vernon, NY, to Acheson, February 8, 1950, 264.111 Vogeler, Robert A./2–850, State Department Decimal File, 1950–54, Box 1090, RG 59, NACP.

93. "A Prisoner for a Crown," *Life*, July 3, 1950, 61–63. U.S. diplomats viewed with alarm the prospect that Budapest would ransom Vogeler for the crown, since an object so precious to the Hungarian Catholic Church (which Mindszenty himself had insisted remain in U.S. custody) was not a price to which Washington could have agreed without furious accusa-

tions of betrayal from Catholics worldwide. As it was, when the rumors were printed, the State Department received numerous telegrams and letters of protest; 264.1111 Vogeler, Robert A., State Department Decimal File, 1950–54, Box 2090, RG 59, NACP.

94. That the crown had *not* been under discussion in April is affirmed in a memorandum by Aaron S. Brown to Lucius D. Battle, June 21, 1950, FRUS, *1950*, 4:1013–14; Davis to Acheson, telegram, #174, September 11, 1950, FRUS, *1950*, 4:1019–22. It seems conceivable that the June press reports caused Budapest to retreat not because it had all along intended to extract the crown but because publication of the deal's terms—in which the United States had not conceded very much other than rescinding the steps immediately taken after Vogeler's arrest—would leave Hungarian officials looking embarrassingly empty-handed.

95. A retrospective on the whole case, dispatched on May 2, 1951, stated that there was "no direct evidence that the Soviet Government has played any part or taken any interest in the Vogeler case, but it would be naïve to suppose that it has not at least been consulted"; Budapest Legation to State Department, "The Vogeler Case," telegram, #737, May 2, 1951, 264.1111 Vogeler, Robert A./5–251, State Department Decimal File, 1950–54, Box 1091, RG 59, NACP.

96. Davis to Acheson, telegram, #174, September 11, 1950, FRUS, *1950*, 4:1019–22.

97. Budapest Legation to State Department, "The Vogeler Case," telegram, #737, May 2, 1951, 264.1111 Vogeler, Robert A./5–251, State Department Decimal File, 1950–54, Box 1091, RG 59, NACP.

98. Davis to Acheson, telegram, #174, September 11, 1950, FRUS, *1950*, 4:1019–22.

99. Davis to Acheson, telegram, #150, February 27, 1950, FRUS, *1950*, 4:994.

100. Acheson to Legation, telegram, #88, February 25, 1950, FRUS, *1950*, 4:993.

101. In April 1950, Davis believed the deal was genuine and that the Hungarian communists were satisfied that they had secured the "best price obtainable" for Vogeler—"whether because he has served their purpose, or is becoming a liability, or for any other reason that dialectic logic may have suggested"; Davis to Acheson, telegram, #428, April 12, 1950, 264.1111 Vogeler, Robert A./4–1250, State Department Decimal File, 1950–54, Box 1091, RG 59, NACP. By September he had reached a very different view of Undersecretary for Foreign Affairs Andor Berei's sincerity; Davis to Acheson, telegram, #174, September 11, 1950, FRUS, *1950*, 4:1021.

102. According to Davis, "Vogeler's appearance at the trial was such that observers found it almost impossible to believe that he had been subjected to serious physical or psychological mistreatment. There was a strong impression that his testimony had been rehearsed, but not necessarily without his cooperation"; ibid.

103. In an article printed in the *Washington Post*, Lucile related that Bob had always said "he would sign any confession they wanted him to. He would do it, he said, because other Westerners in Eastern Europe had done just that. Then their properties had been confiscated and they had been expelled"; "Vogeler's Wife Fights On to Free Him," *WP*, March 18, 1951, B3.

104. Records on the Vogeler case are full of tantalizingly cryptic references as to his possible intelligence activities, and clearly he himself was agitated by the possibility that U.S. Legation staff would believe him guilty of black marketeering. Perkins to Acheson, memo,

"Scheduled Call by Mr. Robert A. Vogeler," June 5, 1951, 264.1111 Vogeler, Robert A./6–551, State Department Decimal File, 1950–54, Box 1091, RG 59, NACP.

105. Davis to Acheson, telegram, #114, February 18, 1950, 264.1111 Vogeler, Robert, A./2–1850, State Department Decimal File, 1950–54, Box 1090, RG 59, NACP.

106. Davis to Acheson, telegram, #119, February 19, 1950, 264.1111 Vogeler, Robert, A./2–1950, State Department Decimal File, 1950–54, Box 1090, RG 59, NACP.

107. Davis to Acheson, telegram, #124, February 20, 1950, 264.1111 Vogeler, Robert, A./2–2050, State Department Decimal File, 1950–54, Box 1090, RG 59, NACP.

108. "Un-American" Americans hardly merited the most vigorous efforts by a state they repudiated, the State Department reasoned, though not in its formal communications with Mrs. Kate Field, Hermann's wife, who strove in vain to attract U.S. media attention to her husband's plight. A confidential memo, justifying the department's dilatory efforts, noted that it had "fulfilled its duties towards the Fields in virtue of their American citizenship, particularly in view of the information indicating that . . . [Hermann] may have been pro-Communist"; Merchant to Barber (State Dept. Division of Eastern European Affairs), memo, May 7, 1953, 248.1151 to 249.1111, State Department Decimal File, 1950–54, Box 0976, RG 59, NACP.

109. Merchant to Dulles, memo, "Background Information for Your Appointment with Mr. and Mrs. Robert A. Vogeler," May 1, 1953, 264.1111 Vogeler, Robert A./5–513, State Department Decimal File, 1950–54, Box 1091, RG 59, NACP.

110. Dowling, Vienna, to Acheson, telegram, #196, July 21, 1952, 264.1111 Vogeler, Robert A./7–2152, State Department Decimal File, 1950–54, Box 1091, RG 59, NACP; Davis to Acheson, telegram, #669, May 4, 1950, 264.1111 Vogeler, Robert A., State Department Decimal File, 1950–54, Box 1090, RG 59, NACP.

111. Memorandum by W. J. Donnelly (American Legation, Vienna), "Conversation with Mrs. Lucille Vogeler," November 8, 1950, 264.1111 Vogeler, Robert A./11–1750, State Department Decimal File, 1950–54, Box 1090, RG 59, NACP.

112. "The Vogeler Mystery," *NYT*, April 22, 1951, 148.

113. "Hungary to Free Vogeler"; "Vogeler, Forgotten by State Dept., Paced Hungarian Red Prison Cell in Solitary," *New York World-Telegram*, April 21, 1951, 1, 2.

114. Diary entry for April 28, 1951, Papers of Nathaniel P. Davis, HSTL.

115. Six months later, Budapest demanded the crown, complaining that the U.S. government was not honoring this part of the agreement, returning only an "insignificant part" of Nazi-seized Hungarian goods; "Hungary Bids US 'Pay Up' on Vogeler," *NYT*, November 25, 1951, 1.

116. Budapest Legation to State Department, "The Vogeler Case," telegram, #737, May 2, 1951, 264.1111 Vogeler, Robert A./5–251, State Department Decimal File, 1950–54, Box 1091, RG 59, NACP.

117. "Vogeler Returns," *NYT*, April 30, 1951, 19; "Stalin's Achilles Heel," *WP*, August 17, 1951, C7. *Life* announced that the United States had agreed to "hand over undisclosed millions of dollars in Hungarian goods seized by the Nazis," "Robert Vogeler Comes Home," *Life*, May 14, 1951, 43, while *Time* reported the rumored value of these looted assets as $82 million; "Hungary: Just Claims," April 30, 1951, 38. More vaguely, *Newsweek* re-

lated that the State Department had "agreed to ransom conditions"; "Out of the Night," May 14, 1951, 30.

118. "Freedom for Vogeler," *Newsweek,* April 30, 1951, 38.

119. "Vogeler Lives Again," *Newsweek,* May 7, 1951, 38; "Hungary: It Could Happen to Anybody," *Time,* May 7, 1951, 35.

120. "Vogeler Bares Torture," *New York World-Telegram,* April 28, 1951, 1.

121. "Vogeler Lives Again," 38.

122. "Vogeler Free, Cites Pressure to Confess; US Agrees to 3 of Terms Set by Hungary," *NYT,* April 29, 1951, 1.

123. "Estimate 4000 PWs Held by Red Chinese," *New York World-Telegram,* April 24, 1951, 46; "Hungary: It Could Happen," 35.

124. "Hungary: It Could Happen," 35.

125. "Vogeler Lands," *New York World-Telegram,* May 1, 1951, 1, 2; "Robert Vogeler Comes Home," 43, 44.

126. "Wife Tells How Cruelty of Red Prison Broke Once-Rugged Vogeler's Spirit," *New York World-Telegram,* May 2, 1951, 1.

127. "Vogeler Warns of Red Plot on Americans," *LAT,* April 30, 1951, 1.

128. "Vogeler Lands," 2.

129. Morris L. Ernst and David Loth devoted a chapter of their *Report on the American Communist* (New York: Holt, 1952) to "Sex Patterns," concluding with the observation that the wife was typically "the more dominant partner" in communist marriages; thus "it was generally assumed that Earl Browder was henpecked," 162–80; "Mrs. Vogeler Has One Aim, Happiness," *New York World-Telegram,* May 2, 1951, 1.

130. Donnelly to Acheson, telegram, #2520, April 30, 1951, 264.1111 Vogeler, Robert A./4–3051, Perkins to Acheson, telegram, June 5, 1951, "Scheduled Call by Mr. Robert A. Vogeler," 264.1111 Vogeler, Robert A./6–551, State Department Decimal File, 1950–54, Box 1091, RG 59, NACP.

131. Donnelly to Acheson, telegram, #1166, May 1, 1951, "Transcript of Consul Tower's Report of Conversation with Mr. Robert A. Vogeler," April 28, 1951, 264.1111 Vogeler, Robert A./5–151, State Department Decimal File, 1950–54, Box 1091, RG 59, NACP.

132. "Vogeler to Enter US Hospital Today," *NYT,* May 3, 1951, 19.

133. "Hungary: It Could Happen," 36.

134. That he might have been a spy was now publicly discussed for the first time, though almost invariably denied; "Mrs. Vogeler Denies Husband Was a Spy," *New York World-Telegram,* June 11, 1951, 22.

135. "Vogeler to Enter," 19; "Vogeler Enters Hospital," *NYT,* May 4, 1951, 29; "Vogeler Talk Postponed," *NYT,* May 15, 1951, 2.

136. "Vogeler Describes Torture Used to Make Him Confess in Hungary," *NYT,* June 9, 1951, 6. The earlier comment that there had been "some truth" to the confession was an attempt "to use irony," he also claimed; "Vogeler's Own Story," *Newsweek,* June 18, 1951, 23.

137. Vogeler's relationship with IT&T ended in late 1952 under circumstances that left it unclear whether he had been dismissed or resigned; "IT&T Liable in His Arrest, Vogeler Says," *CDT,* August 24, 1953, 15.

138. "Vote for Freedom Urged," *NYT,* October 20, 1951, 33.

139. "Vogeler Appeals for Fight on Reds," *NYT*, April 30, 1951, 1; "Vogeler Takes Off on His Way to US," *NYT*, May 1, 1951, 14; "Comfort in Bible Cited by Vogeler," *NYT*, January 11, 1952, 28.

140. "Every American under Red Attack, Vogeler Warns, Cites His Ordeal," *New York World-Telegram*, June 18, 1951, 1.

141. "'Cold War' Tactics Mapped at Parley," *NYT*, February 23, 1952, 4.

142. Donnelly to Acheson, telegram, #2528, April 30, 1951, 264.1111 Vogeler, Robert A./4–3051, State Department Decimal File, 1950–54, Box 1091, RG 59, NACP. Vogeler met, at his request, with Acheson on June 5, 1951, to express "deep gratitude to the Secretary for taking a personal interest in his case throughout the long period of 17 months during which he was held incommunicado" and, in particular, for meeting with Lucile in May 1950; Memorandum for the Vogeler File, June 5, 1951, 2.45 pm, Dean G. Acheson Papers, Secretary of State File, 1945–1972, Memoranda of Conversations File, 1949–1953, Box 69, HSTL. Vogeler's telegrams to Acheson and Truman were published in the *Department of State Bulletin*, May 14, 1951, 770.

143. These lengthy excerpts appeared in the *Saturday Evening Post* issues of October 27, November 3, November 10, November 17, November 24, and December 1, written with Leigh White, former Moscow correspondent of the Chicago *Daily News*.

144. Henry C. Wolfe, "Story of a Shock," *Saturday Review*, May 10, 1952, 14–15. An editorial in the *New York Times* likened Vogeler's first remarks on his release to "a chapter out of Koestler. His examination before the trial? Straight out of *Darkness at Noon*"; "Vogeler Returns," 19.

145. "Dungeon of Fear," 10. Paul Gallico's novel *Trial by Terror* (New York: A. A. Knopf, 1952), which appeared in May 1952, based its fictionalized scenario of a U.S. pressman imprisoned and brainwashed in Hungary on an amalgamation of the Vogeler and Oatis cases.

146. "Vogeler Blasts Red Abductions of Americans," *CDT*, July 3, 1951, 5.

147. Laurence Burd, "US Again Bows to Demands of Red Hungary," *CDT*, July 8, 1951, 2.

148. "The New Barbary Pirates," *NYT*, December 26, 1951, 24; "Vanished World of Jefferson and Theodore Roosevelt," *NYT*, December 27, 1951, 18.

149. "US Studies Ways to Free 4 Fliers Downed in Hungary," *NYT*, December 4, 1951, 1; "Acheson Ridicules Soviet Spy Charge," *NYT*, December 20, 1951, 16; "Vishinsky Asks UN to Make US Cease Help to Anti-Reds," *NYT*, December 20, 1951, 1.

150. "Budapest Hits a New Low," *NYT*, December 24, 1951, 12; "US Debates Ways to Free 4 Airmen Jailed in Hungary," *NYT*, December 25, 1951, 1.

151. "Ransom for Budapest," *NYT*, December 27, 1951, 18.

152. "Angry Public Rallies to Pay 4 Flyers' Fines," *CDT*, December 26, 1951, 1; "New Barbary Pirates," 24.

153. Vogeler, *I Was Stalin's Prisoner*, 283–89; "Vogeler Returns Contributions," *NYT*, December 28, 1951, 3. It was also illegal, the State Department announced on December 27, for private citizens to negotiate with foreign states; "Fliers' Release Put First," *NYT*, December 27, 1951, 5.

154. "'Get Tough' Policy on Hungary Urged," *NYT*, December 28, 1951, 3. Three days later, the *Times* reported the inauguration of "Operation Oatis," headed by a Washington lawyer, to exert pressure on Prague; "Oatis Aid Unit Formed," December 31, 1951, 5.

155. "Group Set to Aid 'Slaves' of Reds," *NYT*, August 23, 1952. Vogeler made common cause with Representative Charles Kersten, whose congressional amendment secured funds from the Mutual Security Act to form "single, young stateless men" fleeing the Soviet sphere into armed units.

156. *I Was Stalin's Prisoner*, dir. Delbert Mann, written by David Swift, episode 6, season 1, Goodyear Television Playhouse, broadcast December 23, 1951 (viewing copy held by UCLA Film & Television Archive).

157. The teleplay was, in *Variety*'s judgment, "an effectively staged documentary with a well-intentioned anti-totalitarian thesis" but ultimately "failed to convey the meaning of Iron Curtain police methods with sufficient vividness," a complaint critics frequently leveled at attempts to condense totalitarianism's nightmarish quality for the small screen; review, *Variety*, December 26, 1951, 30. In the same month, Columbia studios quietly announced that it was shelving a proposed feature on the Vogeler case, *European Edition*, due to "casting difficulties."

158. "Use Red Tactics, Vogeler Urges," *WP*, February 23, 1952, 4; Marquis Childs, "Calling Washington," *WP*, October 5, 1952, 15.

159. Vogeler served as vice chairman of the Volunteers for Taft; "May Put Dixie Democrat in Cabinet: Taft," *CDT*, February 22, 1952, 5; "R. A. Vogeler Aids Taft," *NYT*, March 2, 1952, 76; "McCarthy Assails Democrats for a War 'Prosperity,'" *CDT*, September 28, 1952, 7.

160. Melvin Price to Ben Brown (Acting Assistant Secretary of State), October 18, 1952, 264.1111 Vogeler, Robert A./10–1852, State Department Decimal File, 1950–54, Box 1091, RG 59, NACP.

161. "Critic of UN Backs Bricker Curb on Pacts," *CDT*, October 27, 1953, A1; "Bricker Plan Is Debated by Law Experts," *CDT*, January 27, 1954, 1.

162. His own success aside, Vogeler's representation of publishers' preferences was downright tendentious, as even a cursory glance at the era's best-seller lists or Book of the Month Club and Literary Guild choices would attest.

163. "Vogeler Trial Laid to Reds in State Dept.," *CDT*, March 16, 1954, 16.

164. Kazan quoted in Stephen J. Whitfield, *The Culture of the Cold War* (Baltimore: Johns Hopkins University Press, 1996), 107.

165. "Crowd Hails Vogeler; McCarthy Praises Him," *NYT*, June 17, 1954, 25.

166. This picture was printed on August 24, 1954, in both the *Los Angeles Times* and the *Chicago Daily Tribune*.

167. "Vogeler, Back, Bids US Stay Prepared," *NYT*, May 2, 1951, 14.

168. Far from being an outrage now consigned to the past, lynching remained very much an issue of the present in the South—one that Soviet propaganda emphasized with "particular glee," in the judgment of U.S. psywarriors; Memorandum by W. Bradley Connors, Psychological Coordinating Committee, "Communist 'Hate America' Propaganda," POC D-50/1, January 2 1953, Papers of Howland Sargeant, General File, Clippings and Personal Papers, 1953–54, Box 2, folder "Reports, Public Opinion—1953," HSTL.

169. Bohlen, quoted in T. Michael Ruddy, *The Cautious Diplomat: Charles E. Bohlen and the Soviet Union, 1929–1969* (Kent: Kent State University Press, 1986), 6.

170. "New Dark Continent," 22.

171. "US Forbids Travel to All Soviet Bloc Countries without Consent," *NYT,* May 2, 1952, 1.

172. "Plan Your Vacation Now," *NYT,* May 3, 1951, 28.

173. Davis, Diary (Budapest) 1949–51, entries for December 22 and 30, 1949, Papers of Nathaniel P. Davis, Box 1, HSTL.

174. Deputy Assistant Secretary of State for European Affairs (Bonbright) to the Secretary of State, memo, "Proposed Restrictions on the Travel of Hungarian Legation Personnel in the US," 601.6411/1–2651, FRUS, *1951,* vol. 4, *Europe: Political and Economic Relations* (Washington, DC: Government Printing Office, 1985), 1441–42.

175. Hanson W. Baldwin, "Captives Are Red Pawns," *NYT,* December 21, 1951, 4; "Budapest Hits a New Low," 12.

176. Edward I. Peck, Willoughby, Ohio, to Truman, telegram, February 22, 1950, Papers of Harry S. Truman, General File, Vogel, A-Vogt, A.-K., Box 2543, HSTL.

177. "We Don't Use Our Power," *New York World-Telegram,* February 22, 1950, 14.

178. "GOP Senators Suggest Medics Go behind Lines," *CDT,* July 30, 1951, 4.

5. PRISONERS OF PAVLOV

1. Adam J. Zweiback, "The 21 'Turncoat GIs': Nonrepatriations and the Political Culture of the Korean War," *Historian* 60 (Winter 1998): 345–62; Gary Harold Rice, "The Lost Sheep of Korea" (PhD diss., University of Texas, Austin, 1998); Edward Hunter, *Brainwashing: From Pavlov to Powers* (New York: Bookmailer, 1956), 11.

2. His efforts to spin the story—claiming that as many as "100 or more" American POWs would not want to return "after undergoing the ordeal of mental processing"—were discussed in *Look* magazine, but rarely was prominence given to these deliberately inflated estimates; Richard Wilson, "How US Prisoners Broke under Red 'Brain Washing,'" *Look,* June 2, 1953, 80–83.

3. "Pro-Communist Twenty-three," *America,* October 10, 1953, 35; "The Twenty-two," *Commonweal,* January 1, 1954, 320–21.

4. For a representative example of this genre, see "Case Histories of the 21: What Their Lives Show," *Newsweek,* January 18, 1954, 52–57.

5. George E. Sokolsky, "US Should Expose POW Turncoats," *New York Journal-American,* September 10, 1953, 30.

6. "Fruits of Brainwashing," *NYT,* January 28, 1954, 26.

7. K. S. Thimayya, *Experiment in Neutrality* (New Delhi: Vision Books, 1981), 117.

8. "Jobs Offered 22 GIs Holding Out in Korea," *WP,* November 24, 1953, 18.

9. "Army Bars Korea Trip for 23 GIs' Mothers," *NYT,* October 1, 1953, 3; Rice, "Lost Sheep," 132–52.

10. Rice, "Lost Sheep," 94; Memorandum of Conversation with Walter Williams, September 26, 1953, Telephone Conversations Series, Box 1, file July–October, 1953, Papers of John Foster Dulles, DDEL.

11. "GI's Mother to Fly to Tokyo," *WP,* December 8, 1953, 8; "Mother Still Hopes to See

POW Son," *WP*, December 12, 1953, 3. Mrs. Howe's story was later dramatized (after her son's return to the United States in December 1955) as *Mother of a Turncoat* by NBC's Armstrong Circle Theatre, broadcast on May 1, 1956.

12. "Case of POW Tenneson: His Mother's Explanation," *NYT*, December 20, 1953, E5; "The Lost Sheep," *WP*, December 21, 1953, 10.

13. "'Come Back,' Mom Begs PW," *Chicago Defender*, October 10, 1953, 1. The radio messages recorded by family members received a good deal of press attention; *Time*, for example, devoted a page to the pleas of Arlie Pate's family in Carbondale, Illinois, to return home to the pleasures of squirrel shooting, to care for his ailing mother, and to tell them "all the things that's happening around the world"; "To a Young Progressive," October 19, 1953, 32.

14. "What about Reds among Freed U.S. Prisoners?" *Newsweek*, August 17, 1953, 21.

15. "The Sorriest Bunch," *Newsweek*, February 8, 1954, 40–41.

16. Ibid.; Chalmers M. Roberts, "The GIs Who Went Red," *WP*, December 29, 1953, 11.

17. "Men without a Country," *Newsweek*, February 1, 1954, 32; "Lost Souls," *WP*, February 1, 1954, 6.

18. "Sympathy Wanes for Red-Led GIs," *NYT*, October 20, 1953, 4.

19. "Korea: 22,000 to 22," *Time*, January 4, 1954, 15; "Loud-Speakers Lose to Dances," *US News and World Report*, January 1, 1954, 62–63; Lindesay Parrott, "Korea GI's Spurn Plea to Quit Reds," *NYT*, December 23, 1953, 1.

20. Elie Abel, "21 Pro-Red GI's to Get Dishonorable Discharges," *NYT*, January 26, 1954, 1; Raymond B. Lech, *Broken Soldiers* (Urbana: University of Illinois Press, 2000), 216.

21. "Lost Souls," 6; "Korea: 22,000 to 22," 15.

22. "The Prisoners Go Free," *Time*, February 1, 1954, 16.

23. These statistics are derived from an instant balance sheet drawn up at the end of the war by *US News and World Report*; "Korea: Facts of 3 Years' War," June 26, 1953, 18–19.

24. Dulles address, September 2, 1953, quoted in Barton J. Bernstein, "The Struggle over the Korean Armistice: Prisoners of Repatriation?" in *Child of Conflict: The Korean-American Relationship, 1945–1953*, ed. Bruce Cumings (Seattle: University of Washington Press, 1983), 307.

25. According to the Foreign Affairs Survey conducted by the National Opinion Research Center of the University of Chicago, 42 percent of respondents said in March 1952 that the United States should refuse to return prisoners who had "now turned against communism," a figure that rose to 50 percent in April and 57 percent in June. When it was put to those polled that the communists refused to give back U.S. POWs unless all their prisoners were returned, fewer supported the principle of voluntary repatriation. In those same months, 11 percent, 21 percent, and 28 percent agreed that the United States should still refuse to return disaffected prisoners; Foreign Affairs Survey, March, April, and June 1952, conducted by National Opinion Research Center, University of Chicago, retrieved May 1, 2008, from the iPoll databank, Roper Center for Public Opinion Research, University of Connecticut, www.ropercenter.uconn.edu/ipoll.html.

26. Rosemary Foot, *A Substitute for Victory: The Politics of Peacemaking at the Korean Armistice Talks* (Ithaca: Cornell University Press, 1990), 140.

27. Bernstein, "Struggle," 283–88, 296–97.

28. Demaree Bess, "The Prisoners Stole the Show in Korea," *Saturday Evening Post,* November 1, 1952, 36.

29. Jaro Mayda, "The Korean Repatriation Problem and International Law," *American Journal of International Law* 47, no. 3 (1953): 414–38.

30. Samuel M. Meyers and William C. Bradbury, "The Political Behavior of Korean and Chinese Prisoners of War in the Korean Conflict: A Historical Analysis," in *Mass Behavior in Battle and Captivity: The Communist Soldier in the Korean War,* ed. Samuel M. Meyers and Albert D. Biderman (Chicago: University of Chicago Press, 1968), 213–14.

31. Ibid., 228.

32. Bess, "Prisoners Stole the Show," 53.

33. Of this total, some thirty-eight thousand "loyal South Koreans and civilian internees" were released in the summer of 1952; Meyers and Bradbury, "Political Behavior," 225; Ron Robin, *The Making of the Cold War Enemy: Culture and Politics in the Military-Intellectual Complex* (Princeton: Princeton University Press, 2001), 146.

34. "Truman Endorses UN Truce Stand Rejected by Reds," *NYT,* May 8, 1952, 1.

35. Dean Acheson to George C. Marshall, Secretary of Defense, top-secret letter, August 27, 1951, reproduced as Document Number CK3100054359 in *Declassified Documents Reference System* (Farmington Hills, MI: Gale, 2008).

36. White House, Top Secret, "Notes on Meeting Re. US Policies, from the Psychological Strategy Standpoint, Governing the Exchange of Prisoners of War and Repatriation of North Korean and Chinese Nationals," October 2, 1951, reproduced as Document Number CK3100055672 in *Declassified Documents Reference System.*

37. Dr. Horace S. Craig to Wallace Irwin, memo, "POW Repatriation Issue: Our experience after World War II," Box 26, 383.6, POWs, Records of the Psychological Strategy Board, DDEL.

38. Wallace Carroll to Gordon Gray, "Repatriation of Prisoners of War," top-secret memo, December 28, 1951, Records of the Psychological Strategy Board, reproduced as Document Number CK3100054367 in *Declassified Documents Reference System.*

39. James Cameron, quoted in Foot, *Substitute for Victory,* 111.

40. A. Sabine Chase, chief of the Division of Research for the Far East, quoted in Foot, *Substitute for Victory,* 117.

41. Meyers and Bradbury, "Political Behavior," 334.

42. Frank Stelle of the PPS to Paul Nitze, quoted in Foot, *Substitute for Victory,* 125.

43. Bernstein, "Struggle," 275, 283–84.

44. Foot, *Substitute for Victory,* 96–97.

45. Mayda, "Korean Repatriation Problem," 421; "Screened Reds Given Warning on Allegiance," *WP,* May 22, 1952, 6.

46. This definition was supplied by Colonel George W. Hickman, the senior UN Command staff officer in the POW negotiations; "POW Issue Hardly Dented after One Weary Year," *WP,* December 21, 1952, B3.

47. For its part, the PSB urged a much more limited program of instruction in democracy, restricted to an elite handful of North Korean and Chinese POWs, in the hope that, on return home, these fervent democrats would undermine communist society from within. When camp personnel, with the assistance of imported officers from Taiwan, later insti-

tuted a wider program of indoctrination, their intervention conflicted with Washington's desire to reduce the number of nonrepatriates; Robin, *Making of the Cold War Enemy*, 153–59.

48. Raymond A. Bauer, "Brainwashing: Psychology or Demonology?" *Journal of Social Issues* 13, no. 3 (1957): 41.

49. "The Big Lie," *Life*, November 9, 1953, 51.

50. Virginia Pasley, "21 American GI's Who Chose Communism," *US News and World Report*, July 15, 1955, 119.

51. Hunter, *Brainwashing*, 309.

52. "Red Brainwashing Too Terrible, Expert Says," *LAT*, March 10, 1954, 19.

53. "Pro-Communist Twenty-three," 35. Lenience was also the approach recommended by Edward Hunter, who said that all but a small percentage of "so-called 'progressives'" should be "pitied as sick men, not condemned as traitors"; "Our POWs Are NOT Traitors," *New Leader*, August 24, 1953, 13–14.

54. The corkless bottle metaphor is psychologist Albert Biderman's—a characterization of popular (and, in his estimation, groundless) images of brainwashing; Albert D. Biderman, *March to Calumny: The Story of American POW's in the Korean War* (New York: Macmillan, 1963), 140.

55. Rear Admiral D. V. Gallery, USN, "We Can Baffle the Brainwashers!" *Saturday Evening Post*, January 22, 1955, 94. Orientalist constructions of this sort typified press commentary on the Chinese and North Koreans. "To the Communist, particularly the Oriental Communist, there is no deadline for conquest. Time is endless and the patient instillation of a little poison in the body politic is a means to the ultimate conquest of the world by communism," wrote Hanson W. Baldwin in a *New York Times* article entitled "'Brainwashing' by Reds: A Summary of Problems Created for U.S. by Communists' Treatment of Prisoners," March 1, 1955, 8. See also William A. Ulman, "The GI's Who Fell for the Reds," *Saturday Evening Post*, March 6, 1954, 17–19, 64, 67.

56. William H. Godel, Office of the Secretary of Defense, to Wallace Irwin, PSB, memo, July 23, 1953, "Materials on Mistreatment of UN Captured Personnel in Korea," 729.2, Box 124, Records of the Operations Coordinating Board, DDEL.

57. H. S. Craig, Memorandum for the Record, "POW Exchange," April 21, 1953, 387.4, PSB Central Files, Box 28, Korea (4), DDEL.

58. William Brinkley, "Valley Forge GIs Tell of Their Brainwashing Ordeal," *Life*, May 25, 1953, 108–110, 111–16, 121–22, 124.

59. "A Sorry Blunder," *NYT*, May 5, 1953, 28.

60. "Brainwashing at Valley Forge," *Nation*, May 23, 1953, 425–26. See also "The Brainwashed," *Commonweal*, May 15, 1953, 138.

61. An editorial quoted in "Backing Lifts Valley Forge POWs Spirits," *WP*, May 6, 1953, 3.

62. C. D. Jackson to General Wilton B. Persons, memo, May 11, 1953, Box 5, C. D. Jackson Records, DDEL; Memorandum of a conversation with Ambassador Lodge, May 4, 1953, Records of the PSB, 383.6, POWs, Box 26, DDEL.

63. "Snafu at Valley Forge," *Newsweek*, May 18, 1953, 44.

64. John W. Finney, "All Released POWs to Be Treated Alike," *WP*, May 25, 1953, 3.

65. "'Treat Them Naturally,' the General Said," *Life*, May 11, 1953, 39.

66. Brinkley, "Valley Forge GIs," 121.

67. "Sorriest Bunch," 41.

68. "Washed Brains of POW's: Can They Be Rewashed?" *Newsweek,* May 4, 1953, 37; Mark W. Clark, *From the Danube to the Yalu* (New York: Harper, 1954), 250.

69. Gilbert Bailey, "When an American P.O.W. Comes Home," *NYT Magazine,* May 10, 1953, 9–11.

70. "One Changed His Mind," *Time,* November 2, 1953, 25.

71. "There's Joy in Crackers Neck," *Newsweek,* November 2, 1953, 22–23; "A Prodigal and His Kin," *Life,* November 2, 1953, 45.

72. "GI Who Spurned Reds Welcomed Back Home," *LAT,* November 23, 1953, 37.

73. Malvina Lindsay, "When Men Return from Prison Camps," *WP,* August 12, 1953, 10. Acting on the same principle, the Veterans of Foreign Wars placed two newly returned prisoners from Korea at the center of their May 1953 "Loyalty Parade" in New York, an event presided over by Loyalty Parade Queen Lucile Vogeler, "in recognition of her long effort to free her husband"; "Ex-Captives Ride for Loyalty Today," *NYT,* May 2, 1953, 8.

74. "Into Eager Arms," *Life,* May 11, 1953, 36–39.

75. "Prisoners and Propaganda," *WP,* August 7, 1953, 20. The *Nation* related the experiences of one returning POW, Bennie Smith, who complained that reporters had "felt his arms and legs and commented, 'They sure starved you, didn't they, boy?'" when in fact he just "hadn't had much appetite"; Milton Lowenberg, "'Progressive' POW: Corporal Smith's Story," *Nation,* January 30, 1954, 92.

76. "POW's Back Home, Tell Horrors of Red Slavery," *Chicago Defender,* September 5, 1953, 2.

77. "The Tough Prisoners," *Time,* September 21, 1953, 28; "Eyes of World on Panmunjom as Truce Talks Start Again," *Newsweek,* May 4, 1953, 35–36.

78. E. J. Kahn, "A Reporter at Large: Seeing the Facts Made," *New Yorker,* April 1953, 70–82.

79. "Patriot's Tears," *Newsweek,* December 14, 1953, 41–42.

80. Kahn, "Seeing the Facts Made," 72.

81. I borrow the phrase "excremental assault" from Terrence des Pres, *The Survivor: An Anatomy of Life in the Death Camps* (New York: Oxford University Press, 1976). On the denial of "sanitation privileges" to Lieut. Floyd O'Neal, air force bomber pilot, see "Germ Warfare: Forged Evidence," *Time,* November 9, 1953, 22.

82. "The Prisoners Who Broke: Some 'Chow Rats,' a Few Real Converts," *US News and World Report,* August 21, 1953, 31. This claim wasn't entirely accurate. During and after World War II, the Allies all made concerted attempts to "de-Nazify" POWs in their control; Ron Robin, *The Barbed Wire College: Reeducating German POWs in the United States during World War II* (Princeton: Princeton University Press, 1995); Arthur L. Smith, *The War for the German Mind: Re-educating Hitler's Soldiers* (Providence, RI: Berghahn Books, 1996).

83. "The Prisoners of Pavlov," *Life,* October 5, 1953, 26. It would be hard to overstate the ubiquity of Pavlov in contemporary analyses of brainwashing. He was, for example, extensively discussed during Schwable's investigation; Robert Young, "Brainwashing Impact Told by US Expert," *CDT,* March 4, 1954, B1. Meerloo and Hunter both devoted entire chap-

ters to the man and his dogs—or rats, as populist accounts often had it; Joost Meerloo, *Rape of the Mind: The Psychology of Thought Control, Menticide, and Brainwashing* (Cleveland: World Publishing, 1956), 37–53; Hunter, *Brainwashing*, 17–41.

84. Wilson, "How US Prisoners Broke," 80–83.

85. Gallery, "We Can Baffle the Brainwashers!" 21.

86. "Tough Prisoners," 29.

87. Ibid., 28. The Chinese also apparently reached the same conclusion, abandoning rote indoctrination for all but the most receptive "Progressive" POWs in 1952; Biderman, *March to Calumny*, 43.

88. "Reds Played Race vs. Race," *Chicago Defender*, August 15, 1953, 1; Frederic Sondern, "US Negroes Make Reds See Red," *Reader's Digest*, January 1954, 37–42; "Korean Puzzle: Americans Who Stay," *US News and World Report*, October 9, 1953, 38. Hunter devoted a chapter of his 1956 volume, *Brainwashing*, to "the Negro POW," 89–115.

89. "Prisoners Swayed—Didn't Fall," *US News and World Report*, August 28, 1953, 30; "Washed Brains of POW's," 37.

90. "Korean Puzzle," 39.

91. "Truth vs. Promises in Korea: Prisoners Show Communists Can't Be Trusted," *US News and World Report*, August 14, 1953, 35. Another prisoner described the water treatment in identical language for *Newsweek*, "Terror and Torture: Five Prisoners' Stories," August 17, 1953, 32.

92. "Torture Methods in Korea Detailed: Dr. Mayo Tells How American Fliers Were 'Conditioned' to Level below Animals," *NYT*, October 27, 1953, 4. On POWs' humorous antics, see Major David MacGhee, with Peter Kalischer, "Tortured in Pak's Palace," *Collier's*, 5 February 1954, 74–75; on Christianity as the key to survival, see Pvt. Robert L. Sharpe, as told to Bill Currie, "God Saved My Life in Korea," *Reader's Digest*, April 1951, 21–25.

93. The first phrase comes from a *Time* report on the Army War Crimes Division's efforts to "remind the US of a fact frequently forgotten after long months of stalemate and truce in Korea," namely, that the communists were a "barbarous enemy, capable of savagery and sadism which rival any atrocities in the history of modern warfare"; "Barbarity," *Time*, November 9, 1953, 23–25; "Terror and Torture," 32.

94. Robert J. Lifton, "Home by Ship: Reaction Patterns of American Prisoners of War Repatriated from North Korea," *American Journal of Psychiatry* 10 (1954): 734.

95. Lt. Col. Thomas D. Harrison, USAF, with Bill Stapleton, "Why Did Some GIs Turn Communist?" *Collier's*, November 27, 1953, 25.

96. MacGhee, "Tortured in Pak's Palace," 83.

97. Harrison, "Why Did Some GIs Turn Communist?" 27; "The Ugly Story," *Time*, August 24, 1953, 18.

98. "Prisoners Who Broke," 30; "The 'Rats,'" *Newsweek*, August 24, 1953, 30, 33.

99. On the ship-bound incidents, see Lifton, "Home by Ship," 735. Biderman relates that the KKK tag for "reactionary" organizations in the POW camps came from the Chinese, who attributed all resistance to KKK elements; *March to Calumny*, 60–61.

100. "Prisoners Who Broke," 30.

101. "Tough Prisoners," 28–29.

102. Lowenberg, "'Progressive' POW," 89–93.

103. "What about Reds," 21.

104. For more extensive discussion of these films, see Susan L. Carruthers, "Redeeming the Captives: Hollywood and the Brainwashing of America's Prisoners of War in Korea," *Film History* 10, no. 3 (1998): 275–94; and Charles S. Young, "Missing Action: POW Films, Brainwashing and the Korean War, 1954–1968," *Historical Journal of Film Radio and Television* 18, no. 1 (1998): 49–74.

105. "TV Film Reviews," *Hollywood Reporter,* September 9, 1953, 10.

106. Leo Guild, "On the Air," *Hollywood Reporter,* June 9, 1954, 10.

107. "Detroit Cries 'Sabotage' as U.S. Steel 'P.O.W.' TV Show Blanks Out Midway," *Variety,* November 4, 1953, 26.

108. "Drama: MGM Rushes POW Job," *LAT,* November 5, 1953, B11.

109. *Prisoner of War* (dir. Andrew Marton, MGM, 1954); press book consulted at the British Film Institute, London.

110. *Variety,* March 24, 1954; similarly the *Motion Picture Herald* called it "hardly a convincing portrait" of "the Communist in war," lacking the "realism of the documentary," April 3, 1945, 2245.

111. "War Atrocities Pic Limited in Appeal," *Hollywood Reporter,* March 24, 1954, 3.

112. *The Bamboo Prison* (dir. Lewis Seiler, Columbia Pictures, 1954); *Kinematograph Weekly,* February 19, 1955, 21.

113. Correspondence between the Memphis Board of Censors and Defense Department, reproduced in *Film and Propaganda in America: A Documentary History,* ed. David Culbert; vol. 5, *1945 and After* (microfiche supplement), ed. Larry Suid (New York: Greenwood Press, 1991), 274–81.

114. Anthony Leviero, "Pity or Punishment?" *NYT Magazine,* August 14, 1955, 12.

115. "Army's Ex-POW Trials Cause Nix on 'War,' Rivkin Charges," *Hollywood Reporter,* March 19, 1954, 4; "P.O.W. Film Denied Army Publicity Aid," *NYT,* March 18, 1954, 24; "Defense Dep't Thinks 'P.O.W.' Is Too Fictional," *Hollywood Reporter,* March 18, 1954, 1.

116. Clair E. Towne, Motion Picture Section, to Orville Crouch, MGM, November 20, 1953, in Suid, *1945 and After,* M-459.

117. Elizabeth Lutes Hillman, *Defending America: Military Culture and the Cold War Court-Martial* (Princeton: Princeton University Press, 2005), 47–54.

118. Hanson W. Baldwin, "The Prisoner Issue—I," *NYT,* January 26, 1954, 2.

119. Hanson W. Baldwin, "The Prisoner Issue—II," *NYT,* January 27, 1954, 2.

120. Memorandum for Department of Defense, Office of Public Information, from Department of the Army, November 21, 1953, Document M-459, in Suid, *1945 and After.* Writer Allen Rivkin told the *Hollywood Reporter* that the Defense Department had withdrawn its support because the Adjutant General's Office requested use of *Prisoner of War* to strengthen its stand in the court-martial of former U.S. POWs who had falsely confessed to germ warfare; *Hollywood Reporter,* March 19, 1954, 4.

121. "G.I. Who Chose Reds, Then Quit, Is Seized in Court-Martial Case," *NYT,* January 23, 1954, 1.

122. "Is It a Crime to Crack Up? Test Begins for Prisoners Who Yield to Reds," *US News and World Report,* February 26, 1954, 39.

123. Dr. Philip Bloemsma, a surgeon who had spent four years in a Japanese POW camp,

testified that 98 percent of complaints made by POWs against one another were false. In captivity, POWs developed a mental condition he labeled a "fence complex," which caused the prisoner to lose his "sense of right and wrong"; "Accuser Confused in Dickenson Case," *NYT*, April 28, 1954, 15.

124. Eugene Kinkead, "A Reporter at Large: The Study of Something New in History," *New Yorker*, October 26, 1957, 120.

125. There was also considerable slippage in the accounts Dickenson himself offered of his actions in captivity. Shortly after returning from Korea, the corporal claimed that he stayed behind to gather more dirt on the Chinese, eager to avenge their criminal mistreatment of his buddies—exactly the kind of defense that the Pentagon feared MGM's *Prisoner of War* would inspire; "G.I. Says He Stayed to Expose Red Lies," *NYT*, October 26, 1953, 2. But in other interviews he asserted, contradictorily, that he would never have refused repatriation if he had not been menaced by armed progressives and blackmailed by his Chinese captors with a threat to turn over to U.S. military authorities procommunist propaganda material that Dickenson had written in captivity.

126. "Dickenson Linked to POW's Beating," *NYT*, April 24, 1954, 6.

127. "Former Comrades Accuse Corporal," *NYT*, April 21, 1954, 12; "Abuse of Sick G.I. Laid to Dickenson," *NYT*, April 22, 1954, 8; "Dickenson Called Prison Camp 'Spy,'" *NYT*, April 23, 1954, 3.

128. "Accuser Confused," 15.

129. "Abuse of Sick G.I. Laid to Dickenson," *NYT*, April 22, 1954, 8; "Dickenson Waives Right to Testify," *NYT*, April 30, 1954, 10.

130. During the second army court-martial of a former "nonrepat" prisoner, Dr. Leon Freedom similarly testified that the defendant, Claude Batchelor, suffered from "political psychosis," a sort of compartmentalized paranoia that prevented him from distinguishing right from wrong "in the political field"; Hillman, *Defending America*, 50–51.

131. "Ex-POW Called Unstable by Psychiatrist," *CDT*, April 29, 1954, A10; "Army Hears 2 Psychiatrists," *NYT*, April 29, 1954, 21; "Case of Corporal Dickenson," *WP*, May 8, 1954, 12.

132. Elie Abel, "Army Convicts Dickenson of Collaborating with Reds," *NYT*, May 5, 1954, 1.

133. Sokolsky, "US Should Expose POW Turncoats," 30.

134. "21 Pro-Red G.I.'s to Get Dishonorable Discharges," *NYT*, January 26, 1954, 1. Criticism of the court-martial was by no means confined to more liberal elements of the press. A letter from "Confused" to the conservative *Chicago Daily Tribune* deplored the verdict: "It would take thousands of Dickensons to hurt the United States as much as one Lattimore who is still enjoying freedom"; Letter to Editor, May 17, 1954, 20.

135. Rose Helen Dickenson to Eisenhower, February 6, 1954, quoted in Hillman, *Defending America*, 178 n. 35.

136. "Draft Official Resigns," *NYT*, May 7, 1954, 25.

137. Vogeler quoted in *Winkler County News*, October 7, 1954, quoted in Rice, "Lost Sheep," 375. On the Batchelor court-martial, see Rice, "Lost Sheep," 343–85; Hillman, *Defending America*, 50–51; Lech, *Broken Soldiers*, 241–43, 267–68.

138. "Turncoat GI Finishes 3½ Years in Army Prison," *LAT*, November 24, 1957, 19;

"Korea Turncoat Ends Jail Term," *NYT*, November 24, 1957, 21. Three years later Batchelor was charged with negligent homicide after a collision involving his car; "Korea Turncoat Held," *NYT*, November 9, 1960, 42.

139. According to Biderman, the army investigated 11 percent of its repatriated prisoners, the air force 39 percent, and the marines 26 percent; *March to Calumny*, 30.

140. Many airmen testified that their superiors had briefed them to talk under interrogation rather than suffer prolonged torture—a point that emerged during the Schwable hearing; "Honored POW Signed Reds' Peace Appeal," *WP*, February 25, 1954, 1.

141. When Schwable, a much-decorated officer of "24 years' outstanding service," went to see Marine Commandant Lemuel Shepherd, he "never got past the front door," *Time* related; "Go Slow," November 16, 1953, 24; Lloyd Norman, "Drop Germ War Case against Col. Schwable," *CDT*, April 28, 1954, 7; "The Dreadful Dilemma," *Time*, March 22, 1954, 30.

142. Telephone Conversation with Gen. Smith, October 1, 1953, J. F. Dulles Papers, Telephone Calls Series, Box 1, Telephone Memoranda (July–Oct. 1953), DDEL.

143. "Gallagher Gets a Life Sentence," *NYT*, August 20, 1955, 1.

144. According to Kinkead, "roughly one in three" American prisoners was "guilty of some sort of collaboration," and one in seven of more serious forms; "Something New in History," 102, 108.

145. Biderman, *March to Calumny*, 115.

146. Edgar H. Schein, "Epilogue: Something New in History?" *Journal of Social Issues* 13, no. 3 (1957): 59.

147. Gerald Pratley, *The Films of John Frankenheimer: Forty Years in Film* (Bethlehem, PA: Lehigh University Press, 1998), 40. Several prisoners had, in fact, tried to escape, but conditions in North Korea hardly promoted successful bids to return behind U.S. lines; *March to Calumny*, 84–90. Facing protests on this point, Kinkead changed his original assertion in the *New Yorker* (that "not one of our men escaped from a prison camp") to the slightly different proposition that no prisoner had *successfully* returned to U.S. lines; Eugene Kinkead, *In Every War but One* (New York: W. W. Norton, 1959), 16–17.

148. The *Times* devoted two entire pages to reproducing the report, *P.O.W.: The Fight Continues after Battle* in full; "Text of Report to Defense Secretary by Advisory Committee on Prisoners of War," *NYT*, August 18, 1955, 10–11.

149. Executive Order 10631, "Code of Conduct for Members of the Armed Forces of the United States," Issued by Dwight D. Eisenhower, August 17, 1955, is reproduced as Appendix B of Biderman, *March to Calumny*, 278–79.

150. The description of brainwashing is from Hunter, *Brainwashing*, 4. Throughout the 1950s, the military continued to fund research on communist interrogation and "mind control" techniques; Christopher Simpson, *Science of Coercion: Communication Research and Psychological Warfare, 1945–1960* (New York: Oxford University Press, 1994). More publicly, House and Senate hearings were held on these questions during the later 1950s.

151. Those who missed this charismatic performer in person might have read or heard one of the six hundred thousand copies of his address available in print and on tape; John Greenway, "The Colonel's Korean 'Turncoats,'" *Nation*, November 10, 1962, 302–5; H. H. Wubben, "American Prisoners of War in Korea: A Second Look at the 'Something New in History' Theme," *American Quarterly* 22, no. 1 (1970): 6–7. See also a lengthy interview with

Col. William Erwin Mayer, "Why Did Many GI Captives Cave In?" *US News and World Report*, February 24, 1956, 56–72.

152. Daniel Boorstin, *The Image or What Happened to the American Dream* (Harmondsworth: Pelican Books, 1963), 10.

153. Biderman, *March to Calumny*, 1.

154. These were the conclusions of an unnamed psychiatrist who had worked with the earliest returning POWs; "More about Brainwashing," *WP*, July 3, 1953, 10.

155. Arthur M. Schlesinger Jr., *The Vital Center: The Politics of Freedom* (Boston: Houghton Mifflin, 1949), 1; Betty Friedan, *The Feminine Mystique* (New York: W. W. Norton, 1963), 285–86. Friedan's footnote citing Kinkead remarked "an attempt in recent years to discredit or soft-pedal" his findings, summoning Mayer as the superior authority best placed to shore them up; 393–94 n. 6.

156. "What's Wrong with American Youths?" *US News and World Report*, March 19, 1954, 35. See also Friedan, *Feminine Mystique*, 247.

157. Hunter, *Brainwashing*, 11; Daniel Horowitz, *The Anxieties of Affluence: Critiques of Consumer Culture, 1939–1979* (Amherst: University of Massachusetts Press, 2004).

158. Meerloo, *Rape of the Mind*, 278.

159. Benjamin Spock, "Are We Bringing Up Our Children Too Soft for the Stern Realities They Must Face?" *Ladies' Home Journal* 77 (1960): 20.

160. Mayer, "Why Did So Many GIs Cave In?" 60–61; Philip Wylie, *Generation of Vipers* (New York: Farrar and Rinehart, 1942).

161. Friedan, *Feminine Mystique*, 249.

162. Marya Mannes, "Channels: Two American Women," *Reporter*, November 24, 1953, 41.

163. "Analyze 'Mind Washing," *Science News Letter*, May 16, 1953, 310–11.

164. On *the Rack* (dir. Arnold Laven, MGM, 1956), see Carruthers, "Redeeming the Captives"; on shifts in postwar ideologies of fatherhood, see Robert Griswold, *Fatherhood in America* (New York: Basic Books, 1993), 185–218.

165. "Air Force Trained to Bear Red Jails," *NYT*, September 26, 1954, 25.

166. Darrell Garwood, "Press Invited to Criticized *[sic]* AF Course," *WP*, September 10, 1955, 2; Devers quoted in "The 'School for Survival' . . . Headlines, 'Explanations,' and the Facts," *Newsweek*, September 19, 1955, 38.

167. Garwood, "Press Invited," 2; Devers and Ridgway quoted in " 'School for Survival,'" 38. *Newsweek*'s original story, written from a position of detached neutrality, appeared in an issue the week before, prompting a flurry of explanatory comments from the military; Peter Wyden, "Ordeal in the Desert: Making Tougher Soldiers to Resist Brainwashing," *Newsweek*, September 12, 1055, 33–35.

168. "Bare Cruelty Courses for US Military," *CDT*, September 8, 1955, 1; "AF Disclaims 'Torture' but Backs School," *WP*, September 9, 1955, 1.

169. "Education for Heroism?" *WP*, September 10, 1955, 18; "AF Course in 'Torture' May Soften," *WP*, September 14, 1955, 1. "N. C.," writing the *Saturday Review*'s editorial, was similarly concerned about the consequences of such training for the *trainers*: "A man who is taught to grind another man's face in the dirt with his heel has received a lesson in sadism, pure and simple"; "Schools for Sadists," *Saturday Review*, September 24, 1955, 22.

170. "US Orders Review of 'Torture School,'" *NYT*, September 17, 1955, 9.

171. "*P.O.W.: The Fight Continues*," *NYT*, August 18, 1955, 8.

172. This point was stressed by the first three nonrepatriates to return to the United States from China in September 1955. "The soldiers have to learn what Communism really is," urged Lewis Griggs; "School against Torture Childish, Turncoats Say," *LAT*, September 16, 1955, 6.

173. Greenway, "Colonel's Korean 'Turncoats,'" 303. An editorial in *Commonweal* pointed out, to those who "worry about the seduction of youth in American colleges," that only two of the "nonrepats" had any college education; "Twenty-two," *Commonweal*, 320.

174. Virginia Pasley, *21 Stayed: The Story of the American GI's Who Chose Communist China: Who They Were and Why They Stayed* (New York: Farrar, Straus and Cudahy, 1955), 220.

175. Stephanson draws attention to this passage of NSC 68, a rebuke to liberals and relativists who "wishfully [wait] for evidence that evil design may become noble purpose"; Anders Stephanson, "Liberty or Death: The Cold War as US Ideology," in *Reviewing the Cold War: Approaches, Interpretations, Theory*, ed. Odd Arne Westad (London: Frank Cass, 2000), 86.

176. "A Line Must Be Drawn," *Time*, August 29, 1955, 16.

177. AmVets Auxiliary presents "Code of an American Mother," August 1956, White House Office, Special Assistant, Subject Subseries, Box 2, DDEL.

178. Kenneth Dole, "Religious Faith Urged as Military Code Help," *WP*, August 22, 1955, 7.

179. Virginia Pasley, "21 American GI's," 40–44, 116–27; Harold Lavine, "Twenty-one GI's Who Chose Tyranny," *Commentary*, 18, no. 1 (July 1954) 41–46.

180. "One Who Won't Return," *Time*, October 26, 1953, 27; Pasley, "21 American GI's," 126–27.

181. This was LaRance Sullivan, one of the three African American nonrepatriates, whose mother was murdered in Santa Barbara during his captivity; Pasley, "21 American GI's," 117.

182. Greenway, "Colonel's Korean 'Turncoats,'" 304; Robin, *Making of the Cold War Enemy*, 166.

183. Alonzo M. Mercer, MD, "Daily Brainwashing," *Chicago Defender*, October 24, 1953, 11; "National Grapevine," *Chicago Defender*, May 1, 1954, 2.

184. Kenneth Hansen, *Heroes behind Barbed Wire* (Princeton: D. Van Nostrand, 1957), x.

185. Robin, *Making of the Cold War Enemy*, 145.

186. Bernstein, "Struggle," 285.

187. Thimayya, *Experiment in Neutrality*, 105–6.

188. Callum MacDonald, *Korea: The War before Vietnam* (New York: Free Press, 1986), 250.

189. Foot, *Substitute for Victory*, 199.

190. MacDonald, *Korea*, 252.

191. Foot, *Substitute for Victory*, 197–98.

192. Not only did communist forces in Vietnam fail to surrender en masse, but Washington reverted back to its pre–Korean War position on prisoner repatriation. Thus Henry Kissinger demanded at the end of the war that both sides promptly "return all captured per-

sons" with no delays "for any reason"; quoted in Robert L. Breisner, *Dean Acheson, a Life in the Cold War* (New York: Oxford University Press, 2006), 438.

EPILOGUE

1. Jacques Locquin, "A Turncoat Glories in the Trade He Made," *WP*, August 7, 1955, E1, 5.

2. One of the group died in China; two others, Harold Webb and John Dunn, departed with their wives for Poland and Czechoslovakia, respectively. In the 1990s, Howard Adams and James Veneris continued to live in the People's Republic; Adam J. Zweiback, "The 21 'Turncoat GIs': Nonrepatriations and the Political Culture of the Korean War," *Historian* 60 (Winter 1998): 360.

3. Survey by Gallup Organization, July 14–July 19, 1955, retrieved April 30, 2008, from the iPoll databank, The Roper Center for Public Opinion Research, University of Connecticut. www.ropercenter.uconn.edu/ipoll.html.

4. "The Return of the Turncoats," *CDT*, July 13, 1955, 20. See also a long feature, "Turncoat GI's Tell Story of Red China," *US News and World Report*, July 22, 1955, 20–22, 24, 26, 113–15.

5. The *Washington Post* first used this term in December 1955, reporting Richard Tenneson's change of heart; "Turncoat GI Changes Mind, to Quit China," December 1, 1955, 7. The same Gallup poll cited above (in note 3) found that 37 percent of respondents thought the returnees should be allowed to go free and be "given a second chance," 20 percent thought they should receive a fair trial before being convicted, 25 percent thought they should be punished in some manner, and 11 percent had no opinion on the matter.

6. "Turncoats Facing New Army Charge," *NYT*, July 27, 1955, 8; "Army Arrests 3 American Turncoats after They Greet Relatives in Tears," *WP*, July 30, 1955, 1.

7. "Eisenhower Gets Turncoats' Plea," *NYT*, September 16, 1955, 15.

8. "Three Ex-GI Turncoats Land in San Francisco and Are Jailed by Army," *NYT*, July 30, 1955, 1, 10.

9. "Court Rules Army Can't Try Ex-GI's," *LAT*, November 8, 1955, 7; "Judge Orders Army to Free Turncoat Trio," *CDT*, November 9, 1955, 7.

10. "Turncoats Sue for Pay While Red Prisoners," *LAT*, January 9, 1957, 13.

11. "Peiping Releases 4th US Turncoat," *NYT*, December 13, 1955, 4. In a lengthier report, the *Times* related that Tenneson's remarks at a press conference in Hong Kong "stamped him as a well-indoctrinated victim of the Communist propaganda machine," but his blunt comment that he would "rather face a firing squad than remain in Communist China" hardly suggested one who'd been successfully "brainwashed"; "Turncoat Silent about His Return," *NYT*, December 14, 1955, 24.

12. Wendell Merick, "Two Homesick GI Turncoats Reach Hongkong, Still Searching for Peace," *WP*, December 3, 1956, A3.

13. "Turncoat Sails for US, Blames Homesickness," *LAT*, June 16, 1957, 13; "8th US Turncoat Back from China, Homesick," *WP*, June 16, 1957, A6.

14. "Bitterest US Turncoat Quits China for Home," *LAT*, March 30, 1958, 15; "Turncoat, in Hong Kong, Praises 'Peaceful China,'" *WP*, March 31, 1958, A3.

15. Roy Essoyan, "Returning Turncoat Praises Reds," *WP*, December 20, 1958, A6; "10th 'Turncoat' Home," *NYT*, January 20, 1959, 38.

16. "Ex-GI Voices Disillusion as He Leaves China," *NYT*, August 3, 1963, 2.

17. In time, Adams and his wife would open a string of successful Chinese restaurants in Memphis; Clarence Adams, *An American Dream: The Life of an African American Soldier and POW Who Spent Twelve Years in Communist China* (Amherst: University of Massachusetts Press, 2007).

18. Of mainstream media, *US News and World Report* exhibited the most sustained interest in the story of the "returncoats"; see, for example, a long article, "Story of the GI Turncoats: They Chose Red China and Then—," June 28, 1957, 58–64, 67–74. On return in 1963, Skinner was the subject of a two-hour television inquiry into the "tormented mind" of the voluntary nonrepatriate that also featured Allen Dulles and Albert Biderman; *VNR: The True Story of Lowell Skinner*, produced by WNEW-TV, was aired on August 19, 1963. Three months later, the *NYT* reported Skinner's arrest and subsequent confinement in a "mental institution" after shooting two teenage boys in the apartment of a "convict's wife" while intoxicated. His subsequent breakout was foiled after one day as an escapee; "Ex-Soldier in Korea Held," November 20, 1963, 88; "Onetime Turncoat in Mental Hospital," February 24, 1965, 6; "Turncoat Recaptured," May 20, 1965, 16. Further information about the lives of the returnees can also be found in the memoir of one returnee, Morris R. Wills, *Turncoat: An American's 12 Years in Communist China* (Englewood Cliffs, NJ: Prentice-Hall, 1968), and in a documentary film by Chinese director, Shuibo Wang, about their experiences entitled *They Chose China* (distributed by First Run Icarus Films, 2006).

19. "Mrs. Kasenkina Busy on Novel of Stalin," *NYT*, August 12, 1950, 8; "Faith in US Voiced by Mrs. Kasenkina," *NYT*, August 12, 1953, 14; "People," *Time*, September 2, 1957, 28; "Died," *Time*, August 8, 1960, 82; "Mrs. Oksana Kasenkina Dies; Fled from Russians Here in '48," *NYT*, July 27, 1960, 29.

20. It seems that Michael Garcia had merely knocked on Kravchenko's door in error, triggering an altercation that ended in his shooting; "Assailant Is Shot by Author Reported to Be Kravchenko," *NYT*, October 21, 1956, 1.

21. "Kravchenko Dispels Mystery in Shooting," *NYT*, October 22, 1956, 1; "Kravchenko Kills Himself Here; He Chose Freedom from Soviet," *NYT*, February 26, 1966, 1; "Autopsy Confirms Death of Kravchenko as Suicide," *NYT*, February 27, 1966, 10.

22. "Red Pilot Loses Plea for US Citizenship," *WP*, November 3, 1955, 10.

23. "Flier Who Fled Reds Still Doing It Himself," *WP*, June 17, 1956, A3; "In America, Home-Building Russian Finds Banker Is Comrade and Red Tape Isn't Red," *WP*, November 10, 1956, A1.

24. This characterization of U.S. citizenship was offered by Judge Bryan (who had denied Pirogov's appeal three years earlier) as he presided over the naturalization ceremony; "Air Hero Who Fled Russia Takes Oath as Citizen Here," *WP*, December 11, 1958, B1. Pirogov died on February 27, 1987, a brief obituary notice appearing in the *WP*, February 28, 1987, B6.

25. Pirogov's letter, published in Walter Winchell's *Washington Post* column on June 16, 1950, was read into the *Congressional Record* by George A. Dondero on June 20, 1950;

Congressional Record, Appendix 1950, A4811, Julius Epstein Papers, Box 51, Folder, Pirogov, Peter, Hoover Institution Archives, Stanford University.

26. Kurt Vonnegut, *Slaughterhouse-Five* (London: Triad Grafton, 1979), 13.

27. "A National Strategy for the Soviet Union," address by Rear Adml. L. C. Stevens, U.S. Navy, to the Naval War College, January 25, 1951, SMOF: PSB, 091.411 Drafts of National Psychological Strategy, Box 14, folder 091.411 Drafts of National Psychological Strategy, Papers #1, HSTL. Similarly, Walter Bedell Smith cautioned American readers in 1953 that Russians were "different because wholly different social and political conditions have retarded and perverted their development and set them apart from other civilizations"; introduction to Astolphe de Custine, *Journey for Our Time: The Journals of the Marquis de Custine,* ed. and trans. Phyllis Penn Kohler (London: Arthur Baker, 1953), 13. Not everyone agreed with these propositions, of course. Ardent liberationists often stressed just the opposite, invoking the captive peoples' unquenchable desire for freedom. Dulles, for example, wrote that humans had always rebelled against the kinds of methods used by the Soviets, "and there is no reason to think that human nature has changed even in Russia"; John Foster Dulles, *War or Peace* (New York: Macmillan, 1950), 243.

28. Richard Hofstadter, "The Paranoid Style," in *The Paranoid Style in American Politics, and Other Essays* (New York: Knopf, 1965).

29. Randall Bennett Woods, *Fulbright: A Biography* (Cambridge: Cambridge University Press, 1995), 187.

30. Richard Pells, *Not Like Us: How Europeans Have Loved, Hated, and Transformed American Culture since World War II* (New York: Basic Books, 1997), 80–82.

31. Kenneth Osgood, *Total Cold War: Eisenhower's Secret Propaganda Battle at Home and Abroad* (Lawrence: University Press of Kansas, 2008), chs. 5 and 6; Gunter Bischof, *Cold War Respite: The Geneva Summit of 1955* (Baton Rouge: Louisiana State University Press, 2000).

32. Norman Moss, "Tourism Is Piercing the Iron Curtain," *NYT,* September 11, 1955, X29.

33. Harry Schwartz, "Touring Russia," *NYT,* November 13, 1955, X25.

34. Jack Raymond, "Floridians Flee Moscow's Cold, but Laud Treatment as Tourists," *NYT,* February 27, 1956, 3; David Bird, "The UN Counts Travelers," *NYT,* April 27, 1958, XX21.

35. Harrison E. Salisbury, "Americans Flock to East Europe," *NYT,* July 28, 1957, 1.

36. Frederick C. Barghoorn, "The Partial Reopening of Russia," *American Slavic and East European Review* 16, no. 2 (1957): 146–59; Elie Abel, "US Twits Soviet on Its Own Fingerprinting Rules," *NYT,* June 2, 1956, 1.

37. Barghoorn, "Partial Reopening," 146.

38. Leo Cherne, "Is the 'New Russia' a New Myth?" *NYT Magazine,* June 17, 1956, 54.

39. A Radio Free Europe survey conducted in 1957 among Hungarian refugees bound for the United States found that half of them had expected U.S. support: László Borhi, "Rollback, Liberation, Containment, or Inaction?" *Journal of Cold War Studies* 1, no. 3 (1999): 82. An internal report conducted by Radio Free Europe showed that program guidelines *had* been overstepped—that broadcasts were "crude and unimaginative," their tone "overexcited"; "Policy Review of Voice for Free Hungary Programming, October 23–November

23, 1956," in *The 1956 Hungarian Revolution: A History in Documents*, A National Security Archive Electronic Briefing Book, ed. Malcolm Byrne (2002), www.gwu.edu/~nsarchiv/NSAEBB/NSAEBB76/doc10.pdf.

40. Richard Ferree Smith, "Refugees," *Annals of the American Academy of Political and Social Science* 367 (1967): 46. The Hungarian refugees' heroic image was further burnished by Eisenhower's personal representative for refugee matters, Tracy Voorhees, who hired a public relations firm to amplify strongly supportive signals emitted from Capitol Hill; Gil Loescher and John A. Scanlan, *Calculated Kindness: Refugees and America's Half-Open Door, 1945 to the Present* (New York: Free Press, 1986), 49–60.

41. Aaron Levenstein, *Escape to Freedom: The Story of the International Rescue Committee* (Westport, CT: Greenwood Press, 1983), 36, 55; Loescher and Scanlan, *Calculated Kindness*, 54.

42. Michael R. Marrus, *The Unwanted: European Refugees in the Twentieth Century* (New York: Oxford University Press, 1985), 360–61.

43. "Stalled—and Unwanted," *Life*, November 25, 1957, 135–40.

44. "Vogelers Say They Cannot Find Work," *NYT*, June 30, 1957, 45.

45. Anders Stephanson, *Manifest Destiny: American Expansionism and the Empire of Right* (New York: Hill and Wang, 1995), 99.

46. Elliot Gruner, *Prisoners of Culture: Representing the Vietnam POW* (New Brunswick: Rutgers University Press, 1993), 194. On the notion of "captivity panics" in the context of British imperial history, see Linda Colley, *Captives: Britain, Empire and the World, 1600–1850* (London: Jonathan Cape, 2002).

47. Hanson W. Baldwin, "Captives Are Red Pawns," *NYT*, December 21, 1951, 4.

48. Steven Casey, "Selling NSC-68: The Truman Administration, Public Opinion, and the Politics of Mobilization, 1950–51," *Diplomatic History* 29 (2005): 662.

49. Nelson Poynter of the Office of War Information came up with this phrase in 1942. See Thomas Doherty, *Projections of War: Hollywood, American Culture, and World War II* (New York: Columbia University Press, 1993), 122. The very concept of "cold war" was explicitly conceived as a mobilizing device, though one that some cold war strategists by 1950 had come to believe was counterproductive. A draft NSC paper from May 1950 noted that the "cold war is over. . . . The 'Cold War' was a useful concept to arouse our people in 1947, but it has cost America heavily in moral capital. . . . By a kind of psychological jiu-jitsu, the Soviets have made themselves the 'partisans of peace' and have cast us in the role of 'warmongers' and 'atomic gangsters'"; "Regaining the Psychological Initiative," Draft #2, May 25, 1950, PPS, Working Papers, 1947–53, Box 54, RG 59, NACP.

50. "The Nation: Fighter in a Fighting Year," *Time*, January 3, 1949, 9–10; George Kennan, quoted in Frank Costigliola, "'Unceasing Pressure for Penetration': Gender, Pathology and Emotion in George Kennan's Formation of the Cold War," *Journal of American History* 83, no. 4 (1997):1309–39. Contemplating the best way of exploiting what it called the "Korean atrocity issue," the PSB agreed that it wished to "educate" the public about communist atrocities—but did not want to "inflame and arouse" the U.S. public. A consistent theme of PSB discussions, these concerns grew stronger after the Big Switch, when at least one State Department official feared creating a "Frankenstein that would be hard to handle" if the army continued to press the "domestic publicity campaign on atrocities"; Robinson

McIlvaine (Assistant to the Assistant Secretary for Public Affairs) to Charles Norberg, PSB, memo, September 11, 1953, PSB 383.6, Box 26, folder 5, DDEL. Acheson's caution on the need for discipline is quoted in Casey, "Selling NSC-68," 665.

51. Joost Meerloo, *The Rape of the Mind: The Psychology of Thought Control, Menticide, and Brainwashing* (Cleveland: World Publishing, 1956); Morris L. Ernst and David Loth, *Report on the American Communist* (New York: Holt, 1952), 162–65.

52. Arthur M. Schlesinger Jr., *The Vital Center: The Politics of Freedom* (Boston: Houghton Mifflin, 1949), 151; "Colonel Fleming's Guilt," *WP*, September 26, 1954, B4; Chalmers M. Roberts, "The GIs Who Went Red," *WP*, December 29, 1953, 11.

53. "The Line on 'the Curtain,'" *Newsweek*, May 24, 1948, 8–9; K. A. Cuordileone, *Manhood and American Political Culture in the Cold War* (New York: Routledge, 2005), 82.

54. For example, opinion surveys conducted in October 1949, after the conclusion of the Smith Act trial, which found eleven leaders of the Communist Party USA guilty of "conspiracy to teach and advocate violent overthrow of the government," found 9 percent of college students in favor of "executing" and 43 percent in favor of "deporting" the convicted leaders. Among Catholic students, sampled separately, these figures rose to 22 percent and 47 percent; Maurice L. Farber, "The Communist Trial: College Student Opinion and Democratic Institutions," *Public Opinion Quarterly* 14, no. 1 (1950): 89–92.

55. Robert C. Myers, "Anti-Communist Mob Action: A Case Study," *Public Opinion Quarterly* 12, no. 1 (1948): 57–67.

56. "Apathy and Atrocity," *Newsweek*, August 17, 1953, 21–22; Stephen J. Whitfield, *The Culture of the Cold War* (Baltimore: Johns Hopkins University Press, 1996), 231.

57. "President Proclaims Captive Nations Week," *NYT*, July 18, 1959, 2.

58. These two nonexistent nations were "something called 'Cossackia' and something else called 'Udel-Ural'"; George Kennan, *Memoirs, 1950–1963* (London: Hutchinson, 1973), 99.

59. "Mr Krushchev's Captives," *NYT*, July 28, 1959, 26.

60. "Stir on Captives Laid to Kremlin," *NYT*, July 26, 1959, 5.

61. The Korean War MIA issue was raised most prominently by *US News and World Report* but generated little extensive discussion in 1953–54; "America's 'Vanished' Thousands," February 5, 1954, 34–39; "Americans the Reds Still Hold," June 19, 1955, 36.

62. Cronkite's comment prefaced the sixth episode in CBS's *The Twentieth Century* series, *Brainwashing*, first aired on November 24, 1957; viewing copy held in the Library of Congress, Motion Picture Division; Vance Packard, *The Hidden Persuaders* (New York: David McKay, 1957).

63. *The Fearmakers* (dir. Jacques Tourneur, United Artists, 1958); *The Manchurian Candidate* (dir. John Frankenheimer, United Artists, 1962).

64. Gerald Pratley, *The Films of John Frankenheimer: Forty Years in Film* (Bethlehem, PA: Lehigh University Press, 1998), 40; Packard, *Hidden Persuaders*, 12.

65. J. A. C. Brown, *Techniques of Persuasion: From Propaganda to Brainwashing* (Harmondsworth: Penguin, 1963), 269.

66. According to *Life*, it was the "age of psychology and psychoanalysis as much as it [was] the age of chemistry or the atom bomb"; quoted in Robert Genter, "'Hypnotizzy' in the Cold War: The American Fascination with Hypnotism in the 1950s," *Journal of American Culture* 29, no. 2 (2006): 158.

67. Ibid.; "The Mind: Science's Search for a Guide to Sanity," *Newsweek,* October 24, 1955, 59.

68. A front-page article in the *New York Times* in July 2008 revealed that a 1957 article by Albert Biderman on Chinese communist methods to elicit false confessions has been used in training military interrogators for the "war on terror"; "China Inspired Interrogations at Guantánamo," *NYT,* July 2, 2008, 1, 17; Tim Weiner, "Remembering Brainwashing," *NYT,* July 6, 2008, WK1, 4.

69. "A Study of Brainwashing," *NYT,* August 24, 1954, 20.

70. John Marks, *The Search for the "Manchurian Candidate"* (New York: Norton, 1991). This no longer "secret" history has been thoroughly worked over in the aftermath of the Abu Ghraib story breaking in April 2004, leading to a rediscovery of the alarm occasioned by the confessions of Mindszenty and Vogeler; Michael Otterman, *American Torture: From the Cold War to Abu Ghraib and Beyond* (London: Pluto Press, 2007), 14–27; Gary Younge, "Occupations Abroad Always Lead to the Erosion of Liberties at Home," *Guardian,* June 23, 2008, www.commondreams.org/archive/2008/06/23/9828 on June 24, 2008.

71. Hoover quoted in Alfred W. McCoy, *A Question of Torture: CIA Interrogation, from the Cold War to the War on Terror* (New York: Owl Books, 2006), 25.

72. Ibid., 7.

73. Ibid., 29.

74. "Education for Heroism," *WP,* September 10, 1955, 18.

75. Amnesty International, *Report 2005,* foreword by Irene Khan, Secretary General, www.amnesty.org/en/library/asset/POL10/005/2005/en/dom-POL100052005en.html.

76. Steven Lee Myers, "Above the Arctic Circle, a Gulag Nightmare for Tourists?" *NYT,* June 6, 2005, A4.

77. "The Cold War and Its Spies," *NYT,* April 27, 2008, TR2; Phil Patton, "Visiting the Cold War Today," *American Heritage,* September 2000, 71; Yuri Zarakhovich, "Gulag Fun Park," *Time* (European ed.), May 20, 2002, 75.

78. Osgood, *Total Cold War,* 1.

BIBLIOGRAPHY

PRIMARY SOURCES
Archives and Manuscript Collections
NATIONAL ARCHIVES, COLLEGE PARK, MARYLAND

RG 59 General Records of the Department of State
    Records of the Policy Planning Staff
RG 84 Records of the Foreign Service Posts of the Department of State
    Records of the U.S. Mission to the United Nations and Its Predecessors, 1945–66
RG 200 UN Universal Newsreel Catalog

DWIGHT D. EISENHOWER PRESIDENTIAL LIBRARY, ABILENE, KANSAS

Dwight D. Eisenhower Papers (Ann Whitman File)
    Cabinet Series
    Diary Series
    NSC Series
John Foster Dulles, Telephone Conversations Series
John Foster Dulles, White House Memo Series
C. D. Jackson Papers, 1931–67
C. D. Jackson Records, 1953–54
White House Office; NSC Staff: Papers, 1948–61
    Psychological Strategy Board, Central Files
White House Office; Office of Special Assistant for National Security Affairs
    Policy Paper Subseries
    Subject Subseries

HARRY S. TRUMAN LIBRARY, INDEPENDENCE, MISSOURI

Dean G. Acheson Papers
    Assistant Secretary and Under Secretary of State File, 1941–49
    Secretary of State File, 1945–72
American Institute of Public Opinion Papers
Mark W. Clark Papers
Clark M. Clifford Oral History
Nathaniel P. Davis Papers
Gordon Gray Papers
Charles M. Hulten Papers
Howland Sargeant Papers
Charles W. Thayer Papers
Harry S. Truman Papers
    General File
    President's Personal File
    Staff Member and Office Files: Psychological Strategy Board Files

ARTHUR AND ELIZABETH SCHLESINGER LIBRARY ON THE HISTORY
OF WOMEN IN AMERICA, RADCLIFFE INSTITUTE FOR ADVANCED STUDY,
HARVARD UNIVERSITY

Edith Spurlock Sampson Papers

LAUINGER LIBRARY, GEORGETOWN UNIVERSITY,
WASHINGTON, D.C.

Robert J. Lamphere Papers

HERBERT H. LEHMAN COLLECTIONS, BUTLER LIBRARY,
COLUMBIA UNIVERSITY

Herbert H. Lehman Papers
William B. Welsh Papers

HOOVER INSTITUTION ARCHIVES, STANFORD UNIVERSITY

Eckhardt, Tibor, Papers
Emmet, Christopher T., Jr., Papers
Epstein, Julius, Papers
International Rescue Committee Records
Kertesz, Stephen D., Papers
Kohlberg, Alfred, Papers
Nicolaevsky, Boris I., Collection
Register of the National Republic Records
Tanenhaus, Sam, Papers
Volkov, Boris N., Papers
Wolfe, Bertram D., Papers

SEELEY G. MUDD MANUSCRIPT COLLECTION, PRINCETON UNIVERSITY

American Civil Liberties Union Records, 1947–1995
John Foster Dulles, Papers, 1860–1988

NATIONAL ARCHIVES OF THE UNITED KINGDOM, KEW, SURREY, UK

FO 371   Foreign Office: Political Departments: General Correspondence, 1906–1966
FO 1110   Foreign Office: Records of the Information Research Department: General Correspondence, 1948–67

Commentary/Analysis

Arendt, Hannah. *The Origins of Totalitarianism*. 1951. Reprint, New York: Harcourt, Brace, 1973.

Barghoorn, Frederick C. "The Partial Reopening of Russia." *American Slavic and East European Review* 16, no. 2 (1957): 146–59.

Barnett, Frank R. "America's Strategic Weakness—Redefection." *Russian Review* 15, no. 1 (1956): 29–36.

Bauer, Raymond A. "Brainwashing: Psychology or Demonology?" *Journal of Social Issues* 13 (1957): 41–47.

Bettelheim, Bruno. "Individual and Mass Behavior in Extreme Situations." *Journal of Abnormal and Social Psychology* 38 (1943): 417–52.

Biderman, Albert. "Captivity Lore and Behavior in Captivity." In *The Threat of Impending Disaster,* edited by G. H. Grosser, H. Wechsler, and M. Greenblatt, 223–50. Cambridge, MA: MIT Press, 1964.

———. "Communist Attempts to Elicit False Confessions from Air Force Prisoners of War." *Bulletin of the New York Academy of Medicine* 33, no. 9 (1957): 616–25.

———. "The Image of 'Brainwashing.'" *Public Opinion Quarterly* 26, no. 4 (1962): 547–63.

———. *March to Calumny: The Story of American POW's in the Korean War*. New York: Macmillan, 1963.

Boorstin, Daniel. *The Image or What Happened to the American Dream*. Harmondsworth: Pelican Books, 1963.

Dallin, Alexander, and Ralph S. Mavrogordato. "The Soviet Reaction to Vlasov." *World Politics* 8, no. 3 (1956): 307–22.

Dallin, David J. *The Real Soviet Russia*. New Haven: Yale University Press, 1947.

Dallin, David J., and Boris I. Nicolaevsky. *Forced Labor in Soviet Russia*. New Haven: Yale University Press, 1947.

Elkins, Stanley. *Slavery: A Problem in American Institutional and Intellectual Life*. Chicago: University of Chicago Press, 1959.

Ernst, Morris L., and David Loth. *Report on the American Communist*. New York: Holt, 1952.

Farber, Maurice L. "The Communist Trial: College Student Opinion and Democratic Institutions." *Public Opinion Quarterly* 14, no. 1 (1950): 89–92.

Fischer, George. *Soviet Opposition to Stalin: A Case Study in World War II*. Cambridge, MA: Harvard University Press, 1952.

———. "Vlasov and Hitler." *Journal of Modern History* 23, no. 1 (1951): 58–71.

Friedan, Betty. *The Feminine Mystique*. New York: W. W. Norton, 1963.

Friedrich, Carl J., ed. *Totalitarianism: Proceedings of a Conference Held at the American Academy of Arts and Sciences, March 1953*. Cambridge, MA: Harvard University Press, 1954.

Fromm, Eric. *Escape from Freedom*. New York: Rinehart, 1941.

Ginsburgs, George. "The Soviet Union and the Problem of Refugees and Displaced Persons, 1917–1956." *American Journal of International Law* 51, no. 2 (1957): 325–61.

Hansen, Kenneth. *Heroes behind Barbed Wire*. Princeton: D. Van Nostrand, 1957.

Hofstadter, Richard. *The Paranoid Style in American Politics, and Other Essays*. New York: Knopf, 1965.

Holt, Robert T. *Radio Free Europe*. Minneapolis: University of Minnesota Press, 1958.

Hunter, Edward. *Brainwashing: From Pavlov to Powers*. New York: Bookmailer, 1956.

Jacobson, Harold Karan. "Labor, the UN and the Cold War." *International Organization* 11, no. 1 (1957): 55–67.

Jasny, Naum. "Labor and Output in Soviet Concentration Camps." *Journal of Political Economy* 59, no. 5 (1951): 405–19.

Kinkead, Eugene. *In Every War but One*. New York: W. W. Norton, 1959.

Kirchheimer, Otto. "Asylum." *American Political Science Review* 53, no. 4 (1959): 985–1016.

Kracauer, Siegfried. "National Types as Hollywood Presents Them." *Public Opinion Quarterly* 13 (1949): 66–70.

Lifton, Robert J. "Home by Ship: Reaction Patterns of American Prisoners of War Repatriated from North Korea." *American Journal of Psychiatry* 10 (1954): 732–39.

Liss, Emilia. "A Slave Laborer in Soviet Siberia." *Commentary* 2 (1951): 222–31.

Mattick, Paul. "Obsessions of Berlin." *Partisan Review* 15 (1948): 1108–24.

Mayda, Jaro. "The Korean Repatriation Problem and International Law." *American Journal of International Law* 47, no. 3 (1953): 414–38.

Meerloo, Joost. *The Rape of the Mind: The Psychology of Thought Control, Menticide, and Brainwashing*. Cleveland: World Publishing, 1956.

Miller, James G. "Brainwashing: Present and Future." *Journal of Social Issues* 13, no. 3 (1957): 48–55.

Myers, Robert C. "Anti-Communist Mob Action: A Case Study." *Public Opinion Quarterly* 12, no. 1 (1948): 57–67.

Packard, Vance. *The Hidden Persuaders*. New York: David McKay, 1957.

Packer, Herbert L. *Ex-Communist Witnesses: Four Studies in Fact-Finding*. Stanford: Stanford University Press, 1962.

Preuss, Lawrence. "Consular Immunities: The Kasenkina Case (US-USSR)." *American Journal of International Law* 43 (1949): 37–56.

Proudfoot, Malcolm. *European Refugees, 1939–52: A Study in Forced Population Movement*. London: Faber and Faber, 1957.

Prugh, George S. "The Code of Conduct for the Armed Forces." *Columbia Law Review* 56, no. 5 (1956): 678–707.

Redding, A. David. "Reliability of Estimates of Unfree Labor in the USSR." *Journal of Political Economy* 60, no. 4 (1952): 337–40.

Rees, Elfan. "The Refugee and the United Nations." *International Conciliation* 492 (June 1953): 295–96.

Riesman, David. *Individualism Reconsidered, and Other Essays.* Glencoe, IL: Free Press of Glencoe, 1954.

———. *The Lonely Crowd: A Study of the Changing American Character.* Garden City, NY: Doubleday, 1953.

Rovere, Richard. *Senator Joe McCarthy.* New York: Harcourt, Brace, 1959.

Schein, Edgar H. "Brainwashing and Totalitarianization in Modern Society." *World Politics* 11(1958–59): 430–41.

———. "Epilogue: Something New in History?" *Journal of Social Issues* 13, no. 3 (1957): 56–60.

———. "Reaction Patterns to Severe, Chronic Stress in American Army Prisoners of War of the Chinese." *Journal of Social Issues* 13, no. 3 (1957): 21–30.

Schlesinger, Arthur M., Jr. *The Vital Center: The Politics of Freedom.* Boston: Houghton Mifflin, 1949.

Segal, Julius. "Correlates of Collaboration and Resistance Behavior among US Army POWs in Korea." *Journal of Social Issues* 13, no. 3 (1957): 31–40.

Sheldon, Richard C., and John Dutkowski. "Are Soviet Satellite Interviews Projectable?" *Public Opinion Quarterly* 16, no. 4 (1952–53): 579–94.

Stoessinger, John. *The Refugee and the World Community.* Minneapolis: University of Minnesota Press, 1956.

Suchman, Edward A., Rose K. Goldsen, and Robin M. Williams. "Attitudes toward the Korean War." *Public Opinion Quarterly* 17, no. 2 (1953): 171–84.

Walsh, Warren B. "What the American People Think of Russia." *Public Opinion Quarterly* 8, no. 4 (1944–45): 513–22.

Warren, George L. "The Escapee Program." *Journal of International Affairs* 7, no. 1 (1953): 82–83.

Wylie, Philip. *Generation of Vipers.* New York: Farrar and Rinehart, 1942.

Young, William R. "GULAG—Slavery, Inc.: The Use of an Illustrated Map in Printed Propaganda." In *A Psychological Warfare Casebook,* edited by William E. Daugherty, 597–602. Baltimore: Operations Research Office / Johns Hopkins University Press, 1958.

Memoirs/Reportage

Acheson, Dean. *Present at the Creation: My Years in the State Department.* New York: Norton, 1969.

Adams, Clarence. *An American Dream: The Life of an African American Soldier and POW Who Spent Twelve Years in Communist China.* Amherst: University of Massachusetts Press, 2007.

American Federation of Labor. *Slave Labor in Russia: The Case Presented by the AFL to the United Nations.* Washington, DC: American Federation of Labor, 1949.

Barmine, Alexandre. *One Who Survived: The Life Story of a Russian under the Soviets.* New York: G. P. Putnam's Sons, 1945.

Bentley, Elizabeth. *Out of Bondage: The Story of Elizabeth Bentley.* New York: Devin Adair, 1951.

Bohlen, Charles. *Witness to History: 1929–69.* New York: W. W. Norton, 1973.

Bone, Edith. *Seven Years Solitary.* London: Hamish Hamilton, 1957.

Brown, Wallace L. *The Endless Hours: My Two and a Half Years as a Prisoner of the Chinese Communists.* New York: W. W. Norton, 1961.

Buber-Neumann, Margarete. *Freheit, du bist wieder mein . . .* Munich: Langen Mueller, 1978.

———. *Under Two Dictators.* New York: Dodd, Mead, 1951.

Bucar, Annabelle. *The Truth about American Diplomats.* Moscow: Literaturnaya Gazeta, 1949.

Byrnes, James F. *Speaking Frankly.* New York: Harper and Brothers, 1947.

Callcott, Mary Stevenson. *Russian Justice.* New York: Macmillan, 1935.

Calomiris, Angela. *Red Masquerade: Undercover for the FBI.* Philadelphia: J. B. Lippincott, 1950.

Chambers, Whittaker. *Witness.* New York: Random House, 1952.

Ciliga, Anton. *The Russian Enigma.* London: G. Routledge and Sons, 1940.

Clark, Mark W. *From the Danube to the Yalu.* New York: Harper, 1954.

Crossman, Richard, ed. *The God That Failed.* New York: Harper, 1950.

The Dark Side of the Moon. New York: Charles Scribner's Sons, 1947.

de Beauvoir, Simone. *La force des choses.* Paris: Éditions Gallimard, 1963.

de Custine, Astolphe. *Journey for Our Time: The Journals of the Marquis de Custine.* Edited and translated by Phyllis Penn Kohler. London: Arthur Baker, 1953.

Desanti, Dominique. *Les Staliniens (1944–1956): Une expérience politique.* Paris: Librairie Arthème Fayard, 1975.

Dulles, John Foster. *War or Peace.* New York: Macmillan, 1950.

Ekart, Antoni. *Vanished without Trace: The Story of Seven Years in Soviet Russia.* London: Max Parrish, 1954.

Fábián, Bela. *Cardinal Mindszenty: The Story of a Modern Martyr.* New York: Charles Scribner's Sons, 1949.

Field, Hermann, and Kate Field. *Trapped in the Cold War: The Ordeal of an American Family.* Stanford: Stanford University Press, 1999.

Fischer, Louis. *Soviet Journey.* New York: Harrison Smith and Robert Haas, 1935.

———. *Thirteen Who Fled.* New York: Harper and Brothers, 1949.

Gide, André. *Return from the USSR.* Translated by Dorothy Bussy. New York: McGraw-Hill, 1964.

Gliksman, Jerzy. *Tell the West: An Account of His Experiences as a Slave Laborer in the Union of Soviet Socialist Republics.* New York: Gresham Press, 1948.

Gouzenko, Igor. *The Iron Curtain.* New York: E. P. Dutton, 1948.

Gunther, John. *Behind the Curtain.* New York: Harper and Brothers, 1949.

Harsch, Joseph C. *The Curtain Isn't Iron.* New York: Doubleday, 1950.

Herling, Gustaw. *A World Apart.* New York: New American Library, 1952.

Hermes, Walter G. *Truce Tent and Fighting Front.* Washington, DC: Office of the Chief of Military History, U.S. Army, 1966.

Kasenkina, Oksana. *Leap to Freedom.* Philadelphia: J. B. Lippincott, 1949.

Kennan, George. *Siberia and the Exile System.* Chicago: University of Chicago Press, 1958.

Kennan, George F. *Memoirs, 1950–1963.* London: Hutchinson, 1973.

Kinne, Derek. *The Wooden Boxes.* London: Frederick Muller, 1955.

Kitchin, George. *Prisoner of the OGPU.* London: Longmans, Green, 1935.

Koestler, Arthur. *The Invisible Writing: An Autobiography.* London: Collins with Hamish Hamilton, 1954.

Kravchenko versus Moscow: The Report of the Famous Paris Case with an Introduction by the Rt. Hon. Sir Travers Humphreys, P.C. London: Wingate, 1950.

Kravchenko, Victor. *I Chose Freedom: The Personal and Political Life of a Soviet Official.* New York: Charles Scribner's Sons, 1946.

———. *I Chose Justice.* New York: Charles Scribner's Sons, 1950.

Krivitsky, Walter. *In Stalin's Secret Service: An Exposé of Russia's Secret Policies by the Former Chief of the Soviet Intelligence in Western Europe.* New York: Harper and Brothers, 1939.

Le procès des camps de concentration soviétiques. Paris: Bulletin d'études et d'informations politiques internationales, 1951.

Le procès Kravchenko contre Les Lettres Françaises. Compte rendu des audiences d'après la sténographie suivi d'un index des noms cites. Paris: La jeune parque, 1949.

Lermolo, Elizabeth. *Face of a Victim.* New York: Harper, 1955.

Lipper, Elinor. *Eleven Years in Soviet Prison Camps.* Chicago: Regnery, 1951.

Littlepage, John D. *In Search of Soviet Gold.* New York: Harcourt, Brace, 1938.

Lyons, Eugene. *Assignment in Utopia.* New York: Harcourt, Brace, 1937.

———. *Our Secret Allies: The Peoples of Russia.* London: Arco Publications, 1954.

Millar, Ward M. *Valley of the Shadow.* New York: David McKay, 1955.

Noble, John H. *I Was a Slave in Russia: An American Tells His Story.* New York: Devin-Adair, 1958.

Nurenberg, Thelma. *This New Red Freedom.* New York: Wadsworth Press, 1932.

Orlov, Alexander. *The Secret History of Stalin's Crimes.* London: Jarrolds, 1954.

Pasley, Virginia. *21 Stayed: The Story of the American GI's Who Chose Communist China: Who They Were and Why They Stayed.* New York: Farrar, Straus and Cudahy, 1955.

Pate, Lloyd W. *Reactionary!* New York: Harper and Brothers, 1955.

Petrov, Vladimir. *My Retreat from Russia.* New Haven: Yale University Press, 1950.

———. *Soviet Gold: My Life as a Slave Laborer in the Siberian Mines.* New York: Farrar, Straus, 1949.

Pirogov, Peter. *Why I Escaped: The Story of Peter Pirogov.* New York: Duell, Sloane and Pearce, 1950.

Prychodko, Nicholas. *One of Fifteen Million.* London: J. M. Dent and Sons, 1952.

R. Vogeler, E. Sanders and Their Accomplices before the Criminal Court. Budapest: Hungarian State Publishing House, 1950.

Red Gaols: A Woman's Experiences in Russian Prisons. London: Burns Oates and Washbourne, 1935.

Serge, Victor. *Russia Twenty Years After.* New York: Pioneer Publishers, 1937.

Sheen, Fulton J. *Life Is Worth Living.* New York: McGraw-Hill, 1953.

Shuster, George N. *In Silence I Speak: The Story of Cardinal Mindszenty Today and of Hungary's "New Order."* New York: Farrar, Straus and Cudahy, 1956.

Smith, Walter Bedell. *My Three Years in Moscow.* Philadelphia: J. B. Lippincott, 1950.

Snowden, Ron. *Pak's Palace.* Los Angeles: Spartan Books, 1959.

Souvarine, Boris. *Stalin: A Critical Survey of Bolshevism.* New York: Longmans, Green, 1939.

Stevens, Edmund. *This Is Russia: Uncensored.* New York: Didier, 1950.

Stowe, Leland. *Conquest by Terror.* New York: Random House, 1952.

Tchernavin, Tatiana. *Escape from the Soviets.* New York: E. P. Dutton, 1934.

Tchernavin, Vladimir. *I Speak for the Silent.* Boston: Hale, Cushman and Flint, 1935.

Thimayya, K. S. *Experiment in Neutrality.* New Delhi: Vision Books, 1981.

The Trial of József Mindszenty. Budapest: Hungarian State Publishing House, 1949.

Utley, Freda. *Lost Illusion.* London: George Allen and Unwin, 1949.

van Narvig, William. *East of the Iron Curtain.* Chicago: Ziff Davis, 1946.

Vogeler, Robert. *I Was Stalin's Prisoner.* New York: Harcourt, Brace, 1951.

Von Koerber, Lenka. *Soviet Russia Fights Crime.* London: George Routledge and Sons, 1934.

Webb, Sidney, and Beatrice Webb. *Soviet Communism: A New Civilization?* Vol. 2. New York: Charles Scribner's Sons, 1936.

Weissberg, Alexander. *The Accused.* New York: Simon and Shuster, 1951.

Wills, Morris R. *Turncoat: An American's 12 Years in Communist China.* Englewood Cliffs, NJ: Prentice-Hall, 1968.

Government Publications

U.S. Congress. *Congressional Record.*

U.S. Department of Defense. *P.O.W.: The Fight Continues after Battle. The Report of the Secretary of Defense's Advisory Committee on Prisoners of War.* Washington, DC, 1955.

U.S. Department of State. *Assistance to Escapees—Its Significance for America.* Washington, DC, 1955.

U.S. Department of State, Office of International Information. *Forced Labor in the Soviet Union.* Washington, DC, 1952.

U.S. Foreign Operations Administration. *Escape to Freedom.* Washington, DC, 1954.

U.S. House. Committee on Un-American Activities. *Consultation with Edward Hunter: Communist Psychological Warfare (Brainwashing).* 85th Cong., 2nd sess., 1958.

U.S. Senate. Committee on Government Operations. *Hearings before the Permanent Subcommittee on Investigations: Communist Interrogation, Indoctrination and Exploitation of American Military and Civilian Prisoners.* 84th Cong., 2nd sess., 1956.

U.S. Senate. Committee on Government Operations. *Report of the Committee on Government Operations Made by Its Permanent Subcommittee on Investigations: Communist Interrogation, Indoctrination and Exploitation of American Military and Civilian Prisoners.* 84th Cong., 2nd sess., 1957.

UN Publications

ECOSOC Official Records.

Report of the Ad Hoc Committee on Forced Labour. Geneva: UN International Labour Office, 1953.

Fiction

Condon, Richard. *The Manchurian Candidate.* New York: McGraw-Hill, 1959.

Gallico, Paul. *Trial by Terror.* New York: A. A. Knopf, 1952.

Gouzenko, Igor. *Fall of a Titan.* New York: W. W. Norton, 1954.

Jin, Ha. *War Trash*. New York: Pantheon Books, 2004.

Kafka, Franz. *The Trial*. New York: A. A. Knopf, 1937.

Kern, Alfred. *The Width of Waters*. Boston: Houghton Mifflin, 1959.

Koestler, Arthur. *Darkness at Noon*. New York: Random House, 1941.

Marshall, Bruce. *Vespers in Vienna*. Boston: Houghton Mifflin, 1947.

Orwell, George. *1984, a Novel*. New York: Harcourt, Brace, 1949.

Pollard, Freeman. *Seeds of Turmoil: A Novel of American PW's Brainwashed in Korea*. New York: Exposition Press, 1959.

Serge, Victor. *The Case of Comrade Tulayev*. New York: Doubleday, 1950.

Shalamov, Varlam. *Kolyma Tales*. London: Penguin Books, 1994.

Solzhenitsyn, Alexander. *The Gulag Archipelago, 1918–1956: An Experiment in Literary Investigation*. New York: Harper and Row, 1974.

———. *One Day in the Life of Ivan Denisovich*. New York: Dutton, 1963.

Trilling, Lionel. *The Middle of the Journey*. New York: Viking Press, 1947.

Films

1984 (dir. Michael Anderson, Columbia Pictures, 1956).

The Bamboo Prison (dir. Lewis Seiler, Columbia Pictures, 1954).

Big Jim McLain (dir. Edward Ludwig, Warner Bros., 1952).

Comrade X (dir. King Vidor, MGM, 1940).

Donovan's Brain (dir. Felix Feist, United Artists, 1953).

Escape from East Berlin (dir. Robert Siodmak, MGM, 1962).

A Face in the Crowd (dir. Elia Kazan, Warner Bros. Pictures, 1957).

The Fearmakers (dir. Jacques Tourneur, United Artists, 1958).

A Foreign Affair (dir. Billy Wilder, Paramount Pictures, 1948).

Guilty of Treason (dir. Felix Feist, Eagle Lion, 1950).

I Was a Communist for the FBI (dir. Gordon Douglas, Warner Bros. Pictures, 1951).

Invasion of the Body Snatchers (dir. Don Siegel, Walter Wanger Productions, 1956).

The Iron Curtain (dir. William Wellman, Twentieth Century-Fox, 1948).

Iron Petticoat (dir. Ralph Thomas, London Film Productions/MGM, 1956).

Jet Pilot (dir. Josef von Sternberg, Universal Pictures, 1957).

Man on a Tightrope (dir. Elia Kazan, Twentieth Century-Fox, 1953).

The Manchurian Candidate (dir. John Frankenheimer, United Artists, 1962).

Mission to Moscow (dir. Michael Curtiz, Warner Bros. Pictures, 1943).

Never Let Me Go (dir. Delmer Daves, MGM, 1953).

Night People (dir. Nunnally Johnson, Twentieth Century-Fox, 1954).

Ninotchka (dir. Ernst Lubitsch, MGM, 1939).

One, Two, Three (dir. Billy Wilder, United Artists, 1961).

Operation Manhunt (dir. Jack Alexander, United Artists, 1954).

Panic in the Streets (dir. Elia Kazan, Twentieth Century-Fox, 1950).

Pickup on South Street (dir. Samuel Fuller, Twentieth Century-Fox, 1953).

The Prisoner (dir. Peter Glenville, Columbia Pictures, 1955).

Prisoner of War (dir. Andrew Marton, MGM, 1954).

The Rack (dir. Arnold Laven, MGM, 1956).

The Red Danube (dir. George Sidney, MGM, 1949).

The Searchers (dir. John Ford, Warner Bros. Pictures, 1956).

Shock Corridor (dir. Samuel Fuller, Allied Artists Pictures, 1963).

Silk Stockings (dir. Rouben Mamoulian, MGM, 1957).

The Steel Helmet (dir. Samuel Fuller, Lippert Pictures, 1951).

The Third Man (dir. Carol Reed, British Lion Film Corporation, 1949).

Time Limit (dir. Kurt Malden, United Artists, 1957).

Walk East on Beacon (dir. Alfred Werker, Columbia Pictures, 1952).

Will Success Spoil Rock Hunter? (dir. Frank Tashlin, Twentieth Century-Fox, 1957).

The Wind and The Lion (dir. John Milius, MGM, 1975).

Woman on Pier 13 / I Married a Communist (dir. Robert Stevenson, RKO, 1951).

Teleplays and TV Documentaries

Brainwashing. CBS's The Twentieth Century, November 24, 1957. Viewing copy held in the Library of Congress, Motion Picture Division.

Darkness at Noon. Dir. Delbert Mann, Producers' Showcase, Season 1, Episode 8, May 2, 1955.

I Was Stalin's Prisoner. Dir. Delbert Mann, Goodyear Television Playhouse, Season 1, Episode 6, December 23, 1951.

Mother of a Turncoat. NBC's Armstrong Circle Theatre, May 1, 1956.

POW. Written by David Davidson, United States Steel Hour, Season 1, Episode 1, October 27, 1953.

VNR: The True Story of Lowell Skinner. WNEW-TV, August 19, 1963.

SUPPLEMENTAL SECONDARY SOURCES

Secondary sources that are cited in the notes are not included here.

Adler, Nanci. *The Gulag Survivor: Beyond the Soviet System.* New Brunswick, NJ: Transaction Publishers, 2002.

Alvah, Donna. *Unofficial Ambassadors: American Military Families Overseas and the Cold War, 1946–1965.* New York: New York University Press, 2007.

Appy, Christian, ed. *Cold War Constructions: The Political Culture of United States Imperialism, 1945–1966.* Amherst: University of Massachusetts Press, 2000.

Baldwin, Kate A. *Beyond the Color Line and the Iron Curtain: Reading Encounters between Black and Red, 1922–1963.* Durham: Duke University Press, 2002.

Barrett, Edward W. *Truth Is Our Weapon.* New York: Funk and Wagnalls, 1953.

Bender, Thomas, ed. *Rethinking American History in a Global Age.* Berkeley: University of California Press, 2002.

Biess, Frank. "'Pioneers of a New Germany': Returning POWs from the Soviet Union and the Making of East German Citizens, 1945–50." *Central European History* 32 (1999): 143–80.

Blum, Hester. "Pirated Tars, Piratical Texts: Barbary Captivity and American Sea Narratives." *Early American Studies* 1 (Fall 2003): 133–58.

Bogle, Lori Lynn. *The Pentagon's Battle for the American Mind: The Early Cold War.* College Station: Texas A&M University Press, 2004.

Borstelmann, Thomas. *Apartheid's Reluctant Uncle: The United States and Southern Africa in the Early Cold War.* New York: Oxford University Press, 1993.

———. *The Cold War and the Color Line: American Race Relations in the Global Arena.* Cambridge, MA: Harvard University Press, 2001.

Bowie, Robert, and Richard H. Immerman. *Waging Peace: How Eisenhower Shaped an Enduring Cold War Strategy.* Oxford: Oxford University Press, 1998.

Boyer, John. *By the Bomb's Early Light: American Thought and Culture at the Dawn of the Atomic Age.* Chapel Hill: University of North Carolina Press, 1994.

Carlson, Lewis H. *Remembered Prisoners of a Forgotten War: An Oral History of Korean War POWs.* New York: St. Martin's Press, 2002.

Carmichael, Virginia. *Framing History: The Rosenberg Story and the Cold War.* Minneapolis: University of Minnesota Press, 1993.

Carruthers, Susan L. "Compulsory Viewing: Concentration Camp Film and German Reeducation." *Millennium: Journal of International Studies* 30, no. 3 (2001): 733–59.

———. "*The Manchurian Candidate* (1962) and the Cold War Brainwashing Scare." *Historical Journal of Film, Radio and Television* 18, no. 1 (1998): 75–94.

Cassiday, Julie A. "Marble Columns and Jupiter Lights: Theatrical and Cinematic Modeling of Soviet Show Trials in the 1920s." *Slavic and East European Journal* 42, no. 2 (1998): 640–60.

Caute, David. *The Dancer Defects: The Struggle for Cultural Supremacy during the Cold War.* Oxford: Oxford University Press, 2003.

———. *The Great Fear: The Anti-Communist Purge under Truman and Eisenhower.* New York: Simon and Schuster, 1978.

Cole, Paul M. *POW/MIA Issues.* Vol. 1. *The Korean War.* Santa Monica: RAND, 1994.

Colley, Linda. "Going Native, Telling Tales: Captivity, Collaborations and Empire." *Past and Present* 168 (2000):170–93.

Copfermann, Emile. *David Rousset: Une vie dans le siècle.* Paris: Plon, 1991.

Corber, Robert J. *Homosexuality in Cold War America: Resistance and the Crisis of Masculinity.* Durham: Duke University Press, 1997.

Crockatt, Richard. *The Fifty Years War: The United States and the Soviet Union in World Politics, 1941–1991.* London: Routledge, 1995.

Cuordileone, K. A. "Politics in an Age of Anxiety: Cold War Political Culture and the Crisis in American Masculinity, 1949–60." *Journal of American History* 87 (2000): 515–45.

Dalby, Simon. "Geopolitical Discourse: The Soviet Union as Other." *Alternatives* 13 (1988): 415–42.

Demos, John. *The Unredeemed Captive: A Family Story from Early America.* New York: Vintage, 1995.

Derounian-Stodola, Kathryn Zabelle, ed. *Women's Indian Captivity Narratives.* New York: Penguin Books, 1998.

Derounian-Stodola, Kathryn Zabelle, and James Arthur Levernier. *The Indian Captivity Narrative, 1550–1900.* New York: Twayne, 1993.

Douglas, Ann. "Periodizing the American Century: Modernism, Postmodernism, and Postcolonialism in the Cold War Context." *Modernism/Modernity* 5, no. 3 (1998): 71–98.

Doyle, Robert C. "Unresolved Mysteries: The Myth of the Missing Warrior and the Government Deceit Theme in the Popular Captivity Culture of the Vietnam War." *Journal of American Culture* 15 (1992): 1–18.

Drinnon, Richard. *Facing West: The Metaphysics of Indian-Hating and Empire-Building*. Norman: University of Oklahoma Press, 1997.

Dudziak, Mary L. *Cold War Civil Rights: Race and the Image of American Democracy*. Princeton: Princeton University Press, 2000.

———. "Josephine Baker, Racial Protest, and the Cold War." *Journal of American History* 81, no. 2 (1994): 543–70.

Ebersole, Gary L. *Captured by Texts: Puritan to Postmodern Images of Indian Captivity*. Charlottesville: University of Virginia Press, 1995.

———. "Experience/Narrative Structure/Reading: Patty Hearst and the American Indian Captivity Narratives." *Religion* 18 (1988): 255–82.

Ellwood, Robert S. *The Fifties Spiritual Marketplace*. New Brunswick: Rutgers University Press, 1997.

Endy, Christopher. *Cold War Holidays: American Tourism in France*. Chapel Hill: University of North Carolina Press, 2004.

Engerman, David C. *Modernization from the Other Shore: American Intellectuals and the Romance of Russian Development*. Cambridge, MA: Harvard University Press, 2003.

Fabian, Ann. *The Unvarnished Truth: Personal Narratives in Nineteenth-Century America*. Berkeley: University of California Press, 2000.

Faery, Rebecca Blevins. *Cartographies of Desire: Captivity, Race, and Sex in the Shaping of an American Nation*. Norman: University of Oklahoma Press, 1999.

Fitzpatrick, Tara. "The Figure of Captivity: The Cultural Work of the Puritan Captivity Narrative." *American Literary History* 3 (1991): 1–26.

Foreman, Joel, ed. *The Other Fifties: Interrogating Mid-Century American Icons*. Urbana: University of Illinois Press, 1997.

Foster, Frances Smith. *Witnessing Slavery: The Development of the Ante-Bellum Slave Narratives*. Madison: University of Wisconsin Press, 1994.

Fousek, John. *To Lead the Free World: American Nationalism and the Cultural Roots of the Cold War*. Chapel Hill: University of North Carolina Press, 2000.

Franklin, H. Bruce. *MIA, or, Mythmaking in America*. New Brunswick: Rutgers University Press, 1993.

Fried, Albert. *McCarthyism, the Great American Red Scare: A Documentary History*. New York: Oxford University Press, 1997.

Fried, Richard M. *Nightmare in Red: The McCarthy Era in Perspective*. New York: Oxford University Press, 1990.

Friedman, Andrea. "The Smearing of Joe McCarthy: The Lavender Scare, Gossip, and Cold War Politics." *American Quarterly* 57, no. 4 (2005): 1105–29.

Garber, Marjorie, and Rebecca L. Walkowitz. *Secret Agents: The Rosenberg Case, McCarthyism and Fifties America*. New York: Routledge, 1995.

Gati, Charles. *Failed Illusions: Moscow, Washington, Budapest and the 1956 Hungarian Revolt*. Stanford: Stanford University Press, 2006.

Gilbert, James, ed. *Rethinking Cold War Culture*. Washington, DC: Smithsonian Institution Press, 2001.

Gorsuch, Anne E. "'There's No Place Like Home': Soviet Tourism in Late Stalinism." *Slavic Review* 62, no. 4 (2003): 760–85.

Grimshaw, Allen D. *Racial Violence in the United States.* Chicago: Aldine, 1969.

Hartz, Louis. *The Liberal Tradition in America: An Interpretation of American Political Thought since the Revolution.* New York: Harcourt, Brace, 1955.

Henriksen, Margot A. *Dr. Strangelove's America: Society and Culture in the Atomic Age.* Berkeley: University of California Press, 1997.

Herman, Ellen. *The Romance of American Psychology: Political Culture in the Age of Experts.* Berkeley: University of California Press, 1995.

Hinkle, Lawrence E., and Harold G. Wolff. "Communist Interrogation and Indoctrination of 'Enemies of the State.'" *AMA Archives of Neurology and Psychiatry* 76 (1957): 116–74.

———. "The Methods of Interrogation and Indoctrination Used by the Communist State Police." *Bulletin of the New York Academy of Medicine* 33, no. 9 (1957): 600–615.

Hodos, George H. *Show Trials: Stalinist Purges in Eastern Europe, 1948–1954.* Westport, CT: Praeger, 1987.

Honig, Bonnie. *Democracy and the Foreigner.* Princeton: Princeton University Press, 2001.

Kackman, Michael. *Citizen Spy: Television, Espionage, and Cold War Culture.* Minneapolis: University of Minnesota Press, 2005.

Kaplan, Amy. *The Anarchy of Empire in the Making of U.S. Culture.* Cambridge, MA: Harvard University Press, 2002.

Kirby, Dianne, ed. *Religion and the Cold War.* Basingstoke: Palgrave Macmillan, 2003.

Klein, Christina. *Cold War Orientalism: Asia in the Middlebrow Imagination, 1945–1961.* Berkeley: University of California Press, 2003.

Knight, Amy W. *How the Cold War Began: The Igor Gouzenko Affair and the Hunt for Soviet Spies.* New York: Carroll and Graf, 2005.

Koch, Stephen. *Double Lives: Stalin, Willi Münzenberg and the Seduction of the Intellectuals.* London: HarperCollins, 1996.

Kovel, Joel. *Red Hunting in the Promised Land: Anti-Communism and the Making of America.* London: Cassell, 1997.

Krenn, Michael. *Black Diplomacy: African Americans and the State Department, 1945–1969.* New York: M. E. Sharpe, 1999.

———. "'Unfinished Business': Segregation and U.S. Diplomacy at the 1958 World's Fair." *Diplomatic History* 20, no. 4 (1996): 591–612.

Krylova, Anna. "The Tenacious Liberal Subject in Soviet Studies." *Kritika: Explorations in Russian and Eurasian History* 1, no. 1 (2000): 119–46.

Kutler, Stanley I. *The American Inquisition: Justice and Injustice in the Cold War.* New York: Hill and Wang, 1982.

LaFeber, Walter. *America, Russia and the Cold War, 1945–1996.* New York: McGraw-Hill, 1997.

Leab, Daniel J. "How Red Was My Valley? Hollywood, the Cold War Film and *I Married a Communist.*" *Journal of Contemporary History* 19 (1984): 59–88.

Leffler, Melvyn P. *For the Soul of Mankind: The United States, the Soviet Union and the Cold War.* New York: Hill and Wang, 2007.

———. *The Specter of Communism: The United States and the Origins of the Cold War, 1917–1953.* New York: Hill and Wang, 1994.

Lewis, James R. "Images of Captive Rape in the Nineteenth Century." *Journal of American Culture* 15 (1992): 69–77.

Lipschutz, Ronnie D. *Cold War Fantasies: Film, Fiction and Foreign Policy.* Lanham, MD: Rowman and Littlefield, 2001.

Lucas, Scott. "Campaigns of Truth: The Psychological Strategy Board and American Ideology, 1951–1953." *International History Review* 18, no. 2 (1996): 279–302.

Lucas, Scott, and Helen Laville. "The American Way: Edith Sampson, the NAACP and African-American Identity in the Cold War." *Diplomatic History* 20, no. 4 (1996): 565–90.

Marling, Karal Ann. *As Seen on TV: The Visual Culture of Everyday Life in the 1950s.* Cambridge, MA: Harvard University Press, 1994.

May, Lary, ed. *Recasting America: Culture and Politics in the Age of Cold War.* Chicago: University of Chicago Press, 1988.

McClay, Wilfred M. *The Masterless: Self and Society in Modern America.* Chapel Hill: University of North Carolina Press, 1994.

Medovoi, Leerom. *Rebels: Youth and the Cold War Origins of Identity.* Durham: Duke University Press, 2005.

Meyerowitz, Joanne, ed. *Not June Cleaver: Women and Gender in Postwar America, 1945–1960.* Philadelphia: Temple University Press, 1994.

Namias, June. *White Captives: Gender and Ethnicity on the American Frontier.* Chapel Hill: University of North Carolina Press, 1993.

Nashel, Jonathan. *Edward Lansdale's Cold War.* Amherst: University of Massachusetts Press, 2005.

Nathanson, Charles E. "The Social Construction of the Soviet Threat: A Study in the Politics of Representation." *Alternatives* 13, no. 4 (1988): 443–83.

Navasky, Victor S. *Naming Names.* New York: Hill and Wang, 2003.

Neumann, Iver B. *Uses of the Other: "The East" in European Identity Formation.* Manchester: Manchester University Press, 1999.

Ninkovich, Frank A. *The Diplomacy of Ideas: United States Foreign Policy and Cultural Relations, 1938–50.* Chicago: Imprint Publications, 1995.

Oakes, Guy. *The Imaginary War: Civil Defense and American Cold War Culture.* New York: Oxford University Press, 1994.

Patterson, Thomas G., ed. *Cold War Critics: Alternatives to American Foreign Policy in the Truman Years.* Chicago: Quadrangle Books, 1971.

Pearce, Roy Harvey. *Savagism and Civilization: A Study of the Indian and the American Mind.* Baltimore: Johns Hopkins University Press, 1953.

Pfister, Joel, and Nancy Schnog. *Inventing the Psychological: Toward a Cultural History of Emotional Life in America.* New Haven: Yale University Press, 1997.

Pietz, William. "The 'Post-Colonialism' of Cold War Discourse." *Social Text* 19/20 (1988): 55–75.

Poiger, Uta G. *Jazz, Rock and Rebels: Cold War Politics and American Culture in a Divided Germany.* Berkeley: University of California Press, 2000.

Puddington, Arch. *Broadcasting Freedom: The Cold War Triumph of Radio Free Europe and Radio Liberty.* Lexington: University Press of Kentucky, 2000.

Rev, Istvan. "The Suggestion." *Representations* 80 (2002): 62–98.

———. "*In Mendacio Veritas* (In Lies There Lies the Truth)." *Representations* 35 (1991): 1–20.

Robin, Corey. *Fear: The History of a Political Idea.* New York: Oxford University Press, 2004.

Rogin, Michael. *Ronald Reagan, the Movie: And Other Episodes in Political Demonology.* Berkeley: University of California Press, 1987.

Rojas, Martha Elena. "'Insults Unpunished': Barbary Captives, American Slaves, and the Negotiation of Liberty." *Early American Studies* 1 (Fall 2003): 159–86.

Rosenberg, Emily. "Consuming Women: Images of Americanization in the 'American Century.'" *Diplomatic History* 23 (1999): 479–97.

———. "Foreign Affairs: Connecting Sexual and International Politics after World War II." *Diplomatic History* 18 (1994): 59–70.

Ross, Andrew. *No Respect: Intellectuals and Popular Culture.* New York: Routledge, 1989.

Rotter, Andrew J. "Gender Relations, Foreign Relations: The United States and South Asia, 1947–64." *Journal of American History* 81 (1994): 518–42.

Salomon, Kim. *Refugees in the Cold War: Toward a New International Refugee Regime in the Early Postwar Era.* Lund: Lund University Press, 1991.

Saunders, Frances Stonor. *Who Paid the Piper? The CIA and the Cultural Cold War.* London: Granta, 1999.

Sayre, Gordon M., ed. *American Captivity Narratives.* Boston: Houghton Mifflin, 2000.

Sayre, Nora. *Running Time: The Films of the Cold War.* New York: Dial Press, 1982.

Scott, Catherine V. "Bound for Glory: The Hostage Crisis as Captivity Narrative in Iran." *International Studies Quarterly* 44, no. 1 (2000): 177–88.

Scott-Smith, Giles. *The Politics of Apolitical Culture: The Congress for Cultural Freedom, the CIA and Post-war American Hegemony.* London: Routledge, 2002.

Sharp, Joanne P. *Condensing the Cold War: Reader's Digest and American Identity.* Minneapolis: University of Minnesota Press, 2000.

Simpson, Christopher. *Universities and Empire: Money and Politics in the Social Sciences during the Cold War.* New York: New Press, 1998.

Singh, Nikhil Pal. *Black Is a Country: Race and the Unfinished Struggle for Democracy.* Cambridge, MA: Harvard University Press, 2004.

———. "Cold War Redux: On the 'New Totalitarianism.'" *Radical History Review* 85 (2003): 171–81.

Slotkin, Richard. *Gunfighter Nation: The Myth of the Frontier in Twentieth-Century America.* Norman: University of Oklahoma Press, 1998.

Smith, Arthur L. *Kidnap City: Cold War Berlin.* Westport, CT: Greenwood Press, 2002.

Smith, Geoffrey. "National Security and Personal Isolation: Sex, Gender, and Disease in the Cold War United States." *International History Review* 14 (1992): 307–37.

Sosin, Gene. *Sparks of Liberty: An Insider's Memoir of Radio Liberty.* University Park: Pennsylvania State University Press, 1999.

Spiller, Harry, ed. *American POWs in Korea: Sixteen Personal Accounts.* Jefferson, NC: McFarland, 1998.

Stueck, William. *Rethinking the Korean War: A New Diplomatic and Strategic History.* Princeton: Princeton University Press, 2002.

Todorov, Tzvetan. *Facing the Extreme: Moral Life in the Concentration Camps.* New York: Henry Holt, 1996.

Toker, Leona. *Return from the Archipelago: Narratives of Gulag Survivors.* Bloomington: Indiana University Press, 2000.

Tolczyk, Darius. *See No Evil: Literary Cover-Ups and Discoveries of the Soviet Camp Experience.* New Haven: Yale University Press, 1999.

Tuck, Jim. *McCarthyism and New York's Hearst Press: A Study of Roles in the Witch Hunt.* Lanham, MD: University Press of America, 1995.

Tudda, Chris. *The Truth Is Our Weapon: The Rhetorical Diplomacy of Dwight D. Eisenhower and John Foster Dulles.* Baton Rouge: Louisiana State University Press, 2006.

Urban, George. *Radio Free Europe and the Pursuit of Democracy.* New Haven: Yale University Press, 1997.

Von Eschen, Penny M. *Satchmo Blows Up the World: Jazz Ambassadors Play the Cold War.* Cambridge, MA: Harvard University Press, 2006.

Walker, R. B. J. *Inside/Outside: International Relations as Political Theory.* Cambridge: Cambridge University Press, 1993.

Wark, Wesley K. "Coming in from the Cold: British Propaganda and Red Army Defectors, 1945–1952." *International History Review* 9, no. 1 (1987): 48–72.

Warner, Daniel. "Voluntary Repatriation and the Meaning of Return to Home: A Critique of Liberal Mathematics." *Journal of Refugee Studies* 7 (1994): 160–74.

Wilford, Hugh. *The Mighty Wurlitzer: How the CIA Played America.* Cambridge, MA: Harvard University Press, 2008.

Winkler, Alan. *Life under a Cloud: American Anxiety about the Atom.* Oxford University Press, 1993.

Wright, Patrick. *Iron Curtain: From Stage to Cold War.* Oxford: Oxford University Press, 2007.

INDEX

Page numbers in italics denote illustrations.

TEXT
10/12.5 Minion Pro

DISPLAY
Minion Pro

COMPOSITOR
Integrated Composition Systems

PRINTER AND BINDER
Maple-Vail Book Manufacturing Group